Memory
and Aging

Memory
and Aging

Current Issues and Future Directions

Edited by

Moshe Naveh-Benjamin
and Nobuo Ohta

Psychology Press
Taylor & Francis Group

New York   London

Psychology Press
Taylor & Francis Group
711 Third Avenue
New York, NY 10017

Psychology Press
Taylor & Francis Group
27 Church Road
Hove, East Sussex BN3 2FA

© 2012 by Taylor & Francis Group, LLC
Psychology Press is an imprint of Taylor & Francis Group, an Informa business

Printed in the United States of America on acid-free paper
Version Date: 2011921

International Standard Book Number: 978-1-84872-918-6 (Hardback)

Library of Congress Cataloging-in-Publication Data

Memory and aging : current issues and future directions / edited by Moshe
    Naveh-Benjamin, Nobuo Ohta.
        p. cm.
    Includes bibliographical references and index.
    ISBN 978-1-84872-918-6 (alk. paper)
    1. Memory--Age factors. 2. Aging. I. Naveh-Benjamin, Moshe. II. Ohta, Nobuo.

    BF378.A33M464 2012
    155.67'13--dc23

2011028490

Visit the Taylor & Francis Web site at
http://www.taylorandfrancis.com

and the Psychology Press Web site at
http://www.psypress.com

Contents

Preface

Current demographical patterns predict an aging population worldwide. It is projected that by the year 2050, more than 20% of the US population and 40% of the Japanese population will be older than 65. It is particularly apt, therefore, that psychological research on aging, in general, and on memory and aging, in particular, is growing. This is reflected in scientific databases showing a dramatic increase in articles relating to memory and aging over the last 50 years. It is important to understand these age-related changes in memory because the ability to learn new information and retrieve previously learned information is essential for successful aging, allowing older adults to adapt to changes in their environment, self-concept, and social roles.

This book represents the latest psychological research on different aspects of age-related changes in memory. Its chapters, written by a group of leading international researchers in the field, cover a broad array of issues concerning the changes that occur in memory as people grow older. These include the mechanisms and processes underlying these age-related memory changes, how these changes interact with social and cultural environments, and potential programs intended to increase memory performance in old age. These chapters likewise draw upon diverse methodological approaches, including cross-sectional extreme group experimental designs, longitudinal designs assessing intraparticipant change, and computational approaches and neuroimaging assessment. Together, they provide converging evidence for stability and change in memory as people grow older and for the underlying causes of these patterns, as well as for the heterogeneity in older adults' performance.

The book is divided into four parts. Part 1 deals with behavioral changes and stability in short-term and working-memory functions. Chapter 1, by Paul Verhaeghen, includes a discussion of potential changes in basic processes in working memory, showing an interesting dissociation between age-related changes in updating mechanisms, which seem to stay intact in older adults, and an age-related decline in availability of items once out of the focus of attention. In Chapter 2, Susan Kemper assesses how working-memory limitations affect older adults' use of complex syntactic productions, showing age-related decline in the production and processing of complex sentences. Chapter 3, by Etsuko Harada and her colleagues, assesses relations between experimental laboratory research and real-world behavior in the context of human–information technology interaction.

Part 2 concerns age-related changes in long-term memory. In Chapter 4, Moshe Naveh-Benjamin deals with age-related declines in associative memory, relating them to deficits in effortful-strategic processes at encoding and at retrieval. The fifth chapter, by Leah Light, provides an update of dual-process theories of memory retrieval in old age, describing new studies that show a more complex picture than previously recognized of the typical differential decline in recollection in the face of more intact familiarity. Chapter 6, by Darlene and Jim Howard, describes age-related changes in implicit rather than explicit learning mechanisms showing that different forms of implicit learning age differently, depending on the task and the brain structures that underlie them. In Chapter 7, Gilles Einstein and his colleagues discuss prospective memory, concentrating on the variability in the effects of age on prospective memory and showing that it depends on the types of processes required in a given task.

Whereas Parts 1 and 2 deal primarily with mechanistic age-related changes in memory, Part 3 addresses more pragmatic, functional aspects of age-related changes in ecological contexts. Chapter 8, by Thomas Hess and Lisa Emery, examines memory and aging from a general contextual perspective, considering the importance of memory as an adaptive function and examining the interaction between social and cultural contexts and performance in real-life situations. In Chapter 9, Elizabeth Kensinger focuses on age-related changes in emotion–memory interactions from behavioral and neuroimaging perspectives. The tenth chapter, by Alan Castel and his colleagues, assesses metamemory efficiency in older adults, showing that older adults can use memory efficiently by modifying their attention to prioritize high-value information.

Part 4 of the book deals with neuroscientific, biological, epidemiological, and health aspects with reference to age-related changes in memory. Chapter 11, by Kalpouzos and Nyberg, uses multimodal neuroimaging techniques to examine both structural and functional integrity of the brain, showing complex relationships between the two and also demonstrating different patterns in longitudinal and cross-sectional designs. Shu-Chen Li's Chapter 12 assesses potential neurochemical modulation of memory and aging. It suggests that a decline in dopaminergic activity in the brain as people get older can underlie a decline in memory and shows that computation models based on dopaminergic depletion can simulate well the results of behavioral studies. In Chapter 13, Roger Dixon and his colleagues assess when, how, and why memory shows a decline in older adults. Using longitudinal and epidemiological approaches, it shows that the decline depends on interactive changes of biological and environmental contexts. The final chapter, by Kaarin Anstey, employs a life-course approach linking age-related changes in memory as measured in longitudinal studies to different biomarkers, including measures of change in sensory function.

Some of the chapters in this book are based on presentations at the 8th Tsukuba International Conference on Memory held in April 2010 in Tsukuba, Japan. We believe that this collection brings together a strong and enlightening group of perspectives on memory and aging, and we hope that it will stimulate and inspire innovative new lines of research.

Moshe Naveh-Benjamin
University of Missouri, Columbia, Missouri

Nobuo Ohta
Gakushuin University, Tokyo, Japan

Contributors

Kaarin J. Anstey
Aging Research Unit, Center for
    Mental Health Research
Australian National University
Canberra, Australia

Akihiro Asaro
Chuo University
Tokyo, Japan

Alan D. Castel
University of California,
    Los Angeles
Los Angeles, California

Roger A. Dixon
Department of Psychology
University of Alberta
Edmonton, Alberta, Canada

Gilles O. Einstein
Furman University
Greenville, South Carolina

Lisa Emery
Department of Psychology
Appalachian State University
Boone, North Carolina

Michael C. Friedman
University of California,
    Los Angeles
Los Angeles, California

Etsuko T. Harada
University of Tsukuba
Tsukuba, Japan

Thomas M. Hess
Department of Psychology
North Carolina State University
Raleigh, North Carolina

Darlene V. Howard
Department of Psychology
Georgetown University
Washington, DC

James H. Howard, Jr.
Department of Psychology
The Catholic University
    of America
Washington, DC
Departments of Psychology and
    Neurology
Georgetown University
Washington, DC

Grégoria Kalpouzos
Aging Research Center
Karolinska Institute/Stockholm
    University
Stockholm, Sweden

Susan Kemper
Department of Psychology and
    Gerontology Center
University of Kansas
Lawrence, Kansas

Elizabeth A. Kensinger
Department of Psychology
Boston College
Chestnut Hill, Massachusetts

Shu-Chen Li
Center for Lifespan Psychology
Max Planck Institute for Human
    Development
Berlin, Germany

Leah L. Light
Pitzer College
Claremont, California

Stuart W. S. MacDonald
Department of Psychology
University of Victoria
Victoria, British Columbia, Canada

John J. McArdle
Department of Psychology
University of Southern California
Los Angeles, California

Mark A. McDaniel
Washington University in St. Louis
St. Louis, Missouri

Shannon McGillivray
University of California,
    Los Angeles
Los Angeles, California

Moshe Naveh-Benjamin
Department of Psychological
    Sciences
University of Missouri
Columbia, Missouri

Lars Nyberg
Center for Functional Brain
    Imaging
Umeå University
Umeå, Sweden

Nobuo Ohta
Gakushuin University
Tokyo, Japan

Michael K. Scullin
Washington University in St. Louis
St. Louis, Missouri

Brent J. Small
Department of Psychology
University of South Florida
Tampa, Florida

Satoru Suto
Shizuoka University
Shizuoka, Japan

Paul Verhaeghen
Georgia Institute of Technology
Atlanta, Georgia

Part 1

Psychological perspectives: Short-term and working memory

1 Working memory still working

Age-related differences in working-memory functioning and cognitive control

Paul Verhaeghen

AGING AND WORKING MEMORY: DEFICITS AND THEIR CONSEQUENCES

Working memory is often considered the workplace of the mind. It refers to a temporary memory buffer—lasting for a few seconds at most—which is able to passively store and actively manipulate information (Baddeley & Hitch, 1974; Kane, Bleckley, Conway, & Engle, 2001; Miyake & Shah, 1999). Working memory can be (and has been) studied under quite a number of aspects, such as its structure, the processes that ensure its smooth operation, and its functionality in the broader context of the cognitive system. It is pretty safe to say that there are about as many takes on these aspects as there are researchers (Miyake & Shah, 1999, have an excellent overview of the main theories), but some general principles do stand out.

First, in terms of *structure,* many theorists (perhaps first and foremost Cowan, 2001, in his embedded working-memory model) assume a hierarchy of availability where the amount of information that is available for immediate access is severely limited (depending on the task, one to four items; Verhaeghen, Cerella, & Basak, 2004). Additional items can be accommodated in a different store—in lay terms, "the back of your mind"—where, although information is not immediately accessible, it remains in a state of heightened activation and thus can be retrieved with relative ease (e.g., Oberauer, 2002). The terms I will use here for these two types of stores are *focus of attention* (Cowan's 2001 coinage) and *outer store.* For instance, while cooking a curry with friends, you might need to focus all your attention on cutting peppers and carrots. At the same time, you need to realize that your onions are cooking and not lose track of the exact moment when the spices need to be added to the onions—when they are just past golden brown, not much later. The focus is on the knife, the pan with onions is in the outer store, and from time to time the contents of both will need to be swapped to prevent a culinary (and social) disaster.

Second, in terms of *processes,* many theorists posit that an efficient working memory is helped by a host of control processes sometimes labeled "executive control" processes and sometimes "cognitive control" processes. I will use the terms interchangeably (e.g., Miyake, Friedman, Emerson, Witzki, & Howerter, 2000)—task scheduling, shuffling items in and out of the focus of attention, updating the contents of the focus or the outer store, shielding information from interference, and the like. In the cooking example, at some point you might need to focus your attention wholly on the slicing, then broaden it to include conversation with your friends when the task permits (rinsing the vegetables is a good one), and then again switch it from, say, cutting the carrots to stirring the spices into the browned onions. In general, you also need to update the contents of working memory continuously, making sure you know how the curry is progressing and that the next step in the cooking process is always clear and prepped.

Finally, in terms of *functionality,* researchers like to quantify the workings of working-memory system in a global measure called working-memory capacity: Subjects perform complicated working-memory tasks (e.g., remembering words while also solving arithmetic puzzles) and the number of items they can retain in the face of the interfering tasks and/or items is measured. This capacity is then correlated with other aspects of the cognitive system (e.g., Engle, Kane, & Tuholski, 1999). The underlying reasoning is that an effective working-memory system is crucial for high-level performance in a plethora of cognitive tasks, presumably because an effective working-memory system depends on the efficient implementation of the aforementioned cognitive control operations, which are fundamentally involved in all aspects of the cognitive system. (Obviously, anyone who pulls off the feat of perfect curry must be smart in other domains of life as well.) This type of research has indeed confirmed that significant relations exist between fluid intelligence and working-memory capacity, and between spatial and language abilities and working memory, among others (e.g., Conway, Cowan, Bunting, Therriault, & Minkoff, 2002; Engle et al., 1999; Kemper, Herman, & Lian, 2003; Kyllonen, 1996; Salthouse & Pink, 2008). These correlations are quite respectable in size: In their meta-analysis, for instance, Ackerman, Beier, and Boyle (2005) conclude that the average correlation between working-memory capacity and markers of general fluid ability (g) is .36 (.48 after correcting for unreliability).

The nature of age-related deficits in working memory has received much research attention, precisely because of working memory's functional implications. The brunt of the research shows that working-memory capacity declines with advancing adult age. Small age differences are already found in short-term memory tasks that do not require much cognitive control or attentional resources, such as digit span tasks. Age-related deficits in working memory, as measured by tasks such as reading span, listening span, or operation span, are demonstrably larger. For instance, in a meta-analysis compiling a total of 123 studies from 104 papers, Bopp and Verhaeghen (2005) found a systematic relationship between working-memory capacity measures of younger and older adults: Capacity of older adults could be well described (R^2 = .98) as a simple fraction of that of younger adults. Older adults' capacity in simple short-term memory span tasks was 92% that of the capacity of younger adults; their capacity on true working-memory tasks, however, reached only 74% that of younger adults.

Given working memory's central position in the cognitive system and given age-related declines in its capacity, it is not surprising that working memory explains a substantial part of the age-related deficits observed in higher order aspects of cognition. Figure 1.1 reproduces a relevant path analysis based on a large-scale meta-analysis of the literature (Verhaeghen & Salthouse, 1997), as well as estimates of age-related variance in each of three criterion variables (episodic memory, reasoning ability, and spatial ability) accounted for by processing speed, short-term memory capacity, and working-memory capacity. Depending on the criterion variable, working-memory capacity explains between 30% and 50% of age-related variance, and short-term memory capacity explains much less—between about 10% and about 20% of variance; processing speed explains more—55% to 70%. Importantly, working-memory capacity reliably explains age-related variance over and above the variance already explained by processing speed—the cognitive primitive that is typically most clearly associated with age-related differences in cognition (for a review, see Salthouse, 1996) between 5% and 10%. Combined, then, speed and working-memory capacity account for 60% to 80% of age-related differences in higher order cognition.

All of this suggests that the study of age-related differences in working-memory capacity and its causes and consequences might be a worthwhile endeavor. In the remainder of this chapter, I focus on one class of explanations for its decline and its downstream effects on higher order cognition: those in terms of cognitive control. As stated previously, efficient cognitive control is needed to create an optimally effective working-memory system; these control processes are likely responsible for the close link between working-memory capacity and fluid aspects of cognition (e.g., Heitz et al., 2006).

First, I will give a broad overview, largely based on meta-analysis conducted in my lab; next, I will turn to our own experimental research dealing extensively with one aspect of control: working-memory updating, as examined through the concept of focus switching. Some of the studies in this area of research emphasize the neuropsychological bases of cognitive and executive control and call attention to associations between selected memory deficits and the consequences of brain aging on specific functions associated with the prefrontal and midfrontal regions of the human cortex (e.g., Moscovitch & Winocur, 1995; West, 1996). Alternatively, some researchers take a more integrated view of brain aging effects that includes the integration of multiple brain regions and distributed brain functions (e.g., Adcock, Constable, Gore, & Goldman-Rakic, 2000; Braver et al., 2001; Rosen et al., 2003; Small, Tsai, deLaPaz, Mayeux, & Stern, 2002). I note that my overview will remain firmly at the behavioral level.

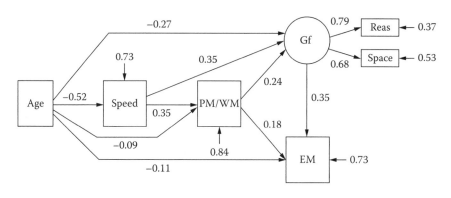

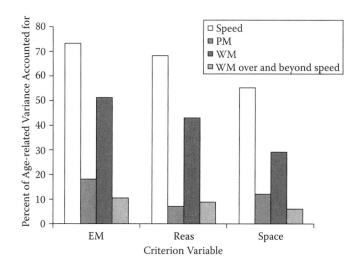

FIGURE 1.1 Working memory mediates age-related differences in higher order cognition. Top panel: path analysis from a large meta-analysis reported by Verhaeghen and Salthouse (Verhaeghen, P., & Salthouse, T. A., 1997. *Psychological Bulletin, 122,* 231–249.) PM/WM = primary memory/working memory; EM = episodic memory; Gf = general fluid ability; Reas = reasoning ability; Space = spatial ability. Bottom panel: reanalysis of these data showing percentages of age-related variance in episodic memory, spatial ability, and reasoning ability explained by speed of processing, short-term memory, and working memory, as well as variance explained by working memory over and beyond variance explained by age.

AGING AND COGNITIVE CONTROL

Control processes have been researched extensively in the field of cognitive aging, but little attempt has been made to tie these efforts to a coherent framework. My own reading of the literature (notably the factor-analytic efforts by Friedman & Miyake, 2004; Engle, Tuholski, Laughlin, & Conway, 1999; Miyake et al., 2000; and Oberauer, Süß, Schulze, Wilhelm, & Wittmann, 2000) suggests that cognitive control can be studied under at least four aspects: resistance to interference, coordinative ability, task switching, and memory updating. I will discuss these in turn, relying heavily on our own meta-analytic work (reviewed in Verhaeghen & Cerella, 2002, 2008; Figure 1.2 presents an overview of these studies).

First, *resistance to interference*, also known as inhibitory control, was a central explanatory construct in aging theories throughout the 1990s (e.g., Hasher, Tonev, Lustig, & Zacks, 2001; Hasher & Zacks, 1988; Hasher, Zacks, & May, 1999; Lövdén, 2003; for a computational approach, see Braver & Barch, 2002). Inhibition theory casts resistance to interference as a true cognitive primitive and posits an age-related breakdown in this resistance. This breakdown would in turn lead to mental clutter in an older adult's working memory, thereby limiting its functional capacity and perhaps also its speed of operation.

The *Stroop* task and negative priming are the procedures most often used to test for age differences in resistance to interference. In the Stroop task, participants are presented with colored stimuli, and have to report the color. Response times (RTs) from a baseline condition where the stimulus is neutral—for instance, a series of colored Xs—are compared with RTs from a critical condition in which the stimulus is itself a word denoting a different color than the one that it is presented in (e.g., the word "yellow" printed in red). Response times are slower in that case, due to interference from the meaning of the word. In the *negative priming* task, participants are shown two stimuli simultaneously; one is the stimulus to be evaluated (the target), while the other is the stimulus to be ignored (the distracter). For instance, the participant can be asked to name a red letter in a display that also contains a superimposed green letter. If the distracter on one trial becomes the target on the next (the critical, negative priming condition), reaction time is slower than in a neutral condition where none of the stimuli are repeated (the baseline condition). Note that this effect is counterintuitive: Higher levels of inhibition are associated with larger costs.

The approach we (Verhaeghen & Cerella, 2002, 2008; Verhaeghen & De Meersman, 1998a, 1998b) have taken to investigate age differences in these processes is to examine whether the presumed age-related deficit observed in the condition requiring high levels of cognitive control (e.g., in the case of Stroop, the color–word condition) is larger than that in the condition requiring lower levels of cognitive control (e.g., in the case of Stroop, the Xs condition). To do so, we use a technique pioneered by Brinley (1965); the Brinley plot is a scatter plot with mean performance of younger adults plotted on the X-axis and mean performance of older adults on the Y-axis. The early plots typically showed that a single straight line (with a small, usually negative intercept), and hence a single linear equation, could describe data drawn from multiple conditions or tasks quite well. A straightforward

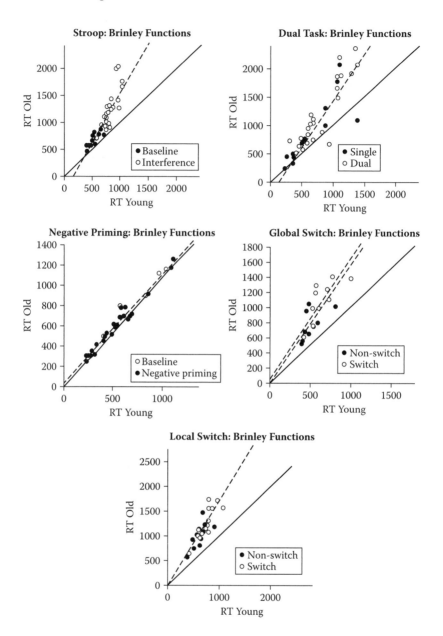

FIGURE 1.2 Brinley plots from meta-analyses on aging and different measures of cognitive control—Stroop, negative priming, dual-task performance, global task switching, and local task switching. (From Verhaeghen, P., & Cerella, J., 2002, *Neuroscience and Biobehavioral Reviews, 26,* 849–857.) Age differences in cognitive control are noted for dual-task performance and global task switching, but not for any of the other measures.

interpretation of this functional relationship is in terms of speed of processing: Older adults are slower than younger adults by a certain constant near-multiplicative factor, regardless of task (Cerella, 1990).

One can also approach this technique with fewer theoretical assumptions or interpretations, simply fitting a linear model to the data and testing explicitly whether a single line (representing both the high-level-of-control type of task and the low-level-of-control type of task) suffices to explain the data, or whether two lines (one for the high-level-of-control type of task, one for the low-level-of-control type of task) are needed. If the former is true, the age deficit is identical for both types of tasks, signaling that there is no specific age-related deficit in the high-level-of-control task; if the latter is true, the conclusion is that there is indeed a specific age-related deficit in cognitive control. (For a mathematical treatment of this result, see Cerella, 1994, and Dunn & Kirsner, 1988.)

The result from our meta-analyses on resistance to interference was quite clear. As can be seen in Figure 1.2, a single line captured both the Stroop data and the negative priming data well; in neither graph was a second line needed. This strongly suggests that there is no specific age-related deficit in the type of interference measured by these two tasks.

Second, age-related deficits have been posited in the ability to *coordinate* distinct tasks or distinct processing streams. Some of the attendant literature pertains to dual-task and task switching performance (Kramer, Hahn, & Gopher, 1999; Verhaeghen, Steitz, Sliwinski, & Cerella, 2003), but the concept has also been investigated using more directly working-memory-inspired tasks (e.g., Bopp & Verhaeghen, 2007; Fisk & Sharp, 2004; Verhaeghen & Basak, 2005; Verhaeghen & Hoyer, 2007; Verhaeghen, Kliegl, & Mayr, 1997). This theory typically sees age differences in coordination as independent of age differences in speed. That is, coordination is considered a mechanism that operates over and above the effects of mere slowing and is presumably necessary to explain age-related differences in more complex tasks.

To examine age-related differences in coordinative ability, we turned to the paradigm most often used in the literature: the dual-task paradigm. In dual-task paradigms, performance on a single task is compared to performance on the same task when a second task has to be performed concurrently (e.g., a visual reaction time task with or without a concurrent auditory reaction time task). Verhaeghen et al. (2003) report a meta-analysis of 33 dual-task studies that included age as a design factor (see Figure 1.2). The pattern observed differs markedly from that observed for resistance to interference: The lines for single- and dual-task performance separate out in the Brinley plot, indicating that the coordination process is slowed by a larger amount than the baseline processes involved in the low-coordination version of the different tasks. Note, however, that the age effect is relatively modest. The slowing factor in the baseline task was 1.6 (measured as the slope of the single-task Brinley function). The degree of slowing in the dual-task effect can be estimated by the old/young ratio of the difference in intercepts, which is where the difference between the single-task curves and the dual-task curves resides. This factor had a value of 1.8—that is, an increase of 20% over baseline slowing (80%–60%). Several moderator variables were examined in our meta-analysis, but none yielded reliable interactions with age.

Third, the late 1990s and early 2000s saw a surge in the number of publications devoted to aging and *task switching* (e.g., Mayr, Spieler, & Kliegl, 2001). Much like the coordination theory, this work considers age differences in task switching as additional to other age-related deficits that might exist in the cognitive system. In task-switching research, the participant is shown a series of stimuli and has to perform one of two possible tasks on each; the required task is indicated by the experimenter. For example, a series of digits may be shown: If the number is printed in red, the participant must report its parity; if the number is printed in blue, the participant must report its relative magnitude. The switch in task can be predictable or not; in the former case, it can be explicitly cued (e.g., by the color coding just described) or not.

Two types of task-switching costs can be calculated. First, one can compare RTs from pure, single-task blocks with RTs from mixed, multiple-task blocks. This is the *global task-switching cost;* it is thought to indicate the setup cost associated with maintaining and scheduling two mental task sets. This cost is similar to a dual-task cost, where performance on a block of dual-task trials is compared to performance on a block of single-task trials. The two paradigms—dual-task performance and global task switching—differ mainly in their temporal dynamics: In task switching, task A and task B are performed in succession; in dual tasking, they are performed concurrently. A second type of task-switching cost involves the comparison, within a mixed block, between trials in which a switch is actually required with nonswitch or repeat trials. This *local task-switching cost* is an indication of the control process associated with the actual switching.

In a meta-analysis of age and task switching based on 10 studies for global switching and 15 studies for local switching, Wasylyshyn, Verhaeghen, and Sliwinski (2003; see Figure 1.2) found that global task switching was clearly age sensitive: The lines for switch and nonswitch blocks in the Brinley plot separate out reliably. The degree of slowing in the global task-switching cost was 2.2 (the old/young ratio of the intercept difference between mixed blocks and pure blocks), compared to a slowing factor of 1.6 in the baseline task. Local task switching was found to be age constant: One Brinley line described the data adequately. Several moderator variables were examined in this meta-analysis, but none yielded reliable interactions with age.

The fourth factor, working-memory *updating*, has been investigated relatively rarely in an aging context (e.g., Fisk & Sharp, 2004; Van der Linden, Brédart, & Beerten, 1994). In lieu of an uninformative meta-analysis, I will highlight my own experimental work in this area in the remaining sections of this chapter.

To summarize, two kinds of outcomes arise from our meta-analyses of aging and executive control. One conclusion—running contrary to many claims in the literature—is that there is no global age-related deficit in cognitive control. Some types of tasks do show decline; others do not. Perhaps most surprisingly (given the attention this explanation has received in the literature), tasks involving resistance to interference (Stroop and negative priming) showed no age sensitivity in the control process. Neither did tasks tapping local task switching. On the other hand, global task switching yielded a larger effect for older adults than would be projected from baseline slowing in pure-task conditions. The same pattern was observed for coordination (dual-task performance).

Thus, we found that control-specific deficits did not emerge in tasks that involved active selection of relevant information, such as determining the ink color of words (Stroop), in actively ignoring or inhibiting a stimulus (negative priming), or in relinquishing attention from one aspect of the stimulus to reattach it to a different aspect (local task-switching). On the other hand, age differences emerged in tasks that involved the maintenance of two distinct mental task sets, as in dual-task performance or global task switching. Multiple task-set maintenance might challenge the control system in several ways. The deficit can arise from the logic implemented in the coordination step itself. But it is also possible that an age-related deficit in the capacity of working memory may be responsible for the difficulty in maintaining multiple sets. In that case, the underlying problem would arise from a structural limit rather than from a specific control process. (Verhaeghen, Cerella, Bopp, & Basak, 2005, expand on this point.)

AGING AND WORKING-MEMORY UPDATING: THE CASE OF FOCUS SWITCHING

Our own recent experimental work has concerned itself with memory updating—the revising of the contents of working memory with newer, more relevant information. There are reasons to be a priori excited about this type of work. Recent individual-differences studies in the area have shown that the updating component of working memory is quite strongly related to fluid intelligence: People who are more effective at updating have higher intelligence scores (Schmiedek, Hildebrandt, Lövdén, Wilhelm, & Lindenberger, 2009; Shelton, Elliott, Matthews, Hill, & Gouvier, 2010; Unsworth & Engle, 2008). Moreover, updating seems to explain quite a bit of age-related variance in at least some aspects of higher order cognition (Chen & Li, 2007). In our own work, we examined working-memory updating from a structural point of view, concentrating on the process of focus switching (a term coined by Voigt & Hagendorf, 2002).

What is focus switching? As stated before, all theories of working memory point at its severely limited capacity; some, most notably Cowan's (e.g.,

2001), posit a hierarchy within those limits: Some items are more accessible than others. Cowan's model proposes a two-store structure for working memory, distinguishing a zone of immediate access, labeled the focus of attention, from a larger, activated portion of long-term memory in which items are stored in a readily available but not immediately accessible state (which we have labeled the "outer store"; Verhaeghen et al., 2004). When the number of items to be retained in working memory is smaller than or equal to the capacity of the focus of attention, they will be contained within the focus. There they will be immediately retrievable, and access times will be fast.

When the number of items to be retained exceeds the capacity of the focus, the excess items will be stored outside the focus of attention. In that case, accessing items for processing will necessitate a retrieval operation; this will slow down response time. This is what we have referred to as focus switching—the process of shunting items in and out of the focus of attention when the focus gets overloaded. The effect has been noted in a multitude of paradigms: the N-back task (McElree, 2001), a running count task in which participants keep multiple counters active (Garavan, 1998), and an arithmetic updating task (Oberauer, 2002). In each of these tasks, a bump in response time is observed when memory load exceeds a critical number: the size of the focus of attention. The critical number in all those studies, it is important to note, is 1, indicating a severely limited focus of attention.

Much of our own work on focus switching and aging uses a variant of the N-back task (Verhaeghen & Basak, 2005). Our version is self-paced. Participants press one of two keys to indicate whether the current stimulus matches the stimulus encountered N positions back; this key press then triggers the next stimulus. To help participants keep track of item positions, stimuli are projected on the computer screen in N virtual columns, one at a time. The first stimulus is in column 1, the second in column 2, and so forth; after (multiples of) N stimuli are presented, a new "row" starts at column 1. What this means in practice is that the participant compares the current stimulus with the stimulus presented previously in the same column. Our paradigm thus allows us to measure the speed of access of an item (we call this an item's accessibility), as well as the accuracy of retrieval, which is an index of an item's availability. (This distinction was first posited by McElree, 2001.)

Figure 1.3 reproduces the results from our first study with this paradigm (Verhaeghen & Basak, 2005, Exp. 1; stimuli were digits). Several aspects of the data are worth pointing out. First, there is clear evidence for a focus-switch cost in response times, pointing at a focus of size 1: The response time by N trace is close to a step function, with a fast response at $N = 1$ and then a jump to slower and statistically equal response times for values of $N > 1$. These results suggest that the focus-switching cost is not driven by memory load per se, but rather by the boundary between $N = 1$ and $N = 2$—that is, by the interjection of a focus-switching operation. The absence of a "search

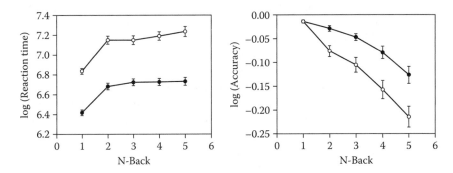

FIGURE 1.3 Data for Exp. 1 from Verhaeghen and Basak (Verhaeghen, P., & Basak, C., 2005, *Quarterly Journal of Experimental Psychology, 58A*, 134–154.) depicting log(response time) and log(accuracy) as a function of N in a group of younger adults in an identity-judgment N-back task. Error bars denote standard errors. The response time data show a step function in passing from N = 1 to N > 1, a cost when items need to be shunted in and out of the focus of attention; the accuracy data show a gradual decline. The focus switch cost is larger for older adults in accuracy but not response time.

slope" for the N = 2 to N = 5 part of the curve is also worth noting. The flat slope suggests that participants, at least in this feed-forward/forward-search paradigm where input and output order are perfectly correlated, can access the correct item efficiently, regardless of memory load.

Second, after we log-transformed the data to take the multiplicative effects of age-related slowing into account, there was no indication of any age difference in the focus-switch cost. The perhaps surprising conclusion is then that older adults can access items in working memory as effectively as younger adults can. The dynamics of focus switching are perfectly preserved in old age. We do note that in this (as in most of our subsequent studies), we found a small and, in this case, nonsignificant response slope over N > 1 for older adults; in subsequent work we noted a trend, sometimes significant, for this slope to be larger than that of younger adults. At this point, our individual-level data are not of sufficient resolution to allow us to trace the source of this age difference. One possibility is that, with advancing age, search processes do become slightly less efficient with increasing memory load. Another possibility is that while younger adults can search at least five items efficiently, older adults may have a lower capacity for efficient search. Individual differences in this capacity limit can produce a slope; if some older adults can retrieve only three items with perfect efficiency, some can retrieve four, and some can retrieve five, the group data will show an RT by set-size slope.

A third important result is that there are clear age-related differences in item availability, as indexed by item accuracy. Both younger and older adults perform with near-perfect accuracy when the item is held within the focus of attention ($N = 1$), but accuracy declines once the items leave the focus and need to be retrieved ($N > 1$). This decline in accuracy is much larger for older adults.

This first study immediately raises a number of questions. First, the finding of preserved dynamics deserves a second look. The finding, taken at face value, is surprising, especially given that this would be one of only a few instances where an age effect in accuracy is not predicated on an age difference in speed of processing. Replication with a more difficult task—pushing the limits of the system—might be a wise next step. Second, the age difference in item availability likewise invites deeper scrutiny. The age difference in item availability could have many origins, including age-related differences in binding items to context (in this case, position in a sequence), age-related differences in dealing with the multiple-task requirement inherent in focus switching (i.e., retrieval in the presence of encoding and vice versa), or age-related differences in resistance to interference (i.e., from other items present in the outer store). In the next few paragraphs, we take up these two questions: (1) Is there really age invariance in item accessibility? (2) What is the origin of the age deficit in item availability?

A CLOSER LOOK AT THE DYNAMICS
OF FOCUS SWITCHING: NO AGE-RELATED
DIFFERENCES IN ITEM ACCESSIBILITY

The data in Figure 1.3 suggest that the focus-switch cost in response time is not larger in older adults than in younger adults once the slowing in baseline processing is taken into account. This conclusion can be challenged on the grounds that our version of the N-back task is still relatively easy: We columnized its presentation, we used very simple stimuli (single digits), and we used a simple forward-feed/forward-search paradigm. Perhaps if we pushed the limits a little bit harder, an age difference would emerge.

In a first experiment (Vaughan, Basak, Hartman, & Verhaeghen, 2008, Exp. 1; results are reproduced in Figure 1.4; RT is log-transformed to take proportional age-related slowing into account), we relaxed the columnization constraint: All items were presented in a single color in the middle of the screen. As can be seen in the figure, this had the effect of increasing the focus-switch cost quite dramatically, likely because participants now need to tag items explicitly for position at encoding, retrieval, or both. (There is independent evidence that position coding indeed does come at a cost; see Lange, Verhaeghen, & Cerella, 2010.) This added cost, however, is proportionally identical in younger and older adults; older adults are not penalized more by the added requirement to keep track.

In a second experiment (Vaughan et al., 2008, Exp. 2; results are reproduced in Figure 1.4), we used more complex stimuli: three-digit numbers, with changes in only one of the three digits for mismatches (e.g., if the

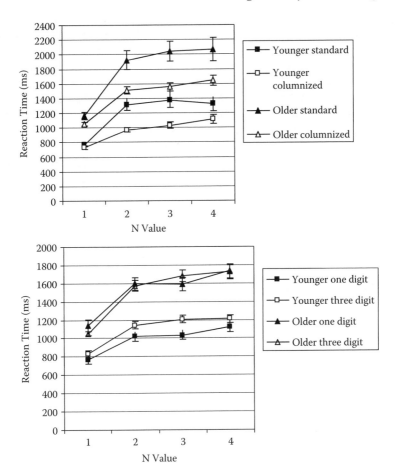

FIGURE 1.4 Increasing task or stimulus complexity does not appear to create age differences in focus switch costs in RT in an N-back task. (Data from Vaughan, L. et al., 2008, *Aging, Neuropsychology, and Cognition*, 15, 703–724.) Top panel: the effects of presenting stimuli in a single location versus N different locations; bottom panel: the effects of using single-digit versus triple-digit stimuli. Error bars denote standard errors.

stimulus was 573, the mismatch would be something like 572, 563, or 473). As can be seen in the figure, this added complexity slowed down younger adults considerably; interestingly, older adults were not fazed at all by this manipulation. Again, we found no evidence for an age-related deficit in item accessibility.

In a third and a fourth experiment (Lange & Verhaeghen, 2009, Exp. 1 and Exp. 2), we abandoned the forward-feed/forward-search requirement. In these two experiments, participants encoded N stimuli (N ranged from 3 to 5) in a forward fashion; then all N locations were probed in the forward order (as in an N-back task), the backward order, a random order, or (in Exp. 1) a fixed but irregular order that participants learned prior to the experiment proper. Experiment 1 used blocked presentation of the four search conditions, allowing participants to adapt their behavior strategically, if possible and if desired. Experiment 2 used a mixed presentation, disallowing for advance preparation of a specific search mode (if any). The motivation for these experiments was that previous experiments from our lab have shown that forward search indeed appears to yield special benefits compared to all other forms of search (Lange et al., 2010; Lange, Verhaeghen, & Cerella, submitted). That is, forward search leads to the perfect efficiency we observed (at least in the young) for our N-back task; any other search order leads to (a) longer RTs, and (b) strong RT by set-size effects.

We examined the data under many aspects; here, I reproduce the serial position curves in Figure 1.5 simply because they are sufficiently complex to pose a challenge to our hypothesis that the dynamics of search are well preserved in old age. It is clear from the figures that the serial position curves of older adults echo those of younger adults closely; we merely needed a linear rescaling of the younger adult data to reproduce the older adult data. This, then, strongly suggests that younger and older adults use the same retrieval processes, regardless of the type of search and whether or not the search can be strategically planned; older adults are just overall more slow in executing those processes.

Taken together, these four experiments confirm and amplify the conclusion from our 2005 paper: There is no evidence for a specific age-related deficit in the dynamics of focus switching. Task difficulty, stimulus complexity, and type of search all yielded identical effect in younger and older adults.

A CLOSER LOOK AT ACCURACY AFTER A FOCUS SWITCH: ITEM AVAILABILITY AS A POTENTIAL COGNITIVE PRIMITIVE

Our first data set suggested that, intact dynamics of the retrieval process notwithstanding, older adults do show a lower probability of retrieving items stored outside the focus of attention than younger adults do. One important question is whether this deficit truly represents a cognitive primitive—a deficit not reducible to another mechanism—or whether a deeper underlying cause for this deficit can be identified. In a series of experiments, we have tried, and so far failed, to locate alternative sources for the deficit.

In a set of three experiments (Bopp & Verhaeghen, 2009), we first investigated the hypothesis that age-related differences in retrieval accuracy might be due to a *source or context binding* memory deficit. The reason to suspect that context binding may be implicated is that in any

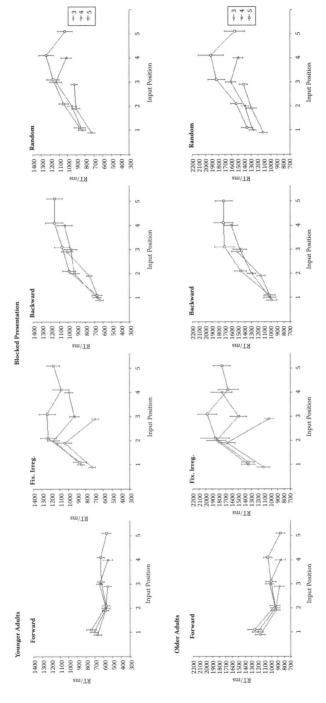

FIGURE 1.5 Serial position curves for younger and older adults in four types of memory search: forward, backward, random, and (in the top panel) fixed irregular. Top panel: search types were blocked; bottom panel: search types were mixed. The data show that the patterns are identical for younger and older adults, suggesting age invariance in the dynamics of memory search processes (Lange, E. B., & Verhaeghen, P., 2009). Error bars denote standard errors.

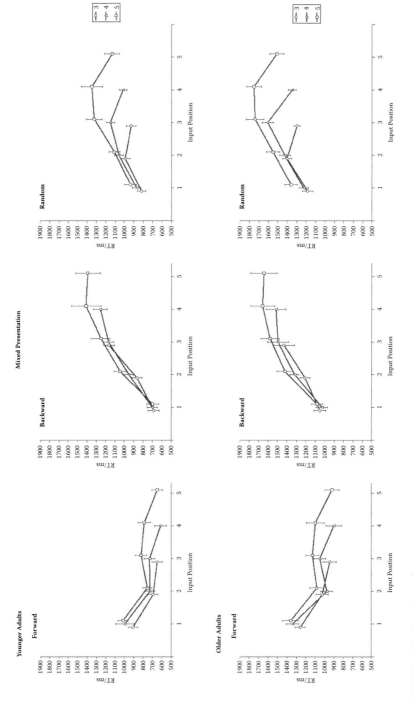

FIGURE 1.5 *(Continued)*

working-memory task at least some item-to-context binding needs to occur. In standard working-memory capacity tasks, the to-be-remembered items need to be distinguished from the to-be-processed items. In an N-back task, participants not only need to remember the item, but also need to be able to remember where in the sequence it occurs—in our version, to what column it belongs. Our repeated finding that age differences remain stable (in both accuracy and RT) when N increases from 2 to 5 lends further credence to this conjecture: If context binding is the culprit, one might expect an all-or-none effect operating between the condition where no binding is necessary (N = 1) and the conditions where it is (N > 1). This also immediately implies that the N-back paradigm is not very well suited to examine the effect of context binding because the presence of binging is completely confounded with memory load.

In these experiments, therefore, we turned to a different paradigm: namely the repetition detection paradigm devised by Bopp (Bopp & Verhaeghen, 2007). In this paradigm, participants view a string of stimuli, one at a time (we have used digits/numbers as well as positions in a grid). One of these stimuli repeats an earlier stimulus, and the participant's task is to identify the repeat. The need for source memory can be easily manipulated by using a single string of stimuli (no context binding required) versus multiple strings (context binding necessary); unlike the N-back task, memory load can be manipulated independently by varying the length of the to-be-remembered series (i.e., the lag between the first item of the list and the second occurrence of the repeating stimulus).

Figure 1.6 presents data from a representative experiment (Exp. 1 from Bopp & Verhaeghen, 2009) in which we contrasted memory for a single string of stimuli, two strings of stimuli, and three strings of stimuli, all the while keeping the working-memory load constant at 16 items. To facilitate context binding, we used separate locations and frame colors for each of the stimuli; the top panel of the figure shows an example of a single-string trial and a dual-string trial. (This constraint was relaxed in Exp. 3 and did not influence the main thrust of the findings concerning age differences.) As can be seen, accuracy declines from the single-string condition to the multiple-string conditions, indicating a cost associated with keeping track of the source/context of an item. The visual stimuli (locations in a 4 × 4 grid) showed a further but less pronounced decrease from dual string to triple string than the verbal stimuli (numbers between 1 and 16). More importantly, there is not even a hint of an age by number of strings interaction, strongly suggesting that older adults' memory for the source of the stimuli (i.e., what string they belong to) is as intact as that of younger adults.

The second and third experiments discussed here (Zhang & Verhaeghen, in preparation) were inspired by an unpublished observation concerning the data from the original Verhaeghen and Basak paper. We noted that age differences increase over the course of a trial in our N-back paradigm. This can

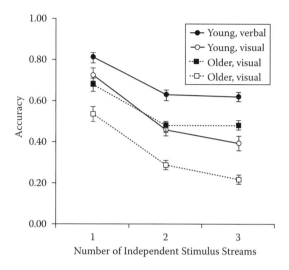

FIGURE 1.6 Accuracy for single versus multiple streams of verbal and visual stimuli for younger and older adults in a repetition detection paradigm
with a constant memory load. (Bopp, K. L., & Verhaeghen, P., 2009,
Psychology and Aging, 24, 968–980, Exp. 1.) The data show that age
differences do not increase for single versus multiple streams, indicating that context binding in short-term memory might be intact in old
age. Error bars denote standard errors.

be due to at least two reasons. First, we noted that younger and older adults
perform almost identically for the first *N* stimuli that are to be retrieved; it
is only after these first *N* stimuli that age differences appear. (The top panel
of Figure 1.7 shows the data for the 5-back condition.) These first *N* stimuli
are retrieved from the first "row"—that is, stimuli that have been encoded
while there were no stimuli to retrieve. It is possible, then, that age differences are minimal when stimuli are encoded under full-attention condition,
but are greatly exacerbated when stimuli have to be encoded while there is a
simultaneous need for updating working-memory representations.

   This *dual-task hypothesis* of age differences in accuracy of retrieval after
a focus switch fits well with the age differences typically found in dual task
performance, as outlined previously. A second interpretation is that age
differences simply grow progressively larger over the course of a trial; this
finding would tie in well with an account in terms of age-related differences
in *resistance to interference*. (Note that this account might not be in opposition to the lack of such age effects found in our meta-analyses. It can be
argued that, in the tasks included in the meta-analyses, all stimuli remain
in focal attention. It is possible that a purported age-related difference in
proneness to interference might appear only when items leave the focus.)

   Figure 1.7 also shows the results of two experiments designed to examine these hypotheses. In the first experiment (lower left panel), the task was

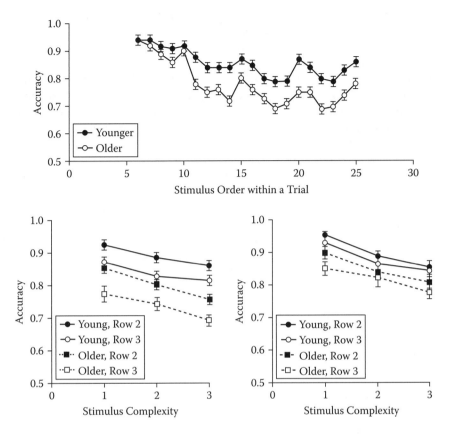

FIGURE 1.7 Age differences in accuracy after a focus switch increase over the course of a trial of 25 stimuli in an N-back task (top panel reanalysis of previously unpublished data from Verhaeghen & Basak, 2005, Exp. 1). The two bottom panels show results from a three-row N-back experiment with (bottom left) and without (bottom right) a requirement to update. The lack of interaction between age group and row suggests that this age difference is not due to either dual-task deficits (bottom left) or deficits in resistance to interference (bottom right), but rather is already present in the second row, suggesting that item availability after focus switching is perhaps a cognitive primitive. (Data from Zhang & Verhaeghen, in preparation.) Error bars denote standard errors.

our version of the 3-back; the stimuli were grid patterns of increasing levels of complexity (as verified by visual search rates; we used these grid patterns to drive accuracy below ceiling). The twist here is that we limited the number of stimuli per trial to three rows. In row 1, only encoding takes place; in row 2, subjects retrieve the stimuli remembered from row 1 and encode the new stimuli into the outer store; in row 3, they retrieve the stimuli remembered from row 2. Thus, accuracy for row 2 reflects accuracy for items encoded under full-attention encoding conditions and accuracy for row 3 reflects accuracy for items encoded under divided-attention conditions (i.e., encoding while also retrieving items).

This experiment then tests the dual-task hypothesis; the decline in accuracy from row 2 to row 3 (if any) is our indicator of the dual-task cost. In the second experiment (lower right panel of Figure 1.7), the number of rows is likewise limited to three, but now we request the participants to compare both the row 2 and row 3 stimuli to row 1. In other words, this experiment presents no updating requirement, and we interpret the potential decline in accuracy from row 2 to row 3 as a measure of the lack of resistance to interference originating from the intervening stimuli in row 2.

The results of the two experiments show a very similar pattern. First, both younger and older adults show a significant decline of accuracy from row 2 to row 3, suggesting, for Exp. 1, a dual-task cost that is quite substantial and, for Exp. 2, an interference cost that is less substantial. Second, there is no hint of a significant age-by-row interaction, strongly suggesting that even with this complex stimulus set, older adults are not more susceptible to dual-task effects or to interference effects than younger adults are. A third and perhaps more important effect also emerged: Age differences are substantial and already present for row 2. This is remarkable, given that this implies that age differences exist for stimuli encoded under full attention less than a few seconds previously. The age difference in Exp. 2 shows that such age differences can even emerge when retrieval is done under full-attention conditions.

What can we conclude from these experiments? Our findings suggest that the age difference in accuracy after a focus switch is not due to specific age differences in source monitoring/context binding, to specific age differences in dealing with the dual-task situation inherent in the kind of memory updating required in these tasks, or to specific age differences in resistance to interference originating from intervening stimuli. We also note that we found such age differences when stimuli encoded under full-attention conditions were retrieved under full-attention conditions, which is about as favorable a circumstance as we can have in working memory. All of this suggests to us that the age difference is tied specifically to the focus switch and that once items need to be stored outside the focus, the probability of accurate retrieval declines more in older adults than in younger adults.

The findings reviewed earlier suggest that the problem is likely not one of capacity, at least when measured in terms of available slots: Older adults are able to access at least five slots as efficiently as younger adults do (which implicates that they possess these slots), and the capacity of the passive short-term memory system declines much less than that of working memory. This in turn suggests that the problem might be one of memory resolution (i.e., how detailed and discriminable the representation within a slot is. Obviously, more research is needed to corroborate this assertion.

AGE-RELATED DIFFERENCES IN PLASTICITY
OF THE SIZE OF THE FOCUS OF ATTENTION

As mentioned before, all of our work to date (as well as work by Garavan, 1998; McElree, 2001; and Oberauer, 2002, among others) suggests the engagement of a focus switch process as soon as more than a single item needs to be attended to, suggesting a focus that can hold only one item. There are, however, strong reasons to believe that under certain circumstances, the focus can hold three to four items. (An excellent review of these data can be found in Cowan, 2001.)

In one of our studies (Verhaeghen et al., 2004), we explored this discrepancy. Our hunch was that the size of the focus might differ according to the number of attentional resources subjects are able to allocate to storage of the memoranda in the presence of ongoing stimulus processing—the trade-off between storage and processing. Our reasoning was that, with continued practice, processing would become more automated and therefore resources otherwise devoted to processing could be freed for storage, perhaps leading to an expansion of the number of immediately accessible items. This is exactly what we found; Figure 1.8 shows data from four younger adults who practiced our N-back task for a total of 10 one-hour sessions.

These individuals were all able to expand the focus of attention from a single item to four: The step function from Session 1 made place for a ramped function with an uptick between $N = 4$ and $N = 5$. When we then subjected four older adults to this same practice regime (Basak, Cerella, & Verhaeghen, unpublished data, likewise reproduced in Figure 1.8), no such expansion was seen. The older adults did show practice effects, becoming faster in each session, but the step function remained firmly in place, its step situated between $N = 1$ and $N = 2$. The result suggests that the focus of attention in older adults is not expandable or at least not as easily as that of younger adults. Perhaps older adults have more difficulties with dual-task requirements, as was demonstrated in our meta-analyses described earlier.

AGE-RELATED DIFFERENCES IN ITEM AVAILABILITY
AFTER A FOCUS SWITCH: POTENTIAL CONSEQUENCES

A final question remains. Finding and cataloguing age differences in one thing, but building a theory with true explanatory power is another. The big question is whether the concept of item availability buys us anything new: Does the age difference in item availability explain anything of interest downstream in the cognitive system?

We already know that age differences in item availability are independent of age differences in item accessibility; we noted an accuracy difference in the absence of a speed difference. What we do not know is how much of the age-related variance in fluid cognition can be explained

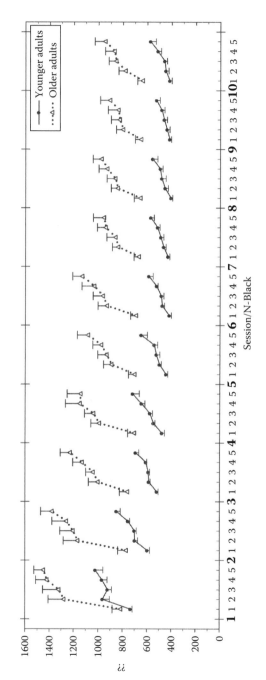

FIGURE 1.8 Ten-session practice data on an *N*-back task, younger and older adults (younger adults: subset of Verhaeghen, P. et al., 2004, *Journal of Experimental Psychology: Learning, Memory, and Cognition, 30*, 1322–1337; older adults: unpublished data collected by Basak, C., Cerella, J., & Verhaeghen, P.). The data suggest that the focus of attention expands to hold four items in younger adults, but does not expand at all for older adults. Error bars denote standard errors.

	WMC	FSA	Raven	Age
Working memory capacity	1			
Focus-switching accuracy	0.14	1		
Raven	0.33	0.44	1	
Age	−0.36	−0.44	−0.49	1

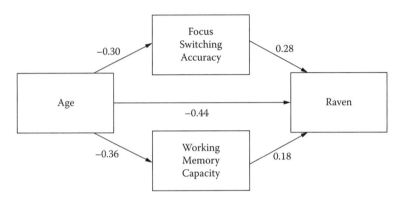

FIGURE 1.9 Correlation matrix between age, working-memory capacity, and accuracy (i.e., item availability) after a focus switch and Raven's test for spatial reasoning, as derived from a meta-analysis of the literature (top panel), as well as one possible path analysis derived from this matrix, indicating that item availability explains age-related variance in Raven over and beyond working-memory capacity.

through this mechanism because no relevant study has been conducted yet. It is possible, however, to simulate such a study by constructing a correlation matrix from the correlations available in the literature. Figure 1.9 shows such a correlation matrix pooled from the relevant correlations reported in Kane, Conway, Miura, and Colflesh (2007), Unsworth and Engle (2008), Vaughan et al. (2008), Verhaeghen and Basak (2005), and Verhaeghen and Salthouse (1997)—correlations between age, accuracy after a focus switch, working-memory capacity, and fluid intelligence. Given its prominence in theories of aging, speed of processing would be on the wish list for this matrix, but I am unaware of focus-switching studies that included this variable in a correlation matrix.

The figure also includes one possible (and well-fitting) path model. What the path analysis suggests is that accuracy after a focus switch mediates some of the age differences in fluid intelligence over and beyond the mediation achieved by working-memory capacity. This then suggest that item availability after a focus switch might be an important new and fundamental variable—a cognitive primitive—necessary for a full understanding of age effects in higher order cognition.

AGE DIFFERENCES IN WORKING MEMORY: AN INTERIM SUMMARY

My goal in this chapter was twofold: to describe age differences in working memory and to examine its causes and consequences. I noted that age differences in working-memory capacity are substantial. They do not appear to stem from deficits in resistance to interference or local task switch costs. There are, however, specific age-related deficits associated with dual-task set maintenance, as evidenced by specific effects on dual-task costs and global task-switch costs.

One additional under-studied aspect of working memory that appears to be age sensitive in some aspects, but not others, is memory updating, which we examined under the aspect of focus switching. First, the dynamics of the process appear to be exquisitely preserved: Older adults are able to access working-memory slots with an efficiency that equals that of younger adults. Second, in sharp contrast to the preserved dynamics, there appear to be severe limits to the availability of the items stored in those slots as soon as these items leave the focus of attention. We were unable to trace the source of this deficit; our experiments failed to support the hypothesis that this age-related decline in accuracy is due to source memory, to the dual-task requirement inherent in updating, or to increased susceptibility to interference. At present, we treat this item availability deficit as a deficit sui generis, of its own kind, irreducible to known control processes. Third, we found that although younger adults were seemingly able to expand the focus of attention from one to four memory items after extensive practice, older adults were not.

ACKNOWLEDGMENTS

The work presented here was supported by grant AG16201 of the National Institute on Aging. I would like to thank all my coauthors on the papers presented here: Chandramallika Basak, Kara Bopp, John Cerella, Bill Hoyer, Elke Lange, Marty Sliwinski, David Steitz, Christina Wasylyshyn, and Yanmin Zhang.

REFERENCES

Ackerman, P. L., Beier, M. E., & Boyle, M. O. (2005). Working memory and intelligence: The same or different constructs? *Psychological Bulletin, 131,* 30–60.

Adcock, R. A., Constable, R. T., Gore, J. C., & Goldman-Rakic, P. S. (2000). Functional neuroanatomy of executive processes involved in dual-task performance. *Proceedings of the National Academy of Sciences, 97,* 3567–3572.

Baddeley, A., & Hitch, G. J. (1974). Working memory. In G. Bower (Ed.), *The psychology of learning and motivation* (vol. 8, pp. 47–90). San Diego, CA: Academic Press.

Bopp, K. L., & Verhaeghen, P. (2005). Aging and verbal memory span: A meta-analysis. *Journal of Gerontology: Psychological Sciences, 60B,* 223–233.

Bopp, K. L., & Verhaeghen, P. (2007). Age-related differences in executive control processes in verbal and visuo-spatial working memory: Storage, transformation, supervision, and coordination. *Journals of Gerontology: Psychological Sciences, 62,* 239–246.

Bopp, K. L., & Verhaeghen, P. (2009). Working memory and aging: Separating the effects of content and context. *Psychology and Aging, 24,* 968–980.

Braver, T. S., & Barch, D. M. (2002). A theory of cognitive control, aging cognition and neuromodulation. *Neuroscience and Biobehavioral Reviews, 26,* 809–817.

Braver, T. S., Barch, D. M., Keys, B., Carter, C. S., Cohen, J. D., Kaye, J. A.,... Reed, B. R. (2001). Context processing in older adults: Evidence for a theory relating cognitive control to neurobiology in healthy aging. *Journal of Experimental Psychology: General, 130,* 746–763.

Brinley, J. F. (1965). Rigidity and the control of cognitive sets in relation to speed and accuracy of performance in the elderly. *Dissertation Abstracts, 26,* 1158–1159.

Cerella, J. (1990). Aging and information processing rate. In J. E. Birren & K. W. Schaie (Eds.), *Handbook of the psychology of aging* (3rd ed., pp. 201–221). San Diego, CA: Academic Press.

Cerella, J. (1994). Generalized slowing in Brinley plots. *Journal of Gerontology, 49,* P65–P71.

Chen, T., & Li, D. (2007). The roles of working memory updating and processing speed in mediating age-related differences in fluid intelligence. *Aging, Neuropsychology, and Cognition, 14,* 631–646.

Conway, A. R. A., Cowan, N., Bunting, M. F., Therriault, D. J., & Minkoff, S. R. B. (2002). A latent variable analysis of working memory capacity, short-term memory capacity, processing speed, and general fluid intelligence. *Intelligence, 30,* 163–183.

Cowan, N. (2001). The magical number 4 in short-term memory: A reconsideration of mental storage capacity. *Behavioral and Brain Sciences, 24,* 87–185.

Dunn, J. C., & Kirsner, K. (1988). Discovering functionally independent mental processes: The principle of reversed association. *Psychological Review, 95,* 91–101.

Engle, R. W., Kane, M. J., & Tuholski, S. W. (1999). Individual differences in working memory capacity and what they tell us about controlled attention, general fluid intelligence, and functions of the prefrontal cortex. In A. Miyake & P. Shah (Eds.), *Models of working memory: Mechanisms of active maintenance and executive control* (pp. 102–134). New York, NY: Cambridge University Press.

Engle, R. W., Tuholski, S. W., Laughlin, J. E., & Conway, A. R. A. (1999). Working memory, short-term memory, and general fluid intelligence: A latent-variable approach. *Journal of Experimental Psychology: General, 128,* 309–331.

Fisk, J. E., & Sharp, C. A. (2004). Age-related impairment in executive functioning: Updating, inhibition, shifting, and access. *Journal of Clinical and Experimental Neuropsychology, 26,* 874–890.

Friedman, N. P., & Miyake, A. (2004). The relations among inhibition and interference control functions: A latent variable analysis. *Journal of Experimental Psychology: General, 133,* 101–135.

Garavan, H. (1998). Serial attention within working memory. *Memory and Cognition, 26,* 263–276.

Hasher, L., Tonev, S. T., Lustig, C., & Zacks, R. T. (2001). Inhibitory control, environmental support, and self-initiated processing in aging. In M. Naveh-Benjamin, M. Moscovitch, & R. L. Roediger, III (Eds.), *Perspectives on human memory and cognitive aging: Essays in honour of Fergus Craik* (pp. 286–297). East Sussex, UK: Psychology Press.

Hasher, L., & Zacks, R. T. (1988). Working memory, comprehension, and aging: A review and a new view. In G. H. Bower (Ed.), *The psychology of learning and motivation* (Vol. 22, pp. 193–225). San Diego, CA: Academic Press.

Hasher, L., Zacks, R. T., & May, C. P. (1999). Inhibitory control, circadian arousal, and age. In D. Gopher & A. Koriat (Eds.), *Attention and performance. XVII, Cognitive regulation of performance: Interaction of theory and application* (pp. 653–675). Cambridge, MA: MIT Press.

Heitz, R. P., Redick, T. S., Hambrick, D. Z., Kane, M. J., Conway, A. R. A., & Engle, R. W. (2006). Working memory, executive function, and general fluid intelligence are not the same. *Behavioral and Brain Sciences, 29,* 135–136.

Kane, M. J., Bleckley, M. K., Conway, A. R. A., & Engle, R. W. (2001). A controlled-attention view of working memory capacity. *Journal of Experimental Psychology: General, 130,* 169–183.

Kane, M. J., Conway, A. R. A., Miura, T. K., & Colflesh, G. J. H. (2007). Working memory, attention control, and the *n*-back task: A question of construct validity. *Journal of Experimental Psychology: Learning, Memory, and Cognition, 33,* 615–622.

Kemper, S., Herman, R. E., & Lian, C. H. T. (2003). The costs of doing two things at once for young and older adults: Talking while walking, finger tapping, and ignoring speech noise. *Psychology and Aging, 18,* 181–192.

Kramer, A. F., Hahn, S., & Gopher, D. (1999). Task coordination and aging: Explorations of executive control processes in the task switching paradigm. *Acta Psychologica, 101,* 339–378.

Kyllonen, P. C. (1996). Is working memory capacity Spearman's *g*? In I. Dennis, & P. Tapsfield (Eds.), *Human abilities: Their nature and measurement* (pp. 49–75). Mahwah, NJ: Lawrence Erlbaum Associates.

Lange, E. B., & Verhaeghen, P. (2009). No age differences in complex memory search: Older adults search as efficiently as younger adults. *Psychology and Aging, 24,* 105–115.

Lange, E. B., Verhaeghen, P., & Cerella, J. (2010). Dual representation of item positions in short-term memory: Evidence for two access modes. *European Journal of Cognitive Psychology, 22,* 463–479.

Lövdén, M. (2003). The episodic memory and inhibition accounts of age-related increases in false memories: A consistency check. *Journal of Memory and Language, 49,* 268–283.

Mayr, U., Spieler, D. H., & Kliegl, R. (2001). *Aging and executive control.* New York, NY: Routledge.

McElree, B. (2001). Working memory and focal attention. *Journal of Experimental Psychology: Learning, Memory, and Cognition, 27,* 817–835.

Miyake, A., Friedman, N. P., Emerson, M. J., Witzki, A. H., & Howerter, A. (2000). The unity and diversity of executive functions and their contributions to complex "frontal lobe" tasks: A latent variable analysis. *Cognitive Psychology, 41,* 49–100.

Miyake, A., & Shah, P. (1999). Toward unified theories of working memory: Emerging general consensus, unresolved theoretical issues, and future research directions. In A. Miyake & P. Shah (Eds.) *Models of working memory: Mechanisms of active maintenance and executive control.* New York, NY: Cambridge University Press.

Moscovitch, M., & Winocur, G. (1995). Frontal lobes, memory, and aging. In J. Grafman, K. J. Holyoak, & F. Boller (Eds.), *Annals of the New York Academy of Sciences: Vol. 769, Structure and functions of the human prefrontal cortex* (pp. 119–150). New York, NY: New York Academy of Sciences.

Oberauer, K. (2002). Access to information in working memory: Exploring the focus of attention. *Journal of Experimental Psychology: Learning, Memory, and Cognition, 28,* 411–421.

Oberauer, K., Süß, H.-M., Schulze, R., Wilhelm, O. & Wittmann, W. W. (2000). Working memory capacity—Facets of a cognitive ability construct. *Personality and Individual Differences, 29,* 1017–1045.

Rosen, A., Prull, M. W., Gabrieli, J. D. E., Stoub, T., O'Hara, R., Friedman, L., Yesavage, J. A., & deToledo-Morrell, L. (2003). Differential associations between entorhinal and hippocampal volumes and memory performance in older adults. *Behavioral Neuroscience, 117,* 1150–1160.

Salthouse, T. A. (1996). The processing speed theory of adult age differences in cognition. *Psychological Review, 103,* 403–428.

Salthouse, T. A., & Pink, J. E. (2008). Why is working memory related to fluid intelligence? *Psychonomic Bulletin & Review, 15,* 364–371.

Schmiedek, F., Hildebrandt, A., Lövdén, M., Wilhelm, O., & Lindenberger, U. (2009). Complex span versus updating tasks of working memory: The gap is not that deep. *Journal of Experimental Psychology: Learning, Memory, and Cognition, 35,* 1089–1096.

Shelton, J. T., Elliott, E. E., Matthews, R. A., Hill, B. D., & Gouvier, W. D. (2010). The relationships of working memory, secondary memory, and general fluid intelligence: Working memory is special. *Journal of Experimental Psychology: Learning, Memory, and Cognition, 36,* 813–820.

Small, S. A., Tsai, W. Y., deLaPaz, R., Mayeux, R., & Stern, Y. (2002). Imaging hippocampal function across the human life span. Is memory decline normal or not? *Annals of Neurology, 51,* 290–295.

Unsworth, N., & Engle, R. W. (2008). Speed and accuracy of accessing information in working memory: An individual differences investigation of focus switching. *Journal of Experimental Psychology: Learning, Memory, and Cognition, 34,* 616–630.

Van der Linden, M., Brédart, S., & Beerten, A. (1994). Age-related differences in updating working memory. *British Journal of Psychology, 85,* 145–152.

Vaughan, L., Basak, C., Hartman, M., & Verhaeghen, P. (2008). Aging and working memory inside and outside the focus of attention: Dissociations of availability and accessibility. *Aging, Neuropsychology, and Cognition, 15,* 703–724.

Verhaeghen, P., & Basak, C. (2005). Aging and switching of the focus of attention in working memory: Results from a modified N-back task. *Quarterly Journal of Experimental Psychology, 58A*, 134–154.

Verhaeghen, P., & Cerella, J. (2002). Aging, executive control, and attention: A review of meta-analyses. *Neuroscience and Biobehavioral Reviews, 26*, 849–857.

Verhaeghen, P., & Cerella, J. (2008). Everything we know about aging and response times: A meta-analytic integration. In S. M. Hofer & D. F. Alwin (Eds.), *The handbook of cognitive aging: Interdisciplinary perspectives* (pp. 134–150). Thousand Oaks, CA: Sage Publications.

Verhaeghen, P., Cerella, J., & Basak, C. (2004). A working memory workout: How to change to size of the focus of attention from one to four in ten hours or less. *Journal of Experimental Psychology: Learning, Memory, and Cognition, 30*, 1322–1337.

Verhaeghen, P., Cerella, J., Bopp, K. L., & Basak, C. (2005). Aging and varieties of cognitive control: A review of meta-analyses on resistance to interference, coordination and task switching, and an experimental exploration of age-sensitivity in the newly identified process of focus switching. In R. W. Engle, G. Sedek, U. von Hecker, & D. N. McIntosh (Eds.), *Cognitive limitations in aging and psychopathology: Attention, working memory, and executive functions* (pp. 160–189). Cambridge, MA: Cambridge University Press.

Verhaeghen, P., & De Meersman, L. (1998a). Aging and negative priming: A meta-analysis. *Psychology and Aging, 13*, 435–444.

Verhaeghen, P., & De Meersman, L. (1998b). Aging and the Stroop effect: A meta-analysis. *Psychology and Aging, 13*, 120–126.

Verhaeghen, P., & Hoyer, W. J. (2007). Aging, focus switching and task switching in a continuous calculation task: Evidence toward a new working memory control process. *Aging, Neuropsychology, and Cognition, 14*, 22–39.

Verhaeghen, P., Kliegl, R., & Mayr, U. (1997). Sequential and coordinative complexity in time-accuracy functions for mental arithmetic. *Psychology and Aging, 12*, 555–564.

Verhaeghen, P., & Salthouse, T. A. (1997). Meta-analyses of age-cognition relations in adulthood: Estimates of linear and non-linear age effects and structural models. *Psychological Bulletin, 122*, 231–249.

Verhaeghen, P., Steitz, D. W., Sliwinski, M. J., & Cerella, J. (2003). Aging and dual-task performance: A meta-analysis. *Psychology and Aging, 18*, 443–460.

Voigt, S., & Hagendorf, H. (2002). The role of task context for component processes in focus switching. *Psychologische Beiträge, 44*, 248–274.

Wasylyshyn, C., Verhaeghen, P., & Sliwinski, M. J. (2011). Aging and task switching: A meta-analysis. *Psychology and Aging, 26*, 15–20.

West, R. L. (1996). An application of prefrontal cortex function theory to cognitive aging. *Psychological Bulletin, 120*, 272–292.

Zhang, Y., & Verhaeghen, P. (in preparation). Aging, dual task performance, resistance to interference, and working memory.

2 The interaction of linguistic constraints, working memory, and aging on language production and comprehension

Susan Kemper

INTRODUCTION

The ability to communicate is essential if older adults are to solicit assistance with daily living activities; fulfill life-long learning goals; gain access to health and legal information from print, broadcast, or electronic media; or enjoy intergenerational contacts with family members. Older adults need to communicate with their families, friends, neighbors, lawyers, and physicians through face-to-face interaction and over the Internet. Older adults' ability to communicate can be compromised by a variety of sensory impairments such as presbyopia and presbycusis as well as by other, more subtle impairments such as limitations of working-memory capacity, processing speed, and inhibitory control. As a result, some aspects of language processing are particularly vulnerable to the effects of aging. These vulnerabilities arise from the interplay of serial and hierarchical aspects of language within a limited capacity processing system.

This chapter provides a brief survey of serial versus hierarchical characteristics of language and a brief survey of age-related changes to working memory before discussing how aging, working memory, and language interact. It will conclude with a consideration of unresolved issues in the study of the interaction of aging, working memory, and language processing that builds on prior reviews in Kemper (1988, 1992).

SERIAL VERSUS HIERARCHICAL CHARACTERISTICS OF LANGUAGE

Although speech is produced "one word at a time," language is inherently hierarchical. A number of phenomena are typically discussed to illustrate the tension between the serial nature of speech and the hierarchical aspects of language:

- In English, datives and objects can alternate in the linear sequence for some verbs such as *give* (compare "Mary gave a cookie to me" to "Mary gave me a cookie") but not for others, such as *donate* ("Mary donated a million dollars to me" versus the ungrammaticality of "*Mary donated me a million dollars").
- Verbs must agree with their subjects in person and number; this constraint is violated in "Efforts to make English the official language is gaining strength throughout the U.S." (*The New Yorker,* November 17, 1986, p. 94); although the verb *is gaining* agrees with the immediately preceding noun, *language,* the grammatical subject of the sentence is the plural noun *efforts.*
- The interpretation of the scope of quantifiers such as *some* or *all* or *everyone* is influenced by word-order variation and clause embedding. Compare "Everyone in this room speaks two languages" to "Two languages are spoken by everyone in this room." Whereas the first sentence implies that each individual is fluent in two languages, the second implies that they are fluent in the same two languages.
- Temporary syntactic ambiguities can arise whenever the linear sequence can be assigned to multiple hierarchical structures. The sequence "The boy chased the dog with two bones" could be interpreted as indicating that the boy had two bones by attaching the prepositional phrase to the verb phrase ([[chased $_V$] [the dog $_{NP}$] [with two bones $_{PP}$] $_{VP}$]) or that the dog had two bones by attaching the prepositional phrase to the object noun phrase ([[chased $_V$] [the dog [with two bones $_{PP}$] $_{NP}$] $_{VP}$]).

As the following four examples show, English, like other languages, provides a number of ways to extend basic sentence structures through the use of different forms of recursion or embedding. One clause can be embedded within another, as a relative clause modifying a noun, as a gerund used as a noun, or as an infinitive complement to a verb. Thus, one clause is nested hierarchically within another.

The serial ordering of these clauses can also vary; two basic variations are demonstrated by the contrast between the sentences in 2 and in 3: In the left-branching constructions in 2, a clause is embedded within the subject of the sentence, which in English is typically to the left of the main verb. In the right-branching constructions in 3, a clause is embedded in the predicate of the sentence, typically to the right of the main verb. Multiple levels of embedding can occur, producing very complex branching patterns, as the examples in 4 demonstrate. Note that the right-branching version is understood easily because the sentence can be segmented into a sequence of noun–verb–noun triplets corresponding to a subject–verb–object clause, whereas the left-branching version is very difficult to understand because each noun must be paired with the correct verb to establish the proper subject–verb–object relations.

1. Relative clause: The baby smiled at the woman *who held him.*
   Gerund: *The baby's smiling* was pleasing to the woman.
   Infinitive complement: The woman tried *to get* the baby *to smile.*
   Subordinate clause: *After the woman picked him up,* the baby smiled.
   Clefts: *It was the baby* who smiled.

2. Left-branching:
   The mare *that I bought over to Wilson's Corners* foaled last night.
   That the stallion would never be a good sire never occurred to me.
   To go to the Chicago Exposition was a grand undertaking.

3. Right-branching:
   We planted the *pasture that Pa bought from old man Silas.*
   We didn't realize *that we had a hard life.*
   For five cents, my father rented me out with a team of horses *to pull gravel out of the riverbed.*

4. Left-branching:
   The painting the woman the man saw owned was stolen from the banker.
   Right-branching: The man saw the woman who owned the painting that was stolen from the banker.

All of these aspects of language must be correctly coordinated in order to produce a well-formed sentence or in order to understand one. This interplay of serial order and hierarchical structure appears to be vulnerable to age-related changes to working memory that limit the ability of older adults to produce and understand the full range of complex syntactic constructions possible in English.

WORKING MEMORY

Working memory is essential to many everyday tasks; it has two functions: the short-term retention of information and the manipulation of information. The prevailing model of working memory, as proposed by Baddeley and Hitch (1974), involves three components: two temporary storage mechanisms that buffer visual (e.g., the visual scratchpad) and auditory (e.g., the phonological loop) information and a central executive processor. A chief characteristic of these multicomponent systems is that the system has limited capacity to store information temporarily or to divide attention among processing tasks. Each component is also assumed to have unique characteristics: the auditory buffer is speech based while the visual buffer is spatially defined. The executive component serves different functions including attentional allocation and selection, inhibition, and information updating.

An age-related decline in working memory is apparent at the end of the life span, although what drives this decline is under debate (Park, Smith, Lautenschlager, Earles, et al., 1996). There is a debate between those who point to an age-related a decline in the storage capacity of working memory (Baddeley, 1986; Dobbs & Rule, 1986) and those that point to age-related declines in attentional control (Cowan, 1999; Engle & Kane, 2004). A variety of mechanisms have been proposed to account for the decline in working memory with advancing age. Salthouse (1988, 1996) has argued for processing speed as the fundamental mechanism; Lindenberger and Baltes (1994) and Baltes and Lindenberger (1997) have argued for neural integrity as measured by sensory acuity as the critical factor, and Hasher and Zacks (1988) have argued for a breakdown in inhibitory functions.

Inhibition is critical for blocking irrelevant information from entering working memory, deleting irrelevant information from working memory, and restraining prepotent responses. Under this hypothesis, older adults with poor inhibitory mechanisms may be not only more susceptible to distraction, but also less able to switch rapidly from one task to another and may rely on well-learned "stereotypes, heuristics, and schemas" (Yoon, May, & Hasher, 1998, p. 123). Recently, McCabe, Roediger, McDaniel, Balota, and Hambrick (2010) have proposed that working-memory capacity measures, measures of processing speed, and measures of inhibition and other executive functions overlap, defining a common executive attention component that is subject to age-related decline.

LANGUAGE AND AGING

The speech of older adults appears simplified in comparison to that of young adults (Kemper, 1987, 1992; Kemper, Kynette, Rash, O'Brien, & Sprott, 1989; Kemper, Rash, Kynette, & Norman, 1990). Although sentence length in words remains constant, older adults show a reduction in their use of complex syntactic constructions such as those involving subordinate and embedded clauses as illustrated in Figure 2.1 based on an analysis of handwritten diaries kept by individuals over seven decades. Consider the two language samples in Table 2.1. Both were produced by men who had completed 4 years of college education. Neither had a history of neurological disease, diabetes, ischemic heart disease, significant hearing loss, or other major medical conditions. Both are fluent and articulate; neither produces many sentence fragments or ungrammatical utterances. Speaker A uses many lexical fillers such as "you know," but he also manages to produce a range of different types of sentences using different forms of embedding. Speaker B tends to use short, grammatically simple sentences. One further difference between Speaker A and Speaker B is their ages: Speaker A is 25; Speaker B is 75.

Not only is there an overall decline in older adults' use of complex syntactic structures involving recursion and embedding, but there is also a specific decline in the types of embedded structures they do produce. Older

Table 2.1 Example language samples

Speaker A

Question: What are some good things and bad things about living in Lawrence?
I really like [MAIN] living [GER] in Lawrence.
You know [FILL] >
There aren't [MAIN] many bad things.
It's [MAIN] cool, you know [FILL].
Lawrence has [MAIN] a lot going [GER] for it.
There's [MAIN] always at lot to do [INF] on weekends and lots of, you know
    [FILL], cool bars and clubs.
Hanging out [GER] downtown is [MAIN] cool.
Club XXX is [MAIN] awesome.
I mean [MAIN] >
Going [GER] to Club XXX is [MAIN] awesome.
They get [MAIN] really great bands to come [INF] in and play.
Frisby golf>
Lawrence has [MAIN] this great frisby golf course, you know [FILL].
It's [MAIN] like [FILL] you know [FILL]>
You throw [MAIN] a frisby around a course, trying [GER] to make [INF] holes in one.
It's [MAIN] cool.
One of the coolest things about Lawrence>
Hanging [GER] out, going [GER] to clubs, playing [GER] frisby golf, that's [MAIN]
what I like [WH] about Lawrence.

Speaker B

Question: What are the good things about Lawrence?
The good things about Lawrence >
Are [MAIN] >
Honestly, uhh, >
I spent [MAIN] some time in Wichita.
And [FILL], umm >
That to me is [MAIN] cultural shock.
Lawrence is [MAIN] neat.
Lawrence is [MAIN] a great place.
There's [MAIN] pretty much everything here.
A lot of people work [MAIN] for KU.
KU brings [MAIN] a lot to Lawrence, all the sports and such.
I don't do [MAIN] that but many go [MAIN] to the games.
I go [MAIN] to the music a lot.
There's [MAIN] a lot of music at KU.
What's [MAIN] bad about Lawrence?
You can't park [MAIN] anywhere.
On a Saturday >
There's [MAIN] no place to park [INF].
I have [MAIN] trouble there.
And I bet [MAIN] a lot of people do [THAT].

Note: All main-clause verbs [MAIN], infinitives [INF], gerunds [GER], that-clauses [THAT], and wh-complement clauses [WH] are marked, as well as all lexical fillers [FILL]. Sentence fragments are marked with angles [>].

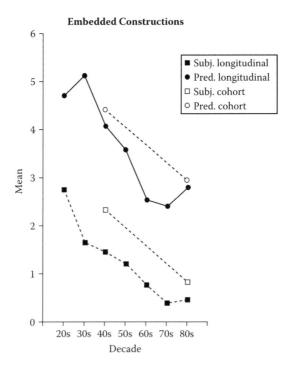

FIGURE 2.1 Comparison of age-related decline in the mean number of subject (subj.) or left-branching and predicate (pred.) or right-branching constructions (per 100 sentences) from longitudinal and cohort-sequential samples of written diary entries. (From Kemper, S., 1987, *Journal of Gerontology, 42,* 232–238. Copyright 1987 by the Gerontological Society of America.)

adults continue to produce coordinate or right-branching constructions (e.g., "She's awfully young to be running a nursery school for our church"), whereas left-branching constructions (e.g., "The gal who runs a nursery school for our church is awfully young") appear to be particularly vulnerable. During the production of the left-branching constructions (in which the embedded clause occurs to the left of the main clause), the form of the subject, *the gal,* must be retained and the grammatical form of the main clause verb, *is* (which must agree with its subject in person and number), must be anticipated while the embedded clause, *who runs a nursery school for our church,* is being produced. Each clause is produced sequentially in the right-branching construction (in which the embedded clause occurs to the right of the main clause), thus minimizing the demands for tracking and temporarily storing the various nouns and verbs.

Kemper, Thompson, and Marquis (2001) documented this decline longitudinally, examining oral language samples elicited from a panel of older adults over a 15-year period. This analysis indicated that the syntactic

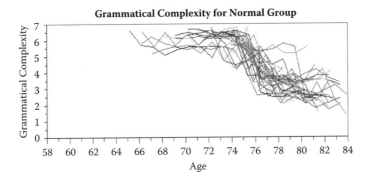

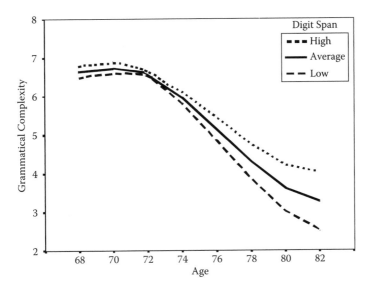

FIGURE 2.2 Longitudinal change in grammatical complexity (top panel) and the effect of individual differences in digit span on grammatical complexity for healthy older adults. (From Kemper, S. et al., 2001, *Psychology and Aging*, *16*, 600–614. Copyright 2001 by the American Psychological Association.)

complexity of healthy adults' speech begins to declines in late adulthood between ages 74 and 78. Their analysis suggested that the pattern of decline is a cubic function of age, such that a period of relative stability is followed by a period of accelerated decline and by a third period of more gradual decline. (See panel 1, Figure 2.2.) The analysis also indicated that there was considerable individual variation in older adults' initial level of grammatical complexity as well as individual variation in their rate of decline.

INTERACTION OF WORKING MEMORY, AGING, AND LANGUAGE

There is widespread agreement that working memory is critical to a wide range of linguistic tasks involving reading and listening comprehension. Performance on the reading- and listening-span tests of Daneman and Carpenter (1980) has been shown to be related to performance on reading and listening comprehension, learning to read, reading ability, arithmetic ability, and reasoning ability (Daneman & Blennerhassett, 1984; Daneman & Green, 1986; Daneman & Merikle, 1996; Daneman & Tardif, 1987; Hitch, Towse, & Hutton, 2001).

Working-memory limitations have also been tied to age-related declines in adults' ability to produce complex syntactic constructions. Kemper et al. (1989) reported that the mean number of clauses per utterance (MCU), a general measure of the complexity of adults' language, is positively correlated with the adults' backward digit span (Wechsler, 1958). See also Kemper and Sumner (2001) and Kemper and Rash (1988) for demonstrations of this linkage between speech complexity and working-memory capacity.

Recall that Kemper et al. (2001) documented a 15-year longitudinal decline in the syntactic complexity of oral language samples elicited from older adults; they sought to relate this decline in syntactic complexity to working memory. They noted that there was considerable individual variation in older adults' initial level of grammatical complexity as well as individual variation in their rate of decline. Their analysis suggested that an individual's initial level of grammatical complexity was predicted in part by the individual's composite score on the forward and backward digit span tests (Wechsler, 1958); further, the grammatical complexity of those with higher initial scores also declined somewhat more rapidly with advancing age. (See panel 2, Figure 2.2.) This line of research, therefore, suggests that working memory limitations may affect older adults' production of complex syntactic constructions by limiting their ability to produce embedded and recursive structures.

Just and his colleagues (Just & Carpenter, 1992; Just & Varma, 2002; King & Just, 1991; MacDonald, Just, & Carpenter, 1992) have also claimed that working-memory capacity limits the ability of older or low-span readers to analyze recursive structures, particularly those resulting in temporary syntactic ambiguities. According to the Just and Carpenter (1992) capacity-constrained (CC) theory (see also the 3CAPS model of Just & Varma, 2002), older or low-span readers should have difficulty processing temporary syntactic ambiguities and should exhibit "garden path" effects, initially misinterpreting ambiguous constructions only to reinterpret the constructions once disambiguating information is encountered. Young or high-span readers should be able to avoid garden path effects by constructing multiple syntactic interpretations of the ambiguous phrases and retaining these interpretations until disambiguating information is encountered.

For example, the fragment "the businessmen loaned money at low interest rates ..." has two interpretations. In the first, "loaned" is the main verb whose subject is "businessmen." This main verb interpretation is confirmed when the sentence ends this way: "The businessmen loaned money at low interest rates during the holiday season." Thus, in answer to the question "Who loaned the money?" the correct answer is "the businessmen."

In the second interpretation, "loaned" is part of a relative clause that has been reduced by deletion of its subject; the unreduced clause might be "the businessmen *who were* loaned money at low interest rates ..." This reduced relative clause interpretation of "loaned" is sustained when a second verb is encountered, as in "The businessmen loaned money at low interest rates recorded their expenses." Now it is clear that the question "Who loaned the money?" is correctly answered by indicating "don't know" or inferring "someone else, maybe a banker." The Just and Carpenter theory would hold that young or high-span readers can form both interpretations and retain them until disambiguating information is provided, whereas older or low-span readers should prefer the simpler, more common main verb interpretation of "loaned" and be forced to abandon this interpretation when the second verb is encountered.

This hypothesis has been carefully examined by Caplan and Waters (1999), who have considered a number of lines of evidence from studies of young and older adults as well as individuals with aphasia and dementia. They distinguish between immediate, interpretive syntactic processing and post interpretive semantic and pragmatic processing. Caplan and Waters argue that there is little evidence to support the hypothesis that working-memory limitations affect immediate syntactic processes; rather, they conclude that working-memory limitations affect postinterpretive processes involved in retaining information in memory in order to recall it or use it (e.g., to answer questions or match sentences against pictures).

In a variety of studies comparing adults stratified into groups based on measures of working memory, Caplan and Waters (1999) note that effects of syntactic complexity do not differentially affect high versus low-span readers or listeners. And they report that secondary tasks that impose additional processing demands on working memory do not differentially affect the processing of complex sentences. Caplan and Waters consider aphasic patients such as B. O., who had a digit span of only two or three digits but was able to perform as well as normal healthy older adults on a wide range of tasks with complex sentences. They also note that patients with Alzheimer's dementia, who also show severely limited working-memory capacity, are able to make speeded acceptability judgments of complex sentences as accurately as nondemented controls.

Waters and Caplan (1996a, 1996b, 1997, 2001) have directly examined the hypothesis that working-memory limitations affect older adults' ability to process complex sentences. These studies have used the auditory moving windows paradigm. This technique allows the listener to start and stop the presentation of sentences and permits the analysis of phrase-by-phrase listening times, analogous to visual moving windows paradigms that permit the analysis of word-by-word or phrase-by-phrase reading times. The studies by Caplan and Waters typically examine the processing of subject- and object-relative clause constructions, such as those in 5:

5. Object subject relative clause:
   The dancer found the music$_j$ that (t_j) delighted the director.
   Subject object relative clause:
   The music$_{i,j}$ that the dancer found (t_i) (t_j) delighted the director.

The object subject relative clause construction imposes few processing demands on the reader or the listener; the object of the main clause, the music, is also the subject of the embedded relative clause, (t_j). The subject object relative clause construction challenges the reader or listener to assign the correct syntactic relations; the subject of the main clause, (t_j), must also be interpreted as the object of the embedded clause, (t_i).

Waters and Caplan (2001) compared how young and older readers allocate listening times to critical phrases of relative clause sentences. Despite differences in working memory, listening times were distributed similarly by young and older listeners. All paused longer when they heard the embedded verb in the complex object relative clause sentences than when they heard the corresponding verb in the simple subject relative clause version; this additional time is attributable to the extra processing required to recover its direct object. They found no evidence that differences in age or working memory lead to different processing strategies, thus supporting their theory.

A recent study by Kemper, Crow, and Kemtes (2004) using eye-tracking methodology reexamined these issues. Eye tracking is a more naturalistic task that imposes few restrictions on readers; they are free to skip words or phrases, read ahead and glance backward, and reread entire segments. Using this technology, Kemper et al. examined three aspects of reading: first fixations to key phrases, regressions to earlier phrases, and the total time key phrases were fixated. They examined reduced relative clause sentences such as those in 6:

6. Reduced relative clause sentence:
   Several angry workers warned about the low wages decided to file complaints.
   Main clause sentence:
   Several angry workers warned about the low wages during the holiday season.
   Focused reduced relative clause sentence:
   Only angry workers warned about the low wages decided to file complaints.

Kemper et al. (2004) found partial support for Waters and Caplan's theory; young and older adults' first-pass fixations were alike and both groups showed a clear garden path effect: a peak in fixation time at the second verb in reduced relative clause sentences but not at the verb in main clause sentences. This garden path effect suggests that all readers initially interpret the first verb as the main verb and must reanalyze it when they encounter the second verb in the reduced relative clause sentence. However, Kemper et al. also observed an increase in regressions and in regression path fixations for older readers for the reduced relative clause sentences, suggesting that older adults were unable to parse these sentences correctly. Further, low-span readers, identified by their scores on a battery of working-memory tests, also produced more regressions and an increase in regression path fixations for reduced relative clause sentences, suggesting that they were unable to parse the sentences correctly.

The results from the eye-tracking analysis of the focused reduced relative clauses sentences also posed problems for Caplan and Waters's theory: High-span readers initially allocated additional processing time to the first noun phrase and then were able to avoid the garden path because the focus operator "only" led them to interpret the first verb phrase correctly as a reduced relative clause.

Kemper and Liu (2007) also used eye tracking to compare young and older adults' processing of unambiguous object-relative sentences and subject-relative sentences, such as the examples in 7 (at the end of this section), which differed in the locus of embedding and the form of the embedded sentences. Young and older adults showed similar patterns of the first pass fixation times, regression path fixations, and leftward regressions to critical regions for both types of cleft sentences and for object-subject relative clause sentences. However, older adults generally needed more time to process subject-object relative clause sentences than young adults did; they made more regressions back to both the main clause subject and the embedded clause subject than did young adults and, consequently, their regression path fixations for these critical regions were longer.

These findings directly contradict Waters and Caplan's hypothesis (2001) that working memory and sentence processing are unrelated. They also indicate that age group differences reflecting differences in working memory arise for some, but not all, types of sentences. Whereas fixation patterns of young and older adults were similar for both cleft subject and cleft object sentences and object subject sentences, subject object sentences gave rise to marked age group differences in regressions and regression path fixations. Cleft subject and object subject sentences can be parsed as two sequential clauses: The main clause is followed by an embedded clause signaled by a "that" complementizer, which is indexed to the preceding noun phrase. Cleft object sentences are somewhat more challenging to parse because the cleft object also serves as the object of the embedded clause and must be temporarily buffered while the embedded clause is processed.

Subject object sentences impose yet greater demands for parsing because the subject of the main clause must also be assigned as the object of the embedded clause; further, the embedded clause interrupts the main clause, so the main clause subject must be temporarily buffered if it is to be correctly linked with its verb.

It may be that there is a threshold for parsing complexity such that differences due to age group and, by inference, working-memory span are not apparent until this threshold is surpassed. What is apparent is that there are differences in the size of the temporary buffer required for syntactic analysis of subject object sentences, mirroring age differences in working memory as measured by traditional span measures. Compared to young adults, older adults, with smaller syntactic processing buffers, must make more regressions and allocate additional processing time to establish the main clause subject and relative clause subject of subject object sentences.

7. Cleft subject: It was the tailor that altered the suit coat.
   Cleft object: It was the suit coat that the tailor altered.
   Object subject: The dancer found the music that delighted the director.
   Subject object: The music that the dancer found delighted the director.

UNRESOLVED ISSUES

This review has shown that both age and working memory interact with the serial and hierarchical characteristics of language to affect the ease and accuracy with which individuals can produce and understand complex sentences. There is an active debate regarding how best to account for these effects: Gibson (1998) has suggested that both storage costs (affecting how long a noun phrase must be retained until it can be mapped onto a verb as its subject or object) and integration costs (affecting how readily semantic and pragmatic factors can be exploited to constrain possible mappings) determine processing costs. Others have suggested a variety of different mechanisms, including how many noun phrases or discourse referents must be simultaneously tracked, how distance is best computed (in words, in morphemes, in clauses), and when semantic and pragmatic information is considered.

Another significant issue that is unresolved is how the choice of language itself enters into this interaction. Consider the examples 8–10 at the end of this section. English, German, and Dutch contrast in their preferred branching structure: English commonly uses a right-branching pattern and, as we have seen, left-branching structures pose difficulty for English. Both Dutch and German commonly produce structures with a concatenation of sentence-final verbs, although the languages differ on how these verbs are mapped onto the preceding nouns. In German, the preferred mapping results in nested clauses; in Dutch, the preferred mapping results in clauses with crossed clauses. Bach, Brown, and Marslen-Wilson (1986) provided evidence that the crossed clauses of Dutch are easier to process than the nested clauses of German.

This debate is, of course, of particular relevance for Japanese; left-branching structures with crossed clauses are commonly produced in Japanese, according to Baker (2001). Baker contrasts the overall typology of English and Japanese, in examples 11 and 12 at the end of this section, as "prepositional" versus "postpositional." In English, the auxiliary verb *is* precedes the main verb *thinking,* the complementizer *that* introduces the embedded clause, the embedded clause follows the main verb, the direct object *picture* follows the verb *showed,* the reflexive *of himself* follows its referent *picture,* and the preposition *to* precedes the dative noun. In contrast, in Japanese, auxiliary verb *iru* follows the main verb *omette,* the complementizer *to* follows the embedded clause, the embedded clause precedes the main verb, the direct object precedes the verb, the reflexive *zibun-no* precedes its referent *syasin,* and the postposition *ni* follows the dative noun.

This preference of Japanese for left-branching structures as well as its preferred postpositional typology may have significant implications for processing models. However, this issue has received little attention, although Nakamura and Miyamoto (2006) and Miyamoto and Nakamura (2004) have suggested that Japanese crossed clauses are easier to process than nested clauses, based on comparing metalinguistic judgments and word-by-word reading time patterns. How age and working memory affect the processing or production of these types of structures in Japanese is unknown.

8. English: right-branching

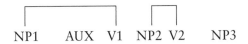

NP1   AUX   V1   NP2 V2   NP3

The men have taught Hans to feed the horses

9. German: nested

NP1   AUX   NP2 NP3   V1   V2

Die Männer haben Hans die Pferde füttern lehern

The men   have Hans the horses feed   teach

10. Dutch: crossed

| NP1 | AUX | NP2 | NP3 | V1 | V2 |

De mannen hebben Hans de paarden leren voeren

The men   have   Hans the horses teach feed

11. English: prepositional

Taro   is thinking   that   Hiro   showed a   picture

Taro-SUBJ PRS thinking   COMPL Hiro-SUBJ showed DET picture

                                of   himself to   Hana

                                PREP reflexive PREP Hana

12. Japanese: postpositional

Taro-ga   Hiro-ga   Hana-ni   zibun-no   syasin-o

Taro-SUBJ Hiro-SUBJ Hana-TO   self-POSS   picture-POSS

                        miseta   to   omette   iru

                        showed COMPL thinking PRS

Thus, there is still much to learn about how the serial and hierarchical characteristics of language, age, and working memory interact to affect language production and comprehension. Recent studies have shown that there is an age-related decline in the production of complex sentences, particularly those involving left-branching forms of embedding, and an age-related increase in the costs of processing such complex structures. While much of this work involves correlational analyses, new techniques including eye tracking provide more sensitive measures of these effects of age and working memory. There is much still to find out about other linguistic variations that challenge the processing abilities of older individuals, limit their access to information, and restrict interpersonal communication.

ACKNOWLEDGMENTS

Preparation of this chapter was supported in part by grants from the NIH to the University of Kansas through the Mental Retardation and Developmental Disabilities Research Center, grant number P30 HD-002528, and the Center for Biobehavioral Neurosciences in Communication Disorders, grant number P30 DC-005803, as well as by grants RO1 AG06319, K04 AG000443, P30 AG10182, RO1 AG09952, and RO1 AG025906 from the National Institute on Aging. Its contents are solely the responsibility of the author and do not necessarily represent the official views of the NIH.

REFERENCES

Bach, E., Brown, C. & Marslen-Wilson, W. (1986). Crossed and nested dependencies in German and Dutch: A psycholinguistic study. *Language and Cognitive Processes, 1*, 249–262.

Baddeley, A., & Hitch, G. J. (1974). Working memory. In G. A. Bower (Ed.), *The psychology of learning and motivation* (Vol. 8, pp. 47–89). New York, NY: Academic.

Baddeley, A. D. (1986). *Working memory.* Oxford, England: Clarendon Press.

Baker, Mark. (2001). *The atoms of language.* New York, NY: Basic Books.

Baltes, P. B., & Lindenberger, U. (1997). Emergence of a powerful connection between sensory and cognitive functions across the adult lifespan: A new window to the study of cognitive aging? *Psychology and Aging, 12*, 12–21.

Caplan, D., & Waters, G. (1999). Verbal working memory and sentence comprehension. *Behavioral and Brain Sciences, 22*, 114–126.

Cowan, N. (1999). An embedded-processes model of working memory. In A. Miyake & P. Shah (Eds.), *Models of working memory: Mechanisms of active maintenance and executive control* (pp. 62–101). Cambridge, England: Cambridge University Press.

Daneman, M., & Blennerhassett, A. (1984). How to assess the listening comprehension skills of prereaders. *Journal of Educational Psychology, 76*, 1372–1381.

Daneman, M., & Carpenter, P. A. (1980). Individual differences in working memory and reading. *Journal of Verbal Learning and Verbal Ability, 19*, 450–466.

Daneman, M., & Green, I. (1986). Individual differences in comprehending and producing words in context. *Journal of Memory and Language, 25*, 1–18.

Daneman, M., & Merikle, P. M. (1996). Working memory and language comprehension: A meta-analysis. *Psychnomic Bulletin and Review, 3*, 422–433.

Daneman, M., & Tardiff, T. (1987). Working memory and reading skill re-examined. In M. Coltheart (Ed.), *Attention and performance XII: The psychology of reading* (pp. 491–508). Hillsdale, NJ: Lawrence Erlbaum Associates.

Dobbs, A. R., & Rule, B. G. (1989). Adult age differences in working memory. *Psychology and Aging, 4*, 500–503.

Engle, R. W., & Kane, M. J. (2004). Executive attention, working memory capacity, and a two-factor theory of cognitive control. In B. Ross (Ed.), *The psychology of learning and motivation* (Vol. 44, pp. 145–199). New York, NY: Elsevier.

Gibson, E. (1998). Linguistic complexity: Locality of syntactic dependencies. *Cognition, 68*, 1–76.

Hasher, L., & Zacks, R. T. (1988). Working memory, comprehension, and aging: A review and a new view. In G. H. Bower (Ed.), *The psychology of learning and motivation* (Vol. 22, pp. 193–225). New York, NY: Academic Press.

Hitch, G. J., Towse, J. N., & Hutton, U. (2001). What limits children's working memory span? Theoretical accounts and applications for scholastic development. *Journal of Experimental Psychology: General, 130*, 184–198.

Just, M., & Varma, S. (2002). A hybrid architecture for working memory: A reply to MacDonald and Christiansen (2002). *Psychology Review, 109,* 55–65.

Just, M. A., & Carpenter, P. A. (1992). A capacity theory of comprehension: Individual differences in working memory. *Psychological Review, 99,* 122–149.

Kemper, S. (1987). Life-span changes in syntactic complexity. *Journal of Gerontology, 42,* 232–238.

Kemper, S. (1988). Geriatric psycholinguistics: Syntactic limitations of oral and written language. In L. Light & D. Burke (Eds.), *Language, memory, and aging.* Cambridge, England: Cambridge University Press.

Kemper, S. (1992). Language and aging. In F. I. M. Craik & T. A. Salthouse (Eds.), *Handbook of aging and cognition.* Hillsdale, NJ: Lawrence Erlbaum Associates.

Kemper, S., Crow, A., & Kemtes, K. (2004). Eye fixation patterns of high and low span young and older adults: Down the garden path and back again. *Psychology and Aging, 19,* 157–170.

Kemper, S., Kynette, D., Rash, S., O'Brien, K., & Sprott, R. (1989) Life-span changes to adults' language: Effects of memory and genre. *Applied Psycholinguistics, 10,* 49–66.

Kemper, S., & Liu, C. J. (2007). Eye movements of young and older adults during reading. *Psychology and Aging, 22,* 84–94.

Kemper, S., & Rash, S. J. (1988). Speech and writing across the life-span. In M. Gruneberg, P. Morris, & R. Sykes (Eds.), *Practical aspects of memory II.* London, England: John Wiley & Sons.

Kemper, S., Rash, S., Kynette, D., & Norman, S. (1990). Telling stories: The structure of adults' narratives. *European Journal of Cognitive Psychology, 2,* 205–228.

Kemper, S. & Sumner, A. (2001). The structure of verbal abilities in young and older adults. *Psychology and Aging, 16,* 312–322.

Kemper, S., Thompson, M., & Marquis, J. (2001). Longitudinal change in language production: Effects of aging and dementia on grammatical complexity and propositional content. *Psychology and Aging, 16,* 600–614.

King, J., & Just, M. A. (1991). Individual differences in syntactic processing: The role of working memory. *Journal of Memory and Language, 30,* 580–602.

Lindenberger, U., & Baltes, P. B. (1994). Sensory functioning and intelligence in old age: A strong connection. *Psychology and Aging, 9,* 339–355.

MacDonald, M., Just, M. A., & Carpenter, P. A. (1992). Working memory constraints on the processing of syntactic ambiguity. *Cognitive Psychology, 24,* 56–98.

McCabe, D. P., Roediger, H. L., III, McDaniel, M. A., Balota, D. A., & Hambrick, D. Z. (2010). The relationship between working memory capacity and executive functioning: Evidence for a common executive attention construct. *Neuropsychology, 24,* 222–243.

Miyamoto, E. T., & Nakamura, M. (2004). Subject/object asymmetries in the processing of relative clauses in Japanese. In G. Garding & M. Tsujimura (Eds.), *Proceedings of the 22nd West Coast Conference on Formal Linguistics,* 342–355.

Nakamura, M., & Miyamoto, E. T. (2006). Crossed dependencies and plausibility factors in the interpretation of double-gap relative clauses in Japanese. *Cognitive Studies, 13,* 369–391.

Park, D. C., Smith, A. D., Lautenschlager, G., Earles, J. L., Frieske, D., Zwahr, M., & Gaines, C. L. (1996). Mediators of long-term memory performance across the life span. *Psychology and Aging, 11,* 621–637.

Salthouse, T. A. (1988). The role of processing resources in cognitive aging. In M. L. Howe & C. J. Brainerd (Eds.), *Cognitive development in adulthood: Progress in cognitive development research* (pp. 185–239). New York, NY: Springer–Verlag.

Salthouse, T. A. (1996). The processing-speed theory of adult age differences in cognition. *Psychological Review, 3,* 403–428.

Waters, G. S., & Caplan, D. (1996a). The capacity theory of sentence comprehension: Critique of Just and Carpenter (1992). *Psychological Review, 103,* 761–772.

Waters, G. S., & Caplan, D. (1996b). The capacity theory of sentence comprehension: New frontiers of evidence and arguments). *Psychological Review, 103,* 773–780.

Waters, G. S., & Caplan, D. (1997). Working memory and on-line sentence comprehension in patients with Alzheimer's disease. *Journal of Psycholinguistic Research, 26,* 337–400.

Waters, G. S., & Caplan, D. (2001). Age, working memory, and on-line syntactic processing in sentence comprehension. *Psychology and Aging, 16,* 128–144.

Yoon, C., May, C. P., & Hasher, L. (1998). *Aging, circadian arousal patterns, and cognition.* Philadelphia, PA: Psychology Press.

Wechsler, D. (1958). *The measurement and appraisal of adult intelligence.* Baltimore, MD: Williams & Wilkins.

3 Error repetition phenomenon and its relation to cognitive control, working memory, and aging

Why does it happen outside the psychology laboratory?

Etsuko T. Harada, Satoru Suto, and Akihiro Asano

AGING AND HUMAN–INFORMATION TECHNOLOGY EQUIPMENT INTERACTION

There is a relatively long history of studies about memory and aging that are particularly insightful about how healthy aging relates to and differs from the cognitive malfunctions associated with illness such as Alzheimer's disease and vascular dementia. Unfortunately, data from the psychology laboratory cannot be applied directly to making a variety of information technology (IT) products easier for healthy older adults to use—even though there is clearly an acute need to understand why older adults often experience problems in using many IT-based products and to investigate how to make these products easier to use (Hara, Naka, & Harada, 2009; Harada, Mori, & Taniue, 2010; Mykityshyn, Fisk, & Rogers, 2002).

Currently, many advanced countries, including Japan, are experiencing two kinds of rapid social change: social aging and dependency on information and communication technology (ICT or IT). Against this background, many community-dwelling older adults frequently experience trouble with IT products. For example, they need to carry mobile phones because the availability of public phones has dramatically decreased in recent years, they must operate automatic teller machines (ATMs) to withdraw money from the bank, and when they wish to receive some forms of social support, they are usually advised to access the websites of local government offices in order to obtain relevant information.

In attempting to understand how and why older adults differ from younger adults in their use of IT, researchers and practitioners within cognitive engineering have started to compare older and younger adults in terms of their performance on usability tests for IT equipment. Interestingly enough, many common characteristics have been identified despite considerable differences in the equipment tested—from personal computer to rice cooker (Harada & Akatsu, 2003).

For example, older adults frequently have difficulty with salient perceptual/cognitive stimuli (e.g., voice instructions). Almost all ATMs at Japanese banks are installed with voice instructions; if a certain period of time elapses without user input, the instructions repeatedly talk to users to provide guidance about how to operate the ATM. During one usability test involving making a remittance using an ATM, an older adult participant was looking for the next operation after she had input her name as the remitter. The voice instructions said, "Please input the name of the remitter." Upon hearing this instruction, the participant input her name again and whispered to herself, "Oh, I input my name twice." This kind of instruction error happens because ATM systems do not monitor the progress of a user's operation on the screen; thus, the machine will simply repeat the relevant instruction for that screen. Older adults make the same kinds of errors when faced with a mechanical device that has a button with an easy word on it (e.g., the "catch" button on a multifunction telephone).

Older adults can also have problems in noticing the appearance or change of information on displays. Because of the characteristics of information in electrical formats, many types of IT equipment have displays where various kinds of information are presented. In fact, when younger adults try to operate a new item, they tend to expect to touch the "soft key" for some new function on the liquid crystal display. However, older participants mainly look for hard (mechanical) buttons. Older adults frequently fail to notice changes to a display, so they sometimes continue to look for *something* even after they have received the needed information from the display.

Based on these and other characteristic behaviors, Harada (2009; based on Harada & Akatsu, 2003) proposed a four-layer model that illustrates why IT equipment can be difficult for older adults to use (Figure 3.1):

Layer 0 incorporates declines in perception and/or physical abilities and reflects the effortful hypothesis (McCoy et al., 2005; Wingfield, Tun, & McCoy, 2005)—namely, that older adults faced with such problems require more effort and energy to regulate perception and their physical selves. This results in fewer resources remaining for higher cognitive processes.

Layer 1 holds problems arising from the cognitive processes associated with aging. Such aging changes include a decrease in working memory capacity (Craik, 1986), slowing of cognitive processing speed (Salthouse, 1991), and/or a decline in inhibition (Hasher & Zacks, 1988). The effects of these cognitive changes have been directly observed in many interactions when older adults use IT

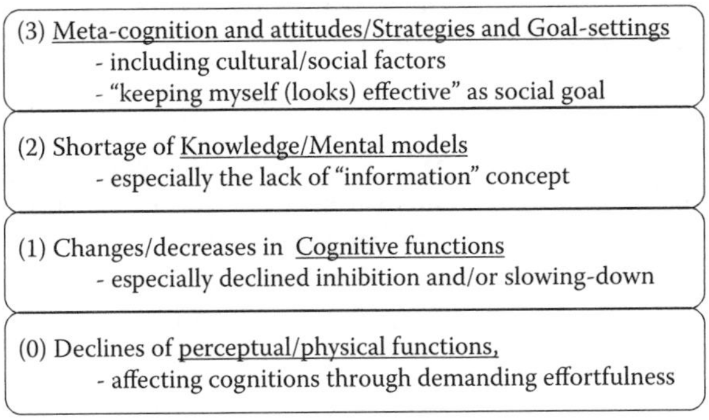

(3) <u>Meta-cognition and attitudes/Strategies and Goal-settings</u>
    - including cultural/social factors
    - "keeping myself (looks) effective" as social goal

(2) Shortage of <u>Knowledge/Mental models</u>
    - especially the lack of "information" concept

(1) Changes/decreases in <u>Cognitive functions</u>
    - especially declined inhibition and/or slowing-down

(0) Declines of <u>perceptual/physical functions,</u>
    - affecting cognitions through demanding effortfulness

FIGURE 3.1 Hypothetical sources of difficulties in using IT artifacts with cognitive aging: a four-layered model. (Harada, E. T., 2009, *Japanese Psychological Review, 52,* 383–395.)

equipment—for example, failures to notice information changes, as described earlier, or the need for more time to understand displayed messages as compared with younger adults (Hara et al., 2009).

Layer 2 describes difficulties faced by older adults when they use IT equipment that are related to the potential lack of knowledge about how to use equipment and/or about general concepts underlying electrical information technology. Adults who are 65 or older are especially likely to have relatively poor mental models of information technology, perhaps because they have encountered the computational concept of information late in life or due to limited opportunities to learn the concepts employed in such technology.

Layer 3 represents another causal feature of older adults' deficits in coping with IT that is related to higher cognition. Older adults often recognize their cognitive changes and are aware of the areas in which they lack knowledge. Such metacognition, blended with social cognition and motivation, results in goal setting, attitudes, and strategies in older adults that are different from those of younger adults. For instance, older adults are likely to avoid using computer-like IT equipment or to rely heavily on the instructions. These kinds of behaviors illustrate computer-stereotype threatening (Harada, 2009) which is an example of stereotype threatening with aging (Chasteen, Bhattacharyya, Horhota, Tam, & Hasher, 2005).

This four-layer model closely resembles the multiple facets of memory and aging (Hess & Emery, Chapter 8, this volume). Observing the activities of older adults within their lives (i.e., in vivo) may reveal the complexity and interrelated natures of cognitive-aging phenomena, which are an amalgam of different causes—from physical/cognitive aging to value setting within social activities.

ERROR REPETITION AS A CHARACTERISTIC PHENOMENON FOR OLDER ADULTS USING IT EQUIPMENT

Harada and Akatsu (2003) listed five different phenomena observed in older adults using IT equipment (Table 3.1). One of the most interesting for cognitive psychologists was the phenomenon of error repetition. Older people using IT equipment often repeat the same erroneous behavior. For example, Figure 3.2(a) is a representation of an ATM screen requesting the user's personal identify number (PIN). Because the four circled options just under the message "please input the PIN" are sufficiently large to push or appear to offer strong encouragement to push them, many older and even some younger adults push these circles in attempting to enter a PIN (usually murmuring the four digits of the PIN at the same time). The cause of this error can be attributed to the poor design of the screen: Even though these four circles are intended to serve as a feedback mechanism indicating how many of the digits have been entered via the 10-key buttons, their location and size encourage users to push them instead.

We have observed that these kinds of poor design are universally misleading across the range of age groups, prompting errors in older adults and eliciting microslips (Suzuki, Mishima, & Sasaki, 1997) or hesitation in younger adults (Akatsu, Harada, Miki, & Komatsubara, 2011; Harada et al., 2010). In fact, it is not unusual for younger adults to make the same error as older adults in such situations.

However, there is a marked difference between younger and older adults after the first error. Younger adults rarely repeat the same mistake. In contrast, older adults frequently make the same error at the next opportunity. In the previous example of pushing the feedback circles on the ATM screen, although the voice guidance system repeatedly gives the instruction, "Please enter your PIN," older adults will persist in pushing the feedback circles rather than touching the number keys.

In another example, when older adults using a simple text communication system known as *sukoyaka-ryota* (Figure 3.2b) want to proceed to

---

Table 3.1 Common features observed for older adult users across usability testing

(1) Vulnerability to (inadequate) perceptual/cognitive salient stimulus

(2) Unawareness of the existence of and/or changes to information within a display

(3) Some commonalities/large differences in learning

(4) Error repetition

(5) Attitudes, especially changes between with- and without computer-like appearances

Source: Harada, E. T., & Akatsu, H. (2003). In E. T. Harada (Ed.), *Cognitive Studies of Human–Artifacts Interaction: What Is "Usability"?* (pp. 119–138). Tokyo, Japan: Kyoritsu-syuppan.

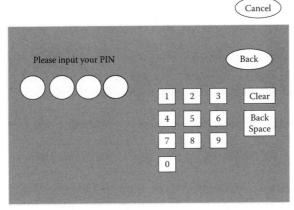

(a) ATM screen: older adults push the circle
(feedback area) under the instruction

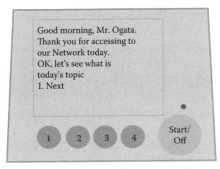

(b) Screen of "Sukoyaka-ryota", a text communication
system: older adults push buttons #2 or #3, when they
are reading the instruction as "1. Next".!

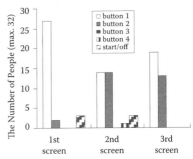

(c) Rates of participants who pushed each
button with the instruction "1. Next"
in function of the screen number.

FIGURE 3.2 Design examples that elicit error repetitions in older adults.

the next "page," they often press the wrong button (e.g., either "2" or "3" when the display instruction is "1. Next"). There are only five buttons on the machine (four buttons, with numbers 1 to 4 on top, and the power supply button, Start/End). When the system asks a question (e.g., "Did you sleep well last night?"), four choices are displayed and participants can select one button (e.g., 1. Yes, I slept well; 2. I slept, but not so well; 3. I slept only briefly; 4. No, I could not sleep).

The prompt message of "1. Next" is a conventional technique with this kind of IT equipment, requiring the user to push button number 1 to proceed to the next page. Although the reasons why older adults have a tendency to push button number 2 when they see the "1. Next" instruction are not clear yet (Ogata, Harada, & Mori, 2005), it is interesting that the error did not occur at the very first screen or the first page (Figure 3.2c). That participants make this error from the second or subsequent pages may reflect the fact that the sources of this error are related to the mental images reflecting the physical book page of the participants. More interestingly for the present context, however, this error was repeated very frequently by certain participants, both at this screen and at other screens (with the same prompt of "1. Next"); the maximum number of repetitions by one participant pushing button number 2 instead of button number 1 was 138.

Such phenomena are rather curious because all the participants were healthy and functioning well, and they appeared to be in good form in general until they made an error. This is quite a famous phenomenon in the usability testing lab, and anyone who regularly conducts such tests with older adults will have encountered it when various kinds of products are tested. The only other phenomenon related to error repetition that is well known to cognitive psychologists is the preservation error on the Wisconsin card sort test (WCST). Error repetition in the usability lab is a little different from the preservation error in WCST, even though we do not have any data for comparing these two phenomena. Error repetition tends to be a quick response to a stimulus, while the preservation error can be very slow. Do participants repeat the error because they do not know that the operation is not correct due to a lack of IT knowledge? Perhaps not—sometimes participants comment out loud that this is not the correct operation, even as they continue the erroneous behavior. Here, we can see some kind of discrepancy between conscious processing and automatic responding that may reflect different characteristics from the errors on the WCST.

WHY DOES ERROR REPETITION OCCUR?
CONSCIOUS CONTROL AND WORKING MEMORY

We think that investigating this error-repetition phenomenon is important for enhancing the usability of interface designs for older adults and for investigating cognitive aging because it seems to be related to declines in inhibition from past experiences when selecting one from multiple response possibilities. From this intuition, we hypothesize a basic mechanism of error repetition, based on the dual process hypothesis (Jacoby, Kelley, & McElree, 1999).

At first, there is an error, which may be elicited by bad design or a cognitive or perceptual "trap" offered by incorrect affordance (Norman, 1988). Due to the universality of design, these errors can occur even with younger adults in many situations (Harada, Mori, & Taniue, 2010). However, younger adults can somehow avoid repeating the same error. How is this possible? The error may be triggered and elicited extrinsically and processed automatically. Remembering the prior error and/or some knowledge that the action does not seem to be the correct way to respond inhibits or stops automatic processing by controlled/conscious processing. Through the full functioning of both automatic processing and conscious control, younger adults do not repeat their errors. However, with weak or delayed processing of conscious control by older adults, erroneous but automatic processing cannot be inhibited and erroneous responses can be repeated, even though the operator knows that they are incorrect.

With this hypothesis, we can understand the phenomenon. That is, it is hypothesized that the phenomenon of error repetition results from the interplay of automatic and controlled processes, which should be related to functions of working memory—especially to central executive processes (Barrett, Tugade, & Engle, 2004). Because aging causes significant changes in working memory, including reductions in cognitive capacity (Craik & Byrd, 1982) as well as various kinds of cognitive control (Braver & West, 2008), it may be no mystery as to why only older adults show the phenomenon of error repetition.

However, we cannot explain why this phenomenon is frequently observed in the usability lab, but not in the cognitive psychology lab. Something special about using IT equipment is eliciting this kind of error repetition, giving rise to misalignments between the two kinds of processing modes. In other words, if we seek out the reason why the error-repetition phenomenon occurs in usage of IT equipment, this would bring out some specific aspects of working memory related to IT equipment use that show a specific susceptibility to aging.

Thus, in order to investigate the condition necessary for the elicitation of the error-repetition phenomenon, we decided to create an experimental task to try to replicate the phenomenon in the psychology lab.

EXPERIMENTAL TASK TO ELICIT THE ERROR-REPETITION PHENOMENON: A KANJI SELECTION TASK

To replicate the phenomenon of error repetition using IT equipment with a simpler psychological task, it was necessary to extract the stimulus characteristics that IT equipment have in common, from the viewpoint of cognitive processing. Within cognitive psychology, the processes of inhibition and their relation to cognitive aging have been investigated using a number of tasks. Generally, these tasks use complicated or difficult stimuli that require participants to inhibit or control some processing. One example is the visual search task, which consists of a target with many dummy stimuli surrounding it. Differentiating dummy stimuli that are similar to the target (e.g., looking for an "O" among a set of "Q" stimuli) is difficult and requires inhibition of responses to the dummy stimuli (compared to differentiating dissimilar dummy stimuli such as "T"). In this kind of inhibitory task, the source of difficulty with the stimulus comes from the similar dummies, which, although generally multiple in number, are all the same. Although identifying a target from many other candidates is a frequent feature of using IT equipment, it is not the same as the visual search task because dummy stimuli are never the same as those found in real IT equipment.

Another popular task is the go/no-go task, which presents a simple target alone; the difficulty comes from the sequence of stimuli. It may be interesting to analyze the sequential characteristics of error repetition observed in the field, but generally these are not a common feature of the phenomenon. The most typical and dramatic stimulus to investigate inhibition might be a Stroop-type stimulus (e.g., the word "green" printed in red ink). Such stimuli are complicated and compound, based on the stimulus itself, and they sometimes include contradictory information. Again, looking for this type of compound stimulus within the context of IT equipment might be interesting, although it seems rare in the real world.

Thus, because we could not find a suitable psychological task with stimuli that have characteristics in common with the kinds of stimuli associated with IT equipment and because of the possibility of eliciting error repetition, we decided to create a new task that would need to meet the following criteria: (1) a target and multiple other candidates, which are all different, and (2) a continuum in terms of the degree of plausibility within candidates, such that one (or two) of the candidates would look similar to the target (referred to as the "lures").

In order to prepare such materials for many trials with adequate control, we created a *kanji* selection task (Harada & Suto, 2004). The Japanese language has many homophones—words that share the same pronunciation: For example, words with the pronunciation of /hasi/ are 端, meaning "edge"; 橋, meaning "bridge"; and 箸, meaning "chopsticks." Japanese speakers can or should determine which kanji orthography representation is appropriate for the particular word within the context of a sentence. Because of this language characteristic, when Japanese people enter Japanese into a computer through a keyboard, they input the pronunciation and then select the appropriate kanji from a list that may include just a few kanji or many tens of candidates.

Mimicking this method of interacting with a computer, our task asks a participant to read a contextual sentence where the pronunciation of one word, written in *katakana* (a syllabic script), is highlighted. Then, four kanji orthography candidate words are presented and the participant is to select the correct one to match the word in the sentence. The four candidates include the correct answer, a homophone as a lure, and two words with different pronunciations (real dummies), which are arranged in a random order along a row. The procedure in a trial is illustrated in Figure 3.3; however, the key point of the task is the procedure that follows when a participant makes an incorrect selection. On such trials, no feedback information is provided and the identical trial (the same context sentence and the same four candidate words) is presented again as the next trial. A particular trial will be presented up to three times if the correct answer is not selected.

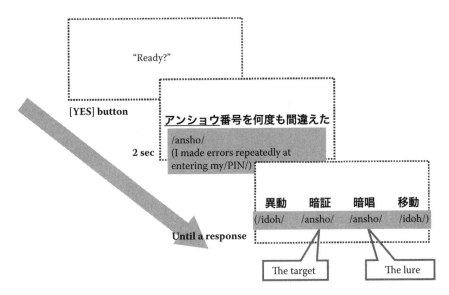

FIGURE 3.3 Task flow and description of the materials for the kanji selection task.

Participants are informed that there might be occasional repetitions of the same problem due to a bug in the computer program (i.e., participants are not told that the same trial will be repeated when they make an error in their answer).

The first experiment (Harada & Suto, 2004) with this kanji selection task was executed with 16 older adults (age 62–78; mean 68.56, SD 4.27) and 24 university students (age 18–22). The older participants were recruited from a senior community center and were paid for their participation, whereas the younger adults were given a partial class credit for their participation. The task was programmed for a personal computer and run with a 15-inch touch panel display (TOTOKU) placed horizontally for easy responding.

Unfortunately, we found that the participants almost never repeated selection errors with this task (mean number of trials for older: 0.56; for younger: 0), even though this error occurred with reasonable frequency on the first trial and there was an aging effect (the mean number of trials for older adults was 7.43 and 5.68 for younger adults over 48 trials). We were quite disappointed, but when we looked at the data closely, we discerned an interesting tendency. There was a systematic difference in the correct response rates as a function of the relative position of the lure to the target (Figure 3.4). The older adults showed poorer performance than the younger adults; however, both age groups showed higher errors for the lure when it was nearer to the target, although this was only when it was located to the

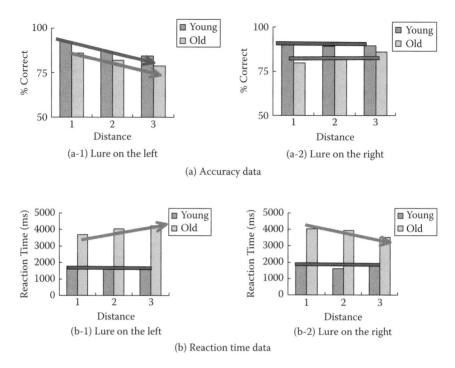

FIGURE 3.4 Accuracy and reaction time data for Exp. 1 as a function of the relative position of the lure from the target.

left side of the target along the horizontal row (Figure 3.4a). Reaction time data also indicated a similar systematic difference as a function of the relative locations of the target and lure, but only for the older adult participants (Figure 3.4b).

The existence of these systematic performance differences associated with the relative locations of the lure and target imply that participants may have employed a spatial strategy that might have helped them to escape error repetition. That is, the multiple candidates in a row may have provided the participants with some clues or a framework for a strategic way of answering without error repetition. Stating that in a different way, if fewer spatial clues were provided to the participants, it might become more difficult to make a selection decision within this task and, with such a shift in the level of task difficulty, it is possible that more error repetition might occur. Accordingly, we decided to add an additional dimension of spatial randomness by arranging the locations of the four candidate responses (as illustrated in Figure 3.5) such that the candidates no longer formed a straight line. Because a pilot study conducted with younger adults indicated a few error repetitions with this random-spatial version of the kanji selection task, a new series of experiments were undertaken.

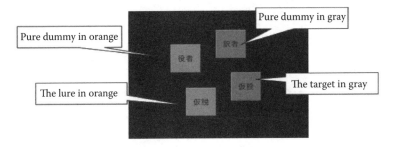

FIGURE 3.5 Example of the task screen for the random spatial version of the kanji selection task.

WHEN DO PEOPLE EXHIBIT ERROR REPETITIONS?
WHAT IS THE NECESSARY CONDITION?

The main purpose of these experiments was to investigate when and how error repetition occurs. In the subsequent experiment, we sought to examine whether cognitive aging and perceptual salience are factors that elicit error repetition. Craik and his colleagues have repeatedly demonstrated that the performance levels of older adults are similar to the performance levels of younger adults under conditions of divided attention (e.g., Anderson, Craik, & Naveh-Benjamin, 1998); this provides the basis for the cognitive capacity hypothesis for cognitive aging. Thus, we included a dual-task condition in order to compare performance on the single-task condition with younger adult participants. At the same time, a factor of perceptual salience was added to examine whether any extrinsic factors are primary causes of the error-repetition phenomenon, on the hypothesis that capturing attention with a salient stimulus could enhance or speed up automatic processing, causing a relative decline in the inhibition on error repetitions.

Thirty-two younger adults were randomly assigned to the two experimental conditions: a single-task condition and a dual-task condition. For the dual-task condition, a single digit was presented auditorily every 2 seconds, and one-back shadowing was executed as the secondary task. Perceptual salience was also introduced as a within-participants factor; for the salient condition, two of four buttons (lures) were vivid orange and the target button was gray.

Figure 3.6 presents the experimental results: Under the divided-attention condition, error repetitions were observed in the younger adult participants. There was a two-way interaction between the task condition (single vs. dual) and the perceptual salience condition. That is, perceptual salience exerted an influence but it was small and only observed in the divided-attention condition, implying that perceptual salience is not an eliciting factor but rather a reinforcement factor for the error-repetition phenomenon (Harada & Suto, 2004).

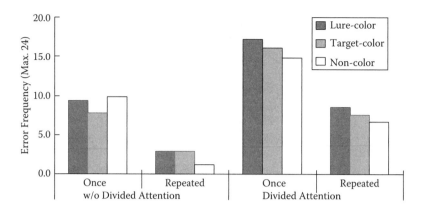

FIGURE 3.6 Results of the kanji selection task for younger adults with/without divided attention.

At that point, we were relatively confident that error repetitions could be easily observed in older adults when employing this version of the kanji selection task. Unfortunately, that proved not to be the case. When we conducted an experiment with three groups of older adult participants that were differentiated in terms of cognitive aging status based on a paper-and-pencil type of cognitive aging test (Kumada, Suto, & Hibi, 2009), we again found that there was very little error repetition by the older adults in all three groups. Why does this happen? Was it not the case that younger adults in the dual-task condition exhibited error repetition because the dual-task condition affected working memory capacity?

Thinking again of the dual-process hypothesis for the error-repetition phenomenon, there are two kinds of cognitive processes. At first, we thought that the combination of cognitive aging with declines in general inhibition and extrinsic conditions as a trap is the necessary condition for error repetition. That is, fast and automatic processing (data driven in nature) presenting a trap caused a user to think, "This is the answer," in an early stage of processing. If such automatic processing is the main factor for error repetitions, older adults and younger adults under a divided-attention condition should show similar results in terms of error repetitions.

However, this was not the case, which indicates that automatic processing itself is not the main factor. Then, what is the main factor of the phenomenon? The other process within dual-process theory—the conscious control process that inhibits the automatic process in proceeding with the "trap" operation—may be a necessary condition underlying the error-repetition phenomenon, but it is not derived from pure cognitive aging. Some special condition for the conscious control processing is necessary in order to observe error repetitions.

Following this line of thinking, we conducted some experiments to burden the participants with greater task loads (Harada, Suto, & Asano, in preparation). If cognitive load influences the conscious control process, we may expect to observe error repetitions in both age groups, as with the younger adults under the divided-attention condition. We prepared two kinds of cognitive loading for that objective. One was a load in terms of task difficulty, where we changed the task instructions to become "Select the kanji with the same pronunciation that is not the appropriate meaning for the sentence context (i.e., select the homophone word)." We called this the *wrong condition.*

The other condition was a *task-switching condition,* where the instructions about which of the candidate stimuli should be selected were changed every three trials. Presentation of the instructions was inserted within every trial before the presentation of the context sentence and consisted of "correct," "wrong" (written in Japanese), or an asterisk (*) indicating "same as last trial." For both the wrong and the task-switching conditions, 16 older adults participated; for the younger adults, we had 16 participants in the wrong condition and 24 participants in the task-switching condition.

Figure 3.7 presents the main results of the experiment. Under the wrong condition, the error rates for the first response were higher; however, error repetitions were not observed in either the older or the younger

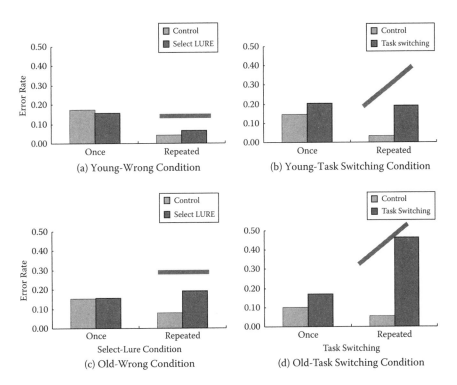

FIGURE 3.7 Results of the kanji selection task for younger and older adults in the cognitive load conditions.

adults (Figure 3.7a,c). In contrast, under the task-switching condition, both groups exhibited error repetitions, with the older adults making more error repetitions than the younger adult participants (Figure 3.7b,d).

ERROR REPETITIONS AND WORKING MEMORY

These results indicate that, using the kanji selection task, the error-repetition phenomenon is not observed under conditions that simply increase task difficulty; however, it is observed under the task-switching and divided-attention conditions. In other words, the necessary requirement of the phenomenon is not purely due to age-related changes in cognitive capacity (i.e., working memory capacity) or to task difficulty that is controlled generally by the central executive. The level of commonality between the task-switching and the divided-attention conditions implies that one of the necessary factors that cause error repetitions would appear to be the maintenance of multiple goals within working memory.

Hence, the phenomenon of error repetitions is related to working memory, which itself is directly related to the executive functions. It seems that working memory, which keeps and monitors multiple goals while executing such tasks in a precise way, is the determining factor for the occurrence of the error-repetition phenomenon; however, the details of this memory system and its processes are not clear yet. These results are related to previous cognitive aging studies on goal neglect and goal maintenance (e.g., De Jong, 2001). However, this study is different from those studies in that, when the experimental task required the maintenance of multiple goals in working memory, young adults showed the same phenomenon as older adults. This is interesting because of the implication that the error repetitions are not a result of cognitive aging, but rather may be a more general phenomenon if the demands of the task involve this condition.

WHY DO OLDER ADULTS MAKE ERROR REPETITIONS WHEN USING IT EQUIPMENT IN PARTICULAR?

Now that we can see the generality of the error-repetition phenomenon, we are faced with the next question: Why do we frequently observe such error repetitions only in the usability lab and only with older adults? What is it about IT equipment that induces older adults to make error repetitions? Part of the reason could be the numerous buttons that are a ubiquitous feature of so much IT equipment or the many vivid colors on the screen (i.e., bad designs) that force older adults to make the first error. However, these characteristics are not the direct causes of error repetitions in situations where the individual needs to maintain multiple goals within working memory.

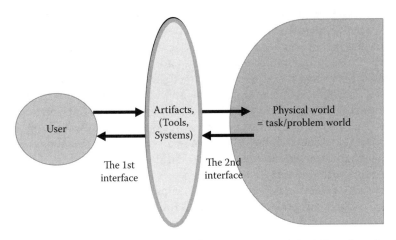

FIGURE 3.8 The dual-interface theory of cognitive engineering. (Based on Sayeki, Y., 1988, in K. Takeuchi (Ed.), *Semantics and Informatics*. Tokyo, Japan: Tokyo University Press.)

An insightful model for human–artifact interaction, called the dual interfaces model, was developed by Sayeki in 1988 (Figure 3.8). The model proposes that any artifacts that humans use are media for acting on the physical world in order to accomplish goals. Thus, there are two kinds of interface: between the human user and the artifact, and between the artifact and the physical environment in which the target exists. Users should know how to act on the artifact through the first interface, and they should know how the artifact will act on the physical world through the second interface. At the same time, users should know how the physical world is being represented by the artifact through the second and first interfaces. That is, individuals should learn to use the artifact because artifacts provide users with new ways of interacting with the target physical world.

The interesting thing is that the artifact becomes transparent as users learn these new ways of accomplishing their goals through using it. For example, when one drives a car and wants to turn right, one turns only the steering wheel while thinking, "I am turning the car." At that point, many veteran drivers do not consciously think that they are acting on the steering wheel because it is now transparent to the driver. Is this the case when one first starts to drive? No. When one has just started to drive, one thing to learn is how to turn the steering wheel; knowing how the car turns when one turns this wheel in a real sense is an important step toward becoming a driver. That is, the artifacts of the steering wheel or the car are initially opaque in terms of their functions as artifacts. However, they become invisible over time and drivers come to have the perception of directly executing their action onto the physical world and accomplishing their goal. Finally, the ultimate form of the individual employing an artifact is realized as the direct manipulation of the physical world (Hutchins, Hollan, & Norman, 1985).

Thinking in terms of this model, after learning to use an artifact, we have only the goal that we wish to achieve, such as turning right while driving. However, when we encounter a new artifact and use it for the first time, we must keep multiple goals in mind: the ultimate goal to execute within the physical world and the immediate goals of operating the artifact. For example, using an unfamiliar ATM in a foreign country, we may have a final goal to withdraw $100 and an immediate goal of operating the ATM (e.g., identifying the appropriate buttons to push). Thinking about this hypothetical shift in the number of goals as we learn to operate ATMs, the fact that error repetitions are observed in older adults using IT equipment makes great sense.

For older adults, many items of IT equipment are new and unfamiliar; they must keep multiple goals in mind and it is not surprising that they show error repetitions. How about younger adults? Assuming that they can learn how to use new equipment very quickly, they would have only one goal to consider in order to accomplish their task. With this hypothesis, it also makes sense that older adults living in their familiar circumstances rarely repeat errors. That is, IT equipment is problematic because it is new and difficult to learn to operate (i.e., difficult to become transparent), especially for older adults compared with younger adults and also compared to other artifacts in older adults' lives.

This hypothesis means that if an artifact is difficult to learn (i.e., difficult to become transparent), even younger adults will repeat errors. There is some anecdotal evidence for this hypothesis; for example, one of the authors made an error repetition when she was reinstalling the operating system on her personal computer during the middle of the night. Given that reinstalling the operating system is a rather complicated task and that the individual in question had lower attentional resources available to her because of fatigue, she persevered in pressing "no" in answer to a question when she should have pressed "yes" to proceed with the reinstallation. The hypothesis is also stimulating because it highlights interactions between semantic memory or skills (procedural memory) and effective executive functioning; this is especially true because aspects of executive functioning or cognitive control may be easily overlooked if we concentrate only on data with experimental tasks in the psychology laboratory.

Based on this hypothesis, now we are thinking that the most effective way to prevent error repetitions might be to support older adults in learning to use IT equipment. This approach may also be a solution for the more general problem—namely, older adults' difficulties with using and tendency to avoid using IT equipment (Harada et al., 2010). It is not so easy to help older adults learn to use IT equipment because such learning is directly influenced by all four of the layers in the model introduced earlier (Figure 3.1) and because we do not know much about how we learn to use artifacts in general, even for younger adults. Endeavors are only now beginning to investigate how human users learn to use artifacts and how to support older adults in learning to use IT equipment (Harada et al., 2010; Mori & Harada, 2010). Of course, we need more intensive research to obtain solid and meaningful results and to make proposals to society in general. However, now that we know what to do, this is a good place for cognitive psychologists to demonstrate our knowledge and skills.

LOOKING AT BOTH SIDES: BASIC RESEARCH AND REAL LIFE

From our curiosity about strange phenomena for older adults in the usability-testing laboratory, we now feel that we are delving into some new problems for cognitive aging research. We have identified the relationship between repeated errors and more general performance on task-switching tasks as individual differences found within older adult populations (Harada & Suto, 2007) or as intraindividual differences related to the time of day (Harada, Asano, & Suto, 2010). The relationship between memory and executive functioning or cognitive control, where dual processes of memory are involved, is a new candidate for a research topic. Accumulating data from such experimental studies will strongly help us to discern the problems in real life with real artifacts from a new viewpoint.

Especially for research into healthy cognitive aging, these kinds of interactions between the experimental laboratory and more real-world research are useful because aging is a phenomenon appearing within the lives of humans. To that purpose, research on human–artifact interaction, or cognitive engineering research, is a useful and effective research area because it is easy to manipulate the conditions surrounding the human participants within a study and to examine the validity of any hypothesis. We hope that many cognitive psychologists will join this research area and cooperate in advancing the research.

REFERENCES

Akatsu, H., Harada, E. T., Miki, H., & Komatsubara, A. (2011). Design principles for IT equipment based on cognitive behavioral characteristics of elderly users—usability test applied to automatic teller machines (ATMs). *Journal of Japan Industrial Management Association, 61,* 303–312 (in Japanese with English abstract).

Anderson, N. D., Craik, F. I. M., & Naveh-Benjamin, M. (1998). The attentional demands of encoding and retrieval in younger and older adults: I. Evidence from divided attention costs. *Psychology and Aging, 13,* 405–423.

Barrett L. F., Tugade, M. M., & Engle, R. W. (2004). Individual differences in working memory capacity and dual-process theories of the mind. *Psychology Bulletin, 130,* 553–573.

Braver, T. S., & West, R. (2008). Working memory, executive control, and aging. In F. M. Craik, T. A. Salthouse, F. M. Craik, & T. A. Salthouse (Eds.), *The handbook of aging and cognition* (3rd ed., pp. 311–372). New York, NY: Psychology Press.

Chasteen, A. L., Bhattacharyya, S., Horhota, M., Tam, R., & Hasher, L. (2005). How feelings of stereotype threat influence older adults' memory performance. *Experimental Aging Research, 31,* 235–260.

Craik, F. I. M. (1986). A functional account of age differences in memory. In F. Klix & H. Hagendorf (Eds.), *Human memory and cognitive capabilities: Mechanisms and performances* (pp. 409–422). Amsterdam, the Netherlands: North-Holland.

Craik, F. I. M., & Byrd, M. (1982). Aging and cognitive deficits: The role of attentional resources. In F. I. M. Craik & S. Trehub (Eds.), *Aging and cognitive processes* (pp. 191–211). New York, NY: Plenum.

De Jong, R. (2001). Adult age difference in goal activation and goal maintenance. *European Journal of Cognitive Psychology, 13,* 71–89.

Hara, N., Naka, T., & Harada, E.T. (2009). How can we make IT appliances easy for older adults? Usability studies of electronic program guide system. In I. Maurtua (Ed.), *Human–computer interaction* (pp. 369–388). Rijeka, Croatia: IN-TECH.

Harada, E. T. (2009). What do cognitive aging studies tell us? Some implications from aging investigations on human memory and cognitive engineering studies. *Japanese Psychological Review, 52,* 383–395 (in Japanese with English abstract).

Harada, E. T., & Akatsu, H. (2003). Usability for old users. In E. T. Harada (Ed.), *Cognitive studies of human–artifacts interaction: What is "usability"?* (pp. 119–138). Tokyo, Japan: Kyoritsu-syuppan (in Japanese).

Harada, E. T., Asano, A., & Suto, S. (2010) *Error repetition and time-of-day effects: Prefrontal function as cognitive control and aging.* Paper presented at the 20th Annual Rotman Research Institute Conference, Toronto, ON.

Harada, E.T., Mori, K., & Taniue, N. (2010). Cognitive aging and the usability of IT-based equipment: Learning is the key. *Japanese Psychological Research, 52,* 227–243.

Harada, E. T., & Suto, S. (2004). *Cognitive aging and interference from "lures" on the same screen.* Paper presented at the 5th Tsukuba International Conference on Human Memory, Tsukuba, Japan.

Harada, E. T., & Suto, S. (2007). *Error repetitions and attention: Examination within the older adults group.* Paper presented at the 48th Annual Meeting of Psychonomic Society, Long Beach, CA.

Hasher, L., & Zacks, R. T. (1988). Working memory, comprehension, and aging: A review and a new view. In G. H. Bower (Ed.), *The psychology of learning and motivation* (Vol. 22, pp. 193–225). New York, NY: Academic Press.

Hutchins, E. L., Hollan, J. D., & Norman, D. A. (1985). Direct manipulation interfaces. *Human–Computer Interaction, 1,* 311–338.

Jacoby, L. L., Kelley, C. M., & McElree, B. D. (1999). The role of cognitive control: Early selection versus late correction. In S. Chaiken & Y. Trope (Eds.) *Dual-process theories in social psychology* (pp. 383–400). New York, NY: Guilford Press,

Kumada, T., Suto, S., & Hibi, Y. (2009). Attention, working memory, and executive function in older adults for cognitive interface design. *Japanese Psychological Review, 52,* 363–378 (in Japanese with English abstract).

McCoy, S. L., Tun, P. A., Cox, L. C., Colangelo, M., Stewart, R. A., & Wingfield, A. (2005). Hearing loss and perceptual effort: Downstream effects on older adults' memory for speech. *Quarterly Journal of Experimental Psychology, 58A*, 22–33.

Mori, K., & Harada, E. T. (2010). Is learning a family matter? Experimental study of the influence of social environment on learning by older adults in the use of mobile phones. *Japanese Psychological Research, 52*(3), 244–255.

Mykityshyn, A. L., Fisk, A. D., & Rogers, W. A. (2002). Learning to use a home medical device: Mediating age-related differences with training, *Human Factors, 44*, 354–364.

Norman, D. A. (1988). *The psychology of everyday things.* New York, NY: Basic Books.

Ogata, K., Harada, E. T., & Mori, K. (2005). *A cognitive engineering study of informational care system at home: From the usability test focusing on workload.* The 5th International Conference of the International Society for Gerontechnology.

Salthouse, T. A. (1991). *Theoretical perspectives on cognitive aging.* Hillsdale, NJ: Lawrence Erlbaum Associates, Inc.

Sayeki, Y. (1988). Information processing between human and machine: An introduction to cognitive engineering. In K. Takeuchi (Ed.) *Semantics and informatics.* Tokyo, Japan: Tokyo University Press (in Japanese; title translated by the authors).

Suzuki, K., Mishima, H., & Sasaki, M. (1997). Affordances and variability of actions: Environment, actions and microslips. *Journal of Japan Society for Fuzzy Theory and Systems, 9*, 826–837 (in Japanese with English abstract).

Wingfield, A., Tun, P. A., & McCoy, S. L. (2005). Hearing loss in older adulthood: What it is and how it interacts with cognitive performance. *Current Directions in Psychological Science, 14*, 144–148.

Part 2
Psychological perspectives: Long-term memory

4   Age-related differences in explicit associative memory

Contributions of effortful-strategic and automatic processes

Moshe Naveh-Benjamin

INTRODUCTION

Past research has shown that memory abilities decline in old age (e.g., Hoyer & Verhaeghen, 2006). This decline, however, seems to be differential, with episodic memory being particularly vulnerable to the effects of aging (e.g., Craik & Jennings, 1992; Light, 1991; Naveh-Benjamin & Old, 2008; Zacks, Hasher, & Li, 2000). The mechanisms underlying this differential decline have drawn considerable research and debate (for a review, see Hoyer & Verhaeghen, 2006; Light, 1991; Salthouse, 1991).

In the current chapter, I will concentrate on associative memory, which seems to be especially vulnerable to the effects of aging (e.g., Bayen, Phelps, & Spaniol, 2000; Chalfonte & Johnson, 1996; Naveh-Benjamin, 2000). Furthermore, considering the large amount of relevant research, in order to make the discussion more manageable, I will address questions related to explicit memory only, in which people need to retrieve information consciously from episodic memory. In particular, after surveying some relevant studies that assessed age-related differences in associative memory, I will evaluate the role of strategic and automatic processes in age-related deficits in associative memory.

Age-related deficits in associative memory have been shown early in the experimental research of aging and memory. For example, several researchers (e.g., Gilbert, 1941; Ruch, 1934a, 1934b; Willoughby, 1927) used the learning of paired associates with a cued-recall task. The results showed robust age-related differences in paired associates, delayed paired associates, and Turkish–English vocabulary tasks, which require the learning and remembering of pairs of words. Salthouse, Kausler, and Saults (1990) showed a monotonic decrease in paired-associates learning from the 20s to the 80s, even when health status was controlled. More recent studies employing a cued-recall task (e.g., Dunlosky & Hertzog, 1998; Hines, Touron, & Hertzog, 2009) showed similar age-related deficits in associative memory.

One of the potential problems with the originally used cued-recall tasks is that it is not clear whether the deficit shown by older adults in these tasks is due to a decline in associative memory or reflects problems with the retrieval of the B item when A is given as a cue to assess memory for the A–B pair studied earlier. Another question is the degree to which such an age-related deficit in associative memory mediates a general episodic memory decline. To resolve these issues, we have suggested (Naveh-Benjamin, 2000; Naveh-Benjamin, Hussain, Guez, & Bar-On, 2003) an associative deficit hypothesis (ADH) based on Underwood's (1969) suggestion that an episode is composed of several attributes (e.g., semantic, acoustic, contextual) that are connected together to create a coherent distinctive unit. According to this hypothesis, an important part of older adults' poorer episodic memory is related to their deficiency in creating and retrieving links between single units of information. The basic units can be two items, an item and its context, two contextual elements, or, more generally, the representation of two mental codes. The extent to which a given memory task requires the creation or use of such associations is a significant determinant of older people's memory performance (see also Bayen et al., 2000; Chalfonte & Johnson, 1996).

The ADH is supported by experiments indicating that older adults tend to preserve the associations between components of an episode poorly, even though their memory for the separate components can be quite good. In particular, several studies have presented young and older adults with small episodes containing two components each (e.g., name–face pairs or word pairs) and then tested their memory of the components (using an item recognition test) and the associations between the components (using an associative recognition test). The typical pattern of results obtained in these studies suggests that older adults show a sizable deficit in memory for the associations, even though memory for the components involved in these associations shows little age-related decline, if at all.

Such results have been reported for associations between paired words (Castel & Craik, 2003; Healy, Light, & Chung, 2005; Light, Patterson, Chung, & Healy, 2004; Naveh-Benjamin, 2000, Experiment 2), paired faces (Bastin & Van der Linden, 2005), paired pictures (Naveh-Benjamin, Hussain, Guez, & Bar-On, 2003), paired names and faces (James, Fogler, & Tauber, 2008; Naveh-Benjamin, Guez, Kilb, & Reedy, 2004; Rendell, Castel, & Craik, 2005), pairings of words and nonwords (Naveh-Benjamin, 2000; Experiment 1), pairings of drawings and colors (Chalfonte & Johnson, 1996; Mitchell, Johnson, Raye, Mather, & D'Esposito, 2000), and pairings between words and their fonts (Naveh-Benjamin, 2000; Experiment 3; see meta-analysis by Old & Naveh-Benjamin, 2008). Note that the interaction between age and type of test is not due to the higher level of difficulty of the associative tests, as Hockley (1992) has shown that associative memory is forgotten at a slower pace than item memory. Furthermore, Kilb and Naveh-Benjamin (2007) have demonstrated an associative memory deficit in older adults even when item and associative memory performance levels were equated.

These findings lead to questions regarding the source of this associative deficit in older adults. One distinction in memory is between automatic and effortful-strategic processes (e.g., Hasher & Zacks, 1979). According to this distinction, memory performance is mediated by the operation of automatic and strategic-effortful processes. Strategic-effortful processes were proposed to reflect slow, effortful, intentional processes, whereas automatic processes seem to occur fast, require little effort, and are to some degree involuntary (e.g., Bargh, 1997; Hasher & Zacks, 1979; Posner & Snyder, 1975; Schneider & Shiffrin, 1977).

Older adults' associative deficit may be underlined by a decline in the use of appropriate strategies to bind together the different components in an episode and retrieve these bindings, by a decline in the ability to bind these components automatically, or by both. Patterns of brain changes in old age point to the potential role of both types of processes in older adults' overall poorer episodic memory. For example, some brain imaging studies show age-related structural as well as functional decline in the prefrontal cortex (PFC). This is assumed to reflect more effortful processes involved in implementing strategies that organize the input to the medial-temporal/hippocampal (MTLH) areas during encoding and that control search and monitoring operations during retrieval (Moscovitch, 1992). Specifically, studies comparing younger and older adults demonstrate that younger adults show more PFC activation during encoding than do older adults (Anderson et al., 2000; Cabeza, Anderson, Mangels, & Nyberg, 2000). Also of interest is a study by Raz, Gunning-Dixon, Head, Depuis, and Acker (1998) that linked age-related PFC shrinkage to increased perseverative errors in the Wisconsin card sorting task, which is an indication of strategic inflexibility. Finally, Raz and Rodrigue (2006) reviewed studies indicating that the PFC shows the greatest amount of age-related atrophy.

Brain imaging studies also indicate a decline in activity and structure of the MTLH areas; this is assumed to reflect the operation of more automatic processes (Moscovitch, 1992). For example, using structural brain imaging in a 5-year longitudinal study, Raz et al. (2005) examined people aged 20–77 to evaluate the degree of deterioration in different brain structures. One area showing the largest volume shrinkage was the hippocampus, which has been implicated as a binder of memories (see Cohen et al., 1999, for a review). Considering the role of these brain structures in episodic memory performance (Moscovitch, 2000), it is reasonable that age-related declines in episodic memory are mediated by declines in strategic-effortful as well as automatic processes.

Evidence from neuropsychology supports the involvement of strategic processes in tasks that require binding and association creation, mediated primarily by the frontal lobes. For example, Glisky (2002; Glisky & Kong, 2008; Glisky, Rubin, & Davidson, 2001) shows that the frontal lobes are responsible for encoding relationships between items and their contexts. Although brain activity was measured somewhat indirectly (through the use of neuropsychological tests), the results indicate that older adults' poorer memory for associations may be due to poor frontal functioning.

The previously mentioned patterns of brain changes in old age point to the potential role of both effortful-strategic and automatic processes in older adults' associative memory deficit. The question that I would like to address in this chapter concerns the empirical evidence that exists in behavioral studies regarding whether older adults' associative deficit is mediated by a decline in strategic-effortful processes or by more automatic ones. In the following, I will discuss several criteria suggested to assess whether a given process is based on controlled-effortful or automatic mode of operation. I will assess whether results regarding older adults' associative memory deficit reflect a decline in one or another type of process, or in both.

In order to ensure that the locus of potential age-related differences is in associative memory and not in the components that make up the association, each of the following studies will include, in addition to a task requiring associative memory, an additional control task involving memory for item/component information. Such a comparison will assess the specificity of age-related memory deficits. In particular, if older adults have a particular deficit in associative memory above and beyond the one in component memory, we would expect an interaction of age (young vs. old) and test (components vs. associations). Even stronger support for the role of specific processes in older adults' associative deficit would be manifested by a triple interaction where the age by test interaction is differentially affected by the comparison used to implement a given strategic-effortful automatic criterion.

The criteria to assess whether a given process is mediated by automatic or controlled-effortful processes were suggested in the memory domain by Hasher and Zacks (1979) and are in line with similar views in other areas of cognition (e.g., Schneider & Shiffrin, 1977). They include the effects of intention to encode the relevant information, whether a given behavior can be interrupted by other behaviors, the effects of strategic interventions, and the type of retrieval processes involved in a given behavior. In the following sections, each of these criteria will be discussed in turn.

INTENTIONALITY OF ENCODING: COMPARING INCIDENTAL AND INTENTIONAL LEARNING INSTRUCTIONS

One criterion (see Hasher & Zacks, 1979) suggests that if the relevant behavior is based on the operation of strategic-effortful processes, encoding the information under intentional learning instructions—where the participants expect a specific memory task—should result in better later memory than when the encoding is performed under incidental learning instructions—where the participants do not expect a later memory task.

However, if the relevant behavior is based on the operation of automatic processes, then intentional learning instructions should not enhance memory performance beyond that achieved under incidental learning instructions. In particular, if older adults' associative memory deficit is mediated by deficient strategic-effortful processes necessary for encoding the associations, then older adults should possess a smaller advantage in the associative test of intentional learning instructions over incidental learning ones relative to younger adults.

Studies using unrelated paired-associates and cued-recall tasks show that when younger and older adults are provided with intentional learning instructions, older adults tend to report less often the use of strategies to relate the two components together. For example, Smith, Park, Earles, Shaw, and Whiting (1998) showed that older adults were using fewer verbal mediators than younger adults to bind picture pairs. Similarly, Dunlosky and Hertzog (2001) showed similar (albeit somewhat smaller) patterns with word pairs. However, as mentioned previously, results of studies using cued recall are potentially ambiguous with respect to the locus of the deficit; this could be due to a deficit in associating the components together or to a deficit in recalling the B target item.

To assess the criterion of intentionality and its differential effects on associative and component memory directly, we ran several studies that manipulated the intention to learn. In one experiment (Naveh-Benjamin, 2000, Experiment 2), we presented to younger (18–25 years old) and older (65–85 years old) adults unrelated word pairs under either associative incidental learning instructions (try to learn the component words in preparation for a word recognition test) or associative intentional learning instructions (try to learn the word pairs in preparation for an associative recognition task). Later on we gave the two age groups a word recognition test where original words (targets) were intermixed with new (distracter) words, as well as an associative recognition test, in which half of the pairs at test were intact (appeared together as such at encoding) and the other half were recombined (included pairs of original words that did not appear together during the study phase). In order to avoid carryover effects, any given stimulus from the study phase appeared in only one of the tests (this is true for the following studies, as well).

Results of proportion hits minus proportion false alarms, which can be seen in Figure 4.1, indicated a triple interaction, and further analysis indicated that the locus of this interaction was the different patterns in the relationships between age and instruction condition for each test. In the item memory test, there was no interaction between age and study instructions, whereas in the associative test there was a significant interaction of age and instructions. The source of this interaction was the age effect, which was much larger in the associative test under instructions to study associations intentionally, than under those to study associations incidentally (study components/items instructions). Put differently, younger adults took

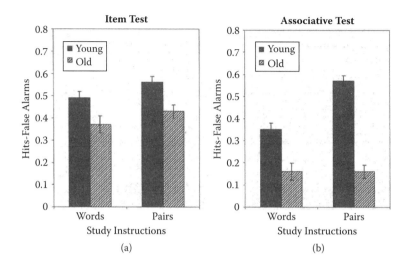

FIGURE 4.1 Proportion hits minus proportion false alarms for younger and older adults in the item and the associative recognition tests in the different study instructions' conditions. Bars depict standard errors. (From Naveh-Benjamin, M., 2000, *Journal of Experimental Psychology: Learning, Memory and Cognition, 26,* 1170–1187. Reprinted with permission of APA.)

advantage of the instructions to encode the word pairs to improve their performance significantly; however, older adults' performance under intentional learning instructions of the associations did not change relative to their performance under incidental learning instructions. Similar results were obtained when the stimuli materials included word–font rather than word–word pairs (Naveh-Benjamin, 2000, Experiment 3).

In another experiment (Naveh-Benjamin, Shing, Kilb, Werkle-Bergner, Lindenberger, & Li, 2009), a somewhat similar procedure was used with face–name pairs presented under incidental and intentional learning instructions. However, whereas the intentional learning instructions were similar to the ones described earlier, under incidental learning instructions, participants judged whether the name and the face "belonged together" with no mention of any upcoming memory test. Results of this experiment show similar triple interaction patterns of performance: Only younger adults took advantage of the intentional learning instructions to improve their associative memory.

The preceding studies are in line with the suggestion that older adults' associative memory deficits are at least partially due to impairment in strategic/controlled processes because older adults do not seem to take advantage of instructions to encode the associative information intentionally, as do younger adults, despite the fact that older adults seem to do so for item/component memory. One interpretation of these results is that, when they are told to learn the associations intentionally, younger adults produce a relevant associative strategy (for example, creating a sentence or a mental image that includes the two words); however, older adults either do not produce such a strategy or use it less effectively. These results are supported by a recent meta-analysis conducted to assess overall patterns of age-related differences in item and associative memory that included 90 studies and a total of more than 7,000 younger and older adults (Old & Naveh-Benjamin, 2008). Results of this meta-analysis indicated a significantly larger effect size for older than for younger adults, reflecting a larger decline in associative than in item memory in comparison to younger adults. This effect size was much larger in those studies that employed intentional learning instructions of the associations than in those that used incidental learning instructions.

INTENTIONALITY OF ENCODING: PERFORMANCE UNDER INCIDENTAL LEARNING INSTRUCTIONS

Information can be encoded and stored incidentally when participants do not encode it in preparation for a test on this information. Under such conditions, people are not expected to engage any effortful type of processing intended to retain the information as they do under intentional learning conditions. If older adults' associative memory deficits were mediated only by strategic-effortful processes, then under conditions in which no strategic-controlled processes are engaged, we would expect older adults to show no associative memory deficit relative to younger adults.

There have been different suggestions on how to operationalize incidental learning (e.g., Block, 2009). One is to ask participants to pay attention to some features of the stimulus that do not include the feature(s) they are being tested on later, with the assumption that, under such conditions, they are not trying to learn the tested-upon feature(s). We ran an experiment with this operationalization by presenting younger and older adults with word pairs and instructions to pay attention to the component words only in order to prepare for a word test (Naveh-Benjamin, 2000, Experiment 2). We later surprised them with an unexpected associative memory test. The results indicated that even under such conditions, older adults showed an associative memory deficit relative to younger adults, although as mentioned before, the deficit was smaller than the one observed under intentional learning instructions (see Figure 4.1b).

Another study, mentioned previously, looked at incidental learning (Naveh-Benjamin et al., 2009). Here, a different operational definition for incidental learning was used. Younger and older adults did not expect any memory test but, in order to make the task meaningful, for each face–name pair presented, they were asked to provide their subjective evaluation of whether or not the name and the face fit together. Results showed that although older adults demonstrated an overall lower memory performance, in this study they did not show a differential larger decline in associative than in item memory in comparison to younger adults.

Finally, in the meta-analysis mentioned previously (Old & Naveh-Benjamin, 2008) for incidental learning, although the age-related effect size for memory for associations was somewhat larger than that for memory for items, these differences did not reach statistical significance. To summarize, although the results of the reported studies are somewhat variable, overall they show a somewhat small age-related associative deficit under incidental learning instructions for the associations. This indicates a modest role of deficient automatic processes in older adults' associative deficit. These results are further discussed later.

EFFECTS OF STRATEGIC INTERVENTIONS

Another criterion to assess the role of strategic-effortful processes in older adults' associative deficit is the degree to which older adults are able to benefit from direct instructions to utilize a given strategy. The assumption behind this criterion is that if older adults either do not spontaneously utilize relevant associative strategies or do not use such strategies effectively, then offering them these strategies and providing them with the opportunity to practice them should improve their associative memory (Kausler, 1994).

To assess this possibility, we ran a study where participants studied lists of unrelated word pairs and then completed item and associative recognition tests (Naveh-Benjamin, Keshet Brav, & Levi, 2007). We tested three separate groups of younger and older adults. One group was tested under standard intentional learning instructions; they were told to try to learn both the words and the word pairs in preparation for the following item and associative recognition tests. A second group was asked, in addition, to employ an associative strategy during encoding involving the creation of a sentence to connect the two words in each given pair. Participants in this group received some practice in the use of the strategy. Finally, a third group was asked, in addition, to use these sentences created during encoding to guide their memory responses during retrieval. The rationale for the third group was that the associative strategic deficit of older adults may occur not only during the encoding of the information, but also during its retrieval. Hence, a suggestion for the use of strategy at both phases of processing could be especially beneficial for older adults if they have a deficit in strategic processes at both encoding and retrieval.

Results of proportion hits minus proportion false alarms (see Figure 4.2) indicated that although older adults exhibited the typical associative deficit under intentional learning instructions, they benefited more than younger participants from the strategy instructions; this was the case especially in the associative memory test. Furthermore, the effect of the strategy

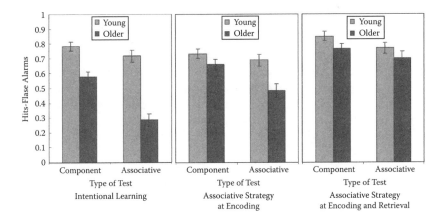

FIGURE 4.2 Proportion hits minus proportion false alarms in the component and the associative recognition tests for younger and older participants in each of the instructions' conditions. Bars depict standard errors. (Reproduced from Naveh-Benjamin, M. et al., 2007, *Psychology and Aging, 22*, 202–208. Reprinted with permission of APA.)

instructions seemed to be additive, with some benefit accruing to associative memory when the strategy was implemented at encoding, and with further benefit resulting from the use of the strategies at retrieval, as well.

Interestingly, there is some independent empirical evidence to support the suggestion that the use of an associative strategy at encoding is mediated by effortful processes. Naveh-Benjamin, Craik, Guez, and Krueger (2005) employed a dual task methodology at encoding to assess the effects of the use of an associative strategy (interactive mental imagery or sentence creation) on younger and older adults' performance in a cued-recall task. The results showed that older (but not younger) adults' improved memory performance in the strategy over the no-strategy condition was associated with a large increase in attentional resources/mental effort during the encoding phase, as reflected by the secondary task costs. Furthermore, Glisky et al. (2001) showed that requiring older adults at study to consider the relations between an item and its context eliminated age-related differences in a source memory task, which requires memory for the associations between the item and its context.

These results are in line with the suggestion that older adults have a particular deficit in associative memory that is due to a lack of a spontaneous use of associative strategies—a production deficiency. Other studies indicate that, in addition, older adults may have problems in an efficient use of associative strategies—a utilization deficit (e.g., Dunlosky & Hertzog, 1998, but see Dunlosky, Hertzog, & Powell-Moman, 2005).

According to this lack-of-efficient-utilization view (differential-quality hypothesis; Dunlosky & Hertzog, 1998), even if older adults are offered an associative strategy that they do not use regularly, their memory performance for associations may not improve to the level of young adults because they might not use the strategy efficiently enough (Craik & Rabinowitz, 1985; Erber, Galt, & Botwinick, 1985; Rabinowitz, 1989; Zelinski, Walsh, & Thompson, 1978). For example, older adults' sentences will not be as cohesive as the ones created by young adults.

Such a view is supported by the conclusions reached by Dunlosky and Hertzog (1998) regarding the overall observed age-related differences in paired-associate recall, suggesting an inefficient use of strategy by older adults as a source of their associative memory deficits. Furthermore, a recent study by Naveh-Benjamin et al. (2005) showed that instructions to use sentence and imagery strategies without training in an efficient creation of sentences or mental images relating word pairs together did not eliminate age-related differences in a cued-recall task.

INTERRUPTION OF STRATEGIC-EFFORTFUL PROCESSES

Another criterion to assess whether memory performance is mediated by automatic or strategic-effortful processes is whether performance is affected by a concurrent mental activity (e.g., Hasher & Zacks, 1979). The underlying assumption is that, with limited cognitive/attentional resources (Craik, 1983, 1986), if a given task requires effortful/controlled processes, then it would draw from a pool of limited resources, leaving too few to complete the concurrent task successfully. Evidence from Craik (1982, 1983, 1986; Craik & McDowd, 1987; Rabinowitz, Craik, & Ackerman, 1982) is consistent with the suggestion that a shortage of available mental resources in older adults results in poorer memory because effortful cognitive operations, such as elaboration, require substantial attentional resources and older adults possess fewer of these resources.

If this is the case, then we should be able to mimic older adults' memory behavior by experimentally manipulating younger adults' available resources through the use of a divided attention (DA) task. Craik and his colleagues were able to simulate older adults' performance in young adults under divided attention in a variety of tasks, including a cued-recall one (e.g., Craik & McDowd, 1987). In the context of our discussion, if the associative deficit shown by older adults is mediated by strategic-effortful processes, then we would expect younger adults under DA conditions to show such a deficit, as well, because their associative memory should be more negatively affected than their item memory when attentional resources are depleted.

Furthermore, if the associative deficit of older adults is mediated by reduced attentional resources necessary to encode the associative information, then we would expect a DA task to reduce further the older adults' available attentional resources and, as a result, to amplify their associative deficit and further reduce their memory for associations.

Finally, an additional way of investigating the role of the involvement of effortful attentional resources in memory performance is by the use of measures from performance on the concurrent task to assess the resources required by the memory task. For example, we can compare performance on the concurrent task under DA to a baseline (where the concurrent task is performed alone), and the difference between these scores can provide a measure of the attentional costs associated with the encoding of the material in the memory task. If having reduced effortful attentional resources is the source of older adults' decline in episodic memory (see Craik, 1983), this cost should be greater for older adults than for younger adults. Several studies have shown this pattern of results (e.g., Anderson, Craik, & Naveh-Benjamin, 1998; Craik & McDowd, 1987; Macht & Buschke, 1983; Naveh-Benjamin et al., 2005).

However, the earlier mentioned studies do not provide separate attentional cost measures for encoding component and associative information. If older adults' associative deficit is mediated by reduced attentional resources, we would expect the encoding of associative information to be especially costly to them in terms of the attentional resources devoted to learning the associations.

We have carried out a series of studies testing all the preceding suggestions (Kilb & Naveh-Benjamin, 2007). In these studies, younger and older adults studied unrelated word pairs under instructions to learn both the words and their associations; this was done with either full or divided attention. Later on, participants were tested on their memory for both the components and their associations. In one of the studies, participants had to concentrate on only one aspect at study, learning (on different trials) either the components or their associations. Finally, in addition to memory performance, we also measured performance on a four-choice concurrent reaction time task, allowing us to assess independently the attentional costs (effort) associated with encoding of component and of associative information.

The results of these studies were somewhat surprising and not in line with the suggestion that reduced attentional resources mediate older adults' associative memory deficit. In particular, although older adults showed an associative memory deficit (see Figure 4.3), younger adults under DA conditions did not. Despite the fact that younger adults' memory performance declined under such conditions, both item and associative memory were affected to the same degree. Furthermore, older adults' associative memory deficit did not increase under DA conditions; it actually decreased somewhat. Finally, relative to younger adults, the older adults did not show a larger attentional cost for learning the associations than for learning the components. This indicates that older adults are not employing more resources to studying combined pieces of information than to studying individual components, relative to the younger adults.

Results showing that younger adults do not exhibit greater deficits in memory for associations than for items when attention is divided at

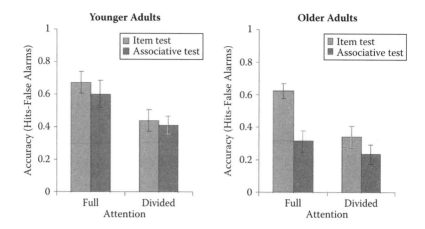

FIGURE 4.3 Proportion hits minus proportion false alarms in the item and the associative recognition tests for younger and older participants under full- and divided-attention conditions. Bars depict standard errors. (Reproduced from Kilb, A., & Naveh-Benjamin, M., 2007, *Memory & Cognition, 35,* 1162–1174. Reprinted with permission of the Psychonomic Society.)

encoding are not unique to the preceding series of studies and are in line with previous studies using somewhat similar procedures and different types of materials (e.g., Naveh-Benjamin et al., 2003, 2004). I will discuss these results further in the discussion section.

STRATEGIC-EFFORTFUL PROCESSES AT RETRIEVAL

Whereas most of the studies mentioned so far have dealt with manipulations during the operation of encoding processes, there is also a need to explore whether the age-related associative deficit is mediated by strategic-effortful or by more automatic processes at retrieval. One potential mediator for older adults' associative deficit is their tendency to rely on automatic retrieval processes rather than on more consciously controlled processes. According to the dual process model, recognition can depend on one of two processes: recollection or familiarity (Yonelinas, 2002). In the context of the current discussion, recollection means that an item is (consciously) retrieved along with its original context, while familiarity refers to (automatic) recognition in the absence of any contextual information. For example, one might rely on familiarity when instantly recognizing someone's face, but recollection must be used in order to remember that person's name or other relevant information about him or her. Evidence from studies using a variety of methodologies converges to suggest that people's ability to use recollection decreases with age, but their ability to use familiarity does not

(Hay & Jacoby, 1999; Java, 1996; Jennings & Jacoby, 1993, 1997; Light et al., 2004; Maylor, 1995; Multhaup, 1995; Rhodes, Castel, & Jacoby, 2008; see also Light, Chapter 5, this volume).

How might older adults' associative memory deficit be mediated by familiarity- and recollection-based processes? Item-component and associative recognition tests may each require different levels of familiarity and recollection. For example, Hockley and Consoli (1999) have shown that participants are more likely to give a familiarity-based response in an item test and are more likely to give a recollection-based response in an associative test, demonstrating that associative tests require more recollective processing than do item tests. Moreover, if a participant is able to rely on recollection, then performance on both tests is likely to be quite high.

On the other hand, if a participant relies mainly on familiarity (i.e., in the absence of recollection), performance in the item recognition test may still be high, but performance in the associative recognition test would suffer. This is because the individual items of a recombined pair (i.e., a new pair created from two studied words) would look familiar, causing the participant mistakenly to recognize the new pairing as old; this would happen especially in the absence of recollective processes to counteract it. For example, participants will not use a recall-to-reject strategy when presented with a recombined A–C pair at test; that is, they will not reject it based on their ability to recollect that A actually appeared with B during the study phase.

To assess the contributions of recollection and familiarity in older adults' associative memory deficit, we looked separately at hits and false alarm rates in the data reported by Kilb and Naveh-Benjamin (2007). The results, which appear in Figure 4.4, show that for hit responses (correctly saying

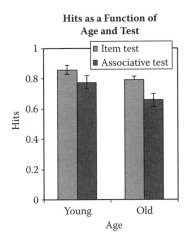
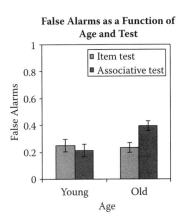

FIGURE 4.4 Proportion hits and proportion false alarms for younger and older adults in the item and the associative recognition tests. Bars depict standard errors.

"yes" to a target that appeared during study), older adults show a similar small decline on both item and associative recognition tests. However, for false alarm responses (incorrectly saying "yes" to a lure), whereas there are almost no age-related differences in the item test, older adults tended to provide a much higher response rate than younger ones.

These results indicate that whereas younger adults' performance is more consistent with patterns predicted by intact recollection, the performance of older adults seems to be more consistent with patterns predicted by a decline in recollection and spared familiarity. Specifically, older adults are much more likely to falsely recognize new pairs in an associative test than new items in an item test, but younger adults show relatively low false alarm rates in both tests. Such patterns of high false alarms by older adults in the associative test were also reported in other studies (e.g., Naveh-Benjamin et al., 2009; Old & Naveh-Benjamin, 2008; Rhodes et al., 2008) and can be interpreted to mean that older adults' associative deficits are due to impaired recollection (for example, the use of recall-to-reject strategy) in the face of spared familiarity (of the components). Overall, this line of research is consistent with the claim that older adults' associative memory deficit is mediated by a decline in strategic-effortful-controlled processes but not by a decline in automatic processes. Interestingly, it seems that the intact automatic processes underlying familiarity actually hamper older adults' associative memory.

Other lines of research also support the claim that impairment in strategic-effortful processes at retrieval contributes to older adults' associative memory deficit. For example, as was mentioned earlier, the study by Naveh-Benjamin et al. (2007) showed that providing older adults with instructions and training to use integrative evaluation strategy at retrieval helped them improve their performance, especially in the associative test. The use of such an associative strategy at retrieval seems to be mediated by controlled effortful processes, as shown by Naveh-Benjamin et al. (2005). These researchers employed a dual task methodology at retrieval (in contrast to encoding, as mentioned earlier) to assess the effects of the use of an associative strategy (interactive mental imagery or sentence creation) on younger and older adults' performance during a cued-recall task. The results showed that both older and younger adults improved memory performance in the strategy over the no-strategy condition. However, only in older adults was such an improvement associated with a large increase in attentional resources/mental effort during the retrieval phase, as reflected by the secondary task costs.

Finally, using a cued-recall paradigm, Dunlosky et al. (2005) instructed younger and older adults to use elaborative strategies (like imagery and sentences) when learning word pairs. Participants also reported the mediator that they created at study to relate the two words together. Results indicated that older adults had much poorer ability to recall the mediator during the test and that such a deficit in mediator recall accounted for a substantial portion of the age-related deficits in the cued-recall task. Such results highlight the role of potential recollection failure in older adults' associative memory deficit.

THE EFFECT OF USE OF PREVIOUS KNOWLEDGE

One factor known to support episodic memory is a reliance on previous knowledge. Studies have shown that people can use semantic memory to support the encoding and retrieval of new information (e.g., the category clustering effect; Bousfield, 1953). Preexisting knowledge may be used to support the formation of richer encoded representations and guide retrieval processes. Use of such knowledge in episodic memory tasks can serve as schematic support (Craik & Bosman, 1992) and may also reduce age-related memory decrements. The activation of previous relevant knowledge seems to happen automatically under varying circumstances and need not require strategies or effortful-controlled processes (e.g., Reder, Park, & Kieffaber, 2009).

One question is whether automatic use of previous knowledge would affect older adults' associative memory deficit. We tested this question in several studies where we compared a standard condition in which pairs of unrelated words were presented to a condition in which the two words in each pair were related semantically to each other. The latter condition allows participants to rely on preexisting knowledge to relate these word pairs at encoding and to use the cue word to access the target at retrieval. We assessed this question using several memory tasks. In one, pairs of mildly related and unrelated words were presented during study under intentional learning conditions; later, a cued-recall task was used in which the first word in a pair was presented as a cue and participants were asked to recall its paired target during study.

Results (reported in Naveh-Benjamin et al., 2005), which can be seen in Figure 4.5a, indicated that in contrast to the large age-related deficit shown with unrelated word pairs, older adults take a greater advantage of the related pairs, in terms of performance improvement, than do younger adults. Similar results were obtained in a paradigm where both item and associative memory tests were administered (Naveh-Benjamin et al., 2003). These results showed that older adults benefit more than the younger ones in the related pairs condition; moreover, this seems to happen more in the associative than in the item memory test. Furthermore, using a dual task methodology, Naveh-Benjamin et al. (2005) assessed the amount of cognitive effort exerted during the encoding of unrelated and related word pairs and found that although older adults exerted overall more effort than younger adults during both encoding and retrieval of the target word, the improvement in memory performance that older adults showed for related pairs was not associated with any increase in attentional resources as

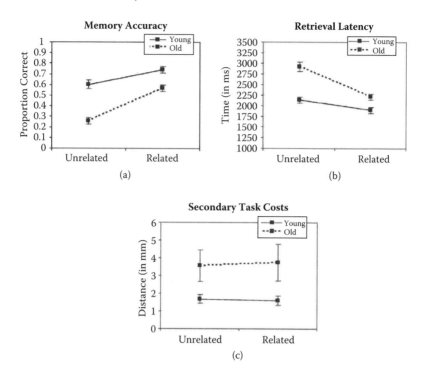

FIGURE 4.5 Memory accuracy, retrieval latency, and secondary task attentional costs at encoding for younger and older adults. Bars depict standard errors. (Reproduced from Naveh-Benjamin, M. et al., 2005, *Journal of Experimental Psychology: Learning, Memory and Cognition, 32,* 520–537. Reprinted with permission of APA.)

measured by the secondary task costs (see Figure 4.5c). Additionally, this improvement was associated with faster response latencies during the test (see Figure 4.5b).

The ability of older adults to rely on previous knowledge in order to remember associations is also nicely illustrated in a series of studies by Castel and colleagues (e.g., Castel, 2005, 2007; McGillivray & Castel, 2010), where younger and older participants had to bind together several pieces of information (grocery items and prices, faces of people and the ages of these people, or numerical and object information). Results indicated that when older adults were able to use previous knowledge or expertise (realistic prices of grocery items, faces of older adults) or when participants were retired accountants and bookkeepers (in the case of numerical information), they showed little or no age-related associative deficits.

The previously mentioned results seem to suggest that older adults can take advantage of prior knowledge and use it to improve their encoding of new associative information. Such a benefit seems not to require controlled-effortful processes.

DISCUSSION

The preceding review was intended to assess whether the deficit shown by older adults in associative episodic memory is mediated by effortful-strategic processes or by more automatic ones. Using several criteria for assessing the involvement of effortful-strategic and automatic processes, the review seems to indicate that, by most criteria, older adults' associative memory deficit is mediated by a decline in the operation of efficient controlled processes, which implement strategic behavior that is effortful. Such a conclusion is based on the fact that older adults show a differential larger associative memory deficit (in comparison to younger adults while using item/component memory as a comparison task) under intentional learning instructions in comparison to incidental learning ones.

Furthermore, it seems that instructions to implement effortful strategies (for example, relating the components of the episode by a sentence), supplemented by practicing such a strategy, are especially beneficial to older adults' associative memory. Such implementation of effortful strategies seems to be helpful at encoding and also at retrieval. This is consistent with a view that the associative strategic deficit of older adults happens at different phases, beginning during the encoding-learning phase and continuing during the retrieval phase. Such implementation of strategic processes seems also to require substantial investment of mental effort on older adults' part—especially during retrieval.

Results assessing the operation of specific processes at retrieval suggest that older adults' associative memory deficits are related to the decline in the ability effortfully to recollect the details of the bound episode. The deficit seems to be especially severe when the memory task provides less environmental support—for example, when a cued-recall rather than a recognition task is used—because older adults have problems in using a relational strategy to retrieve the mediators they have produced during study (e.g., Dunlosky et al., 2005).

One set of results, mentioned before, does not seem to fit the overall picture of the involvement of effortful-strategic processes in older adults' associative memory. These results show that divided attention in younger or in older adults depresses both item and associative memory to the same degree (rather than differentially affecting more associative memory, as expected). There could be several reasons for such results. One is related to the claim that divided attention does not necessarily affect only effortful-strategic processes. For example, Craik and Kester (2000) showed that the effects of divided attention at encoding and the amount of associative elaboration of a given pair during study are additive and not interactive; that is, divided attention affected memory performance negatively to the same degree for pairs for which participants reported the least amount of elaboration during encoding as for pairs that went through extensive elaboration. Another potential reason for the lack of differential effect of divided attention on associative memory is that the concurrent tasks used in the previously mentioned studies were not demanding enough to affect associative memory differentially. Further research should assess this possibility.

With respect to the role of more automatic processes in older adults' associative deficit, the picture emerging is that such processes, either at encoding or at retrieval, are less involved in the deficit than strategic-effortful ones. At encoding, this is manifested by smaller age-related associative deficit under incidental learning instructions. Furthermore, when there is less of a need to engage effortful processes in binding components of an episode (for example, when previous knowledge can be activated to bind these components, as is the case of related word pairs), or in retrieving such binding, older adults show a smaller associative deficit.

Interestingly, although familiarity-based automatic processes involved in component memory may help older adults better recognize previously seen items, under some circumstances, the sparing of automatic processes, such as those based on familiarity, might negatively affect older adults' associative memory performance. This happens, for example, when two familiar components from the study phase create false memories in older adults who seem to endorse the pair as one shown earlier. Such a suggestion is supported by studies showing that enhancing component familiarity— for example, via repetition—increases older but not younger adults' false associative memories (e.g., Light et al., 2004).

Overall, the smaller role of automatic processes in age-related associative deficit could be due to a decline in hippocampal volume and activation. However, it is unclear whether this relatively modest decline in automatic associative processes is in line with the suggestion regarding relatively large age-related declines in the hippocampus (e.g., Raz, 2000) and the important role of the hippocampus in routine intraitem and interitem binding (e.g., Eichenbaum, 1994) and future research is needed on this issue.

LIMITATIONS AND FUTURE RESEARCH

One potential limitation on conclusions regarding the previously surveyed studies is that they are all based on a cross-sectional design with extreme group comparisons. This raises potential issues of confounding (cohort effects) and of generalizability. However, although cohort effects may explain the overall age effects reported in the surveyed studies, the likelihood that the reported complex patterns of triple interactions of age and test with other manipulations can be due to such cohort effects is rather small. As for generalizability, the preceding studies used different samples of older adults, with different stimuli and a variety of procedures. Furthermore, a recent study by Bender, Naveh-Benjamin, and Raz (2010) shows the same age-related differential patterns of decline in associative memory under intentional learning, with age used as a continuous variable, in a sample of people between the ages of 18 and 80.

Second, note that most of the manipulations used to distinguish automatic from effortful-strategic processes were done at a macrolevel. For example, manipulations of intention to learn and of strategic intervention are based on varying the instructions at a general level without the assessment of the microlevel features of behavior. As Jonides, Naveh-Benjamin, and Palmer (1985) suggested, the analysis of automatic and effortful-controlled processes should be done at a microlevel because each given task may be underlined by both types of processes. Although some microlevel analysis was reported in some of the previously reviewed studies (e.g., dual task studies and those assessing different processes at retrieval), further studies should be conducted that use a careful task analysis to dissect potential component processes in order to assess their role in age-related associative deficits.

Finally, note that the studies reviewed in this chapter deal exclusively with explicit memory, in which participants are aware during the test phase that their memory for associations (and items) is tested. Studies assessing the effects of age on implicit associative memory show somewhat mixed results, with recent ones (e.g., Dew & Giovanello, 2010) showing minimal age-related decline in implicit associative memory. These results are in line with the picture that emerged before indicating that older adults do not show a decline in associative memory when performance is based on more familiarity-based automatic retrieval processes, which are probably also those used in implicit memory tasks.

SUMMARY

To summarize, the existing evidence is in line with the suggestion that older adults' associative deficit is mostly mediated by deficits in the employment of controlled processes to initiate and carry out efficient effortful strategies to bind together components of episodes and retrieve these bindings when needed. These results seem to fit the frontal aging hypothesis of cognitive aging (e.g., West, 1996, 2000), which claims that cognitive decline in old age is primarily due to the age-related changes in prefrontal cortex that can be observed in neuropsychological and brain-imaging studies. The role of automatic processes in the associative deficit of older adults, both at encoding and at retrieval, seems to be smaller. Overall, the associative deficit hypothesis seems to capture an important aspect of how memory changes with age as a result of age-related changes in binding components into cohesive units at encoding and unpacking these bindings at retrieval.

ACKNOWLEDGMENTS

The writing of this chapter was supported by a Research Board grant from the University of Missouri. I would like to thank Tina Chen and Max Neal for their help with the references.

REFERENCES

Anderson, N. D., Craik, F. I. M., & Naveh-Benjamin, M. (1998). The attentional demands of encoding and retrieval in younger and older adults: 1. Evidence from divided attention costs. *Psychology and Aging, 13*(3), 405–423.

Anderson, N. D., Iidaka, T., Cabeza, R., Kapur, S., McIntosh, A. R., & Craik, F. I. M. (2000). The effects of divided attention on encoding- and retrieval-related brain activity: A PET study of younger and older adults. *Journal of Cognitive Neuroscience, 12*(5), 775–792.

Bargh, J. A. (1992). The automaticity of everyday life. In R. S. Wyer, Jr. (Ed.). *The automaticity of everyday life: Advances in social cognition* (pp. 1–61). Mahwah, NJ: Lawrence Erlbaum Associates Publishers.

Bastin, C., & Van der Linden, M. (2005). The effects of aging on the recognition of different types of associations. *Experimental Aging Research, 32,* 61–77.

Bayen, U. J., Phelps, M. P., & Spaniol, J. (2000). Age-related differences in the use of contextual information in recognition memory: A global matching approach. *Journals of Gerontology: Series B: Psychological Sciences and Social Sciences, 55B*(3), pp. 131–141.

Bender, A., Naveh-Benjamin, M., and Raz, N. (2010). Associative deficit in recognition memory in a life span sample of healthy adults. *Psychology and Aging, 25*(4), 940–948. doi: 10.1037/a0020595

Block, R. A. (2009). Intent to remember briefly presented human faces and other pictorial stimuli enhances recognition memory. *Memory & Cognition, 37*(5), 667–678. doi: 10.3758/MC.37.5.667

Bousfield, W. (1953). The occurrence of clustering recall of randomly arranged associates. *Journal of General Psychology, 49,* 229–240.

Cabeza, R., Anderson, N. D., Houle, S., Mangels, J. A., & Nyberg, L. (2000). Age-related differences in neural activity during item and temporal-order memory retrieval: A positron emission tomography study. *Journal of Cognitive Neuroscience, 12*(1), 197–206.

Castel, A. D. (2005). Memory for grocery prices in younger and older adults: The role of schematic support. *Psychology and Aging, 20*(4), 718–721.doi: 10.1037/0882-7974.20.4.718

Castel, A. D. (2007). Aging and memory for numerical information: The role of specificity and expertise in associative memory. *Journals of Gerontology: Series B: Psychological Sciences and Social Sciences, 62B*(3), 194–196.

Castel, A. D., & Craik, F. I. M. (2003). The effects of aging and divided attention on memory for item and associative information. *Psychology and Aging, 18*(4), 873–885.

Chalfonte, B. L., & Johnson, M. K. (1996). Feature memory and binding in young and older adults. *Memory & Cognition, 24*(4), 403–416.

Cohen, N. J., Ryan, J., Hunt, C., Romine, L., Wszalek, T., & Nash, C. (1999). Hippocampal system and declarative (relational) memory: Summarizing the data from functional neuroimaging studies. *Hippocampus, 9*(1), 83–98.

Craik, F. I. M. (1982). Selective changes in encoding as a function of reduced processing capacity. In F. Klix, J. Hoffman & E. van der Meer (Eds.), *Cognitive research in psychology* (pp. 152–161). Berlin, Germany: Deutscher Verlag der Wissenschaffen.

Craik, F. I. M. (1983). On the transfer of information from temporary to permanent memory. *Philosophical Transaction of the Royal Society of London, Series B, 302,* 341–359.

Craik, F. I. M. (1986). A functional account of age differences in memory. In F. Klix & H. Hagendorf (Eds.), *Human memory and cognitive capabilities, mechanisms and performance* (pp. 409–422). Amsterdam, the Netherlands: North-Holland and Elsevier.

Craik, F. I. M., & Bosman, E. A. (1992). Age-related changes in memory and learning. In H. Bouma & J. Graafmans (Eds.), *Gerontechnology: Proceedings of the first international conference on technology and aging* (pp. 79–92). Eindhoven, the Netherlands: IOS Press.

Craik, F. I. M., & Jennings, J. M. (1992). In F. I. M. Craik & T. A. Salthouse (Eds.), *The handbook of aging and cognition* (pp. 51–110). Hillsdale, NJ: Lawrence Erlbaum Associates, Inc.

Craik, F. I. M., & Kester, J. D. (2000). Divided attention and memory: Impairment of processing or consolidation? In E. Tulving (Ed.), *Memory, consciousness, and the brain: The Tallinn conference* (pp. 38–51). Philadelphia, PA: Psychology Press.

Craik, F. I. M., & McDowd, J. M. (1987). Age differences in recall and recognition. *Journal of Experimental Psychology: Learning, Memory, and Cognition, 13*(3), 474–479. doi: 10.1037/0278-7393.13.3.474

Craik, F. I. M., & Rabinowitz, J. C. (1985). The effects of presentation rate and encoding task on age-related memory deficits. *Journal of Gerontology, 40*(3), 309–315.

Dew, I. T. Z., & Giovanello, K. S. (2010). Differential age effects for implicit and explicit conceptual associative memory. *Psychology and Aging, 25*(4), 911–921.

Dunlosky, J., & Hertzog, C. (1998). Aging and deficits in associative memory: What is the role of strategy production? *Psychology and Aging, 13*(4), 597–607.

Dunlosky, J., & Hertzog, C. (2001). Measuring strategy production during associative learning: The relative utility of concurrent versus retrospective reports. *Memory and Cognition, 29*(2), 247–253.

Dunlosky, J., Hertzog, C., & Powell-Moman, A. (2005). The contribution of mediator-based deficiencies to age differences in associative learning. *Developmental Psychology, 41*(2), 389–400. doi: 10.1037/0012-1649.41.2.389

Eichenbaum, H. (1994). The hippocampal system and declarative memory in humans and animals: Experimental analysis and historical origins. In D. L. Schacter & E. Tulving (Eds.), *Memory systems* (pp. 147–201). Cambridge, MA: MIT Press.

Erber, J. T., Galt, D., & Botwinick, J. (1985). Age differences in the effects of contextual framework and word-familiarity on episodic memory. *Experimental Aging Research, 11*(2), 101–103.

Gilbert, J. G. (1941). Memory loss in senescence. *Journal of Abnormal and Social Psychology, 36*(1), 73–86. doi: 10.1037/h0057019

Glisky, E. L. (2002). Source memory, aging, and the frontal lobes. In M. Naveh–Benjamin, M. Moscovitch, & H. L. Roediger III (Eds.), *Perspectives on human memory and cognitive aging: Essays in honor of Fergus Craik* (pp. 265–275). Philadelphia, PA: Psychology Press.

Glisky, E. L., & Kong, L. L. (2008). Do young and older adults rely on different processes in source memory tasks? A neuropsychological study. *Journal of Experimental Psychology: Learning, Memory, and Cognition, 34*(4), 809–822.

Glisky, E. L., Rubin, S. R., & Davidson, P. S. R. (2001). Source memory in older adults: An encoding or retrieval problem? *Journal of Experimental Psychology: Learning, Memory, and Cognition, 27*(5), 1131–1146.

Hasher, L., & Zacks, R. T. (1979). Automatic and effortful processes in memory. *Journal of Experimental Psychology: General, 108*(3), 356–388. doi: 10.1037/0096-3445.108.3.356

Hay, J. F., & Jacoby, L. L. (1999). Separating habit and recollection in young and older adults: Effects of elaborative processing and distinctiveness. *Psychology and Aging, 14*(1), 122–134.

Healy, M., R., Light, L. L., & Chung, C. (2005). Dual-process models of associative recognition in young and older adults: Evidence from receiver operating characteristics. *Journal of Experimental Psychology: Learning, Memory, and Cognition, 31*, 768–788.

Hines, J. C., Touron, D. R., & Hertzog, C. (2009). Metacognitive influences on study time allocation in an associative recognition task: An analysis of adult age differences. *Psychology and Aging, 24*(2), 462–475. doi: 10.1037/a0014417

Hockley, W. E. (1992). Item versus associative information: Further comparisons of forgetting rates. *Journal of Experimental Psychology: Learning, Memory, & Cognition, 18*, 1321–1330.

Hockley, W. E., & Consoli, A. (1999). Familiarity and recollection in item and associative recognition. *Memory & Cognition, 27*(4), 657–664.

Hoyer, W. J., & Verhaeghen, P. (2006). Memory aging. In J. E. Birren & K. Schaire (Eds.), *Handbook of the psychology of aging* (pp. 209–232). Amsterdam, Netherlands: Elsevier.

James, L. E., Fogler, K. A., & Tauber, S. K. (2008). Recognition memory measures yield disproportionate effects of aging on learning face-name associations. *Psychology and Aging, 23*(3), 657–664. doi: 10.1037/a0013008

Java, R. I. (1996). Effects of age on state of awareness following implicit and explicit word-association tasks. *Psychology and Aging, 11*(1), 108–111. doi: 10.1037/0882-7974.11.1.108

Jennings, J. M., & Jacoby, L. L. (1993). Automatic versus intentional uses of memory: Aging, attention, and control. *Psychology and Aging, 8*(2), 283–293.

Jennings, J. M., & Jacoby, L. L. (1997). An opposition procedure for detecting age-related deficits in recollection: Telling effects of repetition. *Psychology and Aging, 12*(2), 352–361.

Jonides, J., Naveh-Benjamin, M., and Palmer J. (1985). Assessing automaticity. *Acta Psychologica, 60*, 157–171.

Kausler, D. (1994). *Learning and memory in normal aging.* San Diego, CA: Academic Press.

Kilb, A., & Naveh-Benjamin, M. (2007). Paying attention to binding: Further studies assessing the role of reduced attentional resources in the associative deficit of older adults. *Memory & Cognition, 35*(5), 1162–1174.

Light, L. L. (1991). Memory and aging: Four hypotheses in search of data. *Annual Review of Psychology, 42,* 333–376. doi: 10.1146/annurev.ps.42.020191.002001

Light, L. L., Patterson, M. M., Chung, C., & Healy, M. R. (2004). Effects of repetition and response deadline on associative recognition in young and older adults. *Memory & Cognition, 32*(7), 1182–1193.

Macht, M. L., & Buschke, H. (1983). Age differences in cognitive effort in recall. *Journal of Gerontology, 38,* 695–700.

Maylor, E. A. (1995). Remembering versus knowing television theme tunes in middle-aged and elderly adults. *British Journal of Psychology, 86*(1), 21–25.

McGillivray, S., & Castel, A. D. (2010). Memory for age–face associations in younger and older adults: The role of generation and schematic support. *Psychology and Aging, 25*(4), 822–832. doi: 10.1037/a0021044

Mitchell, K. J., Johnson, M. K., Raye, C. L., Mather, M., & D'Esposito, M. (2000). Aging and reflective processes of working memory: Binding and test load deficits. *Psychology and Aging, 15*(3), 527–541. doi: 10.1037/0882-7974.15.3.527

Moscovitch, M. (1992). Memory and working-with-memory: A component process model based on modules and central systems. *Journal of Cognitive Neuroscience, 4*(3), 257–267. doi: 10.1162/jocn.1992.4.3.257

Moscovitch, M. (2000). Theories of memory and consciousness. In E., Tulving & F. I. M. Craik (Eds.), *The Oxford handbook of memory* (pp. 609–625). New York, NY: Oxford University Press.

Multhaup, K. S. (1995). Aging, source, and decision criteria: When false fame errors do and do not occur. *Psychology and Aging, 10*(3), 492–497.

Naveh-Benjamin, M. (2000). Adult-age differences in memory performance: Tests of an associative deficit hypothesis. *Journal of Experimental Psychology: Learning, Memory and Cognition, 26*(5), 1170–1187. doi: 10.1037/0278-7393.26.5.1170

Naveh-Benjamin, M., Craik, F. I. M., Guez, J., & Kreuger, S. (2005). Divided attention in younger and older adults: Effects of strategy and relatedness on memory performance and secondary task costs. *Journal of Experimental Psychology: Learning, Memory, and Cognition, 31*(3), 520–537.

Naveh-Benjamin, M., Guez, J., Kilb, A., & Reedy, S. (2004). The associative memory deficit of older adults: Further support using face–name associations. *Psychology and Aging, 19*(3), 541–546.

Naveh-Benjamin, M., Hussain, Z., Guez, J., & Bar-On, M. (2003). Adult age differences in episodic memory: Further support for an associative-deficit hypothesis. *Journal of Experimental Psychology: Learning, Memory, and Cognition, 29*(5), 826–837.

Naveh-Benjamin, M., Keshet Brav, T., & Levi, D. (2007). The associative memory deficit of older adults: The role of efficient strategy utilization. *Psychology and Aging, 22,* 202–208.

Naveh-Benjamin, M., & Old, S. R. (2008). Aging and memory. In J. H. Byrne, H. Eichenbaum, R. Menzel, H. L. Roediger, & D. Sweatt (Eds.), *Learning and memory: A comprehensive reference* (pp. 787–808). Oxford, UK: Elsevier.

Naveh-Benjamin, M., Shing, Y.-L., Kilb, A., Werkle-Bergner, M., Lindenberger, U., & Li, S.-C. (2009). Adult age differences in memory for name–face associations: The effects of intentional and incidental learning. *Memory, 17,* 220–232.

Old, S., & Naveh-Benjamin, M. (2008). Differential effects of age on item and associative measures of memory: A meta-analysis. *Psychology and Aging, 23*(1), 104–118. doi: 10.1037/0882-7974.23.1.104

Posner, M. I., & Snyder, C. R. R. (1975). Attention and cognitive control. In R. L. Solso. *Information processing and cognition: The Loyola symposium.* Hillsdale, NJ: Lawrence. Erlbaum Associates.

Rabinowitz, J. C. (1989). Age deficits in recall under optimal study conditions. *Psychology and Aging, 4*(3), 378–380. doi: 10.1037/0882-7974.4.3.378

Rabinowitz, J. C., Craik, F. I., & Ackerman, B. P. (1982). A processing resource account of age differences in recall. *Canadian Journal of Psychology, 36*(2), 325–344.

Raz, N. (2000). Aging of the brain and its impact on cognitive performance: Integration of structural and functional findings. In F. I. M. Craik, & T. A. Salthouse (Eds.), *The handbook of aging and cognition* (pp. 1–90). Mahwah, NJ: Lawrence Erlbaum Associates.

Raz, N., Gunning-Dixon, F. M., Head, D., Depuis, J. H., & Acker, J. D. (1998). Neuroanatomical correlates of cognitive aging: Evidence from structural magnetic resonance imaging. *Neuropsychology, 12*(1), 95–114.

Raz, N., Lindenberger, U., Rodrigue, K. M., Kennedy, K. M., Head, D., Williamson, A.,... Acker, J. D. (2005). Regional brain changes in aging healthy adults: General trends, individual differences and modifiers. *Cerebral Cortex, 15*(11), 1679–1689.

Raz, N., & Rodrigue, K. M. (2006). Differential aging of the brain: Patterns, cognitive correlates and modifiers. *Neuroscience & Biobehavioral Reviews 30*(6), 730–748.

Reder, L. M., Park, H., & Kieffaber, P. D. (2009). Memory systems do not divide on consciousness: Reinterpreting memory in terms of activation and binding. *Psychological Bulletin, 135*(1), 23–49.

Rendell, P. G., Castel, A. D., & Craik, F. I. M. (2005). Memory for proper names in old age: A disproportionate impairment? *Quarterly Journal of Experimental Psychology Section A, 58*(1), 54–71.

Rhodes, M. G., Castel, A. D., & Jacoby, L. L. (2008). Associative recognition of face pairs by younger and older adults: The role of familiarity-based processing. *Psychology and Aging, 23*(2), 239–249. doi: 10.1037/0882-7974.23.2.239

Ruch, F. L. (1934a). The differentiative effects of age upon human learning. *Journal of General Psychology, 11,* 261–286.

Ruch, F. L. (1934b). The differential decline of learning ability in the aged as a possible explanation of their conservatism. *Journal of Social Psychology, 5,* 329–337.

Salthouse, T. A. (1991). *Theoretical perspective on cognitive aging.* Hillsdale, NJ: Lawrence Erlbaum Associates.

Salthouse, T. A., Kausler, D. H., & Saults, J. S. (1990). Age, self-assessed health status, and cognition. *Journals of Gerontology, 45*(4), 156–160.

Schneider, W., & Shiffrin, R. M. (1977). Controlled and automatic human information processing: I. Detection, search, and attention. *Psychological Review, 84*(1), 1–66. doi: 10.1037/0033-295X.84.1.1

Smith, A. D., Park, D. C., Earles, J. L., Shaw, R. J., & Whiting, W. L. (1998). Age differences in context integration in memory. *Psychology and Aging, 13*(1), 21–28. doi: 10.1037/0882-7974.13.1.21

Underwood, B. J. (1969). Attributes of memory. *Psychological Review, 76*(6), 559–573. doi: 10.1037/h0028143

West, R. L. (1996). An application of prefrontal cortex function theory to cognitive aging. *Psychological Bulletin, 120*(2), 272–292. doi: 10.1037/0033-2909.120.2.272

West, R. L. (2000). In defense of the frontal lobe hypothesis of cognitive aging. *Journal of the Neuropsychological Society, 6*(6), 727–729. doi: 10.1017/S1355617700666109

Willoughby, R. R. (1927). Family similarities in mental-test abilities. *Genetic Psychology Monographs, 2*, 235–277.

Yonelinas, A. P. (2002). The nature of recollection and familiarity: A review of 30 years of research. *Journal of Memory and Language, 46*(3), 441–517.

Zacks, R. T., Hasher, L., & Li, K. Z. H. (2000). Human memory. In F. I. M. Craik & T. A. Salthouse (Eds.), *The handbook of aging and cognition* (2nd ed., pp. 293–357). Mahwah, NJ: Lawrence Erlbaum Associates Publishers.

Zelinski, E. M., Walsh, D. A., & Thompson, L. A. (1978). Orienting task effects on EDR and free recall in three age groups. *Journal of Gerontology, 33*(2), 239–245.

5 Dual-process theories of memory in old age

An update

Leah L. Light

INTRODUCTION

Contemporary dual-process models of memory posit two processes—*recollection* and *familiarity*—that underlie both recall and recognition (e.g., Atkinson & Juola, 1974; Jacoby, 1991; Mandler, 1980; see Diana, Reder, Arndt, & Park, 2006; Malmberg, 2008; and Yonelinas, 2002, for reviews). Particular dual-process models differ in various ways (e.g., whether they explicitly elaborate ways to deal with false memory, whether they incorporate assumptions about the architecture of memory representations, whether recollection and familiarity are viewed as independent processes, or whether recollection is treated as a discrete or a continuous variable). Nevertheless, they have much in common.

To illustrate, recollection is generally taken to involve remembering particular aspects of a prior episode, such as perceptual details, spatial or temporal information, the source of information, or thoughts and feelings that accompanied the event. Familiarity, in contrast, usually refers to experiences of prior events that may arise from activated semantic representations (as in the activation monitoring framework of Roediger and McDermott, 2000) or, in some views, from perceptual fluency (e.g., Mandler, 1980). However, these experiences lack the phenomenology associated with recollection. In addition, recollection is typically characterized as being deliberate, attention demanding, and slow in rise time, whereas familiarity is thought to be a relatively automatic process that is recruited more rapidly.

Recollection is usually considered to be the preferred basis for responding in recognition tasks, at least in young adults, unless speeded responding is required or other aspects of the task encourage familiarity-based responding. An assumption, often unstated, is that recollection and familiarity are processes that can be flexibly deployed, with the mix of processes in a given episode of remembering to some measure under the control of the individual and dependent on a person's goals, the quality of the information available in memory, and the way in which memory is probed by researchers (e.g., Benjamin & Bawa, 2004; Malmberg, 2008; Reder, 1988). At one end of the spectrum, when studied items are to be differentiated from randomly similar lures, recognition decisions may depend chiefly on familiarity, with recollection necessary when recognition lures are very similar to studied items. The latter situation arises in the Deese/Roediger–McDermott paradigm in which lures are semantically or phonologically similar to targets (Roediger & McDermott, 1995), as well as in associative recognition in which studied pairs must be discriminated from lures consisting of pairs of items that have both been studied, but with different mates (Yonelinas, 1997).

With respect to memory and aging, the principal questions have been the nature of changes from young to late adulthood (if any) in the relative contribution of recollection and familiarity to performance, and the extent to which such changes can account for changes in true and false memory across the adult life span. For instance, age difference in recollection would be expected because older adults have poorer memory for contextual information, even when item memory is held constant (for meta-analytic reviews, see Old & Naveh-Benjamin, 2008, and Spencer & Raz, 1995), especially when very specific information must be retrieved (Luo & Craik, 2009).

Some of the work in this area has been quantitative, generating model-based estimates of the contributions of recollection and familiarity processes to remembering. Much of it, however, relies on qualitative comparisons of young and older adults to obtain evidence for the shifting roles of the two classes of mental operations in performance (for reviews, see Hoyer & Verhaeghen, 2006; Light, Prull, LaVoie, & Healy, 2000; Yonelinas, 2002). This chapter begins with an examination of efforts to obtain quantitative estimates of the contributions of recollection and familiarity in young and older adults. I then describe research from our laboratory that focuses on the effects of two variables—presentation frequency and the time available to respond during retrieval—on associative recognition in young and older adults.

QUANTITATIVE ESTIMATES OF RECOLLECTION AND FAMILIARITY

Several techniques have been used to derive numerical estimates of recollection and familiarity. These methods include the process dissociation technique (Jacoby, 1991), the remember/know procedure (Gardiner, 1988; Tulving, 1985), the recognition operating characteristic (ROC) fitting approach (Yonelinas, 1994), and the conjoint recognition paradigm (Brainerd, Reyna, & Mojardin, 2009). In the cognitive aging literature, the first three of these approaches have accounted for the bulk of the research, with conjoint recognition paradigms only recently becoming part of the modeling toolkit (e.g., Aizpurua & Koutstaal, 2010; Brainerd, Reyna, & Howe, 2010). Here the first three approaches are considered.

In the process dissociation procedure, estimates of recollection are obtained by contrasting performance on inclusion tasks, in which both recollection and familiarity contribute to accurate performance, and exclusion tasks, where successful performance requires using recollection to oppose familiarity. Estimates from the process dissociation procedure usually show age differences in recollection and age constancy in familiarity, although the latter finding is not universal (Anderson et al., 2008; Davidson & Glisky, 2002; Jennings & Jacoby, 1997; Luo, Hendriks, & Craik, 2007; Salthouse, Toth, Hancock, & Woodard, 1997; Schmitter-Edgecombe, 1999; Toth & Parks, 2006; Zelazo, Muller, Frye, & Marcovitch, 2003; for reviews, see Light et al., 2000; Prull, Crandell Dawes, McLeish, Rosenberg, & Light, 2006; Yonelinas, 2002).

The process dissociation procedure has been subjected to considerable criticism, in part because it assumes that response bias is constant across inclusion and exclusion conditions— something that is not always the case (e.g., Curran & Hintzman, 1995). Hence, it is worth noting that estimates of recollection and familiarity derived solely from exclusion tasks can agree quite nicely with those calculated from separate inclusion and exclusion conditions (Anderson et al., 2008).

In the *remember/know* task, participants are asked not only to decide whether test items have been studied previously, but also to evaluate the conscious experiences that are associated with each decision. A *remember* response is given when elements of the original study episode are recollected, whereas a *know* response is made when study-phase contextual details cannot be retrieved, but the test item feels sufficiently familiar to warrant an *old* judgment. The procedure itself, by forcing participants to choose between *remember* and *know* responses and not permitting participants to say *both,* assumes that these are mutually exclusive states, though they are treated as independent in estimation procedures (Jacoby, 1991). Also, this procedure measures phenomenological states rather than processes that mediate these states.

The proportions of *remember* and *know* responses are nonetheless sometimes treated as relatively pure measures of recollection and familiarity, though it has become routine to convert raw *know* responses proportions to an estimate of familiarity that corrects for independence (Yonelinas & Jacoby, 1995). In the *remember/know* task, older adults generally have reduced *remember* judgments and may also have somewhat greater rates of *know* judgments (e.g., Friedman, de Chastelaine, Nessler, & Malcolm, 2010; Parkin & Walter, 1992; Parks, 2007; Perfect, Williams, & Anderton-Brown, 1995; see Prull et al., 2006, for a discussion).

The *remember/know* paradigm thus appears to yield somewhat inconsistent outcomes with respect to familiarity. This conclusion is perhaps not altogether unexpected. *Know* judgments, like *remember* judgments, assign items to the category of recently studied material. At some level, then, both may tap recollection, although *know* judgments represent less detailed information about acquisition (Wais, Mickes, & Wixted, 2008). By this account, *know* judgments would not yield pure estimates of familiarity in the absence of recollection and would consequently not necessarily show stability across age.

Moreover, *know* judgments and the familiarity estimates based on them may be influenced by noncriterial recollection when people can retrieve contextual information other than that designated by an experimenter as the basis for *remember* responses. The additional contextual information increases the tendency to say that an item has been experienced, but, because it is information that does not meet the experimenter's criterion for *remember* judgments, it instead inflates *know* judgments. Noncriterial recollection is a species of recollection and, unsurprisingly, occurs less strongly or not at all in older adults. In addition to inflating estimates of familiarity in young adults in the *remember/know* task, noncriterial recollection can also affect estimates of familiarity derived from inclusion/exclusion tasks and from the fitting of ROC curves to confidence-rated recognition, though age differences in familiarity estimates can be found in the latter task even in the absence of evidence for noncriterial recognition (Parks, 2007; Toth & Parks, 2006).

The interpretation of age differences in the *remember/know* task is also made challenging by the existence of groups of older adults who are matched in overall accuracy with young adults on recognition as well as on subjective recollection (use of *remember* judgments), but who show objective impairments in recollection (i.e., source memory) (Duarte, Henson, & Graham, 2008; Duarte, Ranganath, Trujillo, & Knight, 2006). However, it is possible that *remember* judgments in this group are based on contextual information other than the source that is tested. Finally, but not trivially, there is some debate about the extent to which responses in the *remember/know* task reflect degrees of confidence rather than subjective manifestations of different underlying processes (Wixted & Stretch, 2004).

In the ROC technique, participants make confidence-rated recognition judgments. To illustrate, with a six-point rating scale, participants might respond *1* (for items that they are very sure were not studied) through *6* (for items that they are very sure were studied). A plot (ROC) is made of the cumulative proportion of hits (old judgments correctly given to studied items) as a function of the cumulative proportion of false alarms (the proportion of old judgments incorrectly given to new items) at various levels of confidence. Theoretical models of the recognition process are fit to the ROC curves, and estimates of recollection and familiarity are derived.

Four investigations that I know of have reported fits of Yonelinas's (1994, 1997) dual-process high-threshold signal detection model to ROCs for item recognition (Howard, Bessette-Symons, Zhang, & Hoyer, 2006; Daselaar, Fleck, Dobbins, Madden, & Cabeza, 2006; Parks, 2007; Prull et al., 2006). This model assumes that recollection is a discrete (high-threshold) process, whereas familiarity is normally distributed. All found higher estimates of recollection in young adults, but Howard et al. and Daselaar et al. observed numerically higher familiarity values in older adults, while Parks and Prull et al. found smaller values of familiarity in this group.

Healy, Light, and Chung (2005) obtained estimates of recollection and familiarity from ROCs for confidence-rated associative recognition tests.

In their studies, young and older adults studied a list of word pairs and then took a recognition test with three kinds of items: intact (studied) pairs, rearranged lures, and completely new lure pairs. Because both intact and rearranged test pairs include two previously studied words, item familiarity is not diagnostic as to the old/new status of test pairs; therefore, correct responding requires recollection.

A number of different models were fit to the resultant ROCs in which both hits to intact pairs and false alarms to rearranged lures were plotted as a function of false alarms to new items. Some of these were dual-process models that included recollection, but the nature of the recollection process varied considerably across models. In models that included recollection, two recollection parameters were estimated. One indexed the extent to which recognition of a previously studied pair is based on recollection that the two words were studied together (recall-to-accept) and the other indexed the extent to which rearranged foils are rejected by recollecting that one of the words in the pair was studied with another item (recall-to-reject).

Healy et al. (2005) included in their analysis Yonelinas's (1994) dual-process signal detection theory model, which assumes that both recall-to-accept and recall-to-reject are threshold processes and that familiarity is normally distributed. Within the framework of this model, associative recognition is a within-task opposition procedure. Intact pairs from the study list represent to-be-included items that benefit from both recollection and familiarity, while rearranged pairs represent to-be-excluded items with recollection needed to oppose item familiarity (because both items in these pairs have been studied). Decisions about old test items that are not recollected and new test items that cannot be recollected are based on familiarity.

Healy et al. (2005) also included two other types of models that make rather different assumptions. One was the multinomial processing tree signal detection model (cf. Macho, 2004) in which familiarity is normally distributed. In this model, recollection responses can be distributed across confidence levels rather than being confined to high-confidence judgments. The second model was based on Kelley and Wixted's (2001) SON (some or nothing) model. In that model, associative recognition judgments are based on item familiarity that can be (sometimes) incremented or (sometimes) decremented by associative familiarity. The recollection parameters in this model represent the probability that associative information is added to item familiarity for the individual words in intact pairs and the probability that associative information is subtracted from item familiarity for rearranged pairs.

The current theoretical consensus is that recollection is not a discrete process as specified in the dual-process signal detection theory, but in fact is continuous (Wixted, 2007; Yonelinas & Parks, 2007). Healy et al. (2005) included a sufficient number of observations in their studies that ROCs could be constructed for individual participants. Interestingly, one version of the SON model was the best performing of the dual-process models across three experiments for both young and older individuals, although a model that did not include recollection also did a very creditable job in fitting the data.

Computing numerical estimates of familiarity and recollection from behavioral data has been described in a fair amount of detail. I believe that such detail is merited, given the energy devoted to this enterprise. Several conclusions seem to be warranted by the extant data. First, for all models examined, recollection parameters were lower for older than for younger adults, with this being especially evident for parameters representing recall-to-reject. Thus, the conclusion that estimates of recollection are lower in later adulthood stands on very firm ground. Second, age effects for familiarity estimates were inconsistent within tasks and were highly model dependent for ROC fitting. Also note that the assumptions underlying the computation of recollection and familiarity in the inclusion/exclusion and *remember/know* tasks and in many studies using ROC fitting may be incorrect to the extent that recollection is a continuously distributed variable. Clearly, conclusions drawn from such models should be accompanied by a caveat emptor. This holds true not only for behavioral studies, but also for neuroimaging studies (Wixted, 2007).

THE TIME COURSE OF RECOLLECTION IN YOUNG AND OLDER ADULTS' ASSOCIATIVE RECOGNITION

Dual-process models of memory make specific predictions about the effects of response deadline and presentation frequency, two variables that are generally deemed difficult (if not impossible) for single-process models of memory to handle with respect to associative recognition (Clark & Gronlund, 1996). In the response deadline procedure, items on a recognition test are presented, but participants are asked not to respond until a signal is presented, at which time they are to respond as rapidly as possible.

As noted previously, one of the assumptions of dual-process models is that familiarity information is available more quickly after the presentation of test pairs than is the associative information needed for recollection-based decisions in associative recognition. Hence, at very short response deadlines when neither item nor associative information is available, recognition decisions reflect guessing. At somewhat longer response deadlines, familiarity information becomes available and false alarms to rearranged pairs increase. With even longer delays between test pair presentation and response signal, associative information becomes available and recall-to-reject mechanisms kick in to reduce false alarms. The net result is that hit rates to intact pairs increase monotonically over the delay period, whereas false alarms to rearranged pairs have a curvilinear relation to response signal delay (Gronlund & Ratcliff, 1989).

The effects of response-signal delay can be exacerbated by increasing the familiarity of lure items on the recognition test. Using a process dissociation paradigm, Jacoby (1999) investigated the influence of both repetition and response pressure in the context of aging. Participants saw a list in which some words appeared one, two, or three times, and then heard a second list of words. At test, they were asked to respond *old* only to words they had heard. When younger adults were given long response deadlines, false alarms on previously studied words decreased with repetition. Ironically, false alarms to previously studied words increased with repetition for older adults, even with quite long deadlines. Thus, for younger adults, exclusion of seen words improved as a function of repetition, but the opposite was true for older adults, consistent with an age-related deficit in the use of contextual information—that is, recollection—to oppose enhanced familiarity produced by repetition.

Interestingly, young adults also showed an increase in false alarms with repetition when forced to respond quickly; this finding accords well with the view that recollection has a longer rise time than familiarity does. Similar ironic effects of repetition for older adults and for young adults tested with short response deadlines have been found in the Deese/Roediger–McDermott task (Benjamin, 2001; Budson, Daffner, Desikan, & Schacter, 2000; Kensinger & Schacter, 1999; Watson, McDermott, & Balota, 2004), in the false-fame paradigm (Bartlett, Strater, & Fulton, 1991), and in a comparison of the effects of massed and spaced practice (Benjamin & Craik, 2001). Such findings are easily explained by the assumption that familiarity is less effectively opposed by recollection in older adults and in young adults who are pressured to respond quickly.

Light, Patterson, Chung, and Healy (2004) generalized these findings to associative recognition, using a paradigm developed by Kelley and Wixted (2001). In their studies, young adults studied lists of word pairs, with half of the pairs presented once (*weak* pairs) and half presented four times (*strong* pairs). After study, participants were given a recognition test that included strong and weak intact pairs (both words studied together), strong and weak rearranged pairs (both words studied but with different partners), and completely new lure pairs. Kelley and Wixted found that with repetition of pairs at study, young adults' hits to intact pairs increased, while their false alarms to rearranged pairs remained constant.

One explanation of their findings is that both familiarity and recollection are increased by repetition of study pairs. For intact pairs, familiarity and recollection work in concert to boost hit rates. Although words in rearranged lures become more familiar with repetition, young adults may recollect the original pairs and reject these lures, successfully opposing the (here misleading) effects of familiarity. However, if recollection fails and both items of a test pair are familiar, participants respond *old*, thus producing false alarms to rearranged lures.

Light et al. (2004) carried out two experiments that extend the Kelley and Wixted (2001) findings to older adults. In both experiments, young and older adults studied a list of word pairs, some presented once and some presented four times. The first experiment used the response signal technique; 26 young adults (aged 8–27 years) and 30 older adults (aged 61–78 years) participated. On each test trial, the participants were shown a focal stimulus for 500 ms, followed by the presentation of the test word pair. Three deadline conditions were used—short, long, and extra long—with young adults tested in the first two and older adults in the last two.

In the short deadline condition, a response cue appeared beneath the test pair 400 ms after presentation. The participants then had 600 ms to respond. The end of this response window was signaled by a beep, and a 1000 ms intertrial interval (blank screen) began immediately thereafter. Thus, each trial lasted 2500 ms, even though test pairs disappeared from the screen if a response occurred within the response window.

In the long deadline condition, the response cue did not appear until after the test pair had been shown for 2400 ms. Durations of all other events within the trial were the same as in the short deadline condition, and each trial lasted 4500 ms. In the extra long deadline condition, the response window was increased to 1600 ms, so each trial lasted 5500 ms. Thus, the shorter of the two deadlines used with older adults was made identical to the longer of the two deadlines used with young adults to compensate for general slowing that occurs with age (see Jacoby, 1999, for a similar design). In the second experiment, no response deadline was used.

The results of the two studies were clear-cut. Those of the first study are shown in Figure 5.1. When compared at their common deadline, hit rates were higher for young adults than for older adults and higher for strong pairs than for weak pairs. False alarm rates for rearranged pairs were higher in older adults than in young adults. More critically, false alarms for rearranged pairs in young adults decreased from .26 to .15 with repetition, but older adults showed an ironic effect of repetition, with false alarms of .40 for weak rearranged pairs and .51 for strong rearranged pairs. Young adults showed an ironic effect of repetition for false alarms at their shorter deadline, but, as noted before, not at their longer deadline.

Older adults, in contrast, had an ironic effect of repetition at both of their deadlines. In the second study, when participants could respond at their own pace with no deadline imposed, older adults continued to show ironic effects of repetition on false alarms to rearranged lures; interestingly, young adults had no effect of pair strength on false alarms to rearranged lures under these conditions. It is possible that young adults responded more quickly in the unspeeded condition of the second study than they did in the long delay condition in the first study. One speculation, then, is that young adults actually had more time for recruitment of recollection in the long delay condition of the first study than in the unspeeded condition of the second study (cf. Malmberg & Xu, 2007).

Our findings are not readily accommodated by simple single-process signal detection theories in which repetition increases the strength of

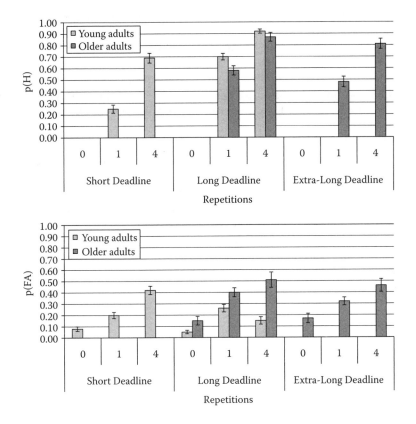

FIGURE 5.1 Mean proportions of hits and false alarms as a function of age, repetition, and response deadline. (Adapted from Light, L. L. et al., 2004, *Memory & Cognition, 32,* 1186. Copyright 2004 by the Psychonomic Society, Inc.)

representations of studied materials and recognition decisions are based on strength or familiarity alone (Clark & Gronlund, 1996; Rotello & Heit, 2000). Without invoking additional machinery, such as slowly recruited recollection or monitoring at retrieval to counter increased familiarity induced by repetition, the difference in outcome patterns across age and deadline conditions cannot be explained (e.g., Hintzman & Curran, 1994; Jacoby, 1999; Jones & Jacoby, 2001; Kelley & Wixted, 2001). Similar conclusions have been reached for the Deese/Roediger–McDermott paradigm (e.g., Benjamin, 2001; Kensinger & Schacter, 1999; McDermott & Watson, 2001; Seamon et al., 2002; Watson et al., 2004). Moreover, parallel results for the effects of repetition, response deadline, and age have been obtained in another task—plurality discrimination, in which participants study nouns in either their singular or plural (plus-*s*) forms and, then, on a recognition task, must differentiate studied words from their plurality-reversed forms and from new items (Light, Chung, Pendergrass, & Van Ocker, 2006).

Light et al. (2004) manipulated familiarity of rearranged lures by varying presentation frequency. In other work, the effects of an additional source of familiarity—namely, preexperimental relatedness of word pairs—on the time course of associative recognition in young and older adults have also been examined (Patterson, Light, Van Ocker, & Olfman, 2009). The Patterson et al. study was based on Dosher and Rosedale (1991). The logic of the research is best understood by reference to Table 5.1, which gives the composition of the study pairs (presented once) and the test pairs.

The participants in the study were 33 young adults (18–22 years) and 28 older adults (aged 60–79). At study, the pairs could be semantically related or unrelated (related pairs re-paired for study). On each test trial, participants were shown a focal stimulus consisting of a row of plus signs for 500 ms, followed by the test word pair. Next, a response cue consisting of a row of asterisks appeared beneath the test pair. Participants were then given 600 ms to respond. The end of this response window was signaled by a beep and a 1000 ms intertrial interval (blank screen) was presented immediately

Table 5.1 Examples of study and test pairs used by Patterson et al.

Study pairs

ABDOMEN/STOMACH
METHOD/CAT
ENVY/JEALOUSY
DOG/TECHNIQUE
HAPPY/NONE
CHAIR/TABLE
ZERO/SAD

Test pairs

Pair type	Example	Correct response
S+E+	ABDOMEN—STOMACH	Old
S-E+	METHOD—CAT	Old
S-E-r	CHAIR—JEALOUSY	New
S+E-	HAPPY—SAD	New
S-E-u	ZERO—TECHNIQUE	New
New-u	DOOR—BOOK	New
New-r	ROBIN—PARROT	New

Source: Adapted from Patterson, M. M. et al., 2009, *Aging, Neuropsychology, and Cognition,* 16, 539. Copyright 2009 by Psychology Press.

Note: S+ = semantically related; S- = semantically unrelated; E+ = episodically related, E- = episodically unrelated.

thereafter. For the short deadline condition, test pairs were presented for 400 ms before the response cue appeared. For the long deadline condition, test pairs were presented for 2400 ms before the response cue appeared.

There were seven types of test pairs, of which five are central to this discussion. These included two types of intact pairs: S+E+ (semantically related, studied together) and S-E+ (semantically unrelated, studied together), and three types of rearranged pairs: S+E- (semantically related, not studied together), S-E-u (semantically unrelated, not studied together, studied in unrelated pairs), and S-E-r (semantically unrelated, not studied together, studied in related pairs). Participants were to respond *old* only when the two words had been studied together (i.e., for semantically related or unrelated intact pairs). Semantic relatedness is irrelevant for judgments of episodic relatedness, but nonetheless can influence associative recognition decisions.

The results of Patterson et al. (2009) are shown in Figure 5.2. Not surprisingly, young adults made fewer false alarms than older adults to completely unrelated lures (S-E-u), so the comparisons of interest are those between these lures and intact pairs and S+E- and S-E-r lures. Like Dosher and Rosedale (1991), Patterson et al. found that performance improved with longer signal-to-response deadlines and that discrimination of intact test pairs was better for S+E+ than for S-E+ pairs (i.e., that related study pairs were better remembered). Critically, and in keeping with work by Naveh-Benjamin, Hussain, Guez, and Bar-On (2003), age differences were obtained for unrelated study pairs but not for related study pairs. Moreover, this age equivalence for related study pairs was observed only at the longer response deadline. With longer deadlines, then, older adults benefited from semantic relatedness, leading to an eradication of age differences on intact semantically related pairs. Presumably, semantically related word pairs encourage more efficient associative binding or strengthening of preexisting connections.

The more interesting results, however, were found for false alarms to S+E- and S+E-r false alarms. Dosher and Rosedale (1991) found that false alarms to S+E- lures were lower at longer response deadlines, suggesting that semantic information becomes available before episodic information and can lead to erroneous judgments, presumably based on semantic activation that is confused with recent experience. Our young adults did not show a benefit of longer response deadlines to counter semantic familiarity of these lures, and older adults actually had *worse* discrimination of these pairs from S-E-u pairs at the longer deadline, again showing an increased impact of semantic relatedness when more time to respond was available.

In addition, and arguably of greatest importance, at the long response deadline both young and older adults had better discrimination of S-E-r pairs from S-E-u pairs; that is, they made fewer false alarms to rearranged pairs whose members had been studied in related pairs. Dosher and Rosedale suggest that this results from an "explicit recall-then-matching strategy" in which participants generate a pair-mate in retrieval mode

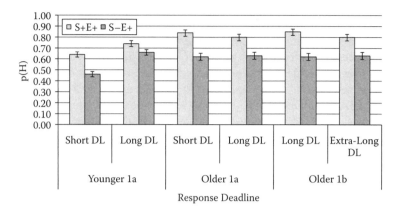

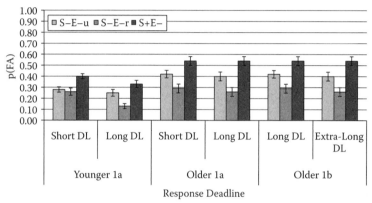

FIGURE 5.2 Mean proportions of hits and false alarms as a function of age, type of test pair, and deadline. (Adapted from Patterson, M. M. et al., 2009, *Aging, Neuropsychology, and Cognition, 16*, 545. Copyright 2009 by Psychology Press.)

and compare it to the tested pair-mate—a recall-to-reject process that takes time and thus manifests only late in the retrieval episode and that is easier to accomplish when the study pair consists of preexperimentally related words. Older adults are known to have difficulty in using recall-to-reject when study pairs consist of unrelated words (Cohn, Emrich, & Moscovitch, 2008; Healy et al., 2005). The ease of retrieval of the original related study pair is presumably the result of increased activation of a previously acquired connection, whereas for S-E-u pairs, the originally studied pairs were unrelated; hence, no preexperimental association was available to facilitate binding, and subsequent retrieval and age differences were seen. As seen in Figure 5.2, giving older adults even more time in a follow-up experiment with an extra long deadline condition, wherein test pairs were presented for 3400 ms before the response cue, had virtually no effect on their performance.

MORE ABOUT EFFECTS OF REPETITION
ON ASSOCIATIVE RECOGNITION

As discussed before, Light et al. (2004) found that strengthening pairs within a list by repetition either had no effect or led to a reduction in false alarms to rearranged pairs in young adults; however, it produced an increase in false alarms in older adults. As discussed later, this ironic effect of repetition on false alarms to rearranged pairs persists for at least eight repetitions of study pairs. Such results strongly argue for preserved familiarity coupled with reduced recollection in older adults, due either to an associative deficit or to a strategic decision not to engage in recall-to-reject processes.

Additional studies to examine further issues raised by these findings have been carried out. Here, two of these experiments are briefly described. The first demonstrates that repetition has similar strengthening effects on familiarity—but not recollection—processes in young and older adults. The second used a variant of the *remember/know* judgment task to explore the subjective experiences of participants during associative recognition.

DIFFERENTIAL EFFECTS OF REPETITION ON ITEM
AND ASSOCIATIVE STRENGTHENING IN YOUNG
AND OLDER ADULTS' ASSOCIATIVE RECOGNITION

This account of why repetition of study pairs produces increases in false alarms in older adults' associative recognition while false alarm rates in young adults remain relatively stable is based on the idea that the rate of change for familiarity is similar across age, while the rate of growth of recollection processes is higher for young than older adults. The Light et al. (2004) data reported for the effects of repetition at long- and short-deadline conditions support this position. Nonetheless, teasing out the separate contributions of repetition to the strengthening of item information and associative information is not possible in the usual paradigm in which pairs are repeated during study. The reason for this is that both associations and the individual items that comprise them are potentially strengthened by increasing presentation frequency.

To examine this question, Buchler, Faunce, Light, Gottfredson, and Reder (2011) manipulated study fan to increase item strength without increasing associative strength. Some study pairs were presented once and some were repeated five times. In addition, word fan was manipulated such that some words were presented multiple times but never in the same pairings. The fans used were 1-1 (study pairs presented once with no repetition of either constituent word), fan 1-5 and fan 5-1 (one member of the pair strengthened through repetition), and fan 5-5 (both left and right members of the pair presented with five different mates during study). The recognition test had intact and rearranged pairs as well as new pair lures in which either the left- or right-hand member of the study pair was presented with a new word. New–new lure pairs were also included. Comparison of word pairs presented once only (fan 1-1) with those for which there were five exact repetitions (rep 5X) constitutes a replication of Light et al. (2004), with pairs and the individual words in them appearing the same number of times.

For this comparison, then, it was expected that older, but not younger, adults would show an increase in false alarms with repetition. In both the rep 5X and fan 5-5 conditions, each word appears five times, so item strength is matched across conditions but pair strength is (obviously) greater in the former than in the latter condition. Here it was expected that older adults would show less benefit than young adults from identical repetitions. Comparison of responses to the fan 1-1, fan 1-5 and fan 5-1, and fan 5-5 conditions was expected to show greater age deterioration for higher fan as a result of associative interference (Cohen, 1990; Gerard, Zacks, Hasher, & Radvansky, 1991).

A novel recognition task introduced by Buchler, Light, and Reder (2008) was used. For each test pair, participants made one of five choices: *old–old (original)*, *old–old (rearranged)*, *old–new*, *new–old*, or *new–new*. This task affords a rich database for making inferences about the role of repetition in strengthening item and associative information in young and older adults. The data from 30 young adults (aged 18–23) and 30 older adults (aged 67–82) are shown in Table 5.2, with correct responses in boldface. As in the standard *yes/no* recognition task, recollection is needed for discriminating intact from rearranged pairs. Item familiarity, however, can be used to differentiate among rearranged pairs with two old words, item lures with one old word, and novel pairs with two new words.

First, the contrast between fan 1-1 and rep X5 pairs was examined to gauge the effect of exact repetition of word pairs. Repetition produced more correct identification of intact pairs (responses of *old-old (original)*) and a reliable age difference. False alarms—responses of *old–old (original)* to rearranged pairs—increased with repetitions, though individual contrasts within age groups showed this was significant only for older adults, as in our previous studies. The effect of repetition on false alarms in older adults appears weaker here than in other studies in our laboratory; the suspicion is that this is due to the fact that the presence of both exact repetitions and fan repetitions in the study list discouraged the use of recollection in *young* adults.

Second, rep X5 and fan 5-5 conditions were compared to examine the effects of repeating items and pairs. Repeating pairs produced higher hit rates and lower false alarm rates than repeating items, implicating exact repetition of pairs in the strengthening of associations. Age effects were found for hits but not false alarms for this contrast. The absence of age interactions suggests that the role of exact repetition is similar across age.

Third, to examine associative interference, the various fan conditions (fan 1-1 vs. fan 1-5, fan 5-1 vs. fan 5-5) were compared to determine the

Table 5.2 Mean proportions of responses to each of the five word-pair types in associative recognition as a function of the number of associates (fan) and repetition for young and older adults

	Response									
	Old–old (original)		Old–old (rearranged)		Old–new		New–old		New–new	
Pair type	Young	Old	Young	Old	Young	Old	Young	Old	Young	Old
Intact										
Fan 1-1	**.45**	**.28**	.11	.14	.06	.12	.10	.10	.28	.36
Fan 1-5	**.40**	**.31**	.19	.27	.04	.03	.29	.30	.07	.09
Fan 5-1	**.40**	**.26**	.19	.30	.31	.32	.02	.03	.08	.09
Fan 5-5	**.53**	**.45**	.37	.42	.04	.07	.05	.03	.01	.03
Rep X5	**.84**	**.75**	.06	.15	.04	.03	.03	.03	.03	.04
Rearranged										
Fan 1-1	.06	.05	**.20**	**.18**	.19	.15	.20	.15	.35	.47
Fan 1-5	.13	.16	**.35**	**.29**	.04	.07	.42	.39	.07	.09
Fan 5-1	.13	.09	**.32**	**.35**	.45	.44	.02	.04	.07	.07
Fan 5-5	.26	.24	**.61**	**.62**	.05	.04	.06	.09	.01	.01
Rep X5	.12	.17	**.53**	**.48**	.14	.16	.14	.14	.08	.05
Item pair										
Fan 1–new	.02	.04	.08	.08	**.29**	**.24**	.08	.10	.53	.53
New–fan 1	.04	.03	.07	.07	.06	.10	**.31**	**.19**	.52	.61
Fan 5–new	.04	.06	.17	.23	**.69**	**.57**	.02	.02	.08	.13
New–fan 5	.07	.11	.10	.18	.02	.04	**.72**	**.59**	.09	.07
Novel pair										
New–new	.01	.02	.05	.07	.10	.12	.10	.11	**.74**	**.69**

Source: Adapted from Buchler, N. G. et al., 2011, *Psychology and Aging, 26*, 111–126.

Note: Correct responses are in boldface.

effects of associative interference. Increasing fan was associated with increments in both hit and false alarm rates. Age effects were again seen only for hits. The absence of exacerbated fan effects for older adults was surprising, but similar age equivalence in fan effects has been observed elsewhere (Overman & Becker, 2009). Thus, age differences favoring young adults were generally observed for hit rates—and, in the analysis of pair repetition, in the false alarm rate as well.

When we look at item information, the picture is different. Several findings suggest that the availability of item information does not decline with age. Examination of Table 5.2 reveals that responses of *old–old (original)* (i.e., false alarms) increase with the number of studied items in a lure pair from zero (novel pairs) to one (lure pairs) to two (rearranged pairs), which is consistent with familiarity-based decision making. However, there is scant evidence for age differences in false alarm rates to these three lure types.

Two types of responses to intact pairs were also considered: correct responses of *old–old (original)* and incorrect responses of *old–old (rearranged)*. The first entails recollection, whereas the second represents correct identification of individual words as old, presumably based on item familiarity, without retrieval of associative information. With the exception of fan 1-1 items, the sum of these two proportions is very similar across age (see entries for fan 1-5, fan 5-1, fan 5-5, and rep X5). What differs, however, is the balance of responses based on recollection. The greater frequency of *old–old (rearranged)* responses to intact pairs in older adults is consistent with their giving greater weight to familiarity in associative recognition decisions when associative information is unavailable to support recollection.

Finally, consider lure pairs in which either the left or right word was old and the other word was new. Both young and older adults were quite good at identifying these pairs and showed little tendency to confuse the position of the presented word. This finding points to the ability of both young and older adults to gauge the familiarity of each member of a pair rather than summing familiarity over both words in a pair to arrive at a single strength indicator on which to base recognition judgments. Such findings are not easily explained by models that postulate a single decision variable, even if that variable incorporates both item familiarity and associative information (Buchler et al., 2008; cf. Hockley & Cristi, 1996).

EFFECTS OF REPETITION ON SUBJECTIVE EXPERIENCE IN ASSOCIATIVE RECOGNITION

Dual-process models predict that, for young adults, repeating pairs of words at study should lead to increased retrieval of information about the study episode when rearranged lures are correctly rejected (Jones, 2005;

Lampinen, Odegard, & Neuschatz, 2004). One question of interest is the nature of claims about the basis for false alarms to rearranged pairs. Using a *remember/know* judgment paradigm, Jones (2005) found an increase in *remember* responses for false alarms to conjunction lures with multiple repetitions of compound words at study.

However, results have not been altogether consistent across studies for young adults. For instance, Lampinen et al. (2004) did not find more reports of specific details about the study experience for false alarms to conjunction lures when the parent compound words were studied several times rather than just once. With respect to older adults, Karpel, Hoyer, and Toglia (2001) found that endorsements of suggested objects in the misinformation paradigm were associated with higher confidence and greater vividness for perceptual details of the nonpresented objects than was the case for young adults; moreover, a second exposure to the original materials led to decreased vividness ratings for suggested objects by young but not older adults.

Older adults may, in general, have higher confidence about the correctness of their responses when they make source errors (e.g., Chua, Schacter, & Sperling, 2009; Dodson, Bawa, & Krueger, 2007; Dodson, Bawa, & Slotnick, 2007; Skinner & Fernandes, 2009) and, indeed, a meta-analysis by McCabe, Roediger, McDaniel, and Balota (2008) found that the age effect size for veridical judgments of remembering and false remembering were of about the same magnitude. In a study pertinent to one to be described, Shing, Werkle-Bergner, Li, and Lindenberger (2009) reported that older adults gave disproportionately higher confidence judgments than young adults for false alarms made in an associative recognition task after a single study opportunity.

Van Ocker, Light, Olfman, and Rivera (2010) examined the effects of repetition on reports from 20 young adults (aged 18–22) and 32 older adults (aged 60–82) of the bases for their correct acceptance of intact pairs, false alarms to rearranged pairs, and correct rejections of rearranged pairs using a variant of the *remember/know* judgment task. Young and older adults studied a list of word pairs and then took an associative recognition test in which they first responded *old* or *new* to each test pair and then indicated whether their response was based on memory for details of the study episode or on familiarity (Jones, 2005).

The results of this study (see Figure 5.3) can be summarized briefly. Hits to intact pairs showed the typical pattern of increases with repetitions and higher levels of performance in younger adults overall. Both of these effects were attributable to changes in *details* responses, with young adults making more of these than older adults, and *details* responses increasing with presentation frequency. The finding that *details* responses dominate associative recognition is consistent with Hockley and Consoli's (1999) report of a preponderance of *remember* judgments in this task. Our usual finding of no systematic change in false alarms to rearranged lures with repetitions

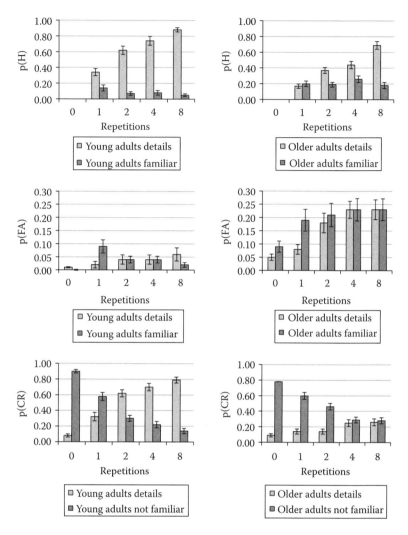

FIGURE 5.3 Mean proportions of hits, false alarms, and correct rejections as a function of age, repetitions, and response type.

in young adults and more false alarms with more frequent study opportunities in older adults was also replicated here and showed no signs of abating with as many as eight repetitions.

Interestingly, older adults made more *details* responses when they false alarmed to rearranged lures than young adults; *details* responses increased with repetitions—but only for older adults, who thus seem to claim that they can recall more details of study episodes that they never experienced. Older adults also made more *familiar* responses than young adults on rearranged lures, but these responses were not sensitive to repetitions. As for correct rejections of rearranged lures, these were, of course, more common in young than in older adults and were more often accompanied by *details* responses for young than older adults. Both young and older adults were more likely to claim that retrieval of details governed their correct rejections as the number of presentations increased, but the effect was more dramatic for young adults.

Correspondingly, older adults were more likely to claim that correctly rejected lure pairs were *not familiar* than were young adults, with both groups showing a drop in such claims over the course of repetitions. These results support the conclusion that both hits on intact pairs and correct rejections of rearranged pairs are based more heavily on recollection in young than older adults and that repetition has a greater impact on recollection in young than in older adults for both categories of response. These findings, then, add to the corpus of work that suggests reduced recollection in older adults.

Perhaps the most intriguing aspect of the results is that increases in false alarms to rearranged pairs made by older adults tended to be accompanied by claims that participants were retrieving specific information about the study episode (e.g., mediators used to link the two words in a study pair). It seems quite reasonable that increases in hit rates to intact pairs and increases in correct rejections occasioned by greater presentation frequency should be accompanied by such reports; however, it is not obvious why *details* responses to rearranged pairs should increase when the test item consists of frequently studied rearranged pairs.

One possibility, based on a suggestion of Dodson and his colleagues (Dodson, Bawa, & Krueger, 2007; Dodson, Bawa, & Slotnick, 2007; also see Kroll, Knight, Metcalfe, Wolf, & Tulving, 1996) is that older adults are prone to forming false bindings at study, so individual words from studied pairs are incorrectly associated with each other. According to this argument, to the extent that repeated pairs are presented more frequently, they would afford more opportunities for false bindings incorporating their constituent words. However, Wixted and Stretch (2004) have questioned the plausibility of explanations that include a greater tendency to false bindings in any group that has a lower rate of veridical binding; this objection would seem to hold for arguments about false binding in older adults. Moreover, because particular pairs are never repeated in close proximity, it seems unlikely that a given false binding would be strengthened by repetition of its constituents to the extent that *details* reports would be more likely to occur with increases in presentation frequency.

Higham and Vokey (2004) suggest that the subjective experience of recollection could be based on very strong familiarity even in the absence of retrieval of details. With increasing repetition, it is possible that the level of familiarity becomes sufficiently high to induce such subjective experiences of recollection in older adults. Our test instructions explicitly informed participants that people could feel very certain that test pairs were old without being able to retrieve details of the study experience and that they should respond *familiar* when this happened rather than *details*. Even so, it is possible that the familiarity process could spuriously give rise to the subjective experience of remembering. However, it is not clear, then, why this would not also occur at least some of the time in young adults, even if they are able to reject some highly familiar rearranged pairs on the basis of recollection of episodic details. Alternatively, false recollection can occur when there are errors of source attribution (see Higham and Vokey for a review), such as might occur if both words in a rearranged lure are familiar but there is only partial contextual information available (e.g., Buchler et al., 2011). This situation could easily occur for older adults if the growth in familiarity of individual words in study pairs materially exceeds the rate of binding of words in those pairs.

ARE RECOLLECTION DEFICITS IN OLDER ADULTS REALLY ENCODING DEFICITS?

Dual-process models focus on retrieval. However, it is highly unlikely that memory deficits in older adults can be localized exclusively to retrieval processes. Naveh-Benjamin and his colleagues (e.g., Naveh-Benjamin, 2000; Naveh-Benjamin et al., 2003) have formulated an associative deficit hypothesis that attributes problems underlying age-related deficits in recall and recognition, including associative recognition, primarily to difficulties in forming associations between items or between items and their contexts (though a role for retrieval problems is also acknowledged). They ascribe a larger role for encoding in effects that have been discussed in terms of retrieval.

Li and her colleagues also have provided evidence from simulations that less distinctive encoding of associations can account for a number of findings (Li, Naveh-Benjamin, & Lindenberger, 2005). For instance, Shing, Werkle-Bergner, Li, and Lindenberger (2008) suggest that less distinct encoding in older adults makes it more difficult to differentiate between studied pairs and rearranged lures in associative recognition. On their account, suboptimal neuromodulation can also lead to more highly activated, though less specific, representations, thus producing a pattern of increased false alarming with high confidence in late adulthood (Chua et al., 2009; Dodson, Bawa, & Krueger, 2007; Shing et al., 2008, 2009; Van Ocker et al., 2010).

Recently, Buchler et al. (2011) produced a good fit to associative recognition data in older adults by modifying the value of only one parameter from the fit of Reder's SAC model (Reder, Park, & Kieffaber, 2009) to young adults' data in the same experiment; that parameter was a working memory resource parameter that affects the efficiency of *both* encoding and retrieval. The findings from the model accord well with those from

Naveh-Benjamin, Craik, Guez, and Krueger (2005); these researchers found disproportionately greater costs of dividing attention in older than young adults at both encoding and retrieval, suggesting that both encoding and retrieval operations place heftier demands on the cognitive resources of older adults.

However, we do not believe that encoding problems per se tell the whole story. Reder, Wible, and Martin (1986) suggest that young adults switch between direct retrieval of actually studied information and plausibility judgments that require only an assessment that a test item is consistent with what was studied, depending, in part, on expectations about the quality of information available in memory and on task demands. Older adults, in contrast, seem to prefer to make plausibility judgments across the board. A related argument has been put forth by Jacoby, Shimizu, Velanova, and Rhodes (2005), who conceptualize familiarity as a less constrained form of memory access than recollection, which involves elaboration of the recognition probe to recapitulate study processing. In their view, familiarity, rather than recollection, is the preferred basis for recognition decisions in older adults, who sometimes may simply not bother to invoke recollection processes at all.

There is also evidence that older adults do not use all of the information that they have at hand in some deliberate memory tasks. For instance, older adults do not differ from young adults in recognition when the criterion for accepting test items includes both actually studied material and similar material—that is, under what constitutes less constrained retrieval instructions (e.g., Chung & Light, 2009; Cohn et al., 2008; Koutstaal, 2006). This result cannot be interpreted in terms of older adults' storage of less contextual information because both young and older adults have higher recognition when the test item is physically identical to the studied item than when it is physically different (i.e., a different picture of an umbrella, a noun studied in singular form but tested in plural form, intact vs. rearranged pairs in associative recognition).

A related finding of age equivalence in performance is observed when study context is reinstated at test, for instance, when words are presented and tested in the same auditory or visual modality (e.g., Light, LaVoie, Valencia-Laver, Albertson Owens, & Mead, 1992). Such findings indicate that perceptual information is available in memory that is not always utilized by older adults, consistent with there being a strategic component in their approach to memory tasks that differs from that of young adults.

Finally, there is evidence that young and older adults have different goals with respect to memory. In particular, older adults may prioritize construction of meaningful narratives that are tailored to the demands of particular audiences over reporting exactly what was experienced. This may occur even in laboratory settings, where researchers typically expect all participants to give verbatim reports of what is in memory (Hasher & Zacks, 1988; see Ornstein & Light, 2010, for a review).

SUMMARY

We believe that both the quantitative and the qualitative data that have been discussed strongly support the existence of age-related declines in recognition memory that are more amenable to explanation by dual-process models than by single-process models (but see Benjamin, 2010, for a different view). Quantitative estimates of recollection, especially recall-to-reject processes, universally find an advantage for young adults. Whether there are age-related differences in the role of familiarity-based mechanisms is less clear. Estimates of the contribution of familiarity are sometimes congruent with the idea that familiarity plays a larger role in recognition decisions in older than in younger adults, but this is by no means a universal finding either in our own work or in research from other laboratories. At present, the source of the discrepant findings is not clear and interpretive issues may not be identical across the different paradigms used to obtain quantitative estimates of familiarity.

The behavioral evidence from studies examining the joint effects of repetition and response pressure is broadly consistent with the view that recollection declines with old age to a greater extent than does familiarity. These effects are typically seen most strongly in age differences in false alarm rates as a function of presentation frequency, though sometimes they show up more clearly in hit rates, as was seen in our five-alternative forced-choice experiment. It is also evident from our research that recall-to-reject processes can be elicited in older adults under some circumstances, such as when the two members of a rearranged lure were originally studied with semantically related words—making retrieval of studied pairs for comparison with test items more likely. (For a discussion of other circumstances in which older adults engage in retrieval-based recognition judgments, see Ornstein and Light, 2010.)

One of the puzzles that have been observed is that the subjective experiences of older adults when they make false alarms to rearranged lures are more confident or more likely to be accompanied by claims that the original study experience is recollected. The theoretical basis for this phenomenon is as yet incompletely understood, but one viable account is that it arises from incomplete retrieval of contextual information by older adults. It is also unknown whether older adults do not engage in recollection principally because encoding is defective, thus making recall-to-reject strategies more difficult to deploy, whether older adults elect to base memory decisions on less complete information because it is simpler to do so than to engage in effortful retrieval processes, or whether the goals of young and older adults are such that direct retrieval of experiences is less important for older than for younger adults.

Our intuition is that future research will reveal that all of these elements are involved.

ACKNOWLEDGMENTS

The research reported here was partially supported by National Institute on Aging grant R01 AG02452. I am grateful to Jason Rivera for assistance in preparation of figures.

REFERENCES

Aizpurua, A., & Koutstaal, W. (2010). Aging and flexible remembering: Contributions of conceptual span, fluid intelligence, and frontal functioning. *Psychology and Aging, 25,* 193–207.

Anderson, N. D., Ebert, P. L., Jennings, J. M., Grady, C. L., Cabeza, R., & Graham, S. J. (2008). Recollection- and familiarity-based memory in healthy aging and amnestic mild cognitive impairment. *Neuropsychology, 22,* 177–187.

Atkinson, R. C., & Juola, J. F. (1974). Search and decision processes in recognition memory. In D. H. Krantz, R. C. Atkinson, R. D. Luce, & P. Suppes (Eds.), *Contemporary developments in mathematical psychology: Volume 1. Learning, memory, and thinking* (pp. 243–293). San Francisco: Freeman.

Bartlett, J. C., Strater, L., & Fulton, A. (1991). False recency and false fame of faces in young adulthood and old age. *Memory & Cognition, 19,* 177–188.

Benjamin, A. S. (2001). On the dual effects of repetition on false recognition. *Journal of Experimental Psychology: Learning, Memory, and Cognition, 27,* 941–947.

Benjamin, A. S. (2010). Representational explanations of "process" dissociations in recognition: The DRYAD theory of aging and memory judgments. *Psychological Review, 117,* 1055–1079.

Benjamin, A. S., & Bawa, S. (2004). Distracter plausibility and criterion placement in recognition. *Journal of Memory and Language, 51,* 159–172.

Benjamin, A. S., & Craik, F. I. M. (2001). Parallel effects of aging and time pressure on memory for source: Evidence from the spacing effect. *Memory & Cognition, 29,* 691–697.

Brainerd, C. J., Reyna, V. F., & Howe, M. L. (2009). Trichotomous processes in early memory development, aging, and neurocognitive impairment: A unified theory. *Psychological Review, 116,* 783–832.

Brainerd, C. J., Reyna, V. F., & Mojardin, A. H. (1999). Conjoint recognition. *Psychological Review, 106,* 160–179.

Buchler, N. G., Faunce, P., Light, L. L., Gottfredson, N., & Reder, L. M. (2011). Effects of repetition on associative recognition in young and older adults: Item and associative strengthening. *Psychology and Aging, 26,* 111–126.

Buchler, N. G., Light, L. L., & Reder, L. M. (2008). Memory for items and associations: Distinct representations and processes in associative recognition. *Journal of Memory and Language, 59,* 183–199.

Budson, A. E., Daffner, K. R., Desikan, R., & Schacter D. L. (2000). When false recognition is unopposed by true recognition: Gist-based memory distortion in Alzheimer's disease. *Neuropsychology, 14,* 277–287.

Chua, E. F., Schacter, D. L., & Sperling, R. A. (2009). Neural basis for recognition confidence in younger and older adults. *Psychology and Aging, 24,* 139–153.

Chung, C., & Light, L. L. (2009). Effects of age and study repetition on plurality discrimination. *Aging, Neuropsychology, and Cognition, 16*, 446–460.

Clark, S. E., & Gronlund, S. D. (1996). Global matching models of recognition memory: How the models match the data. *Psychonomic Bulletin & Review, 3*, 37–60.

Cohen, G. (1990). Recognition and retrieval of proper names: Age differences in the fan effect. *European Journal of Cognitive Psychology, 2*, 193–204.

Cohn, M., Emrich, S. M., & Moscovitch, M. (2008). Age-related deficits in associative memory: The influence of impaired strategic retrieval. *Psychology and Aging, 23*, 93–103.

Curran, T., & Hintzman, D.L. (1995). Violations of the independence assumption in process dissociation. *Journal of Experimental Psychology: Learning, Memory, and Cognition, 21*, 531–547.

Daselaar, S. M., Fleck, M. S., Dobbins, I. G., Madden, D. J., & Cabeza, R. (2006). Effects of healthy aging on hippocampal and rhinal memory functions: An event-related fMRI study. *Cerebral Cortex, 16*, 1771–1782.

Davidson, P. S. R., & Glisky, E. L. (2002). Neuropsychological correlates of recollection and familiarity in normal aging. *Cognitive, Affective, & Behavioral Neuroscience, 2*, 174–186.

Diana, R., Reder, L. M., Arndt, J., & Park, H. (2006). Models of recognition: A review of arguments in favor of a dual-process account. *Psychonomic Bulletin & Review, 13*, 1–21.

Dodson, C. S., Bawa, S., & Krueger, L. E. (2007). Aging, metamemory, and high-confidence errors: A misrecollection account. *Psychology and Aging, 22*, 122–123.

Dodson, C. S., Bawa, S., & Slotnick, S. D. (2007). Aging and a signal detection model of illusory recollection. *Journal of Experimental Psychology: Learning, Memory, and Cognition, 33*, 169–181.

Dosher, B. A., & Rosedale, G. (1991). Judgments of semantic and episodic relatedness: Common time-course and failure of segregation. *Journal of Memory and Language, 30*, 125–160.

Duarte, A., Henson, R. N., & Graham, K. S. (2008). The effects of aging on the neural correlates of subjective and objective recollection. *Cerebral Cortex, 18*, 2169–2180.

Duarte, A., Ranganath, C., Trujillo, C., & Knight, R. T. (2006). Intact recollection memory in high-performing older adults: ERP and behavioral evidence. *Journal of Cognitive Neuroscience, 18*, 33–47.

Friedman, D., de Chastelaine, M., Nessler, D., & Malcolm, B. (2010). Changes in familiarity and recollection across the life span: An ERP perspective. *Brain Research, 1310*, 124–141.

Gardiner, J. M. (1988). Functional aspects of recollective experience. *Memory & Cognition, 16*, 309–313.

Gerard, L., Zacks, R. T., Hasher, L., & Radvansky, G. A. (1991). Age deficits in retrieval: The fan effect. *Journal of Gerontology: Psychological Sciences, 46*, P131–P136.

Gronlund, S. D., & Ratcliff, R. (1989). Time course of item and associative information: Implications for global memory models. *Journal of Experimental Psychology: Learning, Memory, and Cognition, 15*, 846–858.

Hasher, L., & Zacks, R. T. (1988). Working memory, comprehension, and aging: A review and a new view. In G. H. Bower (Ed.), *The psychology of learning and motivation: Advances in research and theory* (Vol. 22, pp. 193–225). New York, NY: Academic Press.

Healy, M. R., Light, L. L., & Chung, C. (2005). Dual-process models of associative recognition in young and older adults: Evidence from receiver operating characteristics. *Journal of Experimental Psychology: Learning, Memory, and Cognition, 31,* 768–788.

Higham, P. A., & Vokey, J. R. (2004). Illusory recollection and dual-process models of recognition memory. *Quarterly Journal of Experimental Psychology, 57A,* 714–744.

Hintzman, D. L., & Curran, T. (1994). Retrieval dynamics of recognition and frequency judgments. Evidence for separate processes of familiarity and recall. *Journal of Memory and Language, 33,* 1–18.

Hockley, W. E., & Consoli, A. (1999). Familiarity and recollection in item and associative recognition. *Memory & Cognition, 27,* 657–664.

Hockley, W. E., & Cristi, C. (1996). Tests of the separate retrieval of item and associative information using a frequency-judgment task. *Memory & Cognition, 24,* 796–811.

Howard, M. W., Bessette-Symons, B., Zhang, Y., & Hoyer, W. J. (2006). Aging selectively impairs recollection in recognition memory for pictures: Evidence from modeling and receiver operating characteristic curves. *Psychology and Aging, 21,* 96–106.

Hoyer, W. J., & Verhaeghen, P. (2006). Memory aging. In J. E. Birren & K. W. Schaie (Eds.), *Handbook of the psychology of aging* (6th ed., pp. 209–232). Amsterdam, the Netherlands: Elsevier.

Jacoby, L. L. (1991). A process dissociation framework: Separating automatic from intentional uses of memory. *Journal of Memory and Language, 30,* 513–541.

Jacoby, L. L. (1999). Ironic effects of repetition: Measuring age-related differences in memory. *Journal of Experimental Psychology: Learning, Memory, and Cognition, 25,* 3–22.

Jacoby, L. L., Shimizu, Y., Velanova, K., & Rhodes, M. G. (2005). Age differences in depth of retrieval: Memory for foils. *Journal of Memory and Language, 52,* 493–504.

Jennings, J. M., & Jacoby, L. L. (1997). An opposition procedure for detecting age-related deficits in recollection: Telling effects of repetition. *Psychology and Aging, 12,* 352–361.

Jones, T. C. (2005). Study repetition and the rejection of conjunction lures. *Memory, 13,* 499–515.

Jones, T. C., & Jacoby, L. L. (2001). Feature and conjunction errors in recognition memory: Evidence for dual-process theory. *Journal of Memory and Language, 45,* 82–102.

Karpel, M. E., Hoyer, W. J., & Toglia, M. P. (2001). Accuracy and qualities of real and suggested memories: Nonspecific age differences. *Journal of Gerontology: Psychological Sciences, 56B,* P103–P110.

Kelley, R., & Wixted, J. T. (2001). On the nature of associative information in recognition memory. *Journal of Experimental Psychology: Learning, Memory, and Cognition, 27,* 701–722.

Kensinger, E. A., & Schacter, D. L. (1999). When true memories suppress false memories: Effects of ageing. *Cognitive Neuropsychology, 16,* 399–415.

Koutstaal, W. (2006). Flexible remembering. *Psychonomic Bulletin & Review, 13,* 84–91.

Kroll, N. E. A., Knight, R. T., Metcalfe, J., Wolf, E. S., & Tulving, E. (1996). Cohesion failure as a source of memory illusions. *Journal of Memory and Language, 35,* 176–196.

Lampinen, J. M., Odegard, T. N., & Neuschatz, J. S. (2004). Robust recollection rejection in the memory conjunction paradigm. *Journal of Experimental Psychology: Learning, Memory, and Cognition, 30,* 332–342.

Li, S-C, Naveh-Benjamin, M., & Lindenberger, U. (2005). Aging neuromodulation impairs associative binding. *Psychological Science, 16,* 445–450.

Light, L. L., Chung, C., Pendergrass, R., & Van Ocker, J. C. (2006). Effects of repetition and response deadline on item recognition in young and older adults. *Memory & Cognition, 34,* 335–343.

Light, L. L., La Voie, D., Valencia-Laver, D., Albertson-Owens, S. A., & Mead, G. (1992). Direct and indirect measures of memory for modality in young and older adults. *Journal of Experimental Psychology: Learning, Memory, and Cognition, 18,* 1284–1297.

Light, L. L., Patterson, M. M., Chung, C., & Healy, M. R. (2004). Effects of repetition and response deadline on associative recognition in young and older adults. *Memory & Cognition, 32,* 1182–1193.

Light, L. L., Prull, M. W., La Voie, D. J., & Healy M. R. (2000). Dual-process theories of memory in old age. In T. J. Perfect & E. A. Maylor (Eds.), *Models of cognitive aging* (pp. 238–300). New York, NY: Oxford University Press.

Luo, L., & Craik, F. I. M. (2009). Age differences in recollection: Specificity effects at retrieval. *Journal of Memory and Language, 60,* 421–436.

Luo, L., Hendriks, T., & Craik, F. I. M. (2007). Age differences in recollection: Three patterns of enhanced encoding. *Psychology and Aging, 22,* 269–280.

Macho, S. (2004). Modeling associative recognition: A comparison of two-high-threshold, two-high-threshold signal detection, and mixture distribution models. *Journal of Experimental Psychology: Learning, Memory, and Cognition, 30,* 83–97.

Malmberg, K. J. (2008). Recognition memory: A review of the critical findings and an integrated theory for relating them. *Cognitive Psychology, 57,* 335–384.

Malmberg, K. J., & Xu, J. (2007). On the flexibility and the fallibility of associative memory. *Memory & Cognition, 35,* 545–556.

Mandler, G. (1980). Recognizing: The judgment of previous occurrence. *Psychological Review, 87,* 252–271.

McCabe, D. P., Roediger, H. L., III, McDaniel, M. A., & Balota, D. A. (2009). Aging reduces veridical remembering but increases false remembering: Neuropsychological test correlates of remember-know judgments. *Neuropsychologia, 47,* 2164–2173.

McDermott, K. B., & Watson, J. M. (2001). The rise and fall of false recall: The impact of presentation duration. *Journal of Memory and Language, 45,* 160–176.

Naveh-Benjamin, M. (2000). Adult age differences in memory performance: Tests of an associative deficit hypothesis. *Journal of Experimental Psychology: Learning, Memory, and Cognition, 26,* 1170–1187.

Naveh-Benjamin, M., Craik, F. I. M., Guez, J., & Krueger, S. (2005). Divided attention in younger and older adults: Effects of strategy and relatedness on memory performance and secondary task costs. *Journal of Experimental Psychology: Learning, Memory, and Cognition, 31,* 520–537.

Naveh-Benjamin, M., Hussain, Z., Guez, J. & Bar-On, M. (2003). Adult age differences in episodic memory: Further support for an associative-deficit hypothesis. *Journal of Experimental Psychology: Learning, Memory, and Cognition, 29,* 826–837.

Old, S., & Naveh-Benjamin, M. (2008). Differential effects of age on item and associative measures of memory: A meta-analysis. *Psychology and Aging, 23,* 104–118.

Ornstein, P. A., & Light, L. L. (2010). Memory development across the life span. In R. M. Lerner & W. F. Overton (Eds.), *The handbook of life-span development. Vol. 1: Cognition, biology, and methods* (pp. 259–300). Hoboken, NJ: John Wiley & Sons.

Overman, A. A., & Becker, J. T. (2009). The associative deficit in older adult memory: Recognition of pairs is not improved by repetition. *Psychology and Aging, 24,* 501–506.

Parkin, A. J., & Walter, B. M. (1992). Recollective experience, normal aging, and frontal dysfunction. *Psychology and Aging, 7,* 290–298.

Parks, C. M. (2007). The role of noncriterial recollection in estimating recollection and familiarity. *Journal of Memory and Language, 57,* 81–100.

Patterson, M. M., Light, L. L., Van Ocker, J. C., & Olfman , D. (2009). Discriminating semantic from episodic relatedness in young and older adults. *Aging, Neuropsychology, and Cognition, 16,* 535–562.

Perfect, T. J., Williams, R. B., & Anderton-Brown, C. (1995). Age differences in reported recollective experience are due to encoding effects, not response bias. *Memory, 3,* 169–186.

Prull, M. W., Dawes, L. L., Martin, A. M., III, Rosenberg, H. F., & Light, L. L. (2006). Recollection and familiarity in recognition memory: Adult age differences and neuropsychological test correlates. *Psychology and Aging, 21,* 107–118.

Reder, L. M. (1988). Strategic control of retrieval strategies. In G. Bower (Ed.), *The psychology of learning and motivation: Advances in research and theory* (Vol. 22, pp. 227–259). San Diego, CA: Academic Press.

Reder, L. M., Park, H., & Kieffaber, P. D. (2009). Memory systems do not divide on consciousness: Reinterpreting memory in terms of activation and binding. *Psychological Bulletin, 135,* 23–49.

Reder, L. M., Wible, C., & Martin, J. (1986). Differential memory changes with age: Exact retrieval versus plausible inference. *Journal of Experimental Psychology: Learning, Memory, and Cognition, 12,* 72–81.

Roediger, H. L., III, & McDermott, K. B. (1995). Creating false memories: Remembering words not presented in lists. *Journal of Experimental Psychology: Learning, Memory, and Cognition, 21,* 803–814.

Roediger, H. L., III, & McDermott, K. B. (2000). Tricks of memory. *Current Directions in Psychological Science, 9,* 123–127.

Rotello, C. M., & Heit, E. (2000). Associative recognition: A case of recall-to-reject processing. *Memory & Cognition, 28,* 907–922.

Salthouse, T. A., Toth, J. P., Hancock, H. E., & Woodard, J. L. (1997). Controlled and automatic forms of memory and attention: Process purity and the uniqueness of age-related influences. *Journal of Gerontology: Psychological Sciences, 52B,* P216–P228.

Schmitter-Edgecombe, M. (1999). Effects of divided attention and time course on automatic and controlled components of memory in older adults. *Psychology and Aging, 14,* 331–345.

Seamon, J. G., Luo, C. R., Schwartz, M. A., Jones, K. J., Lee, D. M., & Jones, S. J. (2002). Repetition can have similar or different effects on accurate and false recognition. *Journal of Memory and Language, 46,* 323–340.

Shing, Y. L., Werkle-Bergner, M., Li, S.-C., & Lindenberger, U. (2008). Associative and strategic components of episodic memory: A life-span dissociation. *Journal of Experimental Psychology: General, 137,* 495–513.

Shing, Y. L., Werkle-Bergner, M., Li, S.-C., & Lindenberger, U. (2009). Committing memory errors with high confidence: Older adults do but children don't. *Memory, 17,* 169–179.

Skinner, E. I., & Fernandes, M. (2009). Illusory recollection in older adults and younger adults under divided attention. *Psychology and Aging, 24,* 211–216.

Spencer, W. D., & Raz, N. (1995). Differential effects of aging on memory for content and context: A meta-analysis. *Psychology and Aging, 10,* 527–539.

Toth, J. P., & Parks, C. M. (2006). Effects of age on estimated familiarity in the process dissociation procedure: The role of noncriterial recollection. *Memory & Cognition, 34,* 527–537.

Tulving, E. (1985). Memory and consciousness. *Canadian Psychology, 26,* 1–12.

Van Ocker, J. C., Light, L. L., Olfman, D., & Rivera, J. (2010). *Effects of repetition and test type on age differences in associative recognition.* Manuscript in preparation.

Wais, P. E., Mickes, L., & Wixted, J. T. (2008). Remember/know judgments probe degrees of recollection. *Journal of Cognitive Neuroscience, 20,* 400–405.

Watson, J. M., McDermott, K. B., & Balota, D. A. (2004). Attempting to avoid false memories in the Deese/Roediger–McDermott paradigm: Assessing the combined influence of practice and warnings in young and old adults. *Memory & Cognition, 32,* 135–141.

Wixted, J. T. (2007). Dual-process theory and signal-detection theory of recognition memory. *Psychological Review, 114,* 152–176.

Wixted, J. T., & Stretch, S. (2004). In defense of the signal detection interpretation of remember/know judgments. *Psychonomic Bulletin & Review, 11,* 616–641.

Yonelinas, A. P. (1994). Receiver-operating characteristics in recognition memory: Evidence for a dual-process model. *Journal of Experimental Psychology: Learning, Memory, and Cognition, 20,* 1341–1354.

Yonelinas, A. P. (1997). Recognition memory ROCs for item and associative information: The contribution of recollection and familiarity. *Memory & Cognition, 25,* 747–763.

Yonelinas, A. P. (2002). The nature of recollection and familiarity: A review of 30 years of research. *Journal of Memory and Language, 46,* 441–517.

Yonelinas, A. P., & Jacoby, L. L. (1995). The relation between remembering and knowing as bases for recognition: Effects of size congruency. *Journal of Memory and Language, 34,* 622–643.

Yonelinas, A. P., & Parks, C. M. (2007) Receiver operating characteristics (ROCs) in recognition memory: A review. *Psychological Bulletin, 133,* 800–832.

Zelazo, P. D., Muller, U., Frye, D., & Marcovitch, S. (2003). The development of executive function in early childhood. *Monographs of the Society for Research in Child Development, 68*(3), Serial No. 274.

6 Dissociable forms of implicit learning in aging

Darlene V. Howard and
James H. Howard, Jr.

INTRODUCTION

Moving to a new home or job can be stressful and tiring because we cannot fall back on routines. But gradually we adjust to the novel physical and social surroundings, getting used to the new rhythms of our days and the layouts of our new spaces, and coming to anticipate the ways in which our new neighbors and colleagues will react. This adaptation involves implicit learning; we are absorbing the structure of our environment without intending to do so and without being aware of exactly what we are learning (Frensch & Ruenger, 2003; Reber, 1993). Such implicit learning contrasts with the more explicit and deliberate way in which we set out to learn the names of the new people we are meeting. Various descriptors have been used to capture the nature of implicit learning. It has been likened to a "structural sponge" (Hoyer & Lincourt, 1998), "learning by osmosis" (Claxton, 2000), the "adaptive unconscious" (Wilson, 2002), and "thinking without thinking" (Gladwell, 2005). Implicit learning is important for many functions, including social intuition (Lieberman, 2000) and language learning (Conway & Pisoni, 2008).

Despite its ubiquity in daily life, the aging of implicit learning has been studied much less than its explicit counterpart. Measures of implicit learning are not typically included in longitudinal studies or used as outcomes in clinical trials testing interventions. One possible reason is that older adults are less likely to notice or complain about changes in this kind of learning because they are typically unaware that it occurs. Another reason is that when implicit learning and memory have been studied, age-related deficits have sometimes been small or nonexistent, in contrast to the notable deficits usually reported for more explicit/declarative learning and memory (for reviews, see Dennis & Cabeza, 2008; Forkstam & Petersson, 2005; Prull, Gabrieli, & Bunge, 2000; Rieckmann & Backman, 2009). This has led to the frequent assumption that implicit learning is relatively spared the effects of aging.

However, we argue here that this is not the case. Rather, there are multiple forms of implicit learning; some do not decline in healthy aging, but others do. We argue further that differentiating among forms of implicit learning will enable us to investigate brain function more directly than using more explicit measures because the latter are more susceptible to differential effects of strategies, which might mask underlying structural and functional differences in brain systems.

TWO IMPLICIT LEARNING TASKS

Many different tasks have been used to study implicit learning. What they all have in common is an attempt to capture in the laboratory people's ability to become sensitive to covariations in the environment. The tasks include artificial grammar learning (Reber, 1967), probabilistic classification learning (Knowlton, Squire, & Gluck, 1994), process control learning (Berry & Broadbent, 1984), invariant feature learning (McGeorge & Burton, 1990), information integration learning (Ashby & Maddox, 1990), and statistical learning (Saffran, Aslin, & Newport, 1996). These tasks differ in many ways, including the nature of the regularity that is present to be learned, the type of stimuli (e.g., visual, auditory, verbal, nonverbal), and in how and when learning is assessed (e.g., by performance measures such as speed collected online during learning versus by judgments collected offline in a subsequent test).

There is no adequate taxonomy of forms of implicit learning. Squire's tree diagram of types of declarative and nondeclarative memory is widely cited (e.g., Squire, 2004), but it does not capture the distinctions on which we focus later, nor does it reflect more recent evidence on the dynamic interactions among learning systems (Henke, 2010; Poldrack & Foerde, 2008). We will not attempt to develop a taxonomy of implicit learning here or to review the relevant literature on the aging. Instead, we will contrast the learning of two kinds of regularities: sequences of events versus spatial contexts. These serve as useful counterpoints because they show different patterns of aging and can be dissociated in several other ways.

Sequence learning:
The Alternating Serial Response Time (ASRT) Task

To study sequence learning, most of the work described here uses an Alternating Serial Response Time (ASRT) task (introduced in Howard & Howard, 1997). This is an adaptation of the SRT task (Nissen & Bullemer, 1987) in which participants view a row of four locations, each with a corresponding response key. An event consists of a single one of these locations filling in. The participant presses the key corresponding to the event as quickly as possible, causing that event to disappear and the next event to occur a few milliseconds later. Unbeknownst to the participant, on most blocks the events occur at a predictable sequence of locations. Learning of the sequence is demonstrated when people come to respond more quickly and/or accurately to blocks that contain this predictable sequence than to those that do not. Such differential response times (RTs) to predictable versus unpredictable events often occur in the absence of any apparent declarative knowledge of the regularity, so the SRT has become the most commonly used assay of implicit sequence learning.

In the ASRT version of the SRT task used here, pattern events alternate with randomly determined ones. For example, a participant assigned the pattern 1324 would see the following sequence throughout training: 1 r 3 r 2 r 4 r 1 r 3 r 2 r 4 r … (where the numbers refer to the locations on the screen, with 1 being the leftmost, and where "r" refers to a randomly determined one of the four locations). Thus, every other event is completely predictable, while the interleaved events are unpredictable, making the lowest level of regularity present second order, in that event *n* is predicted by event *n* – 2. People do not become aware of the alternating regularity, even after 2,100 repetitions of the pattern (D. V. Howard et al., 2004).

Evidence indicates that people are learning implicitly that some runs of three locations (i.e., Triplets) occur more frequently than others. For example, participants assigned the pattern 1324 learn implicitly that Triplets such as 1r3 occur frequently, whereas Triplets such as 3r1 do not. The evidence for this learning is that although the third events in high- versus low-frequency Triplets do not differ in either accuracy or RT at the beginning of training, they do diverge with practice, such that people come to respond more quickly and accurately to high- than low-frequency Triplets. Thus, the amount and rate of sequence learning is assessed via this high- versus low-frequency difference in performance, which we call a *trial-type effect*.

Spatial context learning:
The spatial contextual cueing task (SCCT)

To study the learning of spatial contexts, we have used the spatial contextual cueing task (introduced by Chun & Jiang, 1998). This is a visual search task in which people search arrays of 11 distracter items (offset "L" letters) for one target, the letter "T," which is displayed on its side, with the leg facing either left or right. The participant's task on each trial is to find the T as quickly as possible and to push one of two response keys corresponding to whether the leg of the T is facing left or right. Unbeknownst to participants, there are two types of configurations: *novel*, in which the distracter array and targets are arranged randomly, versus *repeated*, in which certain arrays of distracters repeat over trials. In the latter case, when a given distracter array repeats, the target is always in the same position, though the direction of the T's leg varies randomly. Thus, on repeated trials, the distracter array predicts the position of the target, but not the correct response. At the beginning of training, novel and repeated trials yield identical performance, but, with practice, people come to respond more quickly and accurately to the repeated trials, signaling learning of spatial context. Thus, as in the ASRT, learning can be assessed via a trial-type effect.

Similarities between the two tasks

Although very different from each other, the ASRT and SCCT are similar in at least three important ways.

First, in both cases people are learning relationships, or contexts, and thus the learning is *associative.*

Second, in both cases the instructions are *incidental* in that people are not told to try to learn a regularity, or even that one is present, but are just told to respond to stimuli they encounter. Thus, people are not encouraged to adopt learning strategies, a known source of age differences under intentional instructions.

Third, in both cases the learning is largely *implicit* in that people do not become aware of the underlying regularity. Not only are they unable to give an accurate description of the nature of the regularity, but also, sensitive recognition tests typically reveal no ability to distinguish between predictable and unpredictable events. For example, for the ASRT, people cannot judge above chance which Triplets are high versus low frequency; in the SCCT, people cannot judge which distracter arrays are repeating versus novel, even though they are responding more rapidly and accurately to the high-frequency/repeated than the low-frequency/novel events (e.g., Chun & Jiang, 1998; Howard, Howard, Dennis, Yankovich, & Vaidya, 2004). Thus, any age differences that emerge in learning are unlikely to be attributable to known age differences in more declarative, explicit forms of learning.

AGE DIFFERENCES IN SEQUENTIAL AND SPATIAL CONTEXT LEARNING

We have collected data from healthy young and older adults in a number of studies using these tasks. Our typical study has used an extreme group design in which young college student adults are compared with healthy older adults 65 years of age and older; the age groups are similar on self-reported health, vocabulary score, and years of education.

We find that spatial context learning, as assessed by the SCCT, yields similar learning for young and old adults. For example, Figure 6.1 (based on data reported in J. H. Howard, Jr., et al., 2004) shows the RT trial-type effect (RT on novel minus repeated trials) for young and older adults; both groups are learning to a similar degree.

The relative age constancy we are seeing here is consistent with findings from a number of other studies that examined incidental learning of associations among simultaneously present items. Schmitter-Edgecombe and

Contextual Cueing

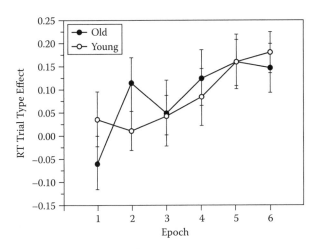

FIGURE 6.1 Associative learning scores (RT in seconds on Novel minus that on repeated trials) as a function of epoch for groups of young and old adults on the spatial contextual cueing task (SCCT). (Based on data reported in Howard, J. H., Jr., et al., 2004, *Neuropsychology, 18,* 124–134, Exp. 1.)

Nissley (2002) reported age constancy in learning on a matrix-scanning task, which is a visual search task similar to the SCCT. Light, LaVoie, Valencia-Laver, Owens, and Mead (1992) showed that older adults benefit as much as young adults from same-modality as opposed to different-modality presentation of words in a repetition priming task, suggesting that both age groups associated words with the context (auditory vs. visual) in which they had occurred. This group also found age constancy in repetition priming of novel nonwords after a single trial of pronunciation in young and old adults (Light, Kennison, Prull, LaVoie, & Zuellig, 1996). Spieler and Balota, using a similar repeated pronunciation task (1996, Experiment 1), showed age constancy in priming for word pairs, suggesting that associations between unrelated words had been formed for both young and older adults after a single pairing.

In addition, Naveh-Benjamin and colleagues (Naveh-Benjamin, Shing, Kilb, Werkle-Bergner, Lindenberger, & Li, 2009; Old & Naveh-Benjamin, 2008) have reported that the associative deficit that is typically seen in paired-associate learning is greatly reduced or eliminated entirely when incidental, as opposed to intentional, encoding instructions are given.

This paired incidental learning is also consistent with Campbell, Hasher, and Thomas's (2010) report of "hyper-binding"; they found that older adults encode extraneous co-occurrences of words superimposed on pictures (e.g., the word "subway" superimposed on a picture of a horse), such that these associations interfere with subsequent learning of conflicting associations for older, but not young, adults. Of course, this finding does not necessarily mean that older adults are encoding these word/picture associations more than or even to the same extent as young adults. It might be that when these associations are detrimental to new learning, the older adults are poorer than the young at suppressing them.

What all of the preceding findings show is that older adults do not appear to have a general associative deficit for *incidental* learning of new associations among simultaneously present items. Thus, all of these results, including ours with the SCCT, are consistent with the often stated conclusion that implicit learning is relatively spared in healthy aging.

The ASRT task, however, yields different results. For example, Figure 6.2 shows trial-type effects from a study in which young and older adults completed 10 sessions of the ASRT spread over several days, with each session taking approximately 40 minutes (based on data from D. V. Howard et al., 2004). Both groups learned, but there are significant age-related deficits which get larger with training. These age differences are not limited to extreme age group comparisons. In a subsequent study, we

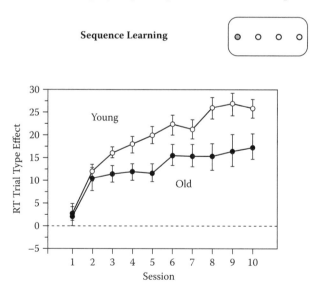

FIGURE 6.2 Associative learning scores (RT in milliseconds on low-frequency minus that on high-frequency trials) as a function of session for groups of young and old adults on the Alternating Serial Response Time (ASRT) task. (Based on data reported in Howard, D. V. et al., 2004, *Psychology and Aging, 19*, 79–92.)

tested middle-aged, midmanagement, career military and government service graduate students who ranged in age from 34 to 53 (Feeney, Howard, & Howard, 2002). We found that those below the age of 45 learned significantly more than those above that age. Figure 6.3 shows the trial-type effects (collapsed across sessions) for each of the 55 people in that study as a function of age, along with the data from individual young and older adults taken from another of our studies (D. V. Howard et al., 2004).

Although longitudinal data are needed for confirmation, these findings suggest that age differences in sequence learning appear gradually throughout the adult years, beginning in early adulthood. Another notable feature of Figure 6.3 is that there are large individual differences at each age. The SCCT task also shows such interindividual variability, which, as discussed later, has enabled us to begin to examine the sources of individual differences in learning.

Of course, the ASRT is motor based, as is the original SRT; in the typical version of these tasks, people respond in rapid succession to approximately 90 events in each block, using four different fingers. Older people respond substantially more slowly than young adults, and they also show more intertrial variability in response time. Because there is a fixed interval between a participant's correct response and the appearance of the next event (120 ms in most studies), older adults are experiencing a slower and more variable event stream than young adults. Sequence learning in young adults is poorer when the event timing is slower and more variable

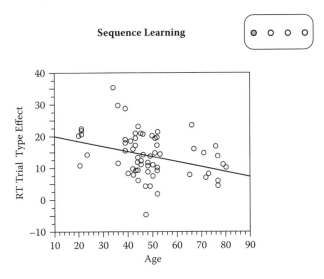

FIGURE 6.3 Associative learning scores (RT in milliseconds on low-frequency minus that on high-frequency trials) for individual adults on the Alternating Serial Response Time (ASRT) task. (Based on data reported in Feeney, J. J. et al., 2002, *Psychology and Aging, 17,* 351–355; and Howard, D. V. et al., 2004, *Psychology and Aging, 19,* 79–92.)

(Howard, Howard, Dennis, & Yankovich, 2007; Stadler, 1995), so it is possible that some of the age-related deficit in learning is due to age differences in the timing of the events and/or to age-related motor-sequencing deficits, rather than to fundamental learning mechanisms.

However, event timing differences and motor sequencing deficits cannot be the whole story. For example, we know that not all learning in the ASRT is motor based because sequence learning occurs even when people only observe the events (Song, Howard, & Howard, 2008). More important, we find substantial and persistent age deficits in a recently developed "Triplets" sequence learning task in which the motor sequencing component is absent and event timing is held constant (Howard, Howard, Dennis, & Kelly, 2008). In the Triplets task, the stimulus array is similar to the ASRT, but rather than responding to every event, participants encounter discrete trials, each containing three sequentially presented events (i.e., three successive event locations filling in) participants respond only to the third, or target, event.

When contingencies are set up such that the first cue predicts the target, thus maintaining the second-order structure in the ASRT motor task, we find substantial and persistent age-related deficits in learning similar to those in the ASRT. In additional work, we have found that even when the high-frequency Triplets are chosen randomly, as opposed to being rule based as in the original ASRT and Triplets studies, age-related deficits still appear, suggesting that the age deficit is not due solely to problems in rule-based learning (Simon, Howard, & Howard, 2010). The deficit does not seem to be due solely to difficulties in learning sequences of locations because we find age deficits even when the stimuli are letters presented in the center of the screen rather than in different spatial locations (Negash, Howard, Japikse, & Howard, 2003) and when the stimuli are sequences of spoken words (Dennis, Howard, & Howard, 2003, 2006).

Our findings of age-related deficits in sequence learning in the ASRT and the related Triplets task are consistent with reports of age differences in sequence learning of complex structures (Curran, 1997) and in information integration category learning (Filoteo & Maddox, 2004; Maddox, Pacheco, Reeves, Zhu, & Schnyer, 2010). These findings suggest, then, that some forms of implicit learning do decline in the course of healthy aging.

A WORKING HYPOTHESIS

How are these task-dependent patterns of aging to be accounted for? As summarized in the upper half of Figure 6.4, although both the ASRT and the SCCT are implicit and associative, they differ in the nature of the regularity present. For the SCCT, the associations to be learned are within an event, in that a particular distracter array is associated with a particular target position, with all present simultaneously. In contrast, for the ASRT (and the Triplets task), the associations to be learned are spread out over

Two Forms of Implicit Learning

- Lack explicit knowledge
- Learning relationships (contexts)
- Associative

Contextual Cueing	*Sequence Learning*
• Co-variation within trials • Deterministic relationships • Medial temporal lobe (MTL)-based system	• Co-variation across trials • Probabilistic relationships • Striatal-based system w/Extended training

	Contextual Cueing	*Sequence Learning*
Healthy Aging	Not affected	Affected
Mild Cognitive Impairment	Affected	Not affected
Corticobasal Syndrome	Not affected	Affected
ApoE	Affected	Not affected
DAT1	Not affected	Affected
Caudate/DLPFC White Matter Integrity	Not affected	Affected
Dyslexia/Reading Ability	Not affected	Affected

FIGURE 6.4 Summary of the contrasts between the two forms of implicit learning compared here, including the dissociations discussed in the text.

time across events, in that the stimuli are not present simultaneously. Thus, integration across nonsimultaneous events is required for the ASRT, but not for the SCCT.

In addition, the regularity in the SCCT is deterministic in that a given repeating distracter array is always a perfect predictor of target position, whereas the ASRT requires learning about probabilities, in that evidence indicates that people are not learning the alternating regularity itself, but rather which Triplets are more or less likely to occur. For example, for participants receiving the regularity 4r3r1r2r, encountering position 3 on trial *n* predicts that the most likely event two trials later will be a 1, but it does not guarantee it.

Due to these different task demands, learning in these two tasks seems to depend on different neural learning systems. Traditionally, it has been thought that implicit learning calls on the striatum, whereas explicit declarative learning calls on the hippocampus and other medial temporal lobe (MTL) structures. However, more recent human and animal evidence indicates that the story is more complicated. That is, the neural systems involved seem to depend on factors such as what is available to be learned and the amount of training, rather than on implicitness per se (Henke, 2010; Poldrack & Packard, 2003).

There is substantial evidence that, for sequence learning, a striatal-based system usually comes to dominate responding with practice, though there is some evidence that the MTL-based system also plays a role early in training (Rauch, Whalen, Savage, Curran, Kendrick, Brown, Bush, Breiter, & Rosen, 1997; Schendan, Searl, Melrose, & Stern, 2003; Simon, Vaidya, Howard, & Howard, in press). Evidence from humans and other species indicates that the striatal-based system is particularly well suited to the gradual acquisition of probabilistic associations (for reviews, see Ashby, Turner, & Horvitz, 2010; White & John, 2008). In contrast, neuroimaging and patient data suggest that contextual cueing calls primarily on an MTL-based system, including the entorhinal cortex (Manns & Squire, 2001; Park, Quinlan, Thornton, & Reder, 2004; Preston & Gabrieli, 2008). This latter finding reflects one way in which Squire's widely cited taxonomy appears inadequate: According to that framework, the MTL-based system is important only for declarative forms of learning.

We propose that the task-dependent patterns of age differences reflect differential aging of the MTL and striatal-based learning systems. There is cross-sectional and longitudinal evidence that the striatum (including the caudate) shows substantial age-related declines in structure and function beginning in early adulthood (Raz et al., 2005). There are also age-related declines in striatal dopamine neurotransmitter function (Backman, Lindenberger, Li, & Nyberg, 2010). In contrast, recent research suggests that the MTL system, particularly the entorhinal cortex, is relatively spared in healthy aging, even though it is affected early in pathological aging such as Alzheimer's disease (Hedden & Gabrieli, 2005; Raz et al., 2005).

Thus, we propose that implicit learning is *not* spared the effects of healthy aging, but rather that age-related declines in a striatal-based learning system result in persistent age deficits in certain forms of implicit learning, but not in others. Related, though different, proposals have been advanced by Poldrack and Foerde (2008), Rieckmann and Backman (2009), and Filoteo, Lauritzen, and Maddox (2010).

DISSOCIATING FORMS OF IMPLICIT LEARNING

We reasoned that if our hypothesis is correct, these two forms of implicit learning should be dissociable under a range of conditions, and that different types of implicit learning might prove to be sensitive and specific indicators of brain function. The rest of this section summarizes the dissociations we have observed, with the overall pattern of results outlined in the lower half of Figure 6.4.

Mild cognitive impairment (MCI)

Amnestic mild cognitive impairment is defined as memory impairment greater than expected for age, but in the absence of dementia (Petersen, Smith, Waring, Ivnik, Tangalos, & Kokmen, 1999). It is a risk factor for

Alzheimer's disease, and is known to be characterized by MTL pathology, with the entorhinal cortex among the first regions to be affected (Stoub, Rogalski, Leurgans, Bennett, & deToledo-Morrell, 2010). The memory tests that are used to diagnose MCI assess explicit memory, but our hypothesis predicts that MTL-based implicit learning should be compromised as well, whereas striatal-based implicit learning should not. Work with collaborators at the Mayo Clinic revealed just such a dissociation when people diagnosed with amnestic MCI via the Mayo Clinic criteria were compared with healthy education- and age-matched controls (mean age of approximately 75 years). The groups learned equally well on a sequence learning task, but, unlike the controls, the patients showed no contextual cueing effect (Negash, Petersen, Geda, Knopman, Boeve, Smith, Ivnik, Howard, Howard, & Petersen, 2007). Thus, the learning and memory deficits in MCI are not limited to explicit learning, but are also detectable via one form of MTL-based implicit learning.

Corticobasal syndrome (CBS)

CBS is a progressive neurological disorder characterized by atrophy of several areas of the brain, including the striatum and other basal ganglia structures (Boeve, Lang, & Litvan, 2003). This suggests that CBS patients should show the reverse of the pattern of learning impairments seen in MCI. Another collaboration with the Mayo group revealed just such a dissociation. When CBS patients were compared with age- and education-matched controls (mean age of approximately 67 years), the groups showed equivalent contextual cueing, but the CBS patients' sequence learning was significantly different from that of the controls (Negash, Boeve, et al., 2007).

ApoE genotype

Genes influence brain structure and function, and recent advances in cognitive neurogenetics have begun to reveal connections between genotype and specific forms of cognitive function (Green et al., 2008), though there has been very little work linking implicit learning and genotype. Nonetheless, it seemed likely that if these different forms of implicit learning call on different brain regions, then they would be influenced differently by genotype.

Apolipoprotein E is known to play a role in brain repair mechanisms, and individuals who carry the e4 variant of the ApoE gene have increased risk for developing Alzheimer's disease and MCI. In addition, there is evidence that individuals who are e4 carriers have smaller medial temporal lobes and poorer explicit memory and spatial processing than noncarriers (Honea, Vidoni, Harsha, & Burns, 2009; Parasuraman, Greenwood, & Sunderland, 2002).

ApoE genotype was available for the healthy control participants in the study of MCI mentioned before, and when healthy e4 carriers were compared with e4 noncarriers, the results revealed the expected dissociation. As a group, the e4 carriers, though of the same mean age (approximately 75 years) and education levels as the noncarriers, showed significantly less contextual cueing than the noncarriers. In fact, the e4 group did not show significant contextual cueing. In contrast, as predicted, the e4 carrier and noncarrier groups learned equally well on a sequence learning task (Negash, Petersen, et al., 2007). These findings suggest that some of the within-group variability in contextual cueing might be linked to genetics.

DAT1 genotype

The dopamine transporter gene DAT1 regulates synaptic dopamine levels, particularly in the striatum; one of its variants, the 9-repeat allele, is associated with higher synaptic dopamine levels and with greater caudate volume and activity (Bertolino et al., 2006; Durston et al., 2005; Jacobsen et al., 2000). We reasoned, therefore, that DAT1 might show the reverse pattern of correlations from the ApoE genotype described previously. In this case, we tested college students who were classified as 9-carriers or as 10/10 homozygotes, and we gave them both the SCCT task and a version of the Triplets task (Simon, Stollstorff, et al., 2010).

As predicted, the DAT1 genotype did not predict SCCT learning but it did predict ASRT learning; 9-repeat allele carriers showed significantly more sequence learning on the Triplets task than the 10/10 homozygotes. Further, this advantage was limited to the last session of training, which, as mentioned earlier, is when the striatal system would be expected to dominate responding in sequence learning. In addition, we observed a significant gene–dose relationship between the number of 9-repeat alleles a person has (i.e., 0, 1, or 2) and the magnitude of his or her last-session sequence learning, but no such relationship with spatial context learning. It is notable that these relations appeared in a group of young adults; such relationships might be magnified in older groups because striatal dopamine levels decline with healthy aging and it is possible that this is particularly so for individuals carrying fewer 9-repeat alleles.

White matter integrity in healthy aging

If these two forms of implicit learning call upon different neural systems, then they should also be related to the structural integrity of different white matter pathways in the brain. We tested groups of healthy young and older adults on the SCCT and the ASRT, and we also conducted MRI scanning and used diffusion tensor imaging (DTI) to assess white matter integrity of selected neural pathways (Bennett, Madden, Vaidya, Howard, & Howard, in press). We first compared the white matter integrity of two tracts in young versus older adults using a measure of fractional anisotropy (FA); high FA signals high integrity. In keeping with the previously cited studies that there is greater age-related decline in the striatum than the MTL (including the hippocampus), we found that our young group had significantly higher FA than the older for a tract linking the caudate and DLPFC (dorsolateral prefrontal cortex), but not for a hippocampal/DLPFC tract. Most earlier evidence for differential decline has been based on comparisons of gray matter, so these findings suggest that similar patterns occur in these different systems for white matter as well.

In addition, when we examined individual differences across all subjects, we found that late-stage sequence learning scores were significantly positively correlated with white matter integrity in the striatal/DLPFC, but not the hippocampal/DLPFC tract. We also found that striatal/DLPFC mediates age differences that appear in late-stage sequence learning. Striatal tract FA alone accounted for approximately 41%, and age alone for 21%, of the variance in ASRT learning scores; when the variance attributable to FA was removed, age no longer predicted sequence learning, accounting for a nonsignificant 1.5% of the variance in learning scores. In contrast, when we examined SCCT learning (unpublished data), we found no significant correlations with either of these white matter tracts. Thus, the findings were in keeping with our prediction that striatal/DLPFC tract integrity would be correlated only with ASRT learning; however, contrary to our original prediction, we did not find hippocampal/DLPFC tract correlations with SCCT learning.

We think that these findings are exciting in that they show that individual differences in white matter integrity in a specific tract interconnecting brain regions previously implicated in sequence learning can account for age differences in such learning. This suggests that a greater emphasis on white matter integrity in future research will be productive.

Reading ability and dyslexia

Dyslexia is defined as poor reading despite normal IQ and opportunity to learn from instruction, and it has been linked to fronto-striatal-cerebellar and sequencing deficits. Most of the literature suggests that explicit forms of learning and memory are spared in dyslexia, but there is debate about whether implicit learning is intact (Russeler, Gerth, & Munte, 2006; Sperling, Lu, & Manis, 2004; Vicari, Marotta, Menghini, Molinari, & Petrosini, 2003). We suspected that this latter inconsistency is due to two factors. In the dyslexia literature, many of the tasks that have been used to assess implicit learning result in considerable explicit awareness and thus might be masking any deficits in implicit learning. In addition, implicit learning has typically been treated as unitary in the dyslexia literature, but as we showed before, it is not.

Given the neural involvement mentioned before, we hypothesized that implicit sequence learning would be impaired in dyslexia, but that spatial context learning would not. Thus, in an initial study, we examined SCCT and ASRT learning in two groups of college students: one diagnosed as dyslexic and the other not (Howard, Howard, Japikse, & Eden, 2006). In addition, we gave all participants real-word (Word Identification) and pseudoword (Word Attack) reading tasks in order to provide a quantitative, continuous measure of reading ability to supplement the categorical dyslexia diagnosis. As predicted, we found significant group differences in sequence learning favoring the controls, but not in contextual cueing. Further, when people from both groups were considered together, Word Attack and Word Identification scores correlated significantly and positively with sequence learning scores, and they correlated significantly and negatively with contextual cueing. Thus, in these college students, poor readers were poor sequence learners but good spatial context learners.

The positive correlation between ASRT learning and reading is as we had predicted, but we are not sure how to interpret the link between poor reading and good spatial context learning. One explanation is based on the evidence that the striatal and MTL learning systems may function competitively, such that one inhibits the other (Poldrack & Packard, 2003). Thus, having a relatively poor striatal system might permit the MTL system to dominate and/or, perhaps, to develop more fully. On the other hand, this could reflect a kind of selection bias in that these students were all able to succeed in college. It might be that they were able to do this because they also happened to possess a very good MTL-based learning system, which they have used to compensate. In any event, we have not found this superior SCCT learning in poor readers in the two studies described next, so it is a topic for future research.

We wondered whether the positive correlation between sequence learning and reading skill was limited to motor sequence learning. To find out, we conducted a second study of college students similar to the one described previously, except that dyslexia and control groups were given the Triplets task (rather than the ASRT) and the SCCT task (Bennett, Romano, Howard, & Howard, 2008). Although we did not find significant group differences in either form of learning, we did find a significant positive correlation between Triplets learning and reading ability when all the subjects were considered together. This study suggests that the implicit sequence learning deficits seen in poor readers are not due solely to motor-sequencing deficits, but rather reflect a more general problem in learning sequential relationships among events.

Both of these studies indicate that, among college students, good sequence learners tend to be good readers. In a subsequent unpublished study of college-educated healthy older adults, we found that the same pattern is true, even among an older group averaging 71 years of age. Real word and nonword reading scores correlated significantly and positively with ASRT learning scores ($r = .52$ and $.54$, respectively) but not with SCCT learning ($r = -.13$ and 0, respectively) (Bennett, Howard, & Howard, 2007).

Overall, then, our results suggest that there is an implicit learning deficit in dyslexia, but that it is not a general one. Rather, poor readers are poor at implicit learning of sequences, but not of spatial context. This suggests that reading and implicit sequence learning may be calling on at least partially overlapping cognitive/brain systems.

IMPLICATIONS

The studies reviewed in this chapter suggest that two forms of implicit learning—sequence learning and spatial context learning—can be dissociated and that they show different age-related trajectories. The motor- and nonmotor-based implicit sequence learning that we have been studying via the ASRT and Triplets tasks show declines with healthy aging, and this decline seems to occur gradually beginning in early adulthood. In contrast, implicit learning of spatial contexts is relatively insensitive to aging in the absence of dementia. These different age trajectories suggest that there is no single answer to the question of whether or not implicit learning (or implicit memory) is spared in aging.

We proposed earlier that these different age trajectories reflect age-related changes in the underlying neural substrates; implicit learning of sequences, which is subserved primarily by the striatal system, is more age sensitive than the learning of spatial context, which is based on the MTL. The preceding review shows a pattern of dissociations in keeping with this hypothesis, as summarized in Figure 6.4. These forms of learning are affected differently by pathology in older adults: Mild cognitive impairment affects spatial context, but not sequence learning, whereas corticobasal syndrome shows the reverse pattern, in keeping with what is known about the effects of these conditions on brain regions.

Genetics also plays a role in dissociating these forms of learning; e4 status, which is associated with MTL structure and function, predicts spatial context learning, but not sequence learning, whereas the dopaminergic gene DAT1 shows the reverse pattern. In terms of brain structure, the white matter integrity of a striatal/DLPFC tract mediates age-related deficits in sequence learning, but not in spatial context learning. Further, these forms of learning are differentially associated with one important skill—reading—in that, for both young and older adults, good readers tend to be good sequence learners, but not necessarily good spatial context learners.

All this suggests that there are different *phenotypes of implicit learning*, with people differing as to the kind of environmental regularities to which they are most sensitive. Some people might be better attuned to spatial context and others to sequential context. The findings reviewed before suggest that these phenotypes depend partly on genetics, but they are likely also influenced by experience, given abundant evidence that practice shapes the brain (e.g., Maguire et al., 2003). For example, we have found that young video gamers and musicians are better at sequence learning, but not contextual cueing, than are controls (Romano Bergstrom, Howard, & Howard, in press). This suggests either that practicing these activities selectively improves sensitivity to sequential structure or that people who are good at picking up sequential structure are more likely to become musicians and gamers. Regardless, it would seem that groups with different kinds of expertise are likely to be characterized by different phenotypes of implicit learning.

Most important for present purposes, our findings indicate that the phenotypes of implicit learning change with age; older people are less sensitive than their younger peers to sequential but not to spatial context. This decline in sequential learning is likely one contributor to the decline across the adult years in the ability to learn second languages via mere exposure (Hakuta, Bialystok, & Wiley, 2003).

Our results suggest that tests of implicit learning may potentially be useful for assessing the biological integrity of different learning systems and as sensitive early behavioral markers of dementia. Backman (2008) has noted that including assessments of multiple domains of cognition (as well as other markers) is likely to improve our ability to detect dementia early. That implicit learning assessments might improve specificity and sensitivity of such batteries is suggested by the finding mentioned earlier (Negash, Petersen, et al., 2007) that healthy elder controls who are e4 carriers are poorer at SCCT learning than non-e4 carriers, even though they show no signs of dementia or even of mild cognitive impairment on the explicit memory tests used for diagnosis. Of course, longitudinal work is necessary to determine whether poor performance on the SCCT predicts subsequent conversion to MCI and/or Alzheimer's disease.

SOME UNANSWERED QUESTIONS

What factors lead to age deficits?

Our goal here has been to show that implicit learning is not unitary and hence that there is no single answer to the question of whether implicit learning and memory decline with healthy aging. To make this case, we have contrasted findings from the ASRT and Triplets tasks, which both tap sequence learning, with those from the SCCT task, which requires spatial context learning. However, as Figure 6.4 suggests, these tasks differ in other ways, including whether the regularity to be learned is deterministic or probabilistic, so we do not yet know what task features determine whether or not age differences appear.

Our hypothesis suggests that *one* determining factor is whether or not the age-sensitive striatal-based learning system must be engaged. Given that the striatal system is well suited to the gradual acquisition of complex, probabilistic associations (Ashby et al., 2010; White & John, 2008), we suspect that age deficits in implicit learning are likely to emerge when the regularity to be learned is probabilistic, rather than deterministic. In keeping with this, we consistently find age deficits in learning the probabilistic second-order structure of the ASRT task. However, Gaillard, Destrebecqz, Michiels, and Cleeremans (2009) did not find age deficits in learning on an SRT task containing a deterministic second-order structure and, in our earlier work with the original deterministic SRT, we found no age deficits (Howard & Howard, 1989, 1992).

Beyond age deficits in learning caused by striatal losses, other task factors are likely to cause age deficits in some implicit learning tasks. For example, to the extent that a given task requires increased capacity, or the ability to inhibit irrelevant material, or perceptual/motor speed, or any other cognitive components known to be influenced by age, apparent age differences in learning (or at least in its manifestation in performance) will appear even if the fundamental learning mechanisms are intact.

In addition, another factor influencing whether age differences will appear in implicit learning is the potential for neural compensation. Research on the cognitive neuroscience of aging, most of it using explicit memory and attention-based tasks, indicates that older brains often perform the same task differently from younger brains, even when there are no age differences in performance, and that these differences are at least sometimes beneficial (e.g., Reuter-Lorenz & Cappell, 2008). There is now evidence that such changes in neural bases may occur for implicit learning as well. Although for young people the striatal-based learning system comes to dominate sequence learning as training progresses, for older people there is evidence that the MTL, prefrontal areas, or other brain regions remain active throughout learning, thus perhaps partially compensating for striatal losses—at least relatively early in training (see the review by Rieckmann & Backman, 2009).

For example, in a probabilistic weather-prediction task, Fera and colleagues (2005) found that young participants revealed greater activation than older participants in bilateral PFC and caudate, and less than older participants in bilateral parietal areas. In addition, correlations with behavioral learning measures (accuracy and RT) were primarily with frontostriatal circuitry in young, but with frontoparietal in old. In an ASRT-like task Aizenstein et al. (2006) found young adults showing significantly more striatal activation than older adults during the second half of training. During motor-based SRT learning, Dennis and Cabeza (2010) found greater MTL activation for older than for young adults, and Rieckmann, Fischer, and Backman (2010) have reported continued activation of the MTL as practice proceeds in old, but not young, adults. In a recent fMRI study using the non-motor-based Triplets task, we have obtained findings similar to these motor-based sequence learning studies (Simon, Vaidya, Howard, & Howard, in press).

Thus, there is emerging evidence that the neural bases of some forms of implicit learning change with aging and that older adults rely more on the MTL-based than the striatal-based learning system than young adults. As Rieckmann and Backman (2009) have argued, this might explain the fact that age deficits have often not been observed in studies of sequence learning (i.e., older adults are compensating for striatal losses by relying more on the MTL or other systems). Nonetheless, our results with the ASRT and Triplets tasks suggest that, for some forms of implicit learning, as training progresses, age deficits do appear in tasks that are typically striatal based in young adults, presumably because the MTL and other systems are unable to compensate completely for the striatal-based system.

This evidence of reduced reliance on the striatal-based system in older adults might at first seem to contradict our previous findings that caudate/DLPFC white matter integrity mediates age differences in sequence learning late in training. However, given that the striatal system is especially suited to late-stage implicit sequence learning, it is likely that these other systems cannot compensate completely; thus, caudate/DLPFC integrity should account for age deficits in late-stage learning, even if older adults are activating other neural systems.

Thus, many questions remain as to the conditions under which age differences appear in implicit learning and whether the underlying neural systems change during healthy and pathological aging. In fact, because age differences in strategy use are likely less important for implicit than explicit learning, implicit learning might be an excellent vehicle for addressing a main question concerning the broader literature on evidence for neural compensation with age: namely, the extent to which such changes in neural activations reflect conscious strategies (Reuter-Lorenz & Cappell, 2008). The findings to date with implicit learning suggest that such compensation can be nonstrategic.

Could the pattern of age effects be due to task differences in reliability?

It is often thought that measures of implicit learning and memory are less reliable than those for explicit tasks. In fact, there is little evidence to support this claim, partly because so few studies have tested the reliability of measures of implicit learning and memory. Indeed, one study of the test–retest reliability of several measures of repetition priming and recognition memory found similar reliability for implicit and explicit measures for young and older adults (Fleischman, Gabrieli, Wilson, Moro, & Bennett, 2005).

Nonetheless, reliability likely varies across types of implicit tests, and we are not aware of any data on the test–retest reliability of the ASRT, Triplets, or SCCT tasks. Split-half reliability of versions of the SRT has been examined in at least two studies, yielding a respectable .74 in one case (Salthouse, McGuthry, & Hambrick, 1999) and a less respectable .44 in another (Kaufman et al., 2010). It is possible that we have found age differences in the ASRT and Triplets tasks, but not in the SCCT, because the latter has poorer reliability and hence is insensitive to task manipulations. We cannot rule out this possibility, and future research needs to assess test–retest reliability of various forms of implicit learning. Nonetheless, differential reliability cannot explain the pattern of dissociations we have reported here because SCCT learning does vary with ApoE genotype and MCI and, in general, the pattern of dissociations we are finding is consistent with predictions based on the neural substrates.

How can implicit learning be maximized?

We know little about how or whether different forms of implicit learning can be maximized over the short or long term because implicit learning is typically not used as an outcome measure in studies of interventions (such as exercise manipulations) or in longitudinal studies. Implicit learning has typically been thought to be uninfluenced by factors such as motivation, but there is now some evidence that young adults' implicit sequence learning is enhanced by a goal-priming manipulation (Eitam, Hassin, & Schul, 2008). In unpublished data, we found that activating negative stereotypes reduced trial-type effects in the ASRT (Ari, Filak, Howard, Howard, & Hess, 2006), while priming goal motivation increased trial-type effects (Lee, Gamble, Simon, Howard, & Howard, 2011). Of course, the findings we have reported here suggest that the factors that maximize learning are likely to differ for different forms of implicit learning.

Can better assays of MTL-based implicit learning be found?

Better assays of implicit learning are needed, particularly those subserved by the MTL. The ASRT and Triplets tasks typically yield very consistent results in that, although individuals vary in the magnitude of their trial-type effects, almost everyone shows some separation of high- and low-probability trials, and rarely do people show the reverse pattern to that predicted; that is, it is rare to find people who are faster on low- than high-frequency trials. This can be seen, for example, in Figure 6.3, where, of the more than 60 participants, only one shows a trial-type effect below 0, and even for that person it is only slightly below 0.

In addition, the amount of implicit learning in the ASRT as assessed via the trial-type effect seems to be largely unaffected by strategies, particularly for young people (Song, Howard, & Howard, 2007) and probably for older people as well (Song, Marks, Howard, & Howard, 2009). Further, although there is a wide range of individual differences at a given age (clear in Figure 6.3), the findings discussed previously suggest that at least some of this variability reflects differences in the efficiency of the underlying neural systems (e.g., in the integrity of white matter pathways; Bennett et al., in press) and factors such as genetics and/or experience, rather than noise.

In contrast, the SCCT often yields so-called "reverse learners" (i.e., people who are significantly faster on novel than repeated trials)—the reverse of what one would expect (Bennett, Barnes, Howard, & Howard, 2009; Hunt & Thomas, 2007). This anomalous pattern seems to be related to the search strategy that people adopt: Young people who are instructed to respond intuitively, using "passive search" to let the target jump out, show larger trial-type effects in the predicted direction than those who are told to search actively for the T (Lleras & von Mühlenen, 2004). Older people who report being "aware" that some arrays repeated (even though they are unable to differentiate above chance between novel and repeated arrays) show smaller trial-type effects than those who report being "unaware" (J. H. Howard, Jr., et al., 2004).

Another puzzle concerning the SCCT is that, contrary to our findings, a recent study reported age-related deficits in SCCT learning, with older groups of adults showing no evidence of spatial context learning at all (Smyth & Shanks, 2011). A number of labs other than our own have shown significant contextual cueing effects in older adults (cf. Manns & Squire, 2001; Negash, Boeve et al, 2007; Negash, Petersen et al, 2007, van Asselen, Almeida, Andre, Januário, Gonçalves, & Castelo-Branco, 2009), so it is unclear why Smyth and Shanks did not. Regardless, their findings suggest that more research on aging and MTL-based implicit learning is needed, as is systematic investigation of the factors affecting such learning in adults of different ages.

Overall, while the SCCT is sensitive enough to reveal effects of pathology and genotype and it is likely that some of the between-subjects variability seen within age groups is due to such factors, there is nonetheless still some question as to how to interpret the SCCT trial-type effects, and any group differences therein. Thus, it would be useful to have additional assays of MTL-based spatial context learning. In addition, the evidence that people do adopt different search strategies in the SCCT, which may affect the learning measure, is a reminder of the importance of well-crafted instructions and postexperimental probing of strategies in all studies of learning.

CONCLUSION

Overall, increasing understanding of implicit learning and how to maximize it at all ages is essential. This is because implicit learning is important for adapting to new environments, new people, and new technologies—all essential to successful aging—and also because it plays a role in rehabilitation and recovery after stroke or physical injury, when people must relearn basic skills such as walking and speaking. We have shown here that implicit learning is not unitary; that different forms age differently, reflecting patterns of brain aging; and that these forms can be dissociated in various ways, revealing different phenotypes of implicit learning. Thus, including assays of implicit learning in longitudinal and intervention studies could yield sensitive and specific early markers of pathology and of the effects of interventions.

ACKNOWLEDGMENTS

The research from our laboratories summarized here and the preparation of this chapter were supported by NIH grants R37AG015450, R01AG036863, F31AG030874, F31NS053388, and F31AG03469. The neuroimaging research was also supported in part by NIH M01RR023942-01 to the Georgetown Clinical Research Center.

REFERENCES

Aizenstein, H. J., Butters, M. A., Clark, K. A., Figurski, J. L., Andrew Stenger, V., Nebes, R. D., et al. (2006). Prefrontal and striatal activation in elderly subjects during concurrent implicit and explicit sequence learning. *Neurobiology of Aging, 27,* 741–751.

Ari, M., Filak, K. L., Howard, D. V., Howard, J. H., Jr., & Hess, T. M. (2006). *Stereotype activation affects implicit sequence learning in old and young adults.* Poster presented at the Association for Psychological Science, New York.

Ashby, F. G., & Maddox, W. T. (1990). Integrating information from separable psychological dimensions. *Journal of Experimental Psychology: Human Perception and Performance, 16,* 598–612.

Ashby, F. G., Turner, B. O., & Horvitz, J. C. (2010). Cortical and basal ganglia contributions to habit learning and automaticity. *Trends in Cognitive Sciences, 14,* 208–215.

Backman, L. (2008). Memory and cognition in preclinical dementia: what we know and what we do not know. *Canadian Journal of Psychiatry, 53,* 354–360.

Backman, L., Lindenberger, U., Li, S. C., & Nyberg, L. (2010). Linking cognitive aging to alterations in dopamine neurotransmitter functioning: Recent data and future avenues. *Neuroscience and Biobehavioral Reviews, 34,* 670–677.

Bennett, I. J., Barnes, K. A., Howard, J. H., Jr., & Howard, D. V. (2009). An abbreviated implicit spatial context learning task that yields greater learning. *Behavior Research Methods, 41,* 391–395.

Bennett, I. J., Howard, J. H., Jr., & Howard, D. V. (2007). *Reading ability and implicit learning in healthy older adults.* Paper presented at the 20th Anniversary Cognitive Aging Conference, Adelaide, Australia.

Bennett, I. J., Madden, D. J., Vaidya, C. J., Howard, J. H., Jr., & Howard, D. V. (in press). White matter integrity correlates of implicit sequence learning in healthy aging. *Neurobiology of Aging.*

Bennett, I. J., Romano, J. C., Howard, J. H., Jr., & Howard, D. V. (2008). Two forms of implicit learning in young adults with dyslexia. *Annals of the New York Academy of Sciences, 1145,* 184–198.

Berry, D. C., & Broadbent, D. E. (1984). On the relationship between task performance and associated verbalizable knowledge. *Quarterly Journal of Experimental Psychology, 36,* 209–231.

Bertolino, A., Blasi, G., Latorre, V., Rubino, V., Rampino, A., Sinibaldi, L.,... Dallapiccola, B. (2006). Additive effects of genetic variation in dopamine regulating genes on working memory cortical activity in human brain. *Journal of Neuroscience, 26,* 3918–3922.

Boeve, B. F., Lang, A. E., & Litvan, I. (2003). Corticobasal degeneration and its relationship to progressive supranuclear palsy and frontotemporal dementia. *Annals of Neurology, 54* (Suppl 5), S15–19.

Campbell, K. L., Hasher, L., & Thomas, R. C. (2010). Hyper-binding: A unique age effect. *Psychological Science, 21,* 399–405.

Chun, M. M., & Jiang, Y. (1998). Contextual cueing: Implicit learning and memory of visual context guides spatial attention. *Cognitive Psychology, 36,* 28–71.

Claxton, G. (2000). *Hare brain, tortoise mind: How intelligence increases when you think less.* New York, NY: Harper Collins.

Conway, C. M., & Pisoni, D. B. (2008). Neurocognitive basis of implicit learning of sequential structure and its relation to language processing. *Annals of the New York Academy of Sciences, 1145,* 113–131.

Curran, T. (1997). Effects of aging on implicit sequence learning: Accounting for sequence structure and explicit knowledge. *Psychological Research, 60,* 24–41.

Dennis, N. A., & Cabeza, R. (2008). Neuroimaging of healthy cognitive aging. In F. I. Craik & T. A. Salthouse (Eds.), *Handbook of cognitive aging* (3rd ed., pp. 1–54), New York, NY: Psychology Press.

Dennis, N. A., & Cabeza, R. (2010). Age-related dedifferentiation of learning systems: An fMRI study of implicit and explicit learning. *Neurobiology of Aging* (online pub.).

Dennis, N. A., Howard, J. H., Jr., & Howard, D. V. (2003). Age deficits in learning sequences of spoken words. *Journals of Gerontology B: Psychological Sciences, 58,* P224–227.

Dennis, N. A., Howard, J. H., Jr., & Howard, D. V. (2006). Implicit sequence learning without motor sequencing in young and old adults. *Experimental Brain Research, 175,* 153–164.

Durston, S., Fossella, J. A., Casey, B. J., Hulshoff Pol, H. E., Galvan, A., Schnack, H. G.,... van Engeland, H. (2005). Differential effects of DRD4 and DAT1 genotype on fronto-striatal gray matter volumes in a sample of subjects with attention deficit hyperactivity disorder, their unaffected siblings, and controls. *Molecular Psychiatry, 10,* 678–685.

Eitam, B., Hassin, R. R., & Schul, Y. (2008). Nonconscious goal pursuit in novel environments: The case of implicit learning. *Psychological Science, 19,* 261–267.

Feeney, J. J., Howard, J. H., Jr., & Howard, D. V. (2002). Implicit learning of higher order sequences in middle age. *Psychology and Aging, 17,* 351–355.

Fera, F., Weickert, T. W., Goldberg, T. E., Tessitore, A., Hariri, A., Das, S.,... Mattay, V. S. (2005). Neural mechanisms underlying probabilistic category learning in normal aging. *Journal of Neuroscience, 25,* 11340–11348.

Filoteo, J. V., Lauritzen, S., & Maddox, W. T. (2010). Removing the frontal lobes: The effects of engaging executive functions on perceptual category learning. *Psychological Science, 21,* 415–423.

Filoteo, J. V., & Maddox, W. T. (2004). A quantitative model-based approach to examining aging effects on information-integration category learning. *Psychology and Aging, 19,* 171–182.

Fleischman, D. A., Gabrieli, J. D., Wilson, R. S., Moro, T. T., & Bennett, D. A. (2005). Repetition priming and recognition memory in younger and older persons: Temporal stability and performance. *Neuropsychology, 19,* 750–759.

Forkstam, C., & Petersson, K. M. (2005). Towards an explicit account of implicit learning. *Current Opinion in Neurology, 18,* 435–441.

Frensch, P. A., & Ruenger, D. (2003). Implicit learning. *Current Directions in Psychological Science, 12,* 13–18.

Gaillard, V., Destrebecqz, A., Michiels, S., & Cleeremans, A. (2009). Effects of age and practice in sequence learning: A graded account of ageing, learning, and control. *European Journal of Cognitive Psychology, 21,* 255–282.

Gamble, K. R., Westbay, L. C., Howard, J. H., Jr., & Howard, D. V. (2011). *Does nonconscious goal pursuit improve implicit learning?* Poster presented at the annual meetings of the American Psychological Association, Washington D.C.

Gladwell, M. (2005). *Blink: The power of thinking without thinking.* New York, NY: Little, Brown, and Company.

Green, A. E., Munafo, M. R., DeYoung, C. G., Fossella, J. A., Fan, J., & Gray, J. R. (2008). Using genetic data in cognitive neuroscience: From growing pains to genuine insights. *Nature Reviews Neuroscience, 9,* 710–720.

Hakuta, K., Bialystok, E., & Wiley, E. (2003). Critical evidence: A test of the critical-period hypothesis for second-language acquisition. *Psychological Science, 14,* 31–38.

Hedden, T., & Gabrieli, J. D. (2005). Healthy and pathological processes in adult development: New evidence from neuroimaging of the aging brain. *Current Opinion in Neurology, 18,* 740–747.

Henke, K. (2010). A model for memory systems based on processing modes rather than consciousness. *Nature Reviews Neuroscience, 11,* 523–532.

Honea, R. A., Vidoni, E., Harsha, A., & Burns, J. M. (2009). Impact of APOE on the healthy aging brain: A voxel-based MRI and DTI study. *Journal of Alzheimer's Disease, 18,* 553–564.

Howard, D. V., & Howard, J. H., Jr. (1989). Age differences in learning serial patterns: Direct versus indirect measures. *Psychology and Aging, 4,* 357–364.

Howard, D. V., & Howard, J. H., Jr. (1992). Adult age differences in the rate of learning serial patterns: Evidence from direct and indirect tests. *Psychology and Aging, 7,* 232–241.

Howard, D. V., Howard, J. H., Jr., Japikse, K., DiYanni, C., Thompson, A., & Somberg, R. (2004). Implicit sequence learning: Effects of level of structure, adult age, and extended practice. *Psychology and Aging, 19,* 79–92.

Howard, J. H., Jr., & Howard, D. V. (1997). Age differences in implicit learning of higher order dependencies in serial patterns. *Psychology and Aging, 12,* 634–656.

Howard, J. H., Jr., Howard, D. V., Dennis, N. A., & Kelly, A. J. (2008). Implicit learning of predictive relationships in three-element visual sequences by young and old adults. *Journal of Experimental Psychology: Learning, Memory, and Cognition, 34,* 1139–1157.

Howard, J. H., Jr., Howard, D. V., Dennis, N. A., & Yankovich, H. (2007). Event timing and age deficits in higher order sequence learning. *Aging, Neuropsychology, and Cognition, 14,* 647–668.

Howard, J. H., Jr., Howard, D. V., Dennis, N. A., Yankovich, H., & Vaidya, C. J. (2004). Implicit spatial contextual learning in healthy aging. *Neuropsychology, 18,* 124–134.

Howard, J. H., Jr., Howard, D. V., Japikse, K. C., & Eden, G. F. (2006). Dyslexics are impaired on implicit higher order sequence learning, but not on implicit spatial context learning. *Neuropsychologia, 44,* 1131–1144.

Hoyer, W. J., & Lincourt, A. E. (1998). Aging and the development of learning. In M. A. Stadler & P. A. Frensch (Eds.), *Handbook of implicit learning* (pp. 445–470). Thousand Oaks, CA: Sage.

Hunt, R. H., & Thomas, K. M. (2007). *Hippocampal recruitment in implicit learning: Neuroimaging evidence from a visual search task.* Paper presented at the Cognitive Neuroscience Society, New York, NY.

Jacobsen, L. K., Staley, J. K., Zoghbi, S. S., Seibyl, J. P., Kosten, T. R., Innis, R. B., & Gelernter, J. (2000). Prediction of dopamine transporter binding availability by genotype: A preliminary report. *American Journal of Psychiatry, 157,* 1700–1703.

Kaufman, S. B., Deyoung, C. G., Gray, J. R., Jimenez, L., Brown, J., & Mackintosh, N. (2010). Implicit learning as an ability. *Cognition, 116,* 321–340.

Knowlton, B. J., Squire, L. R., & Gluck, M. A. (1994). Probabilistic classification learning in amnesia. *Learning and Memory, 1,* 106–120.

Lee, J. M., Gamble, K. R., Simon, J. R., Howard, J. H., Jr., & Howard, D. V. (2010). *The effects of goal motivation on implicit sequence learning.* Poster presented at the annual meetings of the Society for Neuroscience, San Diego, CA.

Lieberman, M. D. (2000). Intuition: A social cognitive neuroscience approach. *Psychological Bulletin, 126,* 109–137.

Light, L. L., Kennison, R., Prull, M. W., LaVoie, D., & Zuellig, A. (1996). One-trial associative priming of nonwords in young and older adults. *Psychology and Aging, 11,* 417–430.

Light, L. L., LaVoie, D., Valencia-Laver, D., Owens, S. A., & Mead, G. (1992). Direct and indirect measures of memory for modality in young and older adults. *Journal of Experimental Psychology: Learning, Memory and Cognition, 18,* 1284–1297.

Lleras, A., & von Mühlenen, A. (2004). Spatial context and top-down strategies in visual search. *Spatial Vision, 17,* 465–462.

Maddox, W. T., Pacheco, J., Reeves, M., Zhu, B., & Schnyer, D. M. (2010). Rule-based and information-integration category learning in normal aging. *Neuropsychologia, 48,* 2998–3008.

Maguire, E. A., Spiers, H. J., Good, C. D., Hartley, T., Frackowiak, R. S., & Burgess, N. (2003). Navigation expertise and the human hippocampus: A structural brain imaging analysis. *Hippocampus, 13,* 250–259.

Manns, J. R., & Squire, L. R. (2001). Perceptual learning, awareness and the hippocampus. *Hippocampus, 11,* 776–782.

McGeorge, P., & Burton, A. M. (1990). Semantic processing in an incidental learning task. *Quarterly Journal of Experimental Psychology A, 42A,* 597–610.

Naveh-Benjamin, M., Shing, Y. L., Kilb, A., Werkle-Bergner, M., Lindenberger, U., & Li, S. C. (2009). Adult age differences in memory for name–face associations: The effects of intentional and incidental learning. *Memory, 17,* 220–232.

Negash, S., Boeve, B. F., Geda, Y. E., Smith, G. E., Knopman, D. S., Ivnik, R. J.,… Petersen, R. C. (2007). Implicit learning of sequential regularities and spatial contexts in corticobasal syndrome. *Neurocase, 13,* 133–143.

Negash, S., Howard, D. V., Japikse, K. C., & Howard, J. H., Jr. (2003). Age-related differences in implicit learning of non-spatial sequential patterns. *Aging Neuropsychology & Cognition, 10*, 108–121.

Negash, S., Petersen, L. E., Geda, Y. E., Knopman, D. S., Boeve, B. F., Smith, G. E.,... Petersen, R. C. (2007). Effects of ApoE genotype and mild cognitive impairment on implicit learning. *Neurobiology of Aging, 28*, 885–893.

Nissen, M. J., & Bullemer, P. (1987). Attentional requirements of learning: Evidence from performance measures. *Cognitive Psychology, 19*, 1–32.

Old, S. R., & Naveh-Benjamin, M. (2008). Differential effects of age on item and associative measures of memory: A meta-analysis. *Psychology and Aging, 23*, 104–118.

Parasuraman, R., Greenwood, P. M., & Sunderland, T. (2002). The apolipoprotein E gene, attention, and brain function. *Neuropsychology, 16*, 254–274.

Park, H., Quinlan, J., Thornton, E., & Reder, L. M. (2004). The effect of midazolam on visual search: Implications for understanding amnesia. *Proceedings of the National Academy of Sciences USA, 101*, 17879–17883.

Petersen, R. C., Smith, G. E., Waring, S. C., Ivnik, R. J., Tangalos, E. G., & Kokmen, E. (1999). Mild cognitive impairment: Clinical characterization and outcome. *Archives of Neurology, 56*, 303–308.

Poldrack, R. A., & Foerde, K. (2008). Category learning and the memory systems debate. *Neuroscience and Biobehavioral Reviews, 32*, 197–205.

Poldrack, R. A., & Packard, M. G. (2003). Competition among multiple memory systems: converging evidence from animal and human brain studies. *Neuropsychologia, 41*, 245–251.

Preston, A. R., & Gabrieli, J. D. (2008). Dissociation between explicit memory and configural memory in the human medial temporal lobe. *Cerebral Cortex, 18*, 2192–2207.

Prull, M. W., Gabrieli, J. D. E., & Bunge, S. A. (2000). Age-related changes in memory: A cognitive neuroscience perspective. In F. I. Craik & T. A. Salthouse (Eds.), *Handbook of aging and cognition* (2nd ed., pp. 91–153). Mahwah, NJ: Lawrence Erlbaum Associates.

Rauch, S. L., Whalen, P. J., Savage, C. R., Curran, T., Kendrick, A., Brown, H. D., ... Rosen, B. R. (1997). Striatal recruitment during an implicit sequence learning task as measured by functional magnetic resonance imaging. *Human Brain Mapping, 5*, 124–132.

Raz, N., Lindenberger, U., Rodrigue, K. M., Kennedy, K. M., Head, D., Williamson, A.,... Acker, J. D. (2005). Regional brain changes in aging healthy adults: General trends, individual differences and modifiers. *Cerebral Cortex, 15*, 1676–1689.

Reber, A. S. (1967). Implicit learning of artificial grammars. *Journal of Verbal Learning & Verbal Behavior, 6*, 855–863.

Reber, A. S. (1993). *Implicit learning and tacit knowledge: An essay on the cognitive unconscious.* New York, NY: Oxford University Press.

Reuter-Lorenz, P. A., & Cappell, K. A. (2008). Neurocognitive aging and the compensation hypothesis. *Current Directions in Psychological Science, 17*, 177–182.

Rieckmann, A., & Backman, L. (2009). Implicit learning in aging: Extant patterns and new directions. *Neuropsychology Review, 19*, 490–503.

Rieckmann, A., Fischer, H., & Backman, L. (2010). Activation in striatum and medial temporal lobe during sequence learning in younger and older adults: Relations to performance. *Neuroimage, 50*, 1303–1312.

Romano Bergstrom, J. C., Howard, J. H., Jr., & Howard, D. V. (In press). Enhanced implicit sequence learning in college-age video game players and musicians. *Applied Cognitive Psychology.* DOI: 10.1002/acp.1800

Russeler, J., Gerth, I., & Munte, T. F. (2006). Implicit learning is intact in adult developmental dyslexic readers: Evidence from the serial reaction time task and artificial grammar learning. *Journal of Clinical and Experimental Neuropsychology, 28,* 808–827.

Saffran, J. R., Aslin, R. N., & Newport, E. L. (1996). Statistical learning by 8-month-old infants. *Science, 274,* 1926–1928.

Salthouse, T. A., McGuthry, K. E., & Hambrick, D. Z. (1999). A framework for analyzing and interpreting differential aging patterns: Application to three measures of implicit learning. *Aging, Neuropsychology, and Cognition, 6,* 1–18.

Schendan, H. E., Searl, M. M., Melrose, R. J., & Stern, C. E. (2003). An FMRI study of the role of the medial temporal lobe in implicit and explicit sequence learning. *Neuron, 37,* 1013–1025.

Schmitter-Edgecombe, M., & Nissley, H. M. (2002). Effects of aging on implicit covariation learning. *Aging Neuropsychology & Cognition, 9,* 61–75.

Simon, J. R., Howard, J. H., Jr., & Howard, D. V. (2010). Age differences in implicit learning of probabilistic, unstructured sequences. *Journal of Gerontology: Psychological Sciences, 66B,* 32–38.

Simon, J. R., Vaidya, C. J., Howard, J. H., Jr., & Howard, D. V. (In press). The effects of aging on the neural basis of implicit associative learning in a probabilistic Triplets Learning Task. *Journal of Cognitive Neuroscience.*

Simon, J. R., Stollstorff, M., Westbay, L. C., Vaidya, C. J., Howard, J. H., Jr., & Howard, D. V. (2010). Dopamine transporter genotype predicts implicit sequence learning. *Behavioral Brain Research, 216,* 452–457.

Smyth, A. C., & Shanks, D. R. (2011). Aging and implicit learning: explorations in contextual cuing. *Psychology and Aging, 26,* 127–132.

Song, S., Howard, J. H., Jr., & Howard, D. V. (2007). Implicit probabilistic sequence learning is independent of explicit awareness. *Learning and Memory, 14,* 167–176.

Song, S., Howard, J. H., Jr., & Howard, D. V. (2008). Perceptual sequence learning in a serial reaction time task. *Experimental Brain Research, 189,* 145–158.

Song, S., Marks, B., Howard, J. H., Jr., & Howard, D. V. (2009). Evidence for parallel explicit and implicit sequence learning systems in older adults. *Behavioral Brain Research, 196,* 328–332.

Sperling, A. J., Lu, Z. L., & Manis, F. R. (2004). Slower implicit categorical learning in adult poor readers. *Annals of Dyslexia, 54,* 281–303.

Spieler, D. H., & Balota, D. A. (1996). Characteristics of associative learning in younger and older adults: Evidence from an episodic priming paradigm. *Psychology and Aging, 11,* 607–620.

Squire, L. R. (2004). Memory systems of the brain: A brief history and current perspective. *Neurobiology of Learning & Memory, 82,* 171–177.

Stadler, M. A. (1995). Role of attention in implicit learning. *Journal of Experimental Psychology: Learning, Memory, & Cognition, 21,* 674–685.

Stoub, T. R., Rogalski, E. J., Leurgans, S., Bennett, D. A., & deToledo-Morrell, L. (2010). Rate of entorhinal and hippocampal atrophy in incipient and mild AD: Relation to memory function. *Neurobiology of Aging, 31,* 1089–1098.

van Asselen, M., Almeida, I., Andre, R., Januário, C., Gonçalves, A. F., & Castelo-Branco, M. (2009). The role of the basal ganglia in implicit contextual learning: a study of Parkinson's disease. *Neuropsychologia, 47,* 1269–1273.

Vicari, S., Marotta, L., Menghini, D., Molinari, M., & Petrosini, L. (2003). Implicit learning deficit in children with developmental dyslexia. *Neuropsychologia, 41,* 108–114.

White, N. M., & John, H. B. (2008). Multiple memory systems in the brain: Cooperation and competition. In H. Eichenbaum (Ed.), *Memory systems* (Vol. 3, pp. 9–46), New York, NY: Elsevier.

Wilson, T. D. (2002). *Strangers to ourselves: Discovering the adaptive unconscious.* Cambridge, MA: Harvard University Press.

7 Prospective memory and aging

Understanding the variability

Gilles O. Einstein, Mark A. McDaniel, and Michael K. Scullin

INTRODUCTION

Since the time of Ebbinghaus, memory researchers have focused on studying explicit retrospective memory or conscious recollection for past events (e.g., free recall, cued recall, and recognition). In recent years there has been increased interest in prospective memory, or remembering to perform actions in the future, such as remembering to put the garbage out on Wednesday nights and remembering to attend a scheduled meeting. Given the prevalence of prospective memory demands in everyday life in both work and nonwork settings (Dismukes, 2008; McDaniel & Einstein, 2007), along with the belief that one of the central functions of human memory is to plan for future actions so that we can respond appropriately to upcoming events (Klein, Robertson, & Delton, 2010), it is surprising that the topic was virtually ignored up until about 25 years ago.

From managing household activities (e.g., remembering to pay bills) to coordinating social relations (e.g., remembering to prepare for and attend a potluck luncheon with friends) to regulating health-related needs (e.g., remembering to take medication), good prospective memory is critical to normal functioning and supporting good interpersonal relations. Prospective memory may be especially important for older adults because forgetting intentions such as turning off the oven or paying bills can threaten independent living. Moreover, given the widespread prevalence of conditions and diseases such as hypertension, cancer, and diabetes among older adults, forgetting intentions like a doctor's appointment or taking medication could be life threatening (Nelson, Reid, Ryan, Willson, & Yelland, 2006).

Although prospective memory tasks vary along a variety of dimensions, the most frequently studied type of prospective memory task is an *event-based* task in which the opportunity for performing an action is signaled by the occurrence of an event or cue, such as remembering to take medication with breakfast. This contrasts, for example, with a *time-based* prospective memory task, where the triggering signal is the passage of time or the occurrence of a particular time, such as remembering to take medication at 10 a.m. In this chapter, our focus will be on understanding the processes involved in successful remembering on event-based prospective memory tasks and how normal aging affects these processes.

WHAT IS DIFFERENT ABOUT EVENT-BASED PROSPECTIVE MEMORY?

Before reviewing the research examining how aging affects prospective memory, we first describe what we and others believe is a fundamental difference between prospective memory and retrospective memory. The standard laboratory paradigm for studying prospective memory involves embedding a prospective memory demand within an ongoing task. For example, participants may be given the ongoing task of performing a lexical decision task as quickly and accurately as possible but then also be asked to press a designated key on the keyboard (e.g., the Q key) whenever they see a particular target event (e.g., the word *building*). Then, in the context of 400 or so lexical decision trials, the target cue *building* may occur three times; prospective memory performance is measured by the proportion of times that participants remember to press the Q key when the target cue *building* occurs.

It is important to note that there has been a great deal of variation using this general paradigm. For example, some researchers present participants with multiple target events (e.g., six different target events) and others present a single target. Some present a prospective memory target very frequently among the ongoing task trials (e.g., every 10th trial) and others infrequently. Some use a target event that is not part of what is being processed for the ongoing task (e.g., the target is a change in the background pattern on the computer screen), whereas others use a target that is processed as part of the ongoing task. As we will describe in a later section, we believe that the specific characteristics of the prospective memory task affect the strategies and processes necessary for successfully remembering on that task and that these, in turn, have important implications for determining the presence and magnitude of age differences.

In any case, a key difference between a prospective memory task and a retrospective memory task (e.g., a cued-recall task) is that participants in a retrospective memory task are put in a retrieval mode at the time of retrieval (Tulving, 1983). That is, in cued recall, participants are presented a cue along with a specific request to retrieve the item that was associated with it during study. In prospective memory, by contrast, the target cue occurs in the context of the ongoing task and there is no external request to engage a retrieval search when the target event occurs. Thus, participants must remember to perform the associated action without an external demand to initiate a retrieval search (e.g., in the paradigm described previously, the ongoing task demand is to classify the string of letters on the screen as a word or nonword). This characteristic of prospective memory was noticed early on by Craik (1986) and led him to characterize prospective memory as especially high in self-initiated retrieval.

ONE THEORY OF PROSPECTIVE MEMORY: ALL PROSPECTIVE MEMORY TASKS REQUIRE CAPACITY-CONSUMING MONITORING PROCESSES

Given this analysis of prospective memory along with his theory that aging disrupts capacity-demanding self-initiated retrieval processes, Craik (1986) made the important prediction that prospective memory should be especially difficult for older adults, and—even more difficult than free recall. The idea is that free recall tasks include a prompt to initiate a search of memory, whereas prospective memory tasks do not. The preparatory attentional and memory processes theory (Smith, 2003; Smith & Bayen, 2006) also predicts that prospective memory tasks will be especially difficult for older adults. The assumption of this theory is that mere exposure to cues that have been associated with prospective memory intentions will not prompt retrieval unless one is in a retrieval mode at the time the target event occurs.

Thus, in order to successfully remember to perform an intended action, the system needs to maintain a retrieval mode via preparatory attentional processes. Specifically, when people have a prospective memory demand and they are in the appropriate retrieval context, Smith and Bayen propose that people initiate preparatory attentional processes, and the purpose of these is to evaluate environmental events as potential prospective memory targets. These processes, which can range from being fully conscious to being outside focal awareness, are needed to initiate recognition checks to evaluate whether the present environmental events include the prospective memory target.

The critical assumptions are that preparatory attentional processes are necessary for prospective memory retrieval and that they draw on limited-capacity working memory resources that have been shown to decline with age (Craik & Byrd, 1982; Park, Lautenschlager, Hedden, Davidson, Smith, & Smith, 2002; Verhaeghen, Chapter 1, this volume). Thus, older adults should be disadvantaged on all prospective memory tasks.

THE STRIKING PATTERN OF AGE EFFECTS ON PROSPECTIVE MEMORY TASKS IS VARIABILITY

The prediction from the just presented views that prospective memory tasks are particularly high in self-initiated retrieval (and more so than free recall; Craik, 1986) has only been partially supported. When examining the change in prospective memory and free recall among older adults ranging in age from 65 to 80, Zeintl, Kliegel, and Hofer (2007) found this predicted pattern. On the other hand, in a large-scale meta-analysis that compared young adults with older adults, Henry, MacLeod, Phillips, and Crawford (2004) found that age effects were significantly smaller on prospective memory tasks than on free recall.

One problem noted by Henry et al. (2004) in comparing performance across prospective and retrospective tasks is that the typical tasks differ on so many dimensions other than self-initiated retrieval. For example, free recall tasks typically have a large number of target events, whereas prospective memory tasks typically have one or only a few target events, and it may be that longer lists (and not the nature of the task, i.e., prospective memory versus free recall) are especially difficult for older adults. Older adults, for example, have been shown to be differentially disadvantaged on prospective tasks that have multiple target events (Einstein, Holland, McDaniel, & Guynn, 1992).

To address this problem partially, Kvavilashvili, Kornbrot, Mash, Cockburn, and Milne (2009) recently compared younger and older participants on a prospective memory task (with one target event) with free recall performance on a short, three-target list. For the free recall task, participants were presented with three targets and then asked to repeat them. Then, after counting backward for a brief time and answering several questions, they were asked to free-recall the targets. For the event-based prospective memory task, participants were given the prospective memory task of pressing a designated key whenever they saw the word *telephone* in the context of performing a general knowledge task. The retention interval between the prospective memory instruction and the first occurrence of the target event was longer (about 13–15 minutes) than the delay in the free recall task. They found that age explained a much larger proportion of the variance on the free recall task (24%) than on the prospective memory task (2%). Thus, the available evidence is not consistent with and, indeed, mostly contradicts the expectation that prospective memory should be more difficult for adults than free recall.

In terms of examining aging effects on prospective memory performance itself, the research to date has produced a strikingly inconsistent pattern of findings, with some studies showing minimal or no age differences in prospective remembering (Cherry & LeCompte, 1999; Einstein & McDaniel, 1990; Einstein, McDaniel, Richardson, Guynn, & Cunfer, 1995; Kvavilashvili et al., 2009; Reese & Cherry, 2002) and others showing robust age-related declines (Maylor, 1993, 1996; Park, Hetzog, Kidder, Morrell, & Mayhorn, 1997; Smith & Bayen, 2006; West, Herndon, & Covell, 2003). Recent meta-analyses of prospective memory and aging (Henry et al., 2004; Kliegel, Jager, & Phillips, 2008) have documented this puzzling wide variability in aging effects. Indeed, the divergent findings can be quite dramatic, sometimes showing identical performance for younger and older adults (e.g., Einstein & McDaniel, 1990, Experiment 1) and other times showing performance for younger adults that is nearly three times higher than that of older adults (Maylor, 1996).

We believe that many factors likely contribute to this variability in age differences in prospective memory, including the relative unreliability of using a paradigm in which only several target events occur during the course of an experiment (Kelemen, Weinberg, Oh, Mulvey, & Kaeochinda, 2006), possible ceiling effects in some studies (Uttl, 2005), age and ability differences in the particular samples of older adults (e.g., Kvavilashvilli et al., 2009; Reese & Cherry, 2002), and whether researchers attempt to equate the demands of the ongoing task for younger and older adults (e.g., Einstein & McDaniel, 1990; Kvavilashvili et al., 2009).

Even so, we believe that an important determiner of this variability is the nature of the prospective memory tasks and the consequent processing demands that they require for successful prospective memory retrieval. The idea here is that different processes may be required for successful prospective memory retrieval in different prospective memory tasks, and these processes may show differential sensitivity to aging.

Consistent with this view, Henry and colleagues' (2004) seminal meta-analysis found that the magnitude of the age differences on prospective memory tasks was significantly larger with event-based prospective memory tasks that required high strategic demands and/or working memory resources (e.g., monitoring) relative to prospective memory tasks assumed to be supported by relatively automatic processes that responded to the occurrence of cues. Indeed, for those tasks categorized as requiring extensive strategic demands, age group accounted for 16.4% of the variance in prospective memory performance. By contrast, for those tasks considered low in their working memory and strategic demands, age group accounted for only 1.9% of the variance.

In the next section, we develop the multiprocess theory, describe the multiple processes that we believe can accomplish prospective memory retrieval, and evaluate the sensitivity of these processes to the effects of aging. We then use the multiprocess theory as an organizational principle for anticipating and evaluating the kinds of prospective memory tasks that should and should not be especially difficult for older adults.

ANOTHER THEORY OF PROSPECTIVE MEMORY: MULTIPLE PROCESSES CAN ACCOMPLISH PROSPECTIVE MEMORY RETRIEVAL

We proposed the multiprocess theory (McDaniel & Einstein, 2000, 2007) in large measure to explain why some studies were finding large age differences in prospective memory performance and others were not. The multiprocess theory assumes that one can accomplish prospective memory retrieval through several different kinds of processes ranging from capacity-consuming monitoring processes to relatively automatic spontaneous retrieval processes. This theory embraces the contextualistic view of memory (Jenkins, 1979) that the process that an individual uses in a particular situation as well as the effectiveness of that process depends on many factors, including the nature of the prospective memory task, the perceived task demands, and the characteristics of the individual.

Importantly from the perspective of understanding age differences in prospective memory, the idea is that some types of prospective memory tasks can be accomplished by relatively automatic, spontaneous retrieval processes that we assume are minimally affected by aging (e.g., Cohn, Emrich, & Moscovitch, 2008; Craik, 1986; Dywan & Jacoby, 1990; McDaniel, Einstein, & Jacoby, 2008). Thus, performance on these tasks should show minimal effects of aging. On the other hand, with prospective memory tasks that demand self-initiated preparatory attentional processes or monitoring for successful retrieval—processes that draw on limited working memory resources that are assumed to decline with age (Braver & West, 2008; Park et al., 2002; Verhaeghen, Chapter 1, this volume)—there should be substantial age differences.

To give the reader a concrete understanding of the spontaneous retrieval processes, we briefly review them here. By "spontaneous retrieval," we mean that the occurrence of a target event can cause the intention to be retrieved even when no resources are devoted to monitoring the environment for the target event (Einstein & McDaniel, 2010). The *reflexive-associative* process assumes that people form an association between the target event and the intended action during planning and store that intention in long-term memory. Later, when the target event is processed, full processing of the target is likely to cause the intended action to be delivered to consciousness (McDaniel, Guynn, Einstein, & Breneiser, 2004). This retrieval is assumed to be rapid and obligatory and to require few cognitive resources; it is assumed to be accomplished by the hippocampal system (Moscovitch, 1994). The idea here is that if you have formed a good encoding of the intention to give your friend Patty a message, later seeing Patty will cause the message to pop into awareness.

A second way in which spontaneous retrieval can occur is through a *discrepancy-plus-search* process (McDaniel et al., 2004). This is based on Whittlesea and Williams's (2001a, 2001b) theory that humans constantly evaluate the processing quality (e.g., fluency of processing) of events and are sensitive to the discrepancy between the actual and the expected quality of processing of these events. As applied to prospective memory, McDaniel et al. proposed that discrepancy can stimulate a controlled search that leads to the retrieval of the prospective memory intention. As an illustration, because you form the intention to give your friend Patty a message, later encountering Patty might cause you to process her more fluently than other friends in the group. This could stimulate a search for the significance of the discrepancy, which is likely to cause the prospective memory intention to be retrieved. The discrepancy reaction may be based on a relatively automatic process and may be preserved in older adults (cf. Dywan & Jacoby, 1990).

Thus, according to the multiprocess theory, participants can rely on spontaneous retrieval processes for prospective memory retrieval, or they can actively monitor the environment for the target events. Which type of process they rely on and the effectiveness of that process will depend on a number of factors, including the nature and demands of the ongoing task, the inclinations of the individual, and the characteristics of the prospective memory task. One important dimension is whether the ongoing task encourages focal or nonfocal processing of the prospective memory task.

As can be seen in Table 7.1, focal processing occurs when the ongoing task encourages processing of the target and especially those features that were processed at encoding. The importance of focal processing follows from the principle of encoding specificity (Tulving, 1983) that retrieval is more likely when the features of the cue that were processed at retrieval match those that were processed at encoding. Indeed, given that a characteristic of prospective memory is that the task itself does not force you to be in a retrieval mode and thus that you cannot assemble additional cues to help guide retrieval (as is the case in retrospective memory tasks like cued recall; Einstein & McDaniel, 2010), the overlap between how an item is processed at encoding and retrieval is likely to be especially important in prospective memory.

Table 7.1 Examples of tasks that are low and high in focal processing

Processing	Ongoing task	Prospective memory task
Nonfocal	Words are presented in the center of a computer monitor and participants have to learn them for recall tests that occur at unpredictable times.	Respond when you see a particular background pattern (background pattern changes every 3 seconds).
Focal	Participants have to keep track of the number of occurrences of each background screen pattern.	Respond when you see a particular background pattern (background pattern changes every 3 seconds).
Nonfocal	Lexical decision task	Respond when you see an item from the "animal" category.
Focal	Lexical decision task	Respond to the word "cat."
Nonfocal	Pairs of words are presented and participants decide whether the word on the left is a member of the category on the right.	Respond when you see a word that begins with the letter "t."
Focal	Pairs of words are presented and participants decide whether the word on the left is a member of the category on the right.	Respond to the word "tortoise."

Nonfocal = low; Focal = high
Source: Adapted from Einstein, G. O., and McDaniel, M. A., 2005.

Nonfocal processing occurs when the ongoing task directs processing away from the target or to features of the target that were not processed at encoding. Thus, nonfocal processing occurs when the ongoing task directs attention to a word in the middle of a computer screen but the prospective memory target occurs on the periphery (see the first example in Table 7.1). It also occurs when the ongoing task draws attention to the meaning of a word but the prospective target is a word that begins with a particular letter (see the third nonfocal example in Table 7.1).

Under nonfocal conditions, we believe that spontaneous retrieval is less likely. Thus, the multiprocess theory prediction is that there should be smaller age differences with a focal prospective memory task relative to a nonfocal prospective memory task; a strong version is that there should be no age differences on a focal task. By contrast, from the perspective that all prospective memory tasks are high in self initiated retrieval and require working memory and/or attentional resources to support monitoring processes (Smith & Bayen, 2006), substantial age differences should occur with both focal and nonfocal prospective memory tasks.

Consistent with the multiprocess theory, in a recent meta-analysis of 46 studies conducted up to November 2006, Kliegel et al. (2008) found significantly larger age effects on nonfocal tasks relative to focal tasks. Because there was still a significant age effect with focal cues, the authors concluded that their meta-analysis supported only a weak version of the multiprocess theory. It did not support the strong prediction of zero effects of age with focal prospective memory tasks.

Although suggestive, the inclusive nature of their meta-analysis compromises the ability to evaluate clearly a stronger version of the multiprocess theory. One limitation is that very few of the studies measured costs of performing a prospective memory task on the ongoing task. Costs are measured by reduced accuracy and/or speed of performing an ongoing task while also performing a prospective memory task relative to performing the ongoing task alone; these are an indication of the extent to which participants are monitoring (Marsh, Hicks, Cook, Hansen, & Pallos, 2003). Thus, it may be that the task demands in some of the studies showing large age effects with a focal prospective memory task encouraged monitoring and that younger adults were more likely to recruit an active monitoring strategy to supplement spontaneous retrieval (which is assumed to be a probabilistic process).

A second limitation is that although the studies were correctly classified as using focal cues, other aspects of the methods may have placed a premium on working memory and executive resources. For example, two experiments classified as focal (Cohen, West, & Craik, 2001, Experiments 1 and 2) had 24 different target events. It is likely that this created a high demand and reward for rehearsing and attempting to keep the 24 targets activated while performing the ongoing task.

Surprisingly little research directly compares focal and nonfocal prospective memory performance of younger and older adults in the same experiment while also examining costs of performing a prospective memory task to the ongoing task. Recently, McDaniel, Einstein, and Rendell (2007) reported two such experiments. Using very different ongoing tasks in the two experiments, they found no age differences in either focal or nonfocal prospective memory performance. Importantly, the age invariance with the focal task occurred when neither younger nor older participants showed any evidence of monitoring. Thus, the results suggest that spontaneous retrieval processes are intact in older adults.

Although prospective memory was lower with a nonfocal prospective memory task, the levels of performance were surprisingly similar across age. There were significant costs in the nonfocal task condition, and this suggests that participants engaged monitoring processes in order to perform the prospective memory task successfully. Importantly, the monitoring costs were exaggerated for older adults in the nonfocal condition (in both experiments), indicating that older adults were able to attain prospective memory performance levels comparable to those of the younger adults only with greater sacrifice to the ongoing task.

One problem in evaluating the just presented experiments is that they did not use focal and nonfocal prospective memory tasks that were comparable in monitoring difficulty (Scullin, McDaniel, Shelton, & Lee, 2010). Scullin et al. recently showed that syllable prospective memory tasks that have been used in many nonfocal prospective memory tasks (e.g., press a designated key whenever you see the target "tor" in the context of a lexical decision task; McDaniel et al., 2007) are more difficult to monitor for than focal prospective memory target events (e.g., press a designated key when you see the target word "tornado"). Thus, from the view that all prospective memory tasks require capacity-consuming monitoring or preparatory attentional processing (Smith & Bayen, 2006), a possible interpretation of the extant findings is that typically found larger age differences on nonfocal prospective memory tasks reflect increased monitoring difficulty for nonfocal than for focal cues.

Toward resolving this problem, Hillary Mullet conducted a study in our laboratories in which she compared the prospective memory of younger and older adults with focal and nonfocal prospective memory cues that were comparable in monitoring difficulty (Scullin et al., 2010). In this experiment, type of prospective memory task was varied within subjects such that all participants performed three blocks of lexical decision trials (with 270 trials per block) and the order of the blocks was counterbalanced across participants. For the control block, participants performed only the ongoing task. For the focal prospective memory block, participants performed the ongoing task after they had been asked also to press the Q key on the keyboard whenever they saw a particular word (e.g., *printer*). In the nonfocal block, participants performed the ongoing task after they had been asked also to press the Q key whenever they saw a word that began with a particular initial letter (e.g., the initial letter *P*). The order for performing these blocks was counterbalanced across the 24 younger and 48 older participants.

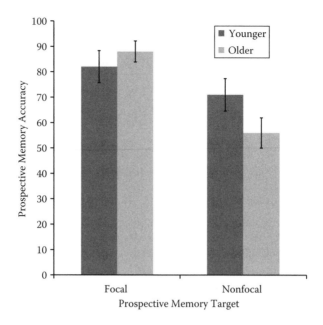

FIGURE 7.1 Proportion of correct prospective memory responses for younger and older adults with focal and nonfocal cues (error bars indicate standard error of the mean).

To encourage similar attentional allocation policies for younger and older participants across the focal and nonfocal tasks, we emphasized the importance of performing the ongoing task as quickly and accurately as possible, and we instructed them that we also had a "secondary interest" in their ability to remember to perform an action in the future. To ensure that older adults did not overly sacrifice ongoing task performance in order to monitor for the prospective memory targets in the nonfocal condition, we gave instructions with especially strong emphasis on speed to half of the older participants.

As can be seen in Figure 7.1, there was a significant interaction between age and type of prospective memory task such that younger and older adults did not differ on the focal prospective memory task (in fact, performance was nominally higher for older adults), although they did differ on the nonfocal prospective memory task (the data are collapsed across the two older age groups who differed in terms of the extent to which we emphasized the speed of performing the ongoing task). Consistent with Kvavilashvili et al. (2009), this interaction was driven by the oldest participants (over 70 years old). As can be seen in Figure 7.2, neither younger nor older participants slowed down during the lexical decision task in the focal condition (relative to the control block, during which they did not perform a prospective memory task). Thus, the high prospective memory performance with a focal cue was likely the result of spontaneous retrieval

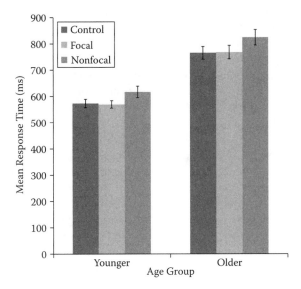

FIGURE 7.2 Mean lexical decision response times for younger and older adults in the control, focal prospective memory, and nonfocal prospective memory blocks (error bars indicate standard error of the mean).

processes, and our results indicate preserved spontaneous retrieval in older adults (even those over 70 years old).

In the nonfocal condition, both younger and older participants slowed down on the ongoing task (relative to the control block), and this slowing was roughly similar for younger (35 milliseconds) and older (57 milliseconds) adults. Taken together, these results are consistent with the thesis presented in this chapter that older adults are more likely to show prospective memory deficits on tasks that are more demanding of capacity-consuming monitoring processes, which presumably involve working memory and/or attentional resources and are assumed to be more limited in older adults.

An important finding in this research is that under conditions in which there was no evidence of monitoring, prospective memory with a focal cue was equivalent for younger and older adults. This result strongly encourages the exciting interpretation that spontaneous retrieval processes are preserved in older adults. We now present converging evidence for this view.

ADDITIONAL EVIDENCE FOR PRESERVED SPONTANEOUS RETRIEVAL PROCESSES IN OLDER ADULTS

One of the principal characteristics of spontaneous retrieval is that prospective memory cues can reflexively trigger retrieval without intention (i.e., without engaging a retrieval mode). If so, then presenting a prospective memory cue during an unexpected context should still elicit retrieval of the associated intention. Once the intention is in conscious awareness, the individual might then employ cognitive control mechanisms to assess whether it is the appropriate context in which to execute the prospective memory task (Braver & Barch, 2002). For example, in the morning, one might form the intention to pick up milk from the grocery store on the way home from work. Then, later, one might see an advertisement for dairy companies (e.g., "Got Milk?"). The ad would spontaneously remind the individual of the intention to pick up milk after work and then require the person to decide to pick up the milk or wait until later to do so.

Recognizing that cues occurring in unexpected contexts often trigger retrieval of a prospective memory intention, we recently developed a laboratory paradigm to examine spontaneous retrieval under such conditions (Einstein et al., 2005). In one example of this paradigm (Scullin, Einstein, & McDaniel, 2009), participants first encoded the prospective memory task of remembering to press the Q key when they saw the word *writer* in the context of an image-rating task. Following encoding, participants were instructed that they would need to perform the prospective memory task during a later image-rating task, but not until after they had performed a lexical decision task. The critical feature of this design is that the target word *writer* was still presented (unexpectedly to the participant) during the lexical decision task.

Because spontaneous retrieval processes are theorized to respond to retrieval cues obligatorily, we predicted that presenting the word *writer* would trigger intention retrieval and that this additional cognitive processing would be evidenced by slower lexical decision times. Termed the *intention interference effect* (Cohen, Dixon, & Lindsay, 2005), younger adults consistently demonstrated slower reaction times to prospective memory target words relative to control words (by approximately 20–30 milliseconds; Einstein et al., 2005; McDaniel & Scullin, 2010; Scullin et al., 2009). Importantly, this retrieval appears to be spontaneous because participants did not monitor during contexts in which the prospective memory task did not need to be performed (confirmed by control groups; Einstein et al., 2005; Marsh, Hicks, & Cook, 2006; Scullin et al.).

In collaboration with Katie Arnold and Rachel Scullin, we used the intention interference paradigm to investigate whether spontaneous retrieval processes are preserved in older adults. Younger adults (*n* = 32) and older adults (*n* = 32) encoded a prospective memory task in the context of an image-rating task. Participants were then instructed that they were going to perform the prospective memory and image-rating tasks at a later point but not until after they performed a lexical decision task. For the lexical decision task, participants were told that they should only make word/non-word decisions; however, the prospective memory target words were still presented during this phase. Both younger and older adults demonstrated significantly slower reaction times to the target words than the control words; importantly, the degree of slowing did not differ between younger and older adults. Thus, the ability to retrieve an intention spontaneously when target cues are processed outside the prospective-memory context is preserved with healthy aging.

One possible concern with the previous finding was that the older adults might have monitored during the lexical decision task. Though this would seem unlikely given prior research showing no monitoring outside the prospective memory context (Marsh et al., 2006; Scullin et al., 2009), we investigated this possibility by including a retrospective memory control condition in which participants encoded the target words for a later recognition memory test. Because recognition memory is experimenter prompted, there is no incentive for participants to monitor for their targets. Therefore, response times to control words in this condition provide a baseline to which to compare the prospective memory group.

Supporting the age-preserved spontaneous retrieval explanation, there were no differences in control trial response times for the prospective memory and recognition memory groups (for younger and older adults). Additionally, the intention interference effect did not obtain in the retrospective memory condition, which suggests that intention interference reflects an associative retrieval process rather than simple familiarity processes. These results collectively indicate that an associative, spontaneous retrieval process is preserved in older adults. Further research is needed, however, to evaluate more fully the extent to which this retrieval process is similar for young and older adults (e.g., see concluding section).

Having provided converging evidence that spontaneous retrieval processes are preserved in older adults, an interesting follow-up question concerns whether younger and older adults can "turn off" these retrieval processes once an intention has been completed. The ability to forget finished prospective memory intentions is critical to normal functioning because, without forgetting, irrelevant intentions would often pop into mind and these retrievals could create problems in reality monitoring (i.e., the ability to discriminate events in memory). Some commission errors (i.e., repetition of an already completed intention) may be relatively benign, such as forgetting whether one has washed one's hair and proceeding to use the shampoo again (as happened recently to one of the authors). Other commission errors have more severe consequences. In the case of medication adherence, retrieving the intention to take one's medication after already taking it could result in an overdose of the medication or aggravated symptoms. Despite the potential importance of commission errors, very little prospective memory research has been conducted on this phenomenon (Einstein, McDaniel, Smith, & Shaw, 1998).

Whereas spontaneous retrieval processes operate relatively automatically and are not predicted to decline with age, there is reason to suspect that older adults are more likely to persist in retrieving and executing finished prospective memories. From the perspective of the inhibition deficit hypothesis, older adults are less capable of "deleting" completed tasks

(Lustig, Hasher, & Zacks, 2007). Therefore, older adults may be more likely than younger adults to retrieve intentions spontaneously, even after they have been completed, if they failed to deactivate adequately or otherwise "delete" the intention upon initial completion. Additionally, according to the inhibitory deficit hypothesis, older adults show declines in the ability to suppress irrelevant information. Therefore, older adults may not only be more likely to retrieve irrelevant intentions but may also be at an increased risk for making commission errors if they are unable to suppress the intention. This theorizing is consistent with cognitive control theories (Braver & Barch, 2002) in which older adults are hypothesized to be more susceptible to the influence of automatic processes (e.g., reflexive associative retrieval) because they cannot exert proper top-down control.

We (Scullin et al., 2009) investigated spontaneous retrieval processes following completion of a prospective memory task by modifying the typical intention interference paradigm. In the modified version, participants first performed a prospective memory task during an image-rating phase. Following completion of the image-rating (and prospective memory) phase, participants were instructed that their prospective memory task was finished and would not need to be performed again. Next, participants performed a lexical decision task and the prospective memory target words were still presented during this phase. Interestingly, younger adults who had been instructed that their prospective memory task was finished no longer demonstrated the intention interference effect.

In a recent study (Scullin, Bugg, McDaniel, & Einstein, in press), we investigated whether older adults could similarly deactivate spontaneous retrieval processes. Consistent with previous findings reported earlier in the chapter, the older adults ($n = 38$, M = .80) performed the prospective memory task at levels statistically equivalent to the younger adults ($n = 40$; M = .87). The novel finding was that whereas the younger adults showed no intention interference following instructions that the prospective memory task was finished, the older adults continued to demonstrate the intention interference effect after the prospective memory task had been completed. Postexperimental questionnaires confirmed that the older adults understood that the prospective memory task was finished and did not need to be performed again. These effects suggest that spontaneous retrieval is not penalized by age; however, age may negatively impact the inhibition or deactivation of the intention.

COMPARING AGE DIFFERENCES
ON FOCAL PROSPECTIVE MEMORY TASKS
WITH TIME-BASED PROSPECTIVE MEMORY TASKS

Continuing the theme that there will be larger age differences on tasks that require working memory resources for monitoring for the appropriate moment to perform an action, in this section we compare age differences on event-based and time-based prospective memory tasks. Although the focus of this chapter is on understanding age differences in event-based prospective memory, given that time-based prospective memory tasks are those in which an action must be performed at a designated time or after a designated time interval, they provide an interesting comparison. With time-based tasks, in the absence of using an external alarm, one needs to monitor the time in order to know when to perform the intended action.

In typical laboratory tests of time-based prospective memory, participants are given an ongoing task to perform and also asked to perform a designated action after certain time intervals have elapsed. Their watches are removed and they can monitor time by looking at a clock that is outside the field of view (e.g., by looking behind them at a clock on the wall or by pressing a key to display a clock on their computer screen). Given that the ongoing task is unrelated to the time-based prospective memory task, there are no external cues in the ongoing task itself to prompt prospective remembering. Thus, time-based tasks are generally considered to require subjects to maintain or revive the intention at the appropriate time without the benefit of external cues and are thought to be more dependent on demanding self-initiated retrieval processes (Einstein et al., 1995).

Although only a few studies have directly compared the performance of younger and older adults on focal event-based prospective memory tasks with that on time-based tasks, they have generally found a larger effect of aging on time-based tasks. Einstein et al. (1995) involved participants in a general knowledge ongoing task and asked them to perform a prospective memory task either every 5 minutes or whenever they encountered the word *president* in a question. Subjects in the time-based condition could monitor the elapsed time by pressing the *F1* key on the keyboard. Einstein et al. found a significant interaction between age and prospective memory performance, with no age difference on the focal event-based task but a significant age difference on the time-based task. Kvavilashvili et al. (2009) found similar results of no age effects with a focal event-based task but significant effects on a time-based task, and the age differences were more pronounced with a stricter criterion for counting correct time-based prospective memory responses.

The general pattern of larger age effects on time-based tasks relative to event-based tasks with low strategic demands like those in a focal prospective memory task was evident in Henry and colleagues' (2004) meta-analysis. They found that the effect size of age was significantly larger in time-based task (age explained 15.4% of the variance) relative to low strategic demand event-based tasks (where age explained 1.9% of the variance). Interestingly, the effect size associated with age on time-based tasks was comparable to that with event-based tasks classified as high in strategic demands (age explained 16.4% of the variance).

Thus, the available research is consistent with the theme that the characteristics of the prospective memory task (and its relation to the ongoing task) have important implications for understanding the magnitude of age differences in prospective memory. Specifically, the idea is that laboratory time-based prospective memory tasks are devoid of cues that can prompt prospective memory retrieval, and the successful prospective memory performance of these tasks seems to be highly dependent on working memory resources for maintaining and reviving the intention while performing an ongoing task.

Interestingly, Kvavilashvili and Fisher (2007) argue that this characteristic of laboratory tests of time-based prospective memory, where the ongoing task provides no cues for the prospective memory task, may not entirely capture time-based prospective memory in natural settings. Kvavilashvili and Fisher asked their participants to call the experimenter 1 week later. They also asked participants to keep a diary and to record all instances of thinking about the prospective memory intention as well as possible cues in the surrounding environment that could have triggered recollection of the intention. They found no age differences and also that participants were often reminded of their prospective memory task by chance encounters with external cues such as seeing someone talking on the telephone or by walking by a telephone pole. Thus, in real-world settings, time-based intentions may often be externally cued.

CHALLENGING THE EXECUTION PHASE OF PROSPECTIVE MEMORY: KEEPING THE INTENTION ACTIVATED OVER BRIEF DELAYS

Successful prospective memory requires a number of cognitive processes, including forming an intention and planning for it, maintaining the intention over a delay, retrieving the intention at the appropriate moment, and then scheduling and executing the response (Ellis, 1996; Guynn, McDaniel, & Einstein, 2001). This latter component may be fairly simple in cases where the prospective memory intended action can be performed as soon as it is retrieved. In some cases, however, the ongoing task may be highly demanding or the timing for performing the action may not be quite right, and we must keep the intention activated until there is an opportune time for disengaging from the ongoing activities and performing the action.

Reflecting on our own experiences, it seems as if these kinds of delays in fulfilling intentions are quite common. For example, while engaged in a conversation with a group of friends, we may retrieve the intention to give a friend a message, but then must hold on to that intention until there is an appropriate break in the conversation. Or, while in the bedroom, we may retrieve the intention to take medication, but then must keep that activated until we get to the kitchen, where the medication is located.

Table 7.2 Sequence of events for each of 20 trials in the delayed-execute task

Ongoing task—paragraph comprehension (This sequence was repeated for 20 trials.)

1. A three-sentence paragraph was presented one sentence at a time.
2. Participants performed a multiple-choice synonym task or took a break for 5–15 seconds
3. Participants answered two multiple-choice trivia questions.
4. Participants answered one or two multiple-choice comprehension questions about the initial three-sentence paragraph.

Prospective memory task

A prospective memory target cue (TECHNIQUE or SYSTEM) occurred in the third sentence of a paragraph on 8 of the 20 trials.

Immediate prospective memory condition: participants were asked to make the prospective memory response as soon as they saw the target.

Delayed-execute condition: upon seeing a target, participants were asked to delay their prospective memory response until they encountered the trivia questions.

Source: From McDaniel, M. A. et al., 2003, *Psychology and Aging, 18,* 807–822.

Given that a core function of working memory is to keep relevant information activated in the face of distraction (Engle, 2002) and, more generally, to actively manipulate information (Baddeley & Hitch, 1974), it would seem that working memory resources would be highly involved in either keeping the intention active over a brief delay or reformulating the intention while performing the task at hand (e.g., reformulating the intention from "I will take my pills" to "When I get to the kitchen, I will take my pills"; see McDaniel, Einstein, Stout, & Morgan, 2003). Given the clear evidence for age-associated declines in working memory capacity (Salthouse, 1996; Verhaeghen, Chapter 1, this volume), older adults should have difficulty performing retrieved intentions that have to be delayed.

To test this prediction, McDaniel et al. (2003; see also Einstein, McDaniel, Manzi, Cochran, & Baker, 2000) tested older and younger adults in situations where they were led to retrieve an intended action but then had to delay that intention for brief intervals (ranging from 5 to 15 seconds). Specifically, in these experiments, the main ongoing task was to read and understand three-sentence paragraphs so that participants could later answer comprehension questions about these paragraphs. In order to create a bit of a delay between reading and answering the comprehension questions, participants were asked to perform a synonym task (or take a break) and then a trivia task (see Table 7.2 for the sequence of events). The prospective memory task was to press a designated key whenever participants saw either of the target words *technique* and *system.*

There were several critical features of this delayed-execute prospective memory task:

- The target event always occurred in upper case letters, whereas the other words in the sentences were always in lower case letters. This was done in order to make the target highly distinctive and virtually to ensure initial retrieval of the prospective memory intention. Indeed, in control conditions in which participants were allowed to respond immediately upon seeing the distinctive target, prospective memory performance was at 95% and 93% for younger and older adults, respectively.
- When the target occurred, it always occurred in the third sentence of the three-sentence paragraph.
- Critically, in the delayed conditions, participants were told not to execute the intended action until they encountered the trivia phase of that trial. Depending on the particular condition, this occurred 5–15 seconds after the offset of the sentence containing the target event.

Given the high prospective memory in the control conditions, in which participants could perform the action immediately, the critical question is whether brief delays interfere with prospective memory performance and whether delays differentially affect older adults. The results were dramatic. Whereas younger adults showed modest declines with delays (still performing above 80% in all delay conditions), older adults showed robust declines when the intention had to be delayed—even with the briefest delays (see also Einstein et al., 2000, and Kelley & Hertzog, 2010, for similar patterns). For example, in contrast to 93% performance when the action could be performed immediately, older adults remembered to perform the action on only 45% of the trials after a 5-second unfilled delay, even when they could take a break during the delay. Einstein et al. (2000) additionally found that working memory span accounted for a large proportion (ranging from 38% to 100%) of the age-associated variance in prospective memory performance.

Taken together, the results indicate that older adults are as capable as younger adults in retrieving intentions when there are strong cues, but that they have great difficulty executing their intentions when they cannot be performed immediately upon retrieval. These findings are consistent with general complaints among older adults that delays and interruptions are highly distracting and interfere with fulfilling planned goals (McDaniel & Einstein, 2007). For example, in the pursuit of the goal of paying a bill, a person may notice that the leaves on a plant are wilting and, after watering the plant, may fail to follow through on the intention to pay the bill.

CHALLENGING THE ENCODING OR PLANNING
PHASE OF PROSPECTIVE MEMORY

As noted at the outset, prospective memory is intimately involved with humans' future-oriented planning. Though planning in prospective memory tasks is not often studied (Dobbs & Reeves, 1996), the available evidence suggests that the nature of plans and encodings of the prospective memory intention that we formulate significantly affects prospective remembering. For instance, plans that are more detailed (Kliegel, McDaniel, & Einstein, 2000) or encodings that create strong associative links between an anticipated event (the target) and an intended action (Cohen & Gollwitzer, 2008; McDaniel, Howard, & Butler, 2008) appear to enhance prospective memory performance.

The preceding observation points to a potentially critical aspect of aging and prospective memory. To the extent that older adults have reduced planning capabilities or associative encoding deficits, older adults' prospective memory would be expected to exhibit decline that is specifically related to these factors. The few available studies indeed indicate that, at least in laboratory paradigms, older adults' plans are less detailed and well formulated than are younger adults' plans.

For instance, Kliegel et al. (2000) gave younger and older adults a complex prospective memory task (patterned on the six-elements tasks developed by Shallice & Burgess, 1991) to perform at some later point in the experiment. At the outset of the experiment, subjects were required to plan aloud how they intended to execute and remember the prospective memory task (see also Kliegel, Martin, McDaniel, Einstein, & Moor, 2007). The older adults' plans were less elaborated and specific than those generated by the younger adults; that is, the older adults were less likely to indicate how they would sequence and initiate the various elements of the prospective memory task. Perhaps not coincidentally, even though older adults remembered their plans with high accuracy, their prospective memory performance was compromised relative to that of the younger adults. Of course, these results, though suggestive, do not definitively establish a link between the age-related impairment in planning and the age-related impairment in prospective remembering.

Accordingly, Kliegel et al. (2007) used a similar paradigm, but in some conditions provided younger and older adults with scaffolding (that could include specific hints) for developing a useful plan. Plan quality (scored as the elaborateness of the plan) improved primarily for older adults and primarily in a scaffolding condition that also included specific hints relative to control conditions that did not receive hints for developing effective plans. Most telling, consistent with the conjecture that plan quality relates to prospective memory performance, scaffolding with specific hints significantly improved the number of subtasks that subjects intended to initiate relative to the no-hint control conditions, and this was particularly the case for older adults.

Also, the age-related difference in prospective memory observed for the no-hint control conditions was eliminated in the plan scaffold plus specific hint conditions. (In this scaffolding condition, younger adults were at ceiling; however, the older adults clearly achieved prospective memory levels equivalent to those of the control younger adults.) This pattern directly supports the idea that age-related declines in prospective memory are at least partially related to deficiencies in planning for older adults.

We should caution, though, that more research is warranted on this topic. Age-related differences in prospective memory planning have been examined only in the paradigm introduced by Kliegel et al. (2000) and, further, the paradigm is limited to the laboratory. In everyday prospective memory tasks, older adults may plan as well as or better than younger adults. Indeed, one suggestion for why age differences do not emerge on naturalistic prospective memory tasks (see Henry et al., 2004, for a meta-analysis) is that older adults may benefit from being able to plan for prospective memory tasks within the normal structure of their daily routine (Rendell & Craik, 2000).

Basic research does converge on the view that older adults have difficulty forming a strong associative link between an anticipated target event and the intended action. One prominent theory of age-related decline in retrospective memory is that older adults have an associative encoding deficit (Naveh-Benjamin, 2000; also see Chapter 4, this volume). Such a deficit could theoretically also compromise prospective memory inasmuch as older adults, upon forming a prospective memory intention and a future anticipated event appropriate for performing the intention, might nevertheless be less able than younger adults to create an associative link between the intention and the target event. On this analysis, if older adults are provided with encoding support for creating the associative link, then significant gains in prospective memory ought to occur.

Park and her colleagues have reported results that support this expectation (Chasteen, Park, & Schwarz, 2001; Liu & Park, 2004). In some conditions, older adults were instructed to link the intention with specific target events by visualizing the setting where they would perform the task and imagining performing the task in that setting (as well as sometimes producing a verbal association: "I intend to write 'Tuesday' on the top right corner of every sheet of paper I receive"; Chasteen et al.). In both a laboratory (remembering to write the day of the week on response sheets) and a naturalistic prospective memory task (remembering to monitor daily for blood glucose levels over 3 weeks), prospective memory performance was significantly better in this guided encoding condition, relative to a nonguided condition, for the older adults in the studies (Chasteen et al.; Liu & Park).

The preceding observations raise an interesting possibility for why some studies have reported age-related declines in focal prospective memory tasks (see Table 7.4 in McDaniel & Einstein, 2007) that, according to the multiprocess theory, generally should be minimally influenced by age. If some older adults have difficulty creating strong associations (during encoding) between the anticipated target and the intended action, then the subsequent encounter of the target event would not as likely stimulate spontaneous retrieval of the intended action. Inasmuch as frontally mediated executive processes are involved in strategic encoding (or binding; Cohn, Emrich,

& Moscovitch, 2008), such encoding deficits (and prospective memory decline) would accordingly be expected to be most prominent for older adults displaying relatively more pronounced frontal decline and, in turn, focal prospective memory would be expected to suffer.

Consistent with this conjecture, McDaniel, Glisky, Rubin, Guynn, and Routhieaux (1999) reported that older adults with lower than normal performance on neuropsychological tests related to frontal functioning performed significantly worse on a focal prospective memory task than older adults with relatively high frontal functioning. The McDaniel et al. study could not rule out the possibility that prospective memory differences were a consequence of differential monitoring across low and high frontal participants. Nevertheless, the interesting issue that researchers could further consider is that age-related focal prospective memory decline, when found, may illuminate age-related encoding challenges (see McFarland & Glisky, 2010, for a similar notion) rather than declines in strategic retrieval processes (e.g., strategic monitoring). In a similar vein, the relation between compromised frontal functioning in older adults and compromised prospective memory may also reflect prospective memory encoding problems, in addition to or instead of declines in demanding strategic retrieval processes.

SUMMARY AND FUTURE DIRECTIONS

Rather than addressing whether age differences do or do not exist in prospective memory, the goal of this chapter has been to attempt to explain some of the substantial variability in age-related performance in laboratory event-based prospective memory tasks. Although many factors likely contribute to this variability, the evidence clearly indicates that age differences are larger to the extent that the components of the prospective memory tasks (encoding, maintenance, retrieval, postresponse monitoring) demand extensive involvement of working memory resources. Thus, age differences in prospective memory are larger with nonfocal prospective memory cues, with time-based prospective memory tasks, when the planning process is complex, and when the execution phase of a prospective memory task is made more challenging. It also appears that older adults are more sensitive to commission errors that can occur in habitual prospective memory tasks (Einstein et al., 2000; McDaniel et al., 2003) and when prospective memory cues are still present after the prospective memory task has been performed (Scullin et al., 2011).

At this point, it is unclear which components of working memory are involved in successful performance on these kinds of prospective memory tasks. We suspect, however, that the executive attentional system is critically involved in maintaining and reactivating monitoring processes, keeping retrieved intentions sufficiently activated in the face of distraction (i.e., the ongoing task) until there is an opportunity to perform the action, and in developing effective plans.

The exciting news, however, is that older adults seem to perform as well as younger adults in cases where there is strong encoding (e.g., when the experimenter provides the planning by associating an action with a particular target event or encourages such planning), the ongoing task encourages focal processing of the target event, and the retrieval demands are straightforward (e.g., the action can be performed as soon as the intention is retrieved). Although spontaneous retrieval processes under these ideal conditions seem to be preserved, further research is needed to determine whether these processes are as robust in older adults as in younger adults. It may be that spontaneous retrieval occurs with a narrower range of cues than is the case in younger adults.

For example, Kvavilashvili et al. (2009) found no age differences on a standard laboratory event-based (focal) prospective memory task, but these same subjects showed large age differences on a "red pen" focal prospective memory task. In this task, participants were told to ask the experimenter for a pen when they were handed a sheet containing a geometric figure. It may be that older adults need a more exact match between their initial encoding (a general representation of a "geometric figure") and the item at retrieval (the actual figure) in order to trigger spontaneous retrieval. Perhaps showing participants the exact figure in advance would have eliminated age differences. It may also be that older adults have more difficulty allowing spontaneously retrieved intentions into awareness under demanding conditions.

Einstein and McDaniel (2008) have proposed that, depending on the demands of the ongoing task, we may set thresholds for allowing spontaneously retrieved thoughts into awareness, and these may operate differently in older and younger adults. In any case, it seems that spontaneous retrieval processes are spared in older adults under at least some conditions, and we believe that examining the sensitivity of these processes to aging is a fruitful avenue for further research, as are strategies for improving prospective memory that capitalize on these preserved processes (such as implementation intentions; Gollwitzer, 1999; Liu & Park, 2004).

ACKNOWLEDGMENTS

We dedicate this chapter to the late Rich Marsh, who died at the prime of his career. A gifted teacher, mentor, and scholar, he played a pivotal role in developing the field of prospective memory. We will miss his contributions, his encouraging yet forthright feedback, his tough warmth, and his friendship.

REFERENCES

Baddeley, A., & Hitch, G. J. (1974). Working memory. In G. Bower (Ed.), *The psychology of learning and motivation* (pp. 47–90). San Diego, CA: Academic Press.

Braver, T. S., & Barch, D. M. (2002). A theory of cognitive control, aging cognition, and neuromodulation. *Neuroscience Biobehavioral Review, 26,* 809–817.

Braver, T. S., & West, R. (2008). Working memory, executive control and aging. In F. I. M. Craik & T. A. Salthouse (Eds.), *The handbook of aging and cognition* (3rd ed., pp. 311–372). New York, NY: Psychology Press.

Chasteen, A. L., Park, D. C., & Schwarz, N. (2001). Implementation intentions and facilitation of prospective memory. *Psychological Science, 12,* 457–461.

Cherry, K. E., & LeCompte, D. C. (1999). Age and individual differences influence prospective memory. *Psychology and Aging, 14,* 60–76.

Cohen, A. L., Dixon, R. A., & Lindsay, D. S. (2005). The intention interference effect and aging: Similar magnitude of effects for young and old adults. *Applied Cognitive Psychology, 19,* 1177–1197.

Cohen, A. L., & Gollwitzer, P. M. (2008). The cost of remembering to remember: Cognitive load and implementation intentions influence ongoing task performance. In M. Kliegel, M. A. McDaniel, & G. O. Einstein (Eds.), *Prospective memory: Cognitive, neuroscience, developmental, and applied perspectives* (pp. 367–390). Mahwah, NJ: Lawrence Erlbaum Associates.

Cohen, A. L., West, R., & Craik, F. I. M. (2001). Modulation of the prospective and retrospective components of memory for intentions in younger and older adults. *Aging, Neuropsychology, and Cognition, 8,* 1–13.

Cohn, M., Emrich, S. M., & Moscovitch, M. (2008). Age-related deficits in associative memory: The influence of impaired strategic retrieval. *Psychology and Aging, 23,* 93–103.

Craik, F. I. M. (1986). A functional account of age differences in memory. In F. Klix & H. Hagendorf (Eds.), *Human memory and cognitive capabilities: Mechanisms and performances* (pp. 409–422). New York, NY: Elsevier Science Publishers.

Craik, F. I. M., & Byrd, M. (1982). Aging and cognitive deficits: The role of attentional resources. In F. I. M. Craik & S. E. Trehub (Eds.), *Aging and cognitive processes* (pp. 191–211). New York, NY: Plenum Press.

Dismukes, R. K. (2008). Prospective memory in aviation and everyday settings. In M. Kliegel, M. A. McDaniel, and G. O. Einstein (Eds.), *Prospective memory: Cognitive, neuroscience, developmental, and applied perspectives* (pp. 411–431). Mahwah, NJ: Lawrence Erlbaum Associates.

Dobbs, A. R., & Reeves, M. B. (1996). Prospective memory: More than just memory. In M. Brandimonte, G. O. Einstein, & M. A. McDaniel (Eds.), *Prospective memory: Theory and applications* (pp. 199–225). Mahwah, NJ: Lawrence Erlbaum Associates.

Dywan, J., & Jacoby, L. L. (1990). Effects of aging in source monitoring: Differences in susceptibility to false fame. *Psychology and Aging, 5,* 379–387.

Einstein, G. O., Holland, L. J., McDaniel, M. A., & Guynn, M. J. (1992). Age-related deficits in prospective memory: The influence of task complexity. *Psychology and Aging, 7,* 471–478.

Einstein, G. O., & McDaniel, M. A. (1990). Normal aging and prospective memory. *Journal of Experimental Psychology: Learning, Memory, and Cognition, 16,* 717–726.

Einstein, G. O., & McDaniel, M. A. (2005). Prospective memory: Multiple retrieval processes. *Current Directions in Psychological Science, 14,* 286–290.

Einstein, G. O., & McDaniel, M. A. (2008). Prospective memory and metamemory: The skilled use of basic attentional and memory processes. In A. Benjamin (Ed.), *The psychology of learning and motivation* (pp. 145–173). San Diego, CA: Elsevier.

Einstein, G. O., & McDaniel, M. A. (2010). Prospective memory and what costs do not reveal about retrieval processes: A commentary on Smith, Hunt, McVay, and McConnell (2007). *Journal of Experimental Psychology: Learning, Memory, & Cognition, 36,* 1082–1088.

Einstein, G. O., McDaniel, M. A., Manzi, M., Cochran, B., & Baker, M. (2000). Prospective memory and aging: Forgetting intentions over short delays. *Psychology and Aging, 15,* 671–683.

Einstein, G. O., McDaniel, M. A., Richardson, S. L., Guynn, M. J., & Cunfer, A. R. (1995). Aging and prospective memory: Examining the influences of self-initiated retrieval processes. *Journal of Experimental Psychology: Learning, Memory, and Cognition, 21,* 996–1007.

Einstein, G. O., McDaniel, M. A., Smith, R. E., & Shaw, P. (1998). Habitual prospective memory and aging: Remember intentions and forgetting actions. *Psychological Science, 9,* 284–288.

Einstein, G. O., McDaniel, M. A., Thomas, R., Mayfield, S., Shank, H., Morrisette, N., & Breneiser, J. (2005). Multiple processes in prospective memory retrieval: Factors determining monitoring versus spontaneous retrieval. *Journal of Experimental Psychology: General, 134,* 327–342.

Ellis, J. (1996). Prospective memory or the realization of delayed intentions: A conceptual framework for research. In M. Brandimonte, G. O. Einstein, & M. A. McDaniel (Eds.), *Prospective memory: Theory and applications* (pp. 1–51). Mahwah, NJ: Lawrence Erlbaum Associates.

Engle, R. W. (2002). Working memory capacity as executive attention. *Current Directions in Psychological Science, 11,* 19–23.

Gollwitzer, P. M. (1999). Implementation intentions: Strong effects of simple plans. *American Psychologist, 54,* 493–503.

Guynn, M. J., McDaniel, M. A., & Einstein, G. O. (2001). *Remembering to perform actions: A different kind of memory.* In M. Marschark (Ed.), Memory for action: A distinct form of episodic memory? (pp. 25–48). New York, NY: Oxford University Press.

Henry, J. D., MacLeod, M. S., Phillips, L. H., & Crawford, J. R. (2004). A meta-analytic review of prospective memory and aging. *Psychology and Aging, 19,* 27–39.

Jenkins, J. J. (1979). Four points to remember: A tetrahedral model of memory. In L. S. Cermak & F. I. M. Craik (Eds.), *Levels of processing in human memory* (pp. 429–446). Hillsdale, NJ: Lawrence Erlbaum Associates.

Kelemen, W. L., Weinberg, W. B., Oh, H. S. Y., Mulvey, E. K., & Kaeochinda, K. F. (2006). Improving the reliability of event-based laboratory tests of prospective memory. *Psychonomic Bulletin & Review, 13,* 1028–1032.

Kelley, A. J., & Hertzog, C. (2010). *Delay–execute prospective memory and aging: Differences in monitoring?* Poster presented at the Cognitive Aging Conference, Atlanta, GA, April 2010.

Klein, S. B., Robertson, T. E., & Delton, A. W. (2010). Facing the future: Memory as an evolved system for planning future acts. *Memory & Cognition, 38,* 13–22.

Kliegel, M., Jager, T., & Phillips, L. H. (2008). Adult age differences in event-based prospective memory: A meta-analysis on the role of focal versus nonfocal cues. *Psychology and Aging, 23,* 203–208.

Kliegel, M., Martin, M., McDaniel, M. A., Einstein, G. O., & Moor, C. (2007). Realizing complex delayed intentions in young and old adults: The role of planning aids. *Memory & Cognition, 35,* 1735–1746.

Kliegel, M., McDaniel, M. A., & Einstein, G. O. (2000). Plan formation, retention, and execution in prospective memory: A new approach and age-related effects. *Memory & Cognition, 28,* 1041–1049.

Kvavilashvili, L., & Fisher, L. (2007). Is time-based prospective remembering mediated by self-initiated rehearsals? Effects of incidental cues, ongoing activity, age, and motivation. *Journal of Experimental Psychology: General, 136,* 12–132.

Kvavilashvili, L., Kornbrot, D. E., Mash, V., Cockburn, J., & Milne, A. (2009). Differential effects of age on prospective and retrospective memory tasks in young, young–old, and old–old adults. *Memory, 17,* 180–196.

Liu, L. L., & Park, D. C. (2004). Aging and medical adherence: The use of automatic processes to achieve effortful things. *Psychology & Aging, 19,* 318–325.

Lustig, C., Hasher, L., & Zacks, R. (2007). Inhibitory deficit theory: Recent developments in a "new view." In D. S. Gorfein & C. M. MacLeod (Eds.), *The place of inhibition in cognition* (pp. 145–162). Washington, DC: American Psychological Association.

Marsh, R. L., Hicks, J. L., & Cook, G. I. (2006). Task interference from prospective memories covaries with contextual associations of fulfilling them. *Memory & Cognition, 34,* 1037–1045.

Marsh, R. L., Hicks, J. L., Cook, G. I., Hansen, J. S., & Pallos, A. L. (2003). Interference to ongoing activities covaries with the characteristics of an event-based intention. *Journal of Experimental Psychology: Learning, Memory, and Cognition, 29,* 861–870.

Maylor, E. A. (1993). Aging and forgetting in prospective and retrospective memory tasks. *Psychology and Aging, 8,* 420–428.

Maylor, E. A. (1996). Age-related impairment in an event-based prospective-memory task. *Psychology and Aging, 11,* 74–78.

McDaniel, M. A., & Einstein, G. O. (2000). Strategic and automatic processes in prospective memory retrieval: A multiprocess framework. *Applied Cognitive Psychology, 14,* S127–S144.

McDaniel, M. A., & Einstein, G. O. (2007). *Prospective memory: An overview and synthesis of an emerging field.* Thousand Oaks, CA: Sage.

McDaniel, M. A., Einstein, G. O., & Jacoby, L. L. (2008). Working memory, executive control and aging. In F. I. M. Craik & T. A. Salthouse (Eds.), *The handbook of aging and cognition* (3rd ed., pp. 251–310). New York, NY: Psychology Press.

McDaniel, M. A., Einstein, G. O., & Rendell, P. G. (2007). The puzzle of inconsistent age-related declines in prospective memory: A multiprocess explanation. In M. Kliegel, M. A. McDaniel, and G. O. Einstein (Eds.), *Prospective memory: Cognitive, neuroscience, developmental, and applied perspectives* (pp. 141–160). Mahwah, NJ: Lawrence Erlbaum Associates.

McDaniel, M. A., Einstein, G. O., Stout, A., & Morgan, Z. (2003). Aging and maintaining intentions over delays: Do it or lose it. *Psychology and Aging, 18,* 807–822.

McDaniel, M. A., Glisky, E. L., Rubin, S. R., Guynn, M. J., & Routhieaux, B. C. (1999). Prospective memory: A neuropsychological study. *Neuropsychology, 13,* 103–110.

McDaniel, M. A., Guynn, M. J., Einstein, G. O., & Breneiser, J. (2004). Cue-focused and reflexive-associative processes in prospective memory retrieval. *Journal of Experimental Psychology: Learning, Memory, and Cognition, 30,* 605–614.

McDaniel, M. A., Howard, D. W., & Butler, K. M. (2008). Implementation intentions facilitate prospective memory under high attention demands. *Memory & Cognition, 36,* 716–724.

McDaniel, M. A., & Scullin, M. K. (2010). Implementation intention encoding does not automatize prospective memory responding. *Memory & Cognition, 38,* 221–232.

McFarland, C. P., & Glisky, E. L. (2010). *The relation between implementation intentions and frontal lobe functions in prospective memory.* Poster presented at the Cognitive Aging Conference, Atlanta, GA, April 2010.

Moscovitch, M. (1994). Memory and working with memory: Evaluation of a component process model and comparisons with other models. In D. L. Schacter & E. Tulving (Eds.), *Memory systems* (pp. 269–310). Cambridge, MA: MIT Press.

Naveh-Benjamin, M. (2000). Adult age differences in memory performance: Tests of an associative deficit hypothesis. *Journal of Experimental Psychology: Learning, Memory, and Cognition, 26,* 1170–1187.

Nelson, M. R., Reid, C. M., Ryan, P., Willson, K., & Yelland, L. (2006). Self-reported adherence with medication and cardiovascular disease outcomes in the second Australian national blood pressure study (ANBP2). *Medical Journal of Australia, 9,* 487–489.

Park, D. C., Hertzog, C., Kidder, D. P., Morrell, R. W., & Mayhorn, C. B. (1997). Effect of age on event-based and time-based prospective memory. *Psychology and Aging, 12,* 314–327.

Park, D. C., Lautenschlager, G., Hedden, T., Davidson, N. S., Smith, A. D., & Smith, P. K. (2002). Models of visuospatial and verbal memory across the adult life span. *Psychology and Aging, 17,* 299–320.

Reese, C. M., & Cherry, K. E. (2002). The effects of age, ability, and memory monitoring on prospective memory task performance. *Aging, Neuropsychology, and Cognition, 9,* 98–113.

Rendell, P. G., & Craik, F. I. M. (2000). Virtual week and actual week: Age-related differences in prospective memory. *Applied Cognitive Psychology, 14,* S43–S62.

Salthouse, T. A. (1996). The processing-speed theory of adult age differences in cognition. *Psychological Review, 103,* 403–428.

Scullin, M. K., Bugg, J. M., McDaniel, M. A., & Einstein, G. O. (2011). Prospective memory and aging: Preserved spontaneous retrieval, but impaired deactivation, in older adults. *Memory & Cognition, 39,* 1232–1240.

Scullin, M. K., Einstein, G. O., & McDaniel, M. A. (2009). Evidence for spontaneous retrieval of suspended but not finished prospective memories. *Memory & Cognition, 37,* 425–433.

Scullin, M. K., McDaniel, M. A., Shelton, J. T., & Lee, J. H. (2010). Focal/nonfocal cue effects in prospective memory: Monitoring difficulty or different retrieval processes? *Journal of Experimental Psychology: Learning, Memory, & Cognition, 36,* 736–749.

Shallice, T., & Burgess, P. (1991). Deficits in strategy application following frontal lobe damage in man. *Brain, 114,* 727–741.

Smith, R. E. (2003). The cost of remembering in event-based prospective memory: Investigating the capacity demands of delayed intention performance. *Journal of Experimental Psychology: Learning, Memory, & Cognition, 29,* 347–361.

Smith, R. E., & Bayen, U. J. (2006). The source of adult age differences in event-based prospective memory: A multinomial modeling approach. *Journal of Experimental Psychology: Learning, Memory, and Cognition, 32,* 623–635.

Tulving, E. (1983). *Elements of episodic memory.* New York, NY: Oxford University Press.

Uttl, B. (2005). Measurement of individual differences: Lessons from memory assessment in research and clinical practice. *Psychological Science, 16,* 460–467.

Verhaeghen, P. (2012). Working memory still working: Age-related difference in working memory functioning and cognitive control. In M. Naveh Benjamin and N. Ohta (Eds.) *Memory and aging: Current issues and future directions* (pp. 1–30). New York, NY: Psychology Press.

West, R. L., Herndon, R. W., & Covell, E. (2003). Neural correlates of age-related declines in the formation and realization of delayed intentions. *Psychology and Aging, 18*(3), 461–473.

Whittlesea, B. W. A., & Williams, L. D. (2001a). The discrepancy-attribution hypothesis: I. The heuristic basis of feelings of familiarity. *Journal of Experimental Psychology: Learning, Memory, and Cognition, 27,* 3–13.

Whittlesea, B. W. A., & Williams, L. D. (2001b). The discrepancy-attribution hypothesis: II. Expectation, uncertainty, surprise, and feelings of familiarity. *Journal of Experimental Psychology: Learning, Memory, and Cognition, 27,* 14–33.

Zeintl, M., Kliegel, M., & Hofer, S. M. (2007). The role of processing resources in age-related prospective and retrospective memory within old age. *Psychology and Aging, 22,* 826–834.

Part 3
Social, emotional, and cultural perspectives

8 Memory in context

The impact of age-related goals on performance

Thomas M. Hess and Lisa Emery

INTRODUCTION

Research has identified many quantitative (e.g., amount of information remembered) and qualitative (e.g., types of information remembered) shifts in memory functioning that appear to characterize normal aging (for review, see McDaniel, Einstein, & Jacoby, 2008). For the most part, it is explicitly or implicitly assumed that memory change is associated with normative alterations in cortical structures associated with basic cognitive processes (e.g., speed, working memory, and inhibitory functions), with change driven by genetically influenced aging processes (McGue & Johnson, 2008), normative neuropathologic processes (Wilson, 2008), or health-related factors that are probabilistically related to aging (Spiro & Brady, 2008).

Although such factors are undoubtedly at work in determining the course of memory change in later life, research is increasingly identifying other causal mechanisms of age-related variability in performance and change in memory functioning. For example, motivational, emotional, and social factors have all been shown to be important influences on memory-related behaviors (for reviews, see Hess, 2005; Kensinger, Chapter 9, this volume; Mather & Carstensen, 2005).

These findings fit well with a general contextual perspective on lifespan development that emphasizes the importance of considering multiple influences and their transactional relationships in determining the course of development (Baltes, 1987). In this chapter, we examine memory and aging from this perspective. We begin by making a case for the importance of a contextual approach and then present a general framework for understanding aging effects on memory performance. We finish by focusing on one particular set of proximal-distal influences representative of a contextual approach. Specifically, we discuss research that addresses the relationship between life circumstances, social context, and personal goals as they relate to memory functioning.

A CONTEXTUAL APPROACH

The lifespan contextualist perspective (Baltes, 1987) has been an influential framework used in guiding theoretical and empirical work on adult development and aging. A primary component of this view is the assertion that age-related changes in behavior are multidimensional and multidirectional, which incorporates the corollary assumption that development is characterized at all points of the life span by both gains and losses. For present purposes, an important implication of multidimensionality and multidirectionality is the assumption of multiple determinants of performance and behavior change. The lifespan perspective also emphasizes the adaptive nature of development as individuals adjust their behavior in response to normative and non-normative changes in life events. This adaptive functioning may result not only in gains as new behaviors are acquired or existing behaviors become more efficient to deal with new circumstances, but also in losses as behaviors are replaced or de-emphasized in response to these same circumstances.

When applied to the study of memory and aging, this perspective argues for consideration of multiple factors at multiple levels of analysis (Hess, 2005). For illustrative purposes, we will make a broad distinction between proximal and distal factors that account for age-related variation in memory performance. Proximal factors are those characteristics that have a relatively direct impact on performance at a given point in time. Interindividual variability and intraindividual change in performance over time can be understood in terms of changes in the constellation of both quantitative and qualitative performance-relevant characteristics of the individual. For the most part, the proximal characteristics considered in the research literature relate to basic characteristics of the information-processing system (e.g., working memory, speed of processing, inhibitory functions) or, more recently, to underlying cortical structures.

In contrast, distal influences refer to the broader context in which development takes place. These factors have a more indirect impact on memory through their determination of the level and form of proximal influences. From a contextual perspective, common patterns of intraindividual change both within and across cohorts are based in stable, age-graded distal influences that have relatively systematic effects on the development of proximal mechanisms. A common implicit or explicit assumption is that much of the age-related change in such mechanisms can be accounted for in terms of distal influences (e.g., neuropathologic processes, health, genetics) that have a relatively systematic but negative effect on underlying biological mechanisms.

It can reasonably be argued that the majority of research on memory and aging has proceeded from a conceptual basis that is consistent with the foregoing characterization of distal and proximal influences. That is, normative changes in cortical structures (e.g., neuronal loss, decreased levels of neurotransmitters) associated with cumulative damage or genetically determined change over the life course has a negative impact on basic mechanisms, such as processing speed, which in turn reduces the efficiency of memory functioning in later life. Note that we are not arguing that this is an inappropriate view or an unfruitful manner in which to study memory and aging. On the contrary, it is abundantly clear that this approach has resulted in important insights into the aging mind.

In addition, this view is quite consistent with a contextualist perspective to the extent that there may be individual differences in characteristics that influence proximal mechanisms and thereby account for variations in age-related change in functioning. For example, whereas there may be some inherent aspects of the aging process that lead to normative changes in memory functioning, lifestyle factors may alter the level of ability and rate of change (see Hertzog, Kramer, Wilson, & Lindenberger, 2009). Our main point is that (a) normative changes in basic cortical and cognitive mechanisms may represent just one category of distal and proximal influences that determine memory functioning in later life and (b) consideration of a broader array of influences as well as the contexts in which individuals use their memory skills will give us a clearer understanding of the nature of age-related change in memory ability as well as insights into factors promoting optimal changes in functioning.

Age-graded changes in social structures, affective functions, goals, and other factors may also be characterized as normative influences that determine the nature of memory functioning and how we use our memory skills (Hess, 2005). To illustrate, older adults often evince reductions in beliefs about the control they have over memory change and performance in later life (Lachman, 2006), which may be based in Western stereotypes about aging and memory (e.g., Levy & Langer, 1994). This, in turn, may result in decreases in the amount of effort that individuals put into a memory task, potentially exaggerating age differences based in ability.

Importantly, these socially based factors may also affect the course of biologically influenced memory change in later life. To the extent that these beliefs result in reduced involvement in memory activities, normative cortical change could also be accelerated due to disuse, thereby potentially hastening the rate of decline in memory ability. Indeed, research (e.g., Levy, Zonderman, Slade, & Ferucci, 2009) has suggested that individual differences in attitudes about aging have important consequences on health and longevity, presumably through their impact on health-related behaviors. It seems reasonable further to infer that this relationship between attitudes and biological change will also be reflected in individual and age-related patterns of memory functioning.

As a means for illustrating a contextual perspective on memory and aging, Figure 8.1 presents a multidimensional model incorporating multiple distal and proximal influences along with causal linkages between influences. The model incorporates what might be thought of as the biologically based "default" mechanism accounting for changes in performance that

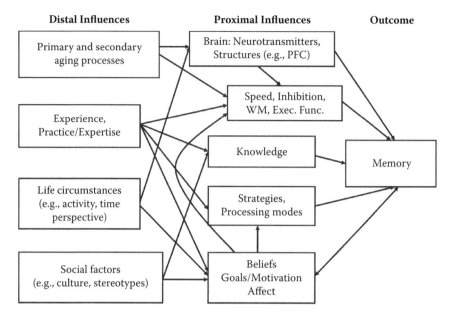

FIGURE 8.1 A contextual perspective on factors associated with age differences in memory performance.

dominates the literature (top). It also identifies other mechanisms along with alternative linkages between factors both within and between levels.

Thus, for example, extensive experience or practice in a given realm or even physical exercise may have a direct positive impact on proximal factors associated with speed, working memory, and executive functions (e.g., Colcombe & Kramer, 2003), thereby helping to maintain levels of performance. These distal factors may also influence one's knowledge base, which may help compensate for losses in processing components of memory by providing organizational structures for encoding and retrieving information in memory. Evidence in support of practice effects on both processes and knowledge comes from studies of expertise (Krampe & Charness, 2006). Experience may also modify control beliefs about one's memory ability, resulting in greater likelihood of both engagement in memory activities and willingness to participate in remediation activities.

Support for a contextual perspective

In a survey of the literature, Hess (2005) examined support for the validity of a contextual approach to the study of aging and memory. While acknowledging strong evidence for systematic age-related change in brain structures and functions (e.g., prefrontal cortex) underlying memory performance (for review, see Dennis & Cabeza, 2008), the bases for such changes and the meaning of differential patterns of activation across individuals of different ages is still open to debate. For example, are the differences that we see in older adults' patterns of cortical activation relative to those of younger adults reflective of changes in processing efficiency associated with neuronal loss or neurochemical change? Or, alternatively, might the observed age differences also reflect the use of inefficient strategies on the part of older adults, which may be related to contextual factors (e.g., task relevance, practice) that influence cognitive engagement?

It is likely that the effects are due to some combination of these factors. Importantly for the contextual perspective, there is evidence that some aging-related variation observed in memory and cognitive performance is attributable to physical health factors (Waldstein, 2000) that have a probabilistic, not inevitable connection to age. In fact, some have suggested that the majority of age-related variance in cognitive outcomes is based in such health factors (e.g., Spiro & Brady, 2008). Of further interest are findings suggesting that lifestyle factors—for example, physical exercise (Colcombe & Kramer, 2003) or engagement in substantively complex activities (Schooler, Malatu, & Oates, 1999)—are associated with memory skills reflective of efficient controlled processing. In addition there is also evidence that lifestyle factors are related to variations in the brain structures and functions thought to underlie observed age differences in memory (e.g., Colcombe et al., 2003; Lupien et al., 1998). Such observations are consistent with the idea that both the environment and individual exert a certain amount of control over the course of memory change as well as the cortical structures undergirding such change.

Hess (2005) also identified evidence for proximal influences on memory performance that were unrelated to the inherent integrity and efficiency of the information-processing system. Rather, these factors were thought to be associated with engagement and direction of this system. Two general classes of such age-graded proximal influences were identified. First, aging is associated with shifts in goals associated with social-cognitive functioning (e.g., Adams, Smith, Pasupathi, & Vitolo, 2002), perspectives of time (e.g., Carstensen & Turk-Charles, 1994), and cognitive resource conservation (e.g., Hess, Germain, Swaim, & Osowski, 2009), which in turn have an impact on memory performance. A second general category of proximal influences is associated with culturally based stereotypes of aging; these may affect performance either indirectly through belief systems (Hertzog & Hultsch, 2000) or through a more direct route associated with their activation from situational cues (e.g., Bargh, Chen, & Burrows, 1996; Hess, Auman, Colcombe, & Rahhal, 2003; Levy, 1996).

Note that the goal- and stereotype-based processes mentioned here may not necessarily be independent of other aging-related changes (e.g., Freund & Baltes, 2002), including those associated with biologically based aspects of development. For example, some intrinsic goals (e.g., need for cognitive structure) that have been found to be predictive of engagement in complex cognitive activity have also been shown to be associated with variation in health-related resources (Hess, 2001; Hess, Emery, & Neupert, in press), suggesting a possible linkage between changing biological and motivational systems. What is important, however, are the facts that (a) not all developmentally relevant goals are driven by changes in biological structures, (b) goals can determine the encoding and retrieval operations underlying mnemonic functioning, and (c) the effects of aging-related changes in biological processes on memory performance may be mediated by goals associated with those changes. We elaborate on these ideas in the next section.

In sum, an examination of existing research on aging and memory does provide evidence consistent with a contextual perspective. Biological, behavioral, and social factors appear to serve as both proximal and distal influences in determining memory performance and change in adulthood. In addition, there are potential cross-linkages among these three types of factors (e.g., Levy et al., 2009), suggesting that a focus on only one level of analysis may be problematic. Thus, the adoption of a contextual perspective along with the consideration of a variety of influences promotes not only our understanding of memory functioning in adulthood, but also the causal mechanisms determining change. This, in turn, has important implications for optimization of functioning as well as remediation.

GOAL-RELATED INFLUENCES
ON MEMORY PERFORMANCE

Proceeding within a contextual perspective, we devote the remainder of this chapter to examining motivational processes and their role in both age differences in ability and intraindividual variation in performance across contexts. One way to think of motivational influences is within the context of goals. One category of goals may be thought of as acute and situation specific, such as those having to do with specific task instructions (e.g., "remember this list of words"). Of greater interest from a contextual perspective are chronic goals that are relatively stable and reflective of an individual's interests, beliefs, and life circumstances. Within the context of chronic goals, we focus primarily on two factors. First, we are interested in identifying *developmentally salient* chronic goals—that is, goals that can be meaningfully tied to age-graded normative influences in an individual's life. Second, we are further interested in specifying the conditions under which these and other types of chronic goals are likely to be operative and whether age-related processes can be meaningfully tied to such conditions.

We argue that chronic goals interact with situational factors (e.g., task demands, information contents) in determining the personal relevance or implications of the task, which influence motivation. Personal relevance is determined by the degree to which chronic goals map onto situational factors that, in turn, will determine the degree of engagement and the direction of processing. Thus, for example, if engaging in the task is somehow tied directly to one's chronic goals, then personal relevance or meaningfulness would be perceived to be high, with concomitant motivational consequences. Tasks may also be reconstrued in a manner consistent with chronic goals so that, for example, acute goals tied to experimenter instructions may be reinterpreted in a more personally meaningful way. In contrast, if the connection to chronic goals is low, motivation—and performance—are likely to be low.

For present purposes, the impact of chronic goals on motivation can be usefully thought of in terms of selection effects. We conceive of selection being related to the directing and energizing functions associated with motivation. With respect to directing, selection effects may be evident when one has a choice of activities and the individual chooses the one of most interest or the one most likely to promote personal goals. The directing effects of selection may also be seen in information search, with attention disproportionately focused on goal-congruent information. In contrast, energizing functions reflective of selection are associated with degree of engagement with the task and the effort devoted to supporting performance in a given situation.

Several different perspectives within the literature on adult development incorporate this notion of selection. We examine these perspectives next, with a focus on the associated research and the implications of each for the understanding of memory and aging. We begin by discussing some initial work on the impact of social-cognitive goals on memory functioning. We then move to discussions of the more formal goal-related frameworks of the selection, optimization, and compensation (SOC) model (e.g., Baltes, Staudinger, & Lindenberger, 1999) and socioemotional selectivity theory (SST; e.g., Carstensen, 1993). We then follow this with an in-depth discussion of selective engagement (e.g., Hess, 2006a). Finally, we discuss work on the impact on memory performance of a specific social context factor—negative stereotypes of aging—and attempt to interpret such findings within the context of goal-related processes.

Social-cognitive goals

One approach to understanding the impact of goals on memory is to consider changes in the social-cognitive context associated with processing information across the adult life span. In other words, what are the dominant tasks associated with different stages of adulthood and how do they affect our cognitive functioning? One theoretical perspective suggests that information-processing goals shift from a focus on information acquisition in early adulthood to an emphasis on interpretation, integration of past and present knowledge, and cross-generation transmission of information in later adulthood (e.g., Greve & Bjorklund, 2009; Labouvie-Vief, 1990; Mergler & Goldstein, 1983). This results in less emphasis on veridical reproduction and greater emphasis on establishment of meaning and sharing of knowledge in later life. Given that many studies focus on verbatim reproduction as a means for assessing memory ability, age differences in memory functioning may be overestimated or misinterpreted due to the mismatch between the demands of the task and the processing goals of the individual.

These ideas were explored in a series of studies by Adams and colleagues that examined age differences in performance as a function of type of memory output and performance context. In two initial studies (Adams, 1991; Adams, Labouvie-Vief, Hobart, & Dorosz, 1990), recall of text material was examined as a means of investigating age differences in memory representations. It was found that the recall of younger adults was dominated by verbatim reproduction of the text. In contrast, middle-aged and older adults exhibited greater evidence of interpretation-based processing in that their recall protocols contained more elaborations and metaphorical propositions. Importantly, these age differences were most evident in unstructured situations, where little guidance was given regarding how to process the information and thus stylistic differences would be most likely to emerge. In addition, older adults' use of more gist-based processes did not appear to be a compensatory response to losses in memory for details. In a subsequent study, Adams, Smith, Nyquist, and Perlmutter (1997) also found that the strength and direction of age differences in memory performance were dependent upon the task. Specifically, young adults were superior to older adults when the task emphasized verbatim recall, whereas older adults outperformed younger adults when the focus was on interpretation.

Adams et al. (2002) also found social context to moderate age differences in recall. They had young and older women learn a story either to retell to the experimenter or to a young child. In the former case, which is analogous to the typical laboratory testing situation, the younger adults outperformed the older adults. In contrast, the performance of older adults was boosted and age differences were nonexistent when they retold the story to a child. Older adults were also more likely than younger adults to adjust the complexity of their output to the characteristics of the audience. These findings are consistent with the idea that knowledge transmission is an important social goal in later life. A recent study examining prospective memory (Altgassen, Kliegel, Brandimonte, & Filippello, 2010) obtained similar results.

Taken together, these results emphasize the importance of social-cognitive goals in determining memory performance. In particular, the match between such goals and the task demands is an important determinant of age differences in memory performance. In addition, these studies suggest that both quantitative and qualitative age differences in memory performance can be understood in part through reference to age-related shifts in the meaning assigned to the contexts in which memory is used.

SOC Model

The SOC model (e.g., Baltes et al., 1999) is a more formal framework of goal-related processes that describes self-regulatory behavior in terms of three inter-related mechanisms. Selection occurs as individuals choose environments, tasks, and social partners that will promote achievement of personally relevant goals. Selectivity may increase as resources having to do with, for example, time and energy become more constrained. Optimization may occur along with selection as individuals focus on specific behavioral domains and devote resources to optimizing functioning therein. For example, middle-aged adults may devote more time and energy to family and profession and less to leisure-time interests as the demands and importance of the former increase. Finally, compensation may occur as individuals adjust to changes in resources or ability by altering aspirations, changing modes of achievement, or de-emphasizing once-valued domains.

An important aspect of the model reflects a shift in chronic developmental goals from early to late adulthood. In young adulthood, growth-based goals are dominant as individuals seek to develop skills and optimize functioning within a context of relatively abundant resources. In old age, as losses come to dominate gains, there is an increased focus on loss-based goals associated with maintenance of functioning and prevention of loss in valued domains. Perceptions of situations in terms of these goals have been shown to have differential effects on motivation in young and older adults. For example, Freund (2006) assessed task persistence as a measure of motivation and found that younger adults expended more effort in tasks focusing on optimizing performance versus those in which maintenance of previous levels of performance was the goal. In contrast, older adults exhibited the opposite pattern of effort, consistent with the enhanced salience of loss-based goals in later life.

There has not been much systematic research examining memory functioning from an SOC perspective, but several findings are supportive of changing life circumstances influencing goals and the motivation to engage in specific behaviors. For example, Li, Lindenberger, Freund, and Baltes (2001) demonstrated that older adults were more likely to shift resources away from memory-related behaviors in order to support sensorimotor functioning (balance while walking), whereas younger adults did the opposite. This type of selection suggests that, as physical resources become more limited, older adults devalue memory behaviors relative to other important life tasks. An interesting further implication of this finding is that this may then negatively affect memory ability due to decreased frequency of exercising associated skills.

The role of changing life circumstances in selection processes can also be seen in the degree to which individuals engage in compensatory behaviors associated with memory. Longitudinal research has found significant changes in self-reported use of compensatory strategies in older adults; the nature of change is moderated by characteristics of the individual. Thus, for example, poor health is associated with declines in the effort associated with compensation, whereas good health is associated with increases in self-reported effort (Dixon & de Frias, 2004). This may reflect changing goals associated with health, with individuals in poor health shifting resources away from cognitive activities and those in good health working to maintain cognitive functioning.

A similar effect was obtained by Dixon and de Frias (2007) when they compared older individuals who had experienced mild memory loss with those exhibiting no impairment. Participants in the latter group reported increasing their use of external and effort-based compensation activities over time, perhaps again indicating a focus on maintenance in relatively high-functioning older adults. In contrast, those experiencing cognitive difficulties may be withdrawing effort from this domain as they adjust goals to be consistent with changing life circumstances. Thus, consistent with SOC, there is evidence that individuals exhibit memory-related compensation and selection behaviors that appear to be tied to changes in personal resources.

Socioemotional selectivity theory

The chronic goals associated with SOC are rooted in changes in the resources available to support behavior. Whereas declining physical and cognitive capabilities are one source of shifting goals and increased selectivity, it is also reasonable to conceive of resources unrelated to these factors. Thus, as young adults transition into midlife, establish careers, and form families, time as a resource becomes limited, and choices are made based upon personal relevance. Similarly, SST (Carstensen, 1993) posits changes in chronic goals that are not necessarily related to physical and cognitive ability. This theory argues that knowledge-based social goals dominate in young adulthood, where an expansive future time perspective is associated with the formulation of long-term goals. A primary function of social exchanges is thus oriented toward gaining knowledge to achieve these goals. In later life or in other cases where the future time perspective becomes compressed (e.g., terminal illness), affective goals become salient as individuals seek to regulate emotions and maintain positive affect.

In recent years, a substantial body of research has been focused on linking the chronic, emotion-regulation goals proposed by SST with age differences in situational information processing of emotional material. For example, the focus on emotion goals may suggest that aging should be associated with a general increase in attention to emotional information. Indeed, evidence in support of this assertion was obtained by Carstensen and Turk-Charles (1994), who found that age differences in memory were greater for the neutral content of a prose passage than for the emotional content. Proponents of SST further posit that older adults direct their attention either toward positively valenced information or away from negatively valenced information in an effort to maintain a positive emotional state

(Mather & Carstensen, 2005). This directing of attention is then thought to cause older adults to remember more positive or less negative information than their younger counterparts, a phenomenon typically known as the "positivity effect."

Some of the most compelling evidence for the positivity effect in attention comes from Isaacowitz and colleagues' eye-tracking studies (e.g., Isaacowitz, Wadlinger, Goren, & Wilson, 2006). A typical study presents older and younger adults with pairs of synthetic faces: one neutral face paired with one emotional face. Gaze pattern comparisons between young and old have suggested that older adults tend to orient away from negative faces and toward positive faces, but that young adults do not (Isaacowitz et al., 2006). Most importantly, subsequent research has demonstrated that older adults are more likely to show this positivity bias in attention when they are in a negative mood—in stark contrast to young adults who tend to show a mood-congruent attentional bias toward negative faces when they are personally unhappy (Isaacowitz, Toner, Goren, & Wilson, 2008). This suggests that older adults truly are using their attentional gaze as a mood regulation technique.

The positivity bias that was found in attention to faces has in some cases been found in memory for emotional material. For example, in one of the first aging studies to examine emotional memory (Charles, Mather, & Carstensen, 2003), older adults showed dampened memory for negative images, resulting in a larger age difference for negative than for positive photographs. It should be noted, however, that the positivity effect in memory is somewhat unreliable across studies; some researchers failed to find a positivity effect (e.g., Grühn, Smith, & Baltes, 2005) and others found the effect only under certain conditions (Emery & Hess, 2008; Kensinger, 2008) or only in older adults with certain characteristics (Mather & Knight, 2005).

Further complicating the issue, a recent meta-analysis (Murphy & Isaacowitz, 2008) found little consistent evidence for age differences in memory for emotional content. The reasons for this inconsistency in the positivity effect for memory may arise from several possible sources. For example, the great variety of materials used across memory studies may be one source of the discrepancy. In particular, some research has found that positivity effects may be dependent on the personal relevance of the material to older adults (Tomaszczyk, Fernandes, & MacLeod, 2008), with a positivity bias only found for materials that were *less* personally relevant to the older adults.

Another factor that has been found to influence the positivity effect in both attention and memory is executive functioning. Older adults with better executive function have been found to show a greater positivity bias in memory (Mather & Knight, 2005), and they are able to maintain their positive mood better when orienting toward positive faces in the eye-tracking tasks (Isaacowitz, Toner, & Neupert, 2009). These studies are particularly relevant in light of our overarching message: When older adults' personal goals match their current situation, they will be more likely to engage the resources necessary for supporting performance. The SST research suggests a tentative corollary to this thesis: Older adults with the resources to spare may be more effective at engagement.

An interesting perspective relevant to this work comes from recent research suggesting that, in some cases, the positivity effect may reflect age differences in response biases. For example, Werheid et al. (2010) found that both young and older adults exhibited a retrieval bias for emotional content in a study examining face memory, but that this bias was significantly stronger for positive items in older adults. They argued that emotional content may serve as gist information that individuals rely upon when item-specific information is poor, with positive items seeming especially familiar to older adults. Spaniol, Voss, and Grady (2008) obtained similar results in examining recognition memory for words, with older adults exhibiting a familiarity bias for positive information in making memory judgments.

In contrast, younger adults were more likely to exhibit a novelty bias for positive information (e.g., interpreting positive items as "new"). (For related findings, see Kapucu, Rotello, Ready, & Seidl, 2008.) Whereas this work may be somewhat inconsistent with the idea that older adults differentially represent positive versus negative information in memory, it is consistent with the SST notion that aging is associated with preferential processing of positive information.

One major limitation to the SST account of positivity effects should be noted, however. Unlike previous SST research into social preferences and network composition (see Carstensen, Isaacowitz, & Charles, 1999, for a review), there has been a relative dearth of data showing that the positivity effect in memory is a result of a limited time perspective. The one exception of which we are aware is a study that showed that first-year college students (e.g., those for whom there was no approaching "ending") paid more attention to sad faces in the eye-tracking paradigm than did college seniors (e.g., those for whom the end of their college years was approaching; Pruzan & Isaacowitz, 2006).

Selective engagement

An alternative approach to understanding goal-related influences suggests that age differences in memory performance are in part related to older adults being more selective in engaging their cognitive resources in support of performance (Hess, 2006a). This selective engagement hypothesis is based in three simple assumptions. First, individuals across the life span are generally more motivated to engage cognitive resources in those situations that have personal implications (e.g., high in relevance or meaningfulness) relative to those low in such implications (e.g., Petty & Cacioppo, 1984).

Second, sustained cognitive activity is effortful in nature, with consequences to both performance and the individual. The most obvious indicator of such costs is that performance deteriorates over time (e.g., Smit, Eling, & Coenen, 2004). There is also evidence, however, that engagement in effortful activity "depletes" resources, which has an effect on both performance (e.g., Schmeichel, Vohs, & Baumeister, 2003) and the effort exerted in subsequent tasks (e.g., Wright et al., 2007). The physiological consequences of effort can also be seen at the cortical level. Specifically, executive functions require a disproportionate supply of blood glucose to support their operation, resulting in quick depletion relative to other types of cognitive operations (for review, see Gailliot, 2008).

The third and most critical assumption is that the costs of sustained cognitive activity are relatively greater in old age than at earlier points in adulthood due to changes in physical capacities. This assumption can be seen as consistent with Craik's (1986) seminal conceptual framework for understanding the effects of aging and memory. Specifically, he argued that aging was associated with a decline in cognitive resources, which in turn had a negative impact on older adults' performance in situations that required the use of self-initiated memory operations. Thus, for example, age differences were expected to be more prevalent in free-recall tasks than in recognition tasks due to the strategic requirements of the former. This notion of self-initiated processing implies that the relative effort (i.e., costs) associated with memory processing increases with age. A similar notion, but from a somewhat different perspective, suggests that the increased effort required by older adults to process sensory information negatively affects the resources available for subsequent encoding and retrieval operations (e.g., Murphy, Craik, Li, & Schneider, 2000; Tun, McCoy, & Wingfield, 2009).

Other research examining stress-related responses also suggests increasing costs with age. For example, Neupert, Miller, and Lachman (2006) found that older adults display stronger cortisol responses during tests of cognitive ability than do younger adults. There is also evidence that older adults are slower to recover from such stress-related responses (e.g., Seeman & Robbins, 1994). Finally, glucose utilization during effortful memory activity is less efficient in later life, and restoration of blood glucose levels to original levels is more problematic (for review, see Gold, 2005). Taken together, these findings suggest that the physical costs of engaging in cognitive activity increase in later life.

The notion of selective engagement is built upon these three assumptions. Namely, it is hypothesized that the increased costs associated with cognitive engagement in later life heighten the salience of personal goals in interactions with the environment. This, in turn, is hypothesized to increase the impact of the personal implications of the task on resource engagement and performance in older relative to younger adults. In particular, age differences in performance would be expected to be attenuated under conditions of high personal relevance.

Note that selective engagement due to resource availability or costs is not specific to older adults. Younger adults would be expected to exhibit similar trends under conditions associated with resource depletion. Thus, for example, Wright et al. (2007) found that prior engagement in a difficult task resulted in reduced effort in a subsequent, demanding task. Rather, it is assumed that selective engagement reflects a response to a more chronic condition in later life and more situational circumstances in young adulthood. Note also that these selection effects should be exacerbated as task difficulty increases.

Research supportive of selective engagement has proceeded from two perspectives. The first has explored linkages between personal resources and trait-like aspects of motivation, with research supporting the idea that age-related declines in resources negatively affect the motivation to engage in cognitively complex behaviors (Hess, 2001; Hess et al., in press; Hess, Waters, & Bolstad, 2000). For example, Hess et al. (in press) found that declines in physical health were associated with changes in cognitive ability (e.g., working memory) and that the relationship between these two factors was mediated by changes in motivation. In other words, individuals who experienced negative changes in physical health exhibited lower motivation to engage in complex cognitive activity; this in turn influenced the performance on tasks assessing basic cognitive functions. In addition, the strength of the relationship between changing resources and motivation was stronger in later adulthood.

A second line of research focuses on the impact of experimental manipulations of motivation on various aspects of cognitive performance, including memory. Support for selective engagement would be evidenced by motivation being a more powerful determinant of performance with increasing age and age differences in performance being attenuated when motivation is high. One line of research testing these predictions examined person memory (i.e., recall of behaviors performed by others). Previous work on social cognition has demonstrated that behavioral information that is inconsistent with the dominant impression of an individual is recalled better than consistent information (see Stangor & McMillan, 1992). This is thought to reflect the more extensive processing associated with resolving inconsistencies (e.g., why is this honest person taking a wallet from someone's desk?) (e.g., Srull & Wyer, 1989).

In addition, an initial study examining age effects (Hess & Tate, 1991) revealed that older adults did not exhibit this recall advantage for inconsistent information. Such a finding is easily interpreted within the context of standard views of cognitive aging that suggest that reductions in cognitive resources in later life negatively affect self-initiated memory operations that are dependent upon such resources. Hess and Tate also found, however, that when older adults spontaneously performed the appropriate encoding operations, they also exhibited enhanced recall of inconsistencies. In other words, older adults were generally capable of engaging in the appropriate type of processing, but did so less consistently. The question, then, is why?

Hess, Rosenberg, and Waters (2001) subsequently examined whether this inconsistent engagement in effortful encoding operations by older adults could, in part, be explained by motivational factors. In a task similar to that of Hess and Tate (1991), participants aged from 20 to 83 were presented with information about a fictitious target person and were asked to form an impression of this person under different conditions of accountability. In the low accountability condition, participants were tested under standard conditions in which the anonymity of their responses was preserved. In the high accountability condition, however, participants publically shared their impressions with other participants, who evaluated their accuracy. All participants were then asked to recall the target information.

Previous research has shown that social accountability boosts cognitive effort and the complexity of thought in situations where people have sufficient capability to perform well (see Lerner & Tetlock, 1999). Given that older adults are quite capable of making sophisticated social judgments (e.g., Hess, Osowski, & Leclerc, 2005)—an ability that is also consistent with the stereotype of increased wisdom in old age—it was thought that public accountability would enhance the salience of the task.

Consistent with expectations, the pattern of age differences observed by Hess and Tate (1991) was replicated under low-accountability conditions. In contrast, individuals of all ages exhibited a similar recall advantage for impression-inconsistent over -consistent behavioral information when accountability was high. Thus, when sufficiently motivated, older adults appear capable of engaging in the same sorts of effortful memory operations as younger adults. Consistent with the notion of selective engagement, the motivational manipulation also had a stronger impact on older than on younger adults' performance.

One complication in interpreting the results of this study in terms of selective engagement is that motivation is thought to operate at the process level, as reflected in effortful memory operations. Such effects were inferred indirectly by Hess, Osowski, et al. (2005) through reference to performance outcomes (e.g., the strength of the inconsistency effect in memory). To deal with this concern, Hess, Germain, et al. (2009) examined the impact of motivation on specific memory processes using Jacoby's (1998) process dissociation procedure. Through appropriate structuring of tests, memory performance can be partitioned in terms of the influence of relatively automatic processes (e.g., familiarity) versus more effortful processes (e.g., conscious recollection).

Once again examining person memory within the context of an impression formation task, Hess, Germain, et al. (2009) found minimal effects of age or accountability on automatic processes. In contrast, conscious recollection was greater for younger than for older adults and for inconsistent than for consistent behaviors. Of greatest interest, however, was the fact that increased social accountability resulted in a disproportionately greater increase in estimates of conscious recollection for older adults relative to younger adults. This was particularly true when memory for impression-inconsistent behaviors was assessed. Thus, in line with the selective engagement idea, motivational factors differentially influenced older adults' effortful cognitive activities.

In another set of studies, Germain and Hess (2007) also examined process-level effects using a different task and different motivational manipulation. Specifically, they examined how distractibility and reading comprehension were influenced by the personal relevance of the text content. Using a task similar to that employed in Carlson, Hasher, Connelly, and Zacks (1995), young and older adults read text with distracting material interspersed throughout. Reading speed is used as a measure of the efficiency of inhibitory functions, with older adults typically exhibiting greater decrements in speed as a function of the distracting material. Germain and Hess varied the text content so that some passages were more relevant to older adults and others were more relevant to younger adults.

In support of the selective engagement hypothesis, older adults read relevant passages more quickly than irrelevant passages and also exhibited greater comprehension for the former (see Figure 8.2). In contrast, younger adults' performance was unaffected by relevance. These results suggest that older adults' engagement in the task is disproportionately enhanced with an increase in personal relevance, with a concomitant impact on the efficiency of reading and memory for text content. Further evidence that efficiency was enhanced with greater motivation was obtained when memory for distracting information was examined. Younger adults demonstrated similar levels

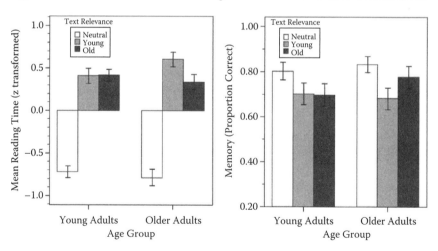

FIGURE 8.2 Reading times and memory (comprehension) scores as a function of participant age and age-group relevance of the text. (From Germain, C. M., and Hess, T. M., 2007, *Aging, Neuropsychology, and Cognition, 14*, 462–486, Experiment 2.) Reading times were standardized within participants to control for age differences in speed. Young- and old-relevant texts contained distracting text, whereas the age-neutral text did not. Bars represent 95% confidence intervals.

of memory for distractors regardless of whether they appeared in relevant or irrelevant passages. In contrast, older adults exhibited poorer memory for distractors appearing in relevant texts than for those in irrelevant texts. This suggests that the enhanced reading speed associated with increased relevance was in part due to more efficient suppression of distracting text.

In sum, these results are consistent with the selective engagement hypothesis in that older adults' memory performance is disproportionately influenced by the personal implications of the task (e.g., accountability, relevance), with age differences in performance attenuated when such implications are high. The motivational impact appears to be specific to cognitively demanding processing mechanisms (e.g., conscious recollection). This suggests that, for example, personal relevance results in increased effort and control of operations during processing.

Similar effects have been observed in other cognitive tasks (e.g., social judgments, decision making), where age differences in performance have been observed to be reduced significantly when (a) the task is personally relevant (Hess, Germain, Rosenberg, Leclerc, & Hodges, 2005), (b) accountability is high (Chen, 2004), and (c) participants report high levels of engagement (Hess, Leclerc, Swaim, & Weatherbee, 2009). It is important to note, however, that the effects of motivation do not necessarily eliminate all age differences in performance. For example, although high accountability did result in older adults remembering inconsistent versus consistent information in a manner similar to that of younger adults, increasing age was still negatively associated with overall levels of memory.

Stereotypes of old age

The contextual approach is particularly relevant in the examination of how cultural stereotypes might impact older adults' performance on a memory test. One of the most pervasive stereotypes in Western culture relates to declining cognitive skills, with memory being a prominent example (e.g., Erber & Prager 1999; Hummert, 1999). In addition, there is accumulating research suggesting that such stereotypes may play an important role in determining age differences in memory performance (for reviews, see Hess, 2006b; McDaniel et al., 2008). It is our contention that such effects might also be construed as goal based. In addition, there are two different mechanisms through which stereotypes might influence memory performance, each of which involves a different type of goal mechanism.

Implicit effects

One way in which stereotypes' influences have been studied is through surreptitious exposure to negative and positive information about aging. In an initial study, Levy (1996) gave young and older adults an initial set of memory tests (recall of words, activity-photo pairs, and dots in a spatial array), subliminally exposed them to words relating to positive or negative age stereotypes, and retested their memory. She found minimal priming effects in younger adults. In contrast, older adults—for whom the stereotype was personally relevant—exhibited stereotype congruent change on several indicators of memory, although the pattern of change was somewhat inconsistent. Stein, Blanchard-Fields, and Hertzog (2002) used a similar procedure, but only partially replicated Levy (1996), with effects being specific to the negative stereotype on one task.

Hess, Hinson, and Statham (2004) examined implicit stereotype effects using a more traditional memory task: free recall of a list of words. Using two different means of implicit priming—a sentence-scramble task (Experiment 1) or a lexical decision task (Experiment 2)—to activate aging stereotypes prior to the free-recall test, they found that older adults exposed to negative stereotypes recalled approximately 13% fewer words than participants exposed to positive stereotypes. Younger adults' recall was unaffected by the priming manipulation. In addition, age differences in recall in the positive condition were attenuated in Experiment 1 and eliminated in Experiment 2. The results of these experiments suggest that implicit stereotype activation may be an important determinant of age differences in performance in conditions where subtle cues about aging stereotypes are present (e.g., laboratory conditions in the typical study on memory and aging).

Implicit priming effects such as these have been viewed as reflections of ideomotor responses (James, 1890), in which activation of a semantic construct (e.g., aging stereotype) leads to activation of associated behaviors (e.g., slowing) (e.g., Bargh et al., 1996). Similar effects have been observed with goals, with implicit activation leading to engagement in goal-consistent behaviors (e.g., Bargh, Gollwitzer, Lee-Chai, Barndollar, & Troetschel, 2001). These similarities suggest that the implicit priming effects associated with aging stereotypes may be similar to the effects associated with implicit goals. Bargh et al. (2001) argue that the effects are somewhat different in that, for example, stereotype-priming effects dissipate over time, whereas goal-priming effects may be maintained until the goal is fulfilled.

It might be argued, however, that the age specificity observed for priming effects in Levy (1996) and Hess at al. (2001) suggests that there is something more to these effects than simple semantic priming of behavioral responses. Specifically, the self-relevant nature of the stereotypes may lead to greater salience of and sensitivity to situational cues in older adults, leading to higher probability of activation and perhaps longer duration. This may result in more goal-like effects, with older adults motivated to behave in a manner that fulfills the goal of "acting like an older adult."

Explicit effects

Stereotypes may also influence behavior through more explicit activation processes through a phenomenon known as *stereotype threat*. Stereotype threat can occur when an individual who is a member of a stereotyped group is performing a task that is thought to be diagnostic of the stereotyped ability (Steele, 1997). This threat can cause an individual to perform below what he or she would otherwise be capable of because the individual may be concerned with potentially confirming that negative stereotype. Much of the general stereotype threat literature focuses on how threat can handicap performance of African Americans and women in academic contexts (for review, see Steele, Spencer, & Aronson, 2002). We argue that stereotype threat also has the potential to handicap older adults' performance on standard laboratory memory tests, thus exaggerating age differences in memory.

Stereotype threat theory would predict that when older adults are made aware of their status as an "older adult" and when they are aware that the test they are taking is meant to test their memory, these broad cultural stereotypes should have a negative impact on their performance. A common laboratory setup, where older adults are recruited for studies about "memory and aging" and given subsequent memory tests, could unintentionally create ideal conditions for producing stereotype threat. A growing body of research has examined this possibility and attempted to determine what other contextual factors might influence the impact of stereotype threat on older adults' memory.

In an initial study, Rahhal, Hasher, and Colcombe (2001) found that age differences in performance on a memory test were significantly reduced when the diagnostic value of the test with respect to the negative aging stereotype was de-emphasized through relabeling of the task. A potential concern with interpretation of their results, however, had to do with the fact that attenuation of the age effect appeared to be in part due to a reduction in younger adults' performance in the nondiagnostic test condition rather than to enhanced performance in older adults.

In a more direct test of stereotype threat effects, Hess, Auman, Colcombe, and Rahhal (2003) examined whether explicitly activating negative cultural stereotypes in older adults would indeed impair performance on a subsequent free-recall test. Older and younger adults were randomly assigned to one of three conditions: negative aging stereotype, positive aging stereotype, and a control condition. Before taking the free-recall test, participants in the experimental conditions read a newspaper article that summarized research on aging and memory in a negative way (e.g., "in order to maintain adequate levels of functioning, older adults may have to increasingly depend upon the help of memory tools as well as friends and family") or a positive way (e.g., "these findings suggest that the degree of memory loss is to a certain extent under control of the environment and the individual"). Participants in the control condition were not exposed to either article before the memory test.

As predicted, the results of the free-recall memory test indicated the presence of stereotype threat effects in the older adults (see Figure 8.3). That

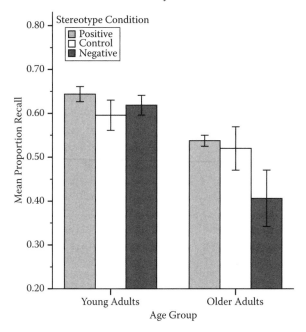

FIGURE 8.3 Proportion recall as a function of positive, neutral, or negative aging stereotype activation. (Hess, T. M. et al., 2003, *Journal of Gerontology: Psychological Sciences, 58B,* 3–1.) Bars represent 95% confidence intervals.

is, although the memory performance of young adults did not vary across conditions, older adults in the negative condition recalled fewer words than older adults in the positive condition. Moreover, statistically significant age differences in memory were found only in the negative condition.

Having established that stereotype threat effects can be found in older adults' memory performance, we now turn to the questions of *how* stereotype threat might impair older adults' memory, and what factors might moderate stereotype threat effects.

Mediators of threat

In the broader stereotype threat literature, a variety of possible mechanisms have been proposed as possible mediators of threat effects. These have included (in part) the possibility that threat decreases working memory capacity (e.g., Schmader & Johns, 2003), increases anxiety (e.g., Osborne, 2001), and/or increases intrusive negative thoughts (e.g., Cadinu, Maass, Rosabianca, & Kiesner, 2005). In the case of older adults' memory performance, Hess and colleagues have found evidence that threat may cause less effective strategy use (Hess et al., 2003) and may also result in changes in people's beliefs and concerns about memory (Hess & Hinson, 2006).

For example, Hess et al. (2003) found that the impact of threat condition on recall was partially mediated by the amount of semantic clustering older adults' used. This suggests that threat disrupts effective strategy use in older adults. Consistent with this conclusion, Kang and Chasteen (2009) found that threat effects were evident in free recall of a prose passage, but not when memory was tested via cued recall or recognition. Hess and Hinson (2006) found that participants exposed to negative aging stereotypes showed reduced scores on the memory controllability index and increased scores on the aging concerns scale (Lachman, Bandura, Weaver, & Elliot, 1995); participants exposed to positive aging stereotypes showed the opposite pattern. Interestingly, threat does not seem to be mediated by more general anxiety or affective responses: Several studies have failed to find evidence of differences in broad affective responses across threat conditions (Hess, Emery, & Queen, 2009; Hess & Hinson, 2006). Threat so far appears to have a relatively specific effect on task-relevant outcomes.

These effects appear to be consistent with the view that threat may operate through reductions in working memory (Schmader, Johns, & Forbes, 2008) as, for example, self-evaluative concerns (e.g., beliefs about one's memory ability) and associated regulatory processes consume resources that interfere with effective strategy use (e.g., clustering). Consistent with this notion, research has also shown that subjective feelings of threat mediate the effects of age on memory performance (Chasteen, Bhattacharyya, Horhota, Tam, & Hasher, 2005) and that feelings of threat are associated with stronger threat-based effects on memory (Kang & Chasteen, 2009). An alternative perspective is that threat effects may be a motivated response to the test situation. We elaborate on this possibility later.

Moderators of threat

Threat effects in older adults have also been found to vary depending on both personal characteristics (e.g., memory achievement motivation, age) and task demands (e.g., type of stereotype activation, time pressure). For example, consistent with the hypothesis that threat effects should be particularly strong in people who identify with the stereotyped ability (Steele, 1997), Hess et al. (2003) found that threat effects were greatest in older adults who placed high value on their memory ability. Thus, those most vulnerable to threat effects may be the people most vested in their memory performance. The finding by Hess, Hinson, and Hodges (2009) that threat effects were greatest in older adults with higher levels of education may represent a similar phenomenon: High education is associated with placing greater value on one's cognitive ability.

One interesting aspect of age-based stereotypes is that age, unlike race or sex, is a characteristic that changes over time. Because of this, being "old" may be more salient at certain times than others as the identification with the stereotyped group changes. In a study examining threat effects on memory across the adult life span, Hess and Hinson (2006) found that threat effects were greater in the young-old than in the old-old. This may occur because being a "new" member of the stereotyped group makes the stereotype more salient as one learns to cope with this new part of the identity. In contrast, middle-aged adults experienced less of an effect of threat on performance than did the young-old. This may reflect a stereotype lift effect (Walton & Cohen, 2003), in which middle-aged adults benefited from contrasting themselves with those who are "old."

Finally, characteristics of the particular task may moderate threat effects as well. We have recently found that imposing an additional constraint on responding may exacerbate threat effects (Hess, Emery, & Queen, 2009). This study examined threat effects on recognition accuracy under time pressure. Threat effects were only found when participants had to respond under deadline pressure, with those in the threat condition showing reduced corrected recognition and reduced "remember" responses (see Tulving, 1985) relative to those in the nonthreat condition. Because age differences in recognition are generally smaller than those found for recall, an additional task constraint may have been necessary to find a negative impact of threat on memory.

In sum, threat may be more "threatening" to old adults (a) who place high value on their memory, (b) who are under demanding and highly constrained task conditions, and (c) for whom identity as an older adult is relatively novel and salient.

Motivational consequences of threat

As mentioned previously, an alternative interpretation of threat effects is a motivational one that draws from ideas about selective engagement and regulatory focus. Specifically, one characteristic of threat is that it is most evident in individuals who value their memory (Hess et al., 2003) or are high in education (Hess, Hinson, & Hodges, 2009). These effects are analogous to the previously discussed findings that older adults will be more engaged in situations that are personally meaningful. In contrast to those situations, however, engagement in this case leads to poorer performance.

It might be argued that engagement in certain situations will lead to performance deficits when evaluation concerns are heightened. It may also be the case, however, that older adults respond to threat-based situations by changing their approach to the task. For example, Seibt and Förster (2004) found that threat was associated with adoption of a prevention regulatory focus. In contrast to a promotion focus, where the motivation is on maximizing success, prevention focus is concerned with avoiding failure. This may be accomplished by adopting more conservative response criteria in a memory task, which could reduce overall level of performance while reducing memory errors.

At present, there are no studies specifically investigating this possibility. However, our finding that older adults perform more poorly and have reduced "remember" responses in a speeded recognition task (Hess, Emery, & Queen, 2009) could be interpreted as consistent with this, with the reduction in remember responses suggesting greater caution. Our main point here is that it may be possible to interpret so-called stereotype threat effects within the selective engagement framework as the self-implications of the situation determine the degree of engagement. The nature and consequences of this motivated response have yet to be understood clearly.

CONCLUSIONS

This chapter adopted an approach to understanding aging effects on memory somewhat different from what is typically found in the literature. Consistent with a lifespan contextualist approach, age differences in memory performance were examined in light of changing life circumstances and individuals' adaptive—and occasionally maladaptive—responses to these circumstances. We attempted to conceptualize such responses in terms of age-related goals and associated selection effects that determine both level of engagement and direction of processing. In doing so, we found clear support for the importance of motivational factors in determining age differences in memory performance.

Four different goal-based conceptual frameworks were used to explore the literature, and each provided a means for understanding various aspects of memory functioning in later life. Thus, for example, age differences in differential focus on content varying in emotional qualities and self-relevance can be explained in terms of changes in shifting importance of socioemotional goals associated with future time perspective and changes in the salience of personal goals with changes in resources in later life. Changes in involvement in specific types of memory tasks, including engagement in compensatory activities, may also be understood in terms of adjustments in the priority that individuals assign to memory functioning and correspondence of activities with growth versus maintenance of functioning. Reference to goals also helps to explain situational variability in the strength of age differences in performance by considering the degree to which the task either meshes with age-related social roles or has personal implications. Goal-related processes might even help us to understand some apparently negative memory outcomes. Thus, although speculative at this point, the negative impact of stereotype threat in older adults might be related to the increased salience of personal goals associated with memory functioning.

The contextual focus in the study of memory and aging can be beneficial in several ways. First, the consideration of multiple distal and proximal influences provides a more complete picture of memory functioning in later life. This may be crucial to the extent that it helps to highlight factors associated with poor memory functioning, which in turn helps inform us about avenues of intervention. Of particular interest is the possibility that certain social factors might prove to be relatively productive targets for remediation attempts.

The work discussed in this chapter also emphasizes the importance of considering memory as part of a broader constellation of abilities and behaviors that contribute to and are reflective of adaptive functions. Thus, for example, instead of just focusing on ability, the SOC model provides a framework for understanding the circumstances under which older adults might choose not to exercise memory skills or to engage in efforts at compensation, both of which have implications for maintenance of functioning.

Likewise, the selective engagement perspective helps to explain the apparent increase in cross-situational variability in memory performance in older adults as a mechanism of resource conservation. In fact, the explanation of variability in older adults' memory performance across different situations may be one of the most important aspects of a contextual perspective. Older adults appear to be more sensitive than younger adults to the contexts in which they are functioning, altering their level of engagement and specificity of behavior in a manner that is specific not only to their available resources and personal interests, but also to the social roles played by members of the older generation.

This situational variability also highlights the important role that a contextual perspective takes when assessment issues are considered. Studies examining age differences in ability typically assess skills using tasks that are relatively devoid of meaning and that are assumed to be equally motivating for young and older adults. The research discussed in this chapter suggests that the social context and the interaction with personal goals are going to be important determinants of both older adults' levels of performance and the strength of any observed age effects. Research on stereotype threat has indicated that activation of positive versus negative aging stereotypes in a typical laboratory testing context can alter older adults' free-recall performance by as much as 15% (e.g., Hess et al., 2003). If recruitment methods and instructions in studies of aging activate such stereotypes (e.g., "the purpose of this study is to examine the effects of aging on memory"), our estimates of age effects may be exaggerated and not reflective of true abilities.

Similar effects may be present in tasks that are not personally meaningful. Note that we are not arguing that age differences in performance can be accounted for solely by factors such as interactions between personal goals and testing context. Even in studies where age differences are significantly attenuated by controlling for such effects, younger adults still typically outperform older adults. Rather, the point is that we may not get an accurate understanding of older adults' competencies when context is not taken into account.

The research presented in this chapter was primarily of the behavioral variety. More recent neuroscience approaches, however, might provide some important insights into the processes described herein. Neuroimaging work relevant to the study of motivational processes in later life is relatively rare. Some work has been done with reactions to emotional stimuli, with a pattern emerging of age differences in responses of the amygdala and prefrontal cortex that appear to reflect an increase in controlled processing of emotional information in later life (St. Jacques, Bessette-Symons, & Cabeza, 2009). Such a pattern is consistent with SST in suggesting that there is an increased emphasis on emotion regulation in later life.

There is also work suggestive of compensatory processes in older adults, who appear to recruit additional processing resources to support high levels of performance when compared with younger adults (e.g., Cabeza, 2002). Such a finding could illustrate the types of compensatory processes discussed in the SOC model, but the interpretation of these effects is still somewhat in doubt. It would be interesting to see if such compensatory processing was more likely in those who were concerned with maintaining current levels of memory functioning.

We were unable to identify any neuroscience research on aging and motivation. Research with younger adults, however, has indicated that high levels of motivation are associated with increased levels of activation in cortical areas associated with working memory and executive functions (Gilbert & Fiez, 2004; Locke & Braver, 2008; Pochon et al., 2002). In addition, several studies have also identified increased activation of areas associated with motivation and self-reflection (Bengtsson, Lau, & Passingham, 2009; Szatkowska, Bogorodzki, Wolak, Marchewka, & Szeszkowski, 2008), suggesting that these areas may be involved in recalibrating available resources to increase levels of performance (Pessoa, 2009). Studies linking behavioral changes in performance to changes in patterns of cortical activation such as these would be valuable in validating the sort of goal-based phenomena discussed in the chapter.

Taking a more global perspective, understanding of aging effects on memory might also be facilitated by examining interactions between the social context and performance. For example, cross-cultural research focusing on societies with more positive versus negative views of aging might foster a better understanding of the role played by aging stereotypes. The main point here is that an incomplete picture of memory and aging is provided by a limited focus on a single set of distal or proximal influences.

ACKNOWLEDGMENT

Writing of this chapter was supported in part by NIH/NIA grants AG05552 (Hess) and AG020153 (Hess and Emery).

REFERENCES

Adams, C. (1991). Qualitative age differences in memory for text: A life-span developmental perspective. *Psychology and Aging, 6,* 323–336.

Adams, C., Labouvie-Vief, G., Hobart, C. J., & Dorosz, M. (1990). Adult age group differences in story recall style. *Journal of Gerontology: Psychological Sciences, 45,* P17–P27.

Adams, C., Smith, M. C., Nyquist, L., & Perlmutter, M. (1997). Adult age-group differences in recall for the literal and interpretive meanings of narrative text. *Journal of Gerontology: Psychological Sciences, 52B,* P187–P195.

Adams, C., Smith, M. C., Pasupathi, M., & Vitolo, L. (2002). Social context effects on story recall in older and younger women: Does the listener make a difference? *Journal of Gerontology: Psychological Sciences, 57B,* P28–P40.

Altgassen, M., Kliegel, M., Brandimonte, M., & Filippello, P. (2010). Are older adults more social than younger adults? Social importance increases older adults' prospective memory performance. *Aging, Neuropsychology, and Cognition, 17,* 312–328.

Baltes, P. B. (1987). Theoretical propositions of life-span developmental psychology: On the dynamics between growth and decline. *Developmental Psychology, 23,* 611–626.

Baltes, P. B., Staudinger, U. M., & Lindenberger, U. (1999). Lifespan psychology: Theory and application to intellectual functioning. *Annual Review of Psychology, 50,* 471–507.

Bargh, J. A., Chen, M., & Burrows, L. (1996). The automaticity of social behavior: Direct effects of trait concept and stereotype activation on action. *Journal of Personality and Social Psychology, 71,* 230–244.

Bargh, J. A., Gollwitzer, P. M., Lee-Chai, A., Barndollar, K., & Troetschel, R. (2001). The automated will: Nonconscious activation and pursuit of behavioral goals. *Journal of Personality and Social Psychology, 81,* 1014–1027.

Bengtsson, S. L., Lau, H. C., & Passingham, R. R. (2009). Motivation to do well enhances responses to errors and self-monitoring. *Cerebral Cortex, 19,* 797–804.

Cabeza, R. (2002). Hemispheric asymmetry reduction in older adults: The HAROLD model. *Psychology and Aging, 17,* 85–100.

Cadinu, M., Maass, A., Rosabianca, A., & Kiesner, J. (2005). Why do women underperform under stereotype threat? Evidence for the role of negative thinking. *Psychological Science, 16,* 572–578.

Carlson, M. C., Hasher, L., Connelly, S. L., & Zacks, R. T. (1995). Aging, distraction, and the benefits of predictable location. *Psychology and Aging, 10,* 427–436.

Carstensen, L. L. (1993). Motivation for social contact across the life span: A theory of socioemotional selectivity. In J. Jacobs (Ed.), *Nebraska symposium on motivation: Vol. 40. Developmental perspectives on motivation* (pp. 209–254). Lincoln, NE: University of Nebraska Press.

Carstensen, L. L., Isaacowitz, D. M., & Charles, S. T. (1999). Taking time seriously: A theory of socioemotional selectivity. *American Psychologist, 54,* 165–181.

Carstensen, L. L., & Turk-Charles, S. (1994). The salience of emotion across the adult life span. *Psychology and Aging, 9,* 259–264.

Charles, S. T., Mather, M., & Carstensen, L. L. (2003). Aging and emotional memory: The forgettable nature of negative images for older adults. *Journal of Experimental Psychology: General, 132,* 310–324.

Chasteen, A. L., Bhattacharyya, S., Horhota, M., Tarn, R., & Hasher, L. (2005). How feelings of stereotype threat influence older adults' memory performance. *Experimental Aging Research, 31,* 235–260.

Chen, Y. (2004). Age differences in the correction of social judgments: Source monitoring and timing of accountability. *Aging, Neuropsychology, and Cognition, 11,* 58–67.

Colcombe, S., Erickson, K. I., Raz, N., Webb, A. G., Cohen, N. J., McAuley, E., & Kramer, A. F. (2003). Aerobic fitness reduces brain tissue loss in aging humans. *Journal of Gerontology: Medical Sciences, 58A,* 176–180.

Colcombe, S., & Kramer, A. F. (2003). Fitness effects on the cognitive function of older adults: A meta-analytic study. *Psychological Science, 14,* 125–130.

Craik, F. I. M. (1986). A functional account of age differences in memory. In F. Klix & H. Hagendorf (Eds.), *Human memory and cognitive capabilities, mechanisms, and performance* (pp. 409–422). Amsterdam, the Netherlands: North-Holland.

Dennis, N. A., & Cabeza, R. (2008). Neuroimaging of healthy cognitive aging. In F. I. M. Craik & T. A. Salthouse (Eds.), *The handbook of aging and cognition* (3rd ed., pp. 1–54). New York: Psychology Press.

Dixon, R. A., & de Frias, C. (2004). The Victoria longitudinal study: From characterizing cognitive aging to illustrating changes in memory compensation. *Aging, Neuropsychology, and Cognition, 11,* 346–376.

Dixon, R. A., & de Frias, C. M. (2007). Mild memory deficits differentially affect 6-year changes in compensatory strategy use. *Psychology and Aging, 22,* 632–638.

Emery, L., & Hess, T. M. (2008). Viewing instructions impact emotional memory differently in older and young adults. *Psychology and Aging, 23,* 2–12.

Erber, J. T., & Prager, I. G. (1999). Age and memory: Perceptions of forgetful young and older adults. In T. M. Hess & F. Blanchard-Fields (Eds.). *Social cognition and aging* (pp. 197–217). San Diego, CA: Academic Press.

Freund, A. M. (2006). Age-differential motivational consequences of optimization versus compensation focus in younger and older adults. *Psychology and Aging, 21,* 240–252.

Freund, A. M., & Baltes, P. B. (2002). Life-management strategies of selection, optimization, and compensation: Measurement by self-report and construct validity. *Journal of Personality and Social Psychology, 82,* 642–662.

Gailliot, M. T. (2008). Unlocking the energy dynamics of executive functioning: Linking executive functioning to brain glycogen. *Perspectives on Psychological Science, 3,* 245–263.

Germain, C. M., & Hess, T. M. (2007). Motivational influences on controlled processing: Moderating distractibility in older adults. *Aging, Neuropsychology, and Cognition, 14,* 462–486.

Gilbert, A. M., & Fiez, J. A. (2004). Integrating reward and cognition in the frontal cortex. *Cognitive, Affective, and Behavioral Neuroscience, 4,* 540–552.

Gold, P. E. (2005). Glucose and age-related changes in memory. *Neurobiology of Aging, 26S,* S60–S64.

Greve, W., & Bjorklund, D. F. (2009). The Nestor effect: Extending evolutionary developmental psychology to a lifespan perspective. *Developmental Review,* *29,* 163–79.

Grühn, D., Smith, J., & Baltes, P. B. (2005). No aging bias favoring memory for positive material: Evidence from a heterogeneity–homogeneity list paradigm using emotionally toned words. *Psychology and Aging, 20,* 579–588.

Hertzog, C., & Hultsch, D. F. (2000). Metacognition in adulthood and old age. In F. I. M. Craik & T. A. Salthouse (Eds.), *The handbook of aging and cognition* (pp. 417–466). Mahwah, NJ: Lawrence Erlbaum Associates.

Hertzog, C., Kramer, A. F., Wilson, R. S., & Lindenberger, U. (2009). Enrichment effects on adult cognitive development: Can the functional capacity of older adults be preserved and enhanced? *Psychological Science in the Public Interest, 9,* 1–65.

Hess, T. M. (2001). Aging-related influences on personal need for structure. *International Journal of Behavioral Development, 25,* 482–490.

Hess, T. M. (2005). Memory and aging in context. *Psychological Bulletin, 131,* 383–406.

Hess, T. M. (2006a). Adaptive aspects of social cognitive functioning in adulthood: Age-related goal and knowledge influences. *Social Cognition, 24,* 279–309.

Hess, T. M. (2006b). Attitudes toward aging and their effects in behavior. In J. E. Birren & K. E. Schaire, (Eds.), *Handbook of the psychology of aging* (pp. 379–406). Amsterdam, the Netherlands: Elsevier.

Hess, T. M., Auman, C., Colcombe, S. J., & Rahhal, T. A. (2003). The impact of stereotype threat on age differences in memory performance. *Journal of Gerontology: Psychological Sciences, 58B,* 3–11.

Hess, T.M., Emery, L., & Neupert, S. (in press). Longitudinal relationships between resources, motivation, and cognitive functioning. *The Journals of Gerontology: Series B: Psychological Sciences and Social Sciences.*

Hess, T. M., Emery, L., & Queen, T. (2009). Task demands moderate stereotype threat effects on memory performance. *The Journals of Gerontology: Series B: Psychological Sciences and Social Sciences, 64B,* 482–486.

Hess, T. M., Germain, C. M., Rosenberg, D. C., Leclerc, C. M., & Hodges, E. A. (2005). Aging-related selectivity and susceptibility to irrelevant affective information in the construction of attitudes. *Aging, Neuropsychology, and Cognition, 12,* 149–174.

Hess, T. M., Germain, C. M., Swaim, E. L., & Osowski, N. L. (2009). Aging and selective engagement: The moderating impact of motivation on older adults' resource utilization. *Journal of Gerontology: Psychological Sciences, 64B,* 447–456.

Hess, T. M., & Hinson, J. T. (2006). Age-related variation in the influences of aging stereotypes on memory in adulthood. *Psychology and Aging, 21,* 621–625.

Hess, T. M., Hinson, J. T., & Hodges, E. A. (2009). Moderators of and mechanisms underlying stereotype threat effects on older adults' memory performance. *Experimental Aging Research, 35,* 153–177.

Hess, T. M., Hinson, J. T., & Statham, J. A. (2004). Implicit and explicit stereotype activation effects on memory: Do age and awareness moderate the impact of priming? *Psychology and Aging, 19,* 495–505.

Hess, T. M., Leclerc, C. M., Swaim, E., & Weatherbee, S. R. (2009). Aging and everyday judgments: The impact of motivational and processing resource factors. *Psychology and Aging, 24,* 735–740.

Hess, T. M., Osowski, N. L., & Leclerc, C. M. (2005). Age and experience influences on the complexity of social inferences. *Psychology and Aging, 20,* 447–459.

Hess, T. M., Rosenberg, D. C., & Waters, S. J. (2001). Motivation and representational processes in adulthood: The effects of social accountability and information relevance. *Psychology and Aging, 16,* 629–642.

Hess, T. M., & Tate, C. S. (1991). Adult age differences in explanations and memory for behavioral information. *Psychology & Aging, 6,* 86–92.

Hess, T. M., Waters, S. J., & Bolstad, S. A. (2000). Motivational and cognitive influences on affective priming in adulthood. *Journal of Gerontology: Psychological Sciences, 55B,* P193–P204.

Hummert, M. L. (1999). A social cognitive perspective on age stereotypes. In T. M. Hess & F. Blanchard-Fields (Eds.), *Social cognition and aging* (pp. 175–196). San Diego, CA: Academic Press.

Isaacowitz, D. M., Toner, K., Goren, D., & Wilson, H. R. (2008). Looking while unhappy: Mood congruent gaze in young adults, positive gaze in older adults. *Psychological Science, 19,* 848–853.

Isaacowitz, D. M., Toner, K., & Neupert, S. D. (2009). Use of gaze for real-time mood regulation: Effects of age and attentional focus. *Psychology and Aging, 24,* 989–994.

Isaacowitz, D. M., Wadlinger, H. A., Goren, D., & Wilson, H. R. (2006). Selective preference in visual fixation away from negative images in old age? An eye-tracking study. *Psychology and Aging, 21,* 40–48.

Jacoby, L. L. (1998). Invariance in automatic influences on memory: Toward a user's guide for the process-dissociation procedure. *Journal of Experimental Psychology: Learning, Memory, and Cognition, 24,* 3–26.

James, W. (1890). *Principles of psychology* (*Vol. 2*). New York, NY: Holt.

Kang, S. K., & Chasteen, A. L. (2009). The moderating role of age-group identification and perceived threat on stereotype threat among older adults. *The International Journal of Aging & Human Development, 69,* 201–220.

Kapucu, A., Rotello, C. M., Ready, R. E., & Seidl, K. N. (2008). Response bias in "remembering" emotional stimuli: A new perspective on age differences. *Journal of Experimental Psychology: Learning, Memory, and Cognition, 34,* 703–711.

Kensinger, E. A. (2008). Age differences in memory for arousing and nonarousing emotional words. *Journals of Gerontology: Series B: Psychological Sciences and Social Sciences, 63B,* P13–P18.

Krampe, R. T., & Charness, N. (2006). Aging and expertise. In K. A. Ericsson, N. Charness, P. J. Feltovich, & R. R. Hoffman (Eds.), *The Cambridge handbook of expertise and expert performance* (pp. 723–742). New York, NY: Cambridge University Press.

Labouvie-Vief, G. (1990). Modes of knowledge and the organization of development. In M. L. Commons, C. Armon, L. Kohlberg, F. A. Richards, T. A. Grotzer, & J. Sinnott (Eds.), *Adult development: Models and methods in the study of adolescent and adult thought* (*Vol. 2,* pp. 43–62). New York, NY: Praeger.

Lachman, M. E. (2006). Perceived control over aging-related declines: Adaptive beliefs and behaviors. *Current directions in Psychological Science, 15,* 282–286.

Lachman, M. E., Bandura, M., Weaver, S. L., & Elliott, E. (1995). Assessing memory control beliefs: The Memory Controllability Inventory. *Aging and Cognition, 2,* 67–84.

Lerner, J. S., & Tetlock, P. E. (1999). Accounting for the effects of accountability. *Psychological Bulletin, 125,* 255–275.

Levy, B. (1996). Improving memory in old age by implicit self-stereotyping. *Journal of Personality & Social Psychology, 71,* 1092–1107.

Levy, B. R., & Langer, E. (1994). Aging free from negative stereotypes: Successful memory in China and among the American deaf. *Journal of Personality and Social Psychology, 66,* 989–997.

Levy, B. R., Zonderman, A. B., Slade, M. D., & Ferrucci, L. (2009). Age stereotypes held earlier in life predict cardiovascular events in later life. *Psychological Science, 20,* 296–298.

Li, K. Z. H., Lindenberger, U., Freund, A. M., & Baltes, P. B. (2001). Walking while memorizing: Age-related differences in compensatory behavior. *Psychological Science, 12,* 230–237.

Locke, H. S., & Braver, T. S. (2008). Motivational influences on cognitive control: Behavior, brain activation, and individual differences. *Cognitive, Affective, and Behavioral Neuroscience, 8,* 99–112.

Lupien, S., De Leon, M. J., de Santi, S., Convit, A., Tarshish, C., Nair, N. P. V., et al. (1998). Cortisol levels during human aging predict atrophy and memory deficits. *Nature Neuroscience, 1,* 69–73.

Mather, M., & Carstensen, L. L. (2005). Aging and motivated cognition: The positivity effect in attention and memory. *Trends in Cognitive Sciences, 9,* 496–502.

Mather, M., & Knight, M. R. (2005). Goal-directed memory: The role of cognitive control in older adults' emotional memory. *Psychology and Aging, 20,* 554–570.

McDaniel, M. A., Einstein, G. O., & Jacoby, L. L. (2008). New considerations in aging and memory: The glass may be half full. In F. I. M. Craik & T. A. Salthouse (Eds.), *The handbook of aging and cognition* (pp. 251–310). New York, NY: Psychology Press.

McGue, M., & Johnson, W. (2008). Genetics of cognitive aging. In F. I. M. Craik & T. A. Salthouse (Eds.), *The handbook of aging and cognition* (pp. 55–96). New York, NY: Psychology Press.

Mergler, N., & Goldstein, M. D. (1983). Why are there old people? Senescence as biological and cultural preparedness for the transmission of information. *Human Development, 26,* 72–90.

Murphy, D. R., Craik, F. I. M., Li, K. Z. H., & Schneider, B. A. (2000). Comparing the effects of aging and background noise on short-term memory performance. *Psychology and Aging, 15,* 323–334.

Murphy, N. A., & Isaacowitz, D. M. (2008). Preferences for emotional information in older and younger adults: A meta-analysis of memory and attention tasks. *Psychology and Aging, 23,* 263–286.

Neupert, S. D., Miller, L. M. S., & Lachman, M. E. (2006). Physiological reactivity to cognitive stressors: Variations by age and socioeconomic status. *International Journal of Aging and Human Development, 62,* 221–235.

Osborne, J. W. (2001). Testing stereotype threat: Does anxiety explain race and sex differences in achievement? *Contemporary Educational Psychology, 26,* 291–310.

Pessoa, L. (2009). How do emotion and motivation direct executive control? *Trends in Cognitive Sciences, 13,* 160–166.

Petty, R. E., & Cacioppo, J. T. (1984). The effects of involvement on responses to argument quantity and quality: Central and peripheral routes to persuasion. *Journal of Personality and Social Psychology, 46,* 69–81.

Pochon, J. B., Levy, R., Fossati, P., Lehericy, S., Poline, J. B., Pillon, B.,... Dubois, B. (2002). The neural system that bridges reward and cognition in humans: An fMRI study. *Proceedings of the National Academy of Sciences, 99,* 5669–5674.

Pruzan, K., & Isaacowitz, D. M. (2006). An attentional application of socioemotional selectivity theory in college students. *Social Development, 15,* 326–338.

Rahhal, T. A., Hasher, L., & Colcombe, S. J. (2001). Instructional manipulations and age differences in memory: Now you see them, now you don't. *Psychology and Aging, 16,* 697–706.

Schmader, T., & Johns, M. (2003). Converging evidence that stereotype threat reduces working memory capacity. *Journal of Personality and Social Psychology, 85,* 440–452.

Schmader, T., Johns, M., & Forbes, C. (2008). An integrated process model of stereotype threat effects on performance. *Psychological Review, 115,* 336–356.

Schmeichel, B. J., Vohs, K. D., & Baumeister, R. F. (2003). Intellectual performance and ego depletion: Role of the self in logical reasoning and other information processing. *Journal of Personality and Social Psychology, 85,* 33–46.

Schooler, C., Mulatu, M. S., & Oates, G. (1999). The continuing effects of substantively complex work on the intellectual functioning of older workers. *Psychology and Aging, 14,* 483–506.

Seeman, T. E., McEwen, B. S., Singer, B. H., Albert, M. S., & Rowe, J. W. (1997). Increase in urinary cortisol excretion and memory declines: MacArthur studies of successful aging. *Journal of Clinical Endocrinology and Metabolism, 82,* 2458–2465.

Seeman, T.E., & Robbins, R.J. (1994). Aging and hypothalamic-pituitary-adrenal response to challenge in humans. *Endocrinology Review, 15,* 233–60.

Seibt, B., & Förster, J. (2004). Stereotype threat and performance: How self stereotypes influence processing by inducing regulatory foci. *Journal of Personality and Social Psychology, 87,* 38–56.

Smit, A. S., Eling, P., & Coenen, A. M. L. (2004). Mental effort affects vigilance enduringly: After-effects in EEG and behavior. *International Journal of Psychophysiology, 53,* 239–243.

Spaniol, J., Voss, A., & Grady, C. L. (2008). Aging and emotional memory: Cognitive mechanisms underlying the positivity effect. *Psychology and Aging, 23,* 859–872.

Spiro, A., III, & Brady, C. B. (2008). Integrating health into cognitive aging research and theory: Quo vadis? In S. M. Hofer & D. F. Alwin (Eds.), *Handbook of cognitive aging: Interdisciplinary perspectives* (pp. 260–283). Los Angeles, CA: Sage.

Srull, T. K., & Wyer, R. S., Jr. (1989). Person memory and judgment. *Psychological Review, 96,* 58–83.

St. Jacques, P. L., Bessette-Symons, B., & Cabeza, R. (2009). Functional neuroimaging studies of aging and emotion: Fronto-amygdalar differences during emotional perception and episodic memory. *Journal of the International Neuropsychological Society, 15,* 819–825.

Stangor, C., & McMillan, D. (1992). Memory for expectancy-congruent and expectancy-incongruent information: A review of the social and social developmental literatures. *Psychological Bulletin, 111,* 42–61.

Steele, C. M. (1997). A threat in the air: How stereotypes shape intellectual identity and performance. *American Psychologist, 52,* 613–629.

Steele, C. M., Spencer, S. J., & Aronson, J. (2002). Contending with group image: The psychology of stereotype and social identity threat. In M. P. Zanna (Ed.), *Advances in experimental social psychology* (pp. 379–440). San Diego, CA: Academic Press.

Stein, R., Blanchard-Fields, F., & Hertzog, C. (2002). The effects of age-stereotype priming on memory performance in older adults. *Experimental Aging Research, 28,* 169–181.

Szatkowska, I., Bogorodzki, P., Wolak, T., Marchewka, A., & Szeszkowski, W. (2008). The effect of motivation on working memory: An fMRI and SEM study. *Neurobiology of Learning and Memory, 90,* 475–478.

Tomaszczyk, J. C., Fernandes, M. A., & MacLeod, C. M. (2008). Personal relevance modulates the positivity bias in recall of emotional pictures in older adults. *Psychonomic Bulletin and Review, 15,* 191–196.

Tulving, E. (1985). Memory and consciousness. *Canadian Psychology, 26,* 1–12.

Tun, P. A., McCoy, S., & Wingfield, A. (2009). Aging, hearing acuity, and the attentional costs of effortful listening. *Psychology and Aging, 24,* 761–766.

Waldstein, S. R. (2000). Health effects on cognitive aging. In P. C. Stern & L. L. Carstensen (Eds.), *The aging mind: Opportunities in cognitive research* (pp. 189–217). Washington, DC: National Academy Press.

Walton, G. M., & Cohen, G. L. (2003). Stereotype lift. *Journal of Experimental Social Psychology, 39,* 456–467.

Werheid, K., Gruno, M., Kathmann, N., Fischer, H., Almkvist, O., & Winblad, B. (2010). Biased recognition of positive faces in aging and amnestic mild cognitive impairment. *Psychology and Aging, 25,* 1–15.

Wilson, R. S. (2008). Neurological factors in cognitive aging. In S. M. Hofer & D. F. Alwin (Eds.), *Handbook of cognitive aging: Interdisciplinary perspectives* (pp. 298–307). Los Angeles, CA: Sage.

Wright, R. A., Junious, T. R., Neal, C., Avello, A., Graham, C., Herrmann, L., et al. (2007). Mental fatigue influence on effort-related cardiovascular response: Difficulty effects and extension across cognitive performance domains. *Motivation and Emotion, 31,* 219–231.

9 Emotion–memory interactions in older adulthood

Elizabeth A. Kensinger

INTRODUCTION

The hallmark of episodic memory is the ability to remember the details of a past experience, including its spatial and temporal context along with other associated details (Tulving, 1972). Although episodic recollections usually bring to mind a rich representation of a past experience, older adults often report that their ability to remember episodic details is not as good as it was when they were younger. Indeed, laboratory studies have confirmed that older adults' memory deficits are particularly noticeable when assessing the ability to remember spatiotemporal contexts (Spencer & Raz, 1995) or other details associated with an experience (e.g., Castel & Craik, 2003; Kausler, 1994; Light, 1991; Naveh-Benjamin, 2000).

Although episodic memory generally declines with aging, the deficits may be lessened when information has emotional significance. It is well known that affectively relevant information holds a privileged status in young adults' memories (reviewed by Buchanan, 2007; Hamann, 2001), and many studies have revealed that the memory advantage for affective information extends to older adults as well (reviewed by St. Jacques, Bessette-Symons, & Cabeza, 2009). The way that affective information is remembered, however, is not identical in young and older adults, and this review will describe two of the ways in which aging affects the interaction between emotion and memory.

The first difference has to do with the types of features that a person remembers about an experience. If I am recalling my trip to Paris, I can remember the sights (how the Eiffel tower looked in the heavy fog), the sounds (the couple laughing behind me as I walked along the Champs Elysees), the spatial layout (the path I walked between the Arc de Triomphe and the Louvre), or the temporal passage of time (the order in which I visited a number of museums). In addition to these details tied to the external unfolding of the events themselves, I can also remember my internal thoughts (how large the Eiffel tower looks in person) or feelings (sadness as I departed from my hotel on the last afternoon). As will be discussed in the following section, older adults seem to remember more affective details, even of experiences that are not themselves highly emotional.

The second difference relates to the valence of emotional experiences that young and older adults remember best. When we think back on our past, it usually is not the mundane moments that come to mind, but rather the events that elicited an affective response. Some of these events may be pleasant, while others may be unpleasant. A few lines of research have suggested that young adults may be more likely to remember negative events, whereas older adults may not show this effect and, in fact, may be prone to remember positive experiences (reviewed by Mather & Carstensen, 2005). There has been tremendous discussion about the reasons for this effect and about the possible implications for older adults' mental health. The second section will discuss this "positivity effect" in older adults' memories, with particular consideration of the circumstances and processes that may yield such an effect. The third section will discuss some of the general proposals that have been put forth to explain age-related changes in emotional memory as well as a few avenues of ongoing research that may help to elucidate the basis for the changes.

MEMORY FOR AFFECTIVE DETAILS OF EXPERIENCES

Although declines in episodic memory are a typical effect of cognitive aging, older adults do not have equal difficulty in remembering all types of episodic details. One area that tends to show relative preservation is the ability for older adults to remember how an experience made them feel and to recall affect-relevant dimensions of a past event. For example, older adults do well when asked to remember whether a name is associated with a "good person" or a "bad person," but they have difficulty remembering whether the name was read by a male or female voice (Rahhal, May, & Hasher, 2002). Similarly, older adults are as capable as young adults when asked to remember whether food is "safe" or "unsafe" to eat, but they are impaired at remembering nonaffective information about the food, such as whether it should be served hot or cold (May, Rahhal, Berry, & Leighton, 2005). Older adults also remember proportionally more affect-relevant information from prose passages than do young adults (Adams, Labouvie-Vief, Hobart, & Dorosz, 1990; Carstensen & Turk-Charles, 1994; Yoder & Elias, 1987), confirming their tendency to focus on the affective meaning of information rather than on other types of details.

More generally, focusing on how information makes them feel tends to improve older adults' memories. Older adults remember more information when it is presented in a way that references feelings (e.g., an advertisement with the slogan "capture those special moments") rather than in a manner that references other goals (e.g., "capture the unexplored world"; Fung & Carstensen, 2003). They also remember what they thought of an event or how they felt during it much better than they remember other event features (Comblain, D'Argembeau, Van der Linden, & Aldenhoff, 2004; Hashtroudi, Johnson, & Chrosniak, 1990; Schaefer & Philippot, 2005). Their memory for these internal details appears to take on such importance to older adults that they base their confidence in a memory upon their ability to remember their emotional reactions (e.g., Comblain et al., 2004).

The benefit for remembering affective information in older adulthood is consistent with evidence that, with aging, emotion-related goals become particularly salient and older adults become more focused on emotional information in their environment (e.g., Carstensen, Fung, & Charles, 2003; Gross et al., 1997). One explanation for why older adults do so well at remembering affective meaning, therefore, is that they attend more to this affective information and it therefore gains prioritized encoding into memory. In other words, older adults' memories' benefit for the affective context may reflect the way in which they process and rehearse the information (top box of Figure 9.1).

Evidence to support this hypothesis has come from studies that manipulate the way in which participants are asked to focus on experiences: If older adults are encouraged to focus on the facts rather than on the affective tone of information, they no longer show a bias to remember affective contexts, and their ability to remember nonaffective details improves (Hashtroudi, Johnson, Vnek, & Ferguson, 1994). Similarly, if young adults are asked to attend to the affective meaning of information, they will often show a bias to remember these sorts of details (Hashtroudi et al., 1994). Thus, the types of details attended and thus remembered can be altered by changing people's encoding orientations. However, it appears that the default for older adults is to focus upon the affect-relevant features of information, leading those details to be remembered well.

Although this explanation suggests that older adults' enhanced memory for affective information stems from the increased salience that this information

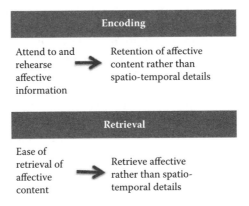

FIGURE 9.1 Processes proposed to lead to older adults' memory for affective event details.

has for them, another explanation focuses instead on the way that older adults' retrieval orientation biases them to remember affective information (bottom box in Figure 9.1). By this conjecture, older adults' good memory for affective information does not represent its increased salience so much as the fact that it is a type of information that older adults can easily retrieve. There is evidence that less retrieval effort is required to bring to mind affective information than to retrieve nonaffective information (Zajonc, 1980). Because older adults do better on tasks with lower retrieval demands (Kausler, 1994; Light, 1991), affective information may simply represent a category of information that older adults can retrieve easily (see Kensinger & Schacter, 2006; Brown & Ridderinkhof, 2009; Burke & Light, 1981; Nielsen & Phillips, 2008). This hypothesis aligns with the claims of Adams et al. (1990), who describe how older adults may remember the moral or gist of a story because memory for those aspects requires fewer information-processing resources than memory for the story's specific details.

A different level of explanation, focusing on neural changes with aging, may also explain why older adults would be able to retrieve affective details: Retrieval of such information may rely on dissociable neural processes from those that support memory for nonaffective details. For instance, an fMRI study by Smith, Stephan, Rugg, and Dolan (2006) provided evidence for dissociable processes corresponding with retrieval of affective context versus nonaffective context, at least in young adults.

These researchers found that when young adults were asked to determine whether information had been studied in an affective context (i.e., to decide whether information had been presented in a negative or neutral context), there was increased connectivity between the orbitofrontal cortex and the amygdala as compared to a condition in which participants were asked to discriminate in which of two nonaffective contexts information had been studied (i.e., to decide whether information had been presented in a context with people or without people). Similarly, Somerville, Wig, Whalen, and Kelley (2006) demonstrated that the amygdala is involved in retrieval of whether someone is a "good" or "bad" person, whereas this region is not typically implicated in the ability to retrieve other types of contextual details (e.g., Paller & Wagner, 2002; Ranganath & Knight, 2003).

Instead, retrieval of nonaffective context often relies on regions within the lateral prefrontal cortex (Paller & Wagner, 2002; Ranganath & Knight, in press). To the extent that orbitofrontal and amygdalar cortices are less impaired with aging than are the lateral prefrontal cortices (see Rajah & D'Esposito, 2005; Raz et al., 2004; Salat, Kaye, & Janowsky, 2001; Salat et al., 2004; Wright, Dickerson, Feczko, Negeira, & Williams, 2007), it may follow that older adults' memory for affective context is preserved because the ability to retain this information relies on neural circuitry that is preserved despite advancing age.

Although the results described so far have explained how older adults' focus on affective information can benefit their memory for those types of details, this focus often comes at the cost of memory for nonaffective details. For example, Comblain, D'Argembeau, and Van der Linden (2005) found that older adults remembered the thoughts and feelings elicited by pictures better than the perceptual or semantic details. Older adults also have more difficulty than young adults when required to process nonaffective elements within a scene that includes affective content (e.g., to process a forest that contains a snake; Kensinger, Garoff-Eaton, & Schacter, 2007; Kensinger, Piguet, Krendl, & Corkin, 2005). As has been discussed in more detail elsewhere (Kensinger, 2008b), it is plausible that older adults cannot strategically redirect their attention once it is focused on the affective content, causing them to be susceptible to these memory trade-offs (see also Waring & Kensinger, 2009).

MEMORY FOR EMOTIONAL EVENTS

The previous section focused on the effects of aging on the types of details remembered about an experience. But aging also appears to affect the types of experiences that are remembered. As noted in the introduction to this chapter, a "positivity effect" can arise with aging (e.g., Carstensen & Mikels, 2005; Carstensen, Mikels, & Mather, 2006; Kennedy, Mather, & Carstensen, 2004). This effect occasionally has been noted in studies of attention, with older adults sustaining attention on positive information longer than young adults (Isaacowitz, Wadlinger, Goren, & Wilson, 2006) and diverting attention away from negative information more quickly (Isaacowitz et al., 2006; Mather & Carstensen, 2003). The effect is more reliable in studies of memory (see Murphy & Isaacowitz, 2008): Older adults remember their prior decisions as more optimal (Mather & Johnson, 2000), and they retrieve more positive events from their past (e.g., Gruhn, Scheibe, & Baltes, 2007; Kennedy et al., 2004).

There have been different conceptualizations of the "positivity effect," but the most rigorous definition requires an interaction between the effect of age and the effect of valence on memory, with the benefit in memory for positive versus negative information being larger in older adults than in young adults (e.g., Mather, 2006). This interaction can arise because of a few different patterns of performance (see Figure 9.2):

It can result when young adults show a bias to remember negative versus positive information but older adults do not show such a bias (i.e., a lack of a "negativity bias" in older adults).

It can occur when older adults show a bias to remember positive versus negative information, whereas young adults do not (i.e., the presence of a "positivity bias" in older adults).

It can occur because of a combination of these effects.

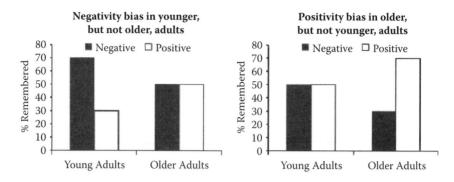

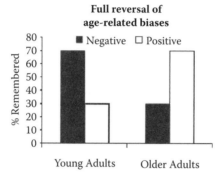

FIGURE 9.2 Possible instantiations of the "positivity effect" in memory: The age × valence interaction can result when there is a negativity bias in young adults but not older adults (left panel), when there is a positivity bias in older adults but not younger adults (middle panel), or when young adults show a negativity bias and older adults show a positivity bias (right panel).

In this section, I will try to be clear about which type of bias creates the positivity effect because the different manifestations of the effect may reflect different underlying processes (see Murphy & Isaacowitz, 2008, for further discussion).

The occurrence of the positivity effect

The positivity effect has occurred reliably in studies comparing young and older adults' memories, but the effect appears to be a modest one, and it is not always replicated. It has therefore become important to clarify the circumstances under which the effect occurs, in the hopes that understanding the constraints on the effect will better elucidate the processes that underlie it. In a comprehensive meta-analysis examining studies that assessed emotional memory in young adults or in older adults, Murphy and Isaacowitz (2008) demonstrated that tests of recognition memory were particularly likely to lead

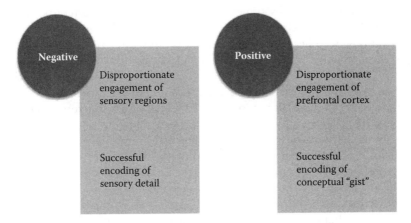

FIGURE 9.3 Emotional valence may affect the types of processes engaged during encoding and the types of details remembered. Older adults' positivity effect may be noted more frequently when tasks assess the "gist"-based information readily encoded for positive information.

to a positivity effect in memory because of a lack of a negativity bias in older adults. Recall tasks, by contrast, were less likely to lead to a positivity effect.

Murphy and Isaacowitz (2008) suggested that this pattern might be tied to the purported role of cognitive control in the positivity effect. Mather and colleagues (see Mather, 2006, for review) have proposed that the positivity effect may reflect a cognitively demanding set of processes that older adults implement because they are motivated to process positive information and to avoid negative information. If this is true, then the positivity effect should be most likely to arise under circumstances that allow older adults to implement cognitive control while processing emotional information. Consistent with this conjecture, the positivity effect has been shown to be greatest in older adults who have good cognitive control ability and when older adults can devote their full resources toward processing emotional information (Mather & Knight, 2005).

The manipulations by Mather and Knight (2005) either focused on altering the cognitive control resources available during encoding (Experiment 3) or could not easily distinguish the role of cognitive control during retrieval versus encoding (or reencoding; Experiments 2 and 3). However, Murphy and Isaacowitz (2008) propose that the cognitive effort required during *retrieval* may influence whether the positivity effect is manifest. They suggest that when memory tasks create high retrieval demands, they may deplete older adults' cognitive resources, thus lessening the likelihood that the positivity effect is revealed. By contrast, memory tasks that are low in retrieval demands may increase the likelihood that older adults can exert control over the type of information they retrieve and may therefore be more likely to reveal positivity effects.

Although motivated by somewhat different theoretical interests, studies from our laboratory seem to support this hypothesis. We had been interested in examining whether memory assessments that require retention of specific episodic details would be less likely to yield positivity effects than those that rely only on retrieval of the "gist" or general theme of information. Although we had couched these distinctions in terms of differences in memory specificity rather than in terms of retrieval demands, the retrieval of specific details will generally make higher retrieval demands than will retrieval of gist information. For this reason, it may be informative to consider these findings in light of the proposal of Murphy and Isaacowitz (2008).

In one set of studies (Kensinger, Garoff-Eaton, & Schacter, 2006, 2007), young and older adults were asked to distinguish *same* items (identical to those that they had studied) from *similar* items (sharing the same verbal label as a studied item, but differing in visual details) and *new* items (unrelated to any studied item). Both young and older adults were more accurate at distinguishing *same* from *similar* items when those items were negative (e.g., a snake) than when they were positive (e.g., a cake) or neutral (e.g., a rake). Thus, when scoring required memory for the specific visual details of the items to be remembered, young and older adults performed similarly, with both groups showing a "negativity bias" in memory. No positivity effect was noted.

When scoring was relaxed so that participants merely needed to identify an item as studied (i.e., as *same* or *similar* rather than *new*), without regard to whether the *same* versus *similar* selection was correct, a different pattern of results emerged. With these scoring rules, young adults again showed a negativity bias in memory, recognizing more of the negative items as studied. Older adults, in contrast, did not show a negativity bias; they were just as likely to recognize the positive items as studied as they were to recognize the negative items. Thus, only the scoring system that did not require retrieval of specific item details revealed a positivity effect in older adults' memories, brought about by a lack of a negativity bias in the older adults.

Similar results were revealed on a task of reality-monitoring performance. Young and older adults were better at discriminating items they had seen from items they had imagined if those items were negative versus positive (Kensinger, O'Brien, Swanberg, Garoff-Eaton, & Schacter, 2007; Kensinger & Schacter, 2006). Thus, when memory for specific episodic detail was required, young and older adults both showed a negativity bias in memory. However, when scoring required participants only to know that they had encountered an item previously, without penalizing for an incorrect assignment to visual perception versus mental imagery, only young adults showed a negativity bias. With these relaxed scoring rules, older adults showed equivalently good performance for positive and negative items—again revealing a lack of negativity bias in the older adults.

Studies of autobiographical memory have provided additional evidence that when episodic details must be remembered, adults of all ages may show a negativity bias. In a retrospective study, Bohn and Berntsen (2007) asked individuals from former East and West Germany to recall the details of the fall of the Berlin Wall. Some of these individuals had found the event to be highly positive, while others had experienced it as highly negative. The authors found that those individuals who experienced the event as negative remembered it more accurately than those who experienced it as positive. Because the age of their participants ranged from 29 to 82, their findings suggest that negative emotion may enhance memory accuracy across the adult life span.

In a direct examination of the effect of age on memory for the details of negative and positive experiences, Holland and Kensinger (submitted) compared the ability of young and older adult participants to remember details about the 2008 presidential race. Because of different political preferences, some participants felt the outcome to be positive, whereas others perceived it to be negative. The results revealed that regardless of the age group, memory consistency was higher if individuals had found the outcome to be negative rather than positive. Thus, these studies suggest that a negativity bias is commonly revealed when individuals must retrieve the details of past autobiographical experiences.

Although to my knowledge no study has directly compared detailed versus gist-based retrieval of positive and negative autobiographical events in young and older adults, a number of studies have shown that older adults tend to remember more positive than negative autobiographical experiences when the scoring relies only on recovery of the general theme of past events (e.g., "a trip to Paris") and does not factor the detail of the recollections into the equation (e.g., Kennedy et al., 2004). By contrast, positivity effects may not arise when memory for affective details is considered more directly (e.g., Alea, Bluck, & Semegon, 2004). This pattern of results is consistent with the proposal that the positivity effect may be elicited more reliably when mnemonic retrieval demands are low and when memory for gist is sufficient.

Future research will be required to determine when the factors of retrieval demand or memory specificity influence whether a positivity effect is noted, but the extant data suggest that, at least in some circumstances, these factors can be powerful predictors. In the following sections, I will address two questions that arise from this set of findings:

Why would a negativity bias arise for young and older adults when mnemonic demands are high and when a detailed recollection is required?
Why would a positivity effect arise more often when mnemonic demands are low and when memory for gist is sufficient?

Negativity biases arise when mnemonic demands are high and detailed recollection is required

One reason why adults of all ages might show a negativity bias when mnemonic demands are high or when detailed recollection is required relates to differences in the ways that negative and positive information are processed. It has been proposed that whereas negative information is processed in a detail-oriented and analytical fashion, positive information is processed in a more heuristic or schematic fashion (e.g., Bless et al., 1996; Gasper & Clore, 2002). Thus, individuals tend to focus on the local features of negative information, whereas their attention is broadened when they process positive information (e.g., Fredrickson & Branigan, 2005; Gasper & Clore, 2002; Rowe, Hirsch, & Anderson, 2007). It would make sense that these differences in processing could have pronounced effects on memory, leading negative information to be remembered more vividly and with more contextual detail than positive events (e.g., Comblain et al., 2005; Kensinger, 2008a; Kensinger & Corkin, 2003; Ochsner, 2000).

The neural data are consistent with these differences in processing. Negative information appears to be processed in a manner that recruits more sensory regions than does the processing of positive information, and this additional recruitment appears to enhance participants' abilities to remember the sensory details of negative items. For instance, in one study (Mickley & Kensinger, 2008), young adults studied positive, negative, and neutral photographs. After a short delay, participants performed a recognition memory task on which they were asked to indicate whether they vividly "remembered" an item, "knew" an item had been presented but did not remember any details about its presentation, or believed the item was "new" (see Jacoby, 1991; Mandler, 1980; Yonelinas, 2002, for discussion about the remember/know distinction).

This study revealed that, during encoding, negative items that were later "remembered" recruited temporo-occipital regions associated with sensory processing more than positive or neutral items that later were "remembered." There were no regions disproportionately recruited during the encoding of positive items that would later be "remembered," suggesting that negative valence is especially likely to enhance the encoding processes that allow vivid episodic recollections. By contrast, the encoding of positive information that was later "known" recruited regions associated with conceptual and self-referential processing (e.g., the cingulate gyrus and bilateral frontal and parietal areas) to a greater extent than negative or neutral items that were later "known." Similar dissociations have been revealed in other studies conducted in young adults, suggesting that the additional recruitment of sensory processes during the encoding of negative items may allow these items to be vividly "remembered" (e.g., Mickley Steinmetz & Kensinger, 2009) and to be remembered with specific episodic detail (e.g., Kensinger & Schacter, 2008). Thus, when memory tasks require retention of these types of details, negativity biases may appear.

Although much of this research has been restricted to young adult samples, two studies have suggested that older adults may show a similar tendency to engage sensory processes during the encoding of negative information. In one study (Kensinger & Schacter, 2008), young and older adults underwent an fMRI scan as they viewed negative or positive images. By employing the recognition paradigm that required participants to distinguish "same" from "similar" exemplars, we could examine how valence influenced participants' abilities to remember the precise visual details of an object. Consistent with the behavioral studies described in "The Occurrence of the Positivity Effect," young and older adults were better able to discriminate "same" from "similar" images when the images were of negative content versus positive content.

At a neural level, the successful encoding of negative information resulted in disproportionate activity within sensory processing regions including the occipital (visual) cortex and along the fusiform gyrus (a region specialized for processing high-level features of objects and faces and for encoding those stimuli; e.g., Bernstein, Beig, Siegenthaler, & Grady, 2002; Garoff, Slotnick, & Schacter, 2005; Kirchhoff, Wagner, Maril, & Stern, 2000; Kuskowski & Pardo, 1999). This pattern was stable for young and older adults, and in fact there were no age differences in the neural activity corresponding with subsequent memory for negative information. Addis, Leclerc, Muscatell, and Kensinger (2010) similarly found that connectivity between the amygdala, hippocampus, and fusiform gyrus is particularly strong during the encoding of negative information and that the strength of these connections does not differ between young and older adults.

Taken together, this research suggests that individuals may remember the specific sensory details associated with a negative item's presentation relatively easily because they engage more sensory processing during the encoding of that negative information. The incorporation of that additional information into a memory trace may make it easier for participants to recollect negative information (e.g., Ochsner, 2000) and to remember the sensory details of those experiences (e.g., Kensinger, Garoff-Eaton, & Schacter, 2007).

Tasks that capitalize on these abilities may therefore be the ones most likely to show a negativity bias. To the extent that this effect of negative valence is preserved into older adulthood, this negativity bias should be demonstrated by adults of all ages, and the extant data are consistent with that hypothesis. However, relatively little research has directly assessed the tie between negativity biases, memory specificity, and retrieval demands; there is still more work to be done before we fully understand when negativity biases occur, and under what conditions they will emerge in adults of all ages.

Positivity effects arise when mnemonic demands are low and memory for "gist" is sufficient

As noted earlier (in the section, "The Occurrence of the Positivity Effect"), when memory for the general theme of presented information is assessed, young adults often show a negativity bias, whereas older adults do not (Kensinger, Garoff-Eaton, & Schacter, 2007; Kensinger, O'Brien, et al., 2007). Similarly, when memory is assessed via recognition, positivity effects with aging are often revealed (Murphy & Isaacowitz, 2008). This section will explore the hypothesis that the reason why these types of tasks are likely to reveal age differences in memory relates to three factors: (1) the way that older adults process affective information in general (i.e., with more of a self-referential orientation toward their internal, affective responses), (2) differences in the way that positive versus negative information is processed, and (3) differences in the retrieval demands of the tasks.

Older adults are more likely to focus on how information makes them feel than are young adults (as reviewed in "Memory for Affective Details of Experiences"), and they are more likely to process information in a self-relevant fashion, with concern for how the information impacts them (discussed by Kensinger & Leclerc, 2009). It is well known that this type of self-referential processing conveys mnemonic benefits (Rogers, Kuiper, & Kirker, 1977; Symons & Johnson, 1997) in older adults as well as in young adults (Gutchess, Kensinger, Yoon, & Schacter, 2007; Mueller, Wonderlich, & Dugan, 1986). But it also is possible that orienting toward our internal states may benefit memory for the gist of an event more than memory for the specific details (Hashtroudi et al., 1994). To the extent that older adults' positivity effect results because they disproportionately engage in self-referential, internally focused processing of positive stimuli, it would make sense that their positivity effect would be more likely to be revealed on tasks that rely only on memory for the gist-based information so readily processed when individuals are focused on how information relates to them.

Although it has been difficult to ascertain, from behavioral studies, the degree to which older adults are relying on self-referential processing of positive information (however, see Tomaszczyk, Fernandes, & MacLeod, 2008, for some evidence), neuroimaging studies have begun to provide evidence that older adults may disproportionately engage self-referential processes when encoding positive information as compared to negative information.

In a few studies, age-related reversals have been revealed in the valence of information that elicits the most activity within self-referential processing regions (Leclerc & Kensinger, 2008a, 2009, 2010, 2011). In each of these studies, regions within the ventromedial prefrontal cortex and anterior cingulate gyrus have shown an age-related valence reversal: Young adults have shown more activity in these regions during the processing of negative compared to positive stimuli, whereas older adults have shown the opposite pattern of results, engaging these regions more during the processing of positive information. The midline cortical regions that have shown these valence reversals have been associated with self-referential processing (see meta-analysis by Northoff & Bermpohl, 2004), suggesting that age differences in engagement of these regions are linked to differences in the likelihood that individuals connect information to themselves.

Importantly, the extent of recruitment of these midline regions also corresponds with older adults' ability to remember positive information. The positive items that engage the medial prefrontal cortex most strongly are the items that older adults will later remember (Kensinger & Schacter, 2008). Moreover, more midline cortical regions show a connection to subsequent memory for older adults than for young adults (Kensinger & Schacter, 2008), and the medial prefrontal regions are more strongly connected to other limbic regions when older adults process positive information than when young adults do (Addis et al., 2010). These findings suggest that the tie between self-referential processing and memory for positive items may be particularly strong in older adults, contributing to their positivity effect in memory.

Older adults' positivity effect may also be more apparent when assessing gist memory or recognition ability because of the more heuristic fashion in which positive information is processed. The prior section highlighted fundamental differences in the way that negative and positive information is processed. These differences may lead not only to negativity biases when retrieval demands are high and memory for detail is required, but also to positivity effects when retrieval demands are low and memory for gist is sufficient.

When individuals are in a positive mood, they often ignore the local item-specific features of information and instead broaden their attention to the global or heuristic features of an event (e.g., Fredrickson & Branigan, 2005; Gasper & Clore, 2002; Rowe et al., 2007). At a neural level, this effect of positive valence is often revealed as a shift from posterior sensory processing toward frontal-based processes, likely because those frontal processes are the ones that support schema reliance and conceptual elaborations. The disproportionate engagement of frontal processes for positive information is apparent during encoding as well as retrieval (Markowitsch, Vandekerckhove, Lanfermann, & Russ, 2003; Piefke, Weiss, Ziles, Markowitsch, & Fink, 2003), suggesting increased reliance on schematic, conceptual processing during both phases of memory.

Part of the reason for this overlap may relate to the fact that retrieval activity often reflects the recapitulation of processes engaged during encoding (e.g., Kahn, Davachi, & Wagner, 2004; Nyberg, Habib, McIntosh, & Tulving, 2000; Wheeler, Petersen, & Buckner, 2000; Vaidya, Zhao, Desmond, & Gabrieli, 2002): When we remember an event, we bring online those processes that we initially recruited to encode the event. Moreover, retrieval is most successful when there is a match between the processes engaged during encoding and those engaged during retrieval (e.g., Craik & Lockhart, 1972). It therefore makes sense that the retrieval processes or retrieval cues that would be most effective in guiding memory retrieval would be linked to the types of processes that were engaged as people initially encoded information.

In other words, asking participants to retrieve the gist of positive information may convey a particular memory advantage because that is the type of information that they initially encoded about positive experiences. The correspondence between gist-based orientation and good memory for positive information may be particularly large for older adults because they are more likely to focus on gist-based information than young adults (see

Koutstaal, 2006; McDowd & Botwinick, 1984) and even more likely to engage in conceptual and self-referential processing of positive information (reviewed by Kensinger & Leclerc, 2009).

Older adults are also more likely to process information in a frontally mediated fashion, an effect that Cabeza and colleagues have referred to as the posterior-to-anterior shift with aging (PASA; Davis, Dennis, Daselaar, Fleck, & Cabeza, 2008). Although this shift has been noted even for neutral stimuli (reviewed by Davis et al., 2008), the shift to frontal-based processing may be particularly pronounced for emotional information. Across a number of studies, older adults have shown enhanced recruitment of prefrontal regions while they process emotional information (reviewed by St. Jacques, Bessette-Symons, & Cabeza, 2009).

It remains an open question as to whether this prefrontal recruitment is the result of compensatory efforts by older adults (see Cabeza, 2002) or of an inefficiency or dedifferentiation of function in the older adult brain (see Li et al., 2001). One way to distinguish these possibilities may be to use connectivity analyses to examine whether these prefrontal regions are well connected with the rest of the networks (consistent with a compensatory view) or whether they show weak connectivity (consistent with an inefficiency or dedifferentiation viewpoint). The few studies examining neural connectivity as older adults process emotional information have so far provided evidence most consistent with a compensatory view: Older adults have shown enhanced connectivity between prefrontal regions and medial temporal-lobe regions, particularly during the encoding of positive information (Addis et al., 2010), although the increased tie between prefrontal engagement and emotional memory may also exist for negative information (St. Jacques, Dolcos, & Cabeza, 2009).

Indeed, although initial studies had suggested that older adults' positivity effect might stem from changes in amygdala recruitment (Mather et al., 2004), more recent studies have suggested that the amygdala may undergo less age-related change than prefrontal regions when it comes to processing emotional information (Kensinger & Leclerc, 2009; St. Jacques, Bessett-Symons, & Cabeza, 2009). It will be important for future research to continue to investigate this possibility that older adults are recruiting prefrontal regions into an emotion-processing network to compensate for declines in other parts of the network.

Older adults' prefrontal recruitment may explain the propensity for gist-based measures of memory to reveal more age differences than measures that require retention of sensory details. Prefrontal processes probably play a dominant role in processing and encoding the conceptual meaning of information that would lead to gist memory, whereas sensory cortices are likely to be more involved in the processing of sensory detail. Given the tie between prefrontal activity and gist memory and the link between prefrontal activity and older adults' memory for emotional (and perhaps specifically positive) information, it makes sense that memory tasks that rely more on prefrontal processes and less on posterior sensory processes would reveal older adults' positivity effect most strongly.

As suggested by Murphy and Isaacowitz (2008), the reduced retrieval demands required for retrieval of gist may also benefit older adults' memories for positive information through another means (see the section, "The Occurrence of the Positivity Effect"). If older adults' positivity effect is connected to controlled processes (Mather, 2006) of limited capacity, then retrieval tasks that do not tax these cognitive resources will leave them available to guide the selection of positive information from memory. Although this is an intriguing hypothesis put forth by Murphy and Isaacowitz (2008), more research is needed to clarify the link between cognitive control processes and the positivity effect. Initial research by Mather and Knight (2005) suggested an important influence of cognitive control processes and, indeed, in some contexts the time course over which older adults' positivity effect emerges is consistent with the suggestion that it requires cognitive control (e.g., Isaacowitz, Allard, Murphy, & Schlangel, 2009).

However, other research has revealed that full deployment of cognitive control may not be necessary for the positivity effect to occur. For instance, Allard and Isaacowitz (2008) found that even when cognitive control resources were occupied by a secondary task, older adults were able to demonstrate a positivity effect in their eye gaze. Most likely, the secondary task did not fully deplete older adults' cognitive resources; nevertheless, this finding suggests that positivity effects can occur even without older adults' full cognitive control. In other words, older adults' positivity effect may require the availability of some cognitive resources, but it may not be impeded by tasks that divert a fraction of the cognitive resources away from emotion processing.

DIRECTIONS FOR FUTURE RESEARCH

One of the largest questions motivating current research on emotion–memory interactions with aging is the question of why some aspects of the interaction are altered by aging whereas others are not. A number of explanations have been proposed to explain the effects of aging on emotional memory, and I believe that understanding the conditions under which each is relevant should be an important goal for future research. In this section, I briefly outline three of the proposals that have been put forth and note some avenues that may prove fruitful in investigating the proposal in more detail.

Preserved arousal-based processing but altered valence-based processing

Some research has suggested that young and older adults may show similar processing of high-arousal information, whereas age differences may be more apparent when information is low in arousal and varies in valence. In one study, young and older adults showed a similar memory advantage for high-arousal information, regardless of its valence; however, age differences were apparent when information was lower in arousal. Young adults remembered negative nonarousing information better than positive nonarousing information, whereas older adults showed the opposite pattern of retention (Kensinger, 2008b). Thus, valence mattered for the types of nonarousing information remembered by young and older adults, whereas there was no effect of valence upon the types of arousing items remembered by the two age groups.

Compatible results were revealed in a study examining young and older adults' abilities to remember the phenomenological characteristics associated with an item's presentation (Mickley & Kensinger, 2009). Young and older adults remembered similar characteristics about high-arousal events, but there were age differences in the types of details remembered about low-arousal events. Particularly for internal details (thoughts and feelings), young adults' phenomenological ratings were higher for negative low-arousal information and older adults' ratings were higher for positive low-arousal information. Interestingly, these effects were evidenced even though there was no positivity effect in the recognition memory scores.

In fact, the corrected recognition scores revealed that older adults showed better memory for *negative* low-arousal items than for positive low-arousal ones. These results suggest that assessing people's abilities to retain the internal qualities of an experience may be a robust way to reveal positivity effects, possibly because these are the types of details that older adults focus upon most readily (see "Memory for Affective Details of Experiences") or because retrieval of internal, affective details requires less cognitive demand than the retrieval of other types of event details (see "The Occurrence of the Positivity Effect").

At a more general level, it appears that there may be more consistency in the way that young and older adults process high-arousal information and more divergence in the way that the two age groups process low-arousal information. For instance, on a visual search task, no effects of age were found when examining the influence of arousal on target detection times; both age groups were faster at detecting high-arousal targets than low-arousal targets. However, older adults showed a broader detection advantage than young adults: Older adults were faster to detect low-arousal targets than neutral targets, whereas this was not true for young adults (Leclerc & Kensinger, 2008b).

The fact that both age groups detect and remember high-arousal information well is consistent with research indicating that arousing information can be detected rapidly and automatically by participants (Anderson, Christoff, Panitz, De Rosa, & Gabrieli, 2003; Hahn, Carlson, Singer, & Gronlund, 2006; Mather & Knight, 2006; Ohman & Mineka, 2001) and that the memory boost for arousing information is also supported by relatively automatic processes (reviewed by Kensinger, 2004). For example, a number of experiments have demonstrated that arousing information benefits from prioritized processing (e.g., Anderson & Phelps, 2001; Pessoa, 2005) and can be detected and remembered even when attentional resources are taxed (Bush & Geer, 2001; Dolan & Vuilleumier, 2003; Kensinger & Corkin, 2004). Given the relative preservation of automatic processing with aging (Fleischman, Wilson, Gabrieli, Bienias, & Bennett, 2004; Jennings & Jacoby, 1993), it makes sense that older adults would be able to take advantage of these automatic systems for detecting and remembering high-arousal information.

By contrast, age-related changes in the processing of low-arousal information may reflect the fact that this type of information recruits more elaborative and strategic processing and relies less on automatic processing (Buchanan, Etzel, Adolphs, & Tranel, 2006; Kensinger, 2004; Talmi, Luk, McGarry, & Moscovitch, 2007). Thus, memory for low-arousal words is more likely to be disrupted by divided attention than is memory for high-arousal words (Bush & Geer, 2001; Kensinger & Corkin, 2004; Kern, Libkuman, Otani, & Holmes, 2005), and subsequent memory for low-arousal words is more likely to be associated with the engagement of lateral prefrontal regions associated with semantic elaboration (Kensinger & Corkin, 2004).

This elaborative processing could include conceptual linkages, connections to autobiographical experiences, or other forms of self-referential processing (see "Negativity Biases Arise When Mnemonic Demands Are High and Detailed Recollection Is Required" for further discussion). It may be that these types of elaborative processes are more likely to be altered by the aging process. These hypotheses still require further testing, so it will be important for future research to examine under what conditions age-related changes in emotion processing are more apparent for low-arousal than for high-arousal information.

Changes in emotion regulation and top-down processing of emotion

The positivity effect has commonly been interpreted within the framework of socioemotional selectivity theory (SST; Carstensen, 1993), which states that aging is associated with a changing perception of time. As adults approach the end of their life, they perceive time as more limited. As a result of this shifting time perspective, they begin to prioritize goals related to emotional fulfillment (Carstensen, Isaacowitz, & Charles, 1999). The positivity effect has been interpreted as one means through which older adults can achieve these goals (Carstensen & Mikels, 2005; Mather & Carstensen, 2005).

There is some evidence that older adults may continually regulate their emotions, perhaps in an attempt to maximize their emotional well-being.

In one study, older adults showed mood-incongruent gaze choices, focusing their attention toward positive images and away from negative images when they were in a negative mood. Young adults, in contrast, showed mood-congruent gaze choices (Isaacowitz, Toner, Goren, & Wilson, 2008). These results suggest that older adults may be more motivated to regulate their affect than young adults and are consistent with the proposal that older adults' regulatory goals are chronically active whereas young adults' regulatory goals are not (discussed by Mather & Knight, 2005; see also Xing & Isaacowitz, 2006, for evidence that young adults do not spontaneously use gaze to regulate their emotions but can do so when instructed).

Neuroimaging data have also been interpreted as reflecting enhanced emotion regulation in older adults. As noted earlier (see "Positivity Effects Arise When Mnemonic Demands Are Low and Memory for 'Gist' Is Sufficient" section), older adults often show increased prefrontal activation, as compared to young adults, during the processing of emotional information (e.g., Gunning-Dixon et al., 2003; Tessitore et al., 2005; Williams et al., 2006), and these differences are exacerbated depending on the extent of the older adults' cognitive decline (Krendl, Heatherton, & Kensinger, 2009). The particular prefrontal regions that are often over-recruited by older adults (e.g., the ventrolateral and ventromedial prefrontal cortex) are thought to be brought online during the controlled maintenance and manipulation of information (reviewed by Courtney, Petit, Haxby, & Ungerleider, 1998) and during the regulation of emotional information (e.g., Ochsner, Bunge, Gross, & Gabrieli, 2002; Urry et al., 2006).

Thus, these results are consistent with the proposal that older adults control and regulate their processing of emotional information more than young adults. These controlled processes may interact with other regions of the limbic system to dampen older adults' responses to negative images or to increase their responses to positive images (Tessitore et al., 2005; Williams et al., 2006). It is important to note, however, that frontal activity could reflect processes aside from regulation; more research is therefore needed to confirm whether this shift to frontal-based processing of emotional information reflects older adults' efforts to regulate their affect or whether it reflects other age-related differences in emotional processing (discussed in Kensinger & Leclerc, 2009). If future evidence does support an emotion-regulation interpretation of the findings, it will also be important to determine whether this regulation is engaged effortfully by the older adults, or whether they may engage more automatic regulatory processes (see Scheibe & Blanchard-Fields, 2009, for evidence that, in some instances, regulation may be more automatic for older adults).

The studies discussed so far have investigated whether there is a tie between age-related changes in emotion regulation and the initial allocation of processing resources and attention toward emotional information. In other words, these studies have looked at how *attention* toward emotional information is affected by regulatory changes with aging. It additionally has been proposed, however, that age-related changes in regulatory processes may be tied to changes in older adults' *memory* for emotional information. To my knowledge only one study has directly assessed this connection between emotion regulation and emotional memory in older adults (Leclerc, Carpenter, & Kensinger, submitted).

In this study, young and older adults were asked to increase, decrease, or maintain their emotional responses to positive and negative images (following the reappraisal task instructions of Ochsner et al., 2002, 2004). Participants' memories for the images were later assessed. The results revealed that age affected the valence of information that was retained, but only when information was regulated in a nonhedonic mode (i.e., when participants increased negative affect or decreased positive affect). When participants viewed the images without instructions to reappraise or when they viewed the images with instructions to regulate their affect in a hedonic mode, both age groups recalled more negative than positive images. However, when participants regulated in a nonhedonic mode, only the younger adults showed a negativity bias; the older adults recalled a comparable proportion of positive and negative information.

These results suggest that older adults may have an additional tool in their emotion-regulation toolbox: Even when they make themselves feel worse in the moment, older adults are able to recruit strategies to help them recall the situation in a less negative light. Young adults may not create this same type of retrospective memory bias.

The link between emotion regulation and the positivity effect remains a topic with many open questions. One conundrum is that there are significant age-related declines in executive function (for reviews, see Braver & Barch, 2002; Braver & West, 2007; Park & Payer, 2006; Park & Schwarz, 2000; Verhaeghen, Marcoen, & Goosens, 1993), yet executive functions are required for many forms of emotion regulation, including reappraisal (Baumeister, Vohs, & Tice, 2007; Richards & Gross, 2000). Considered together, these two lines of evidence would suggest that older adults should be *less* effective at emotion regulation than young adults. Yet many studies have suggested the opposite (Carstensen et al., 1999; Labouvie-Vief & Medler, 2002; Lawton, Kelban, Rajagopal, & Dean, 1992; Mather & Knight, 2005).

It remains unclear whether older adults devote a larger portion of their available resources to regulation (discussed by Mather, 2006), whether regulation is more automatic for older adults (e.g., Scheibe & Blanchard-Fields, 2009) or can occur more rapidly (Larcom & Isaacowitz, 2009), or whether older adults' expertise in regulation allows them to utilize distinct processes from young adults (Blanchard-Fields, 2009). More generally, although there has been much speculation about the tie between emotion regulation and the positivity effect, few data sets speak directly to the association. It makes sense that such a link would be present, but it will be important for future research to clarify the conditions under which the positivity effect is directly tied to differences in how young and older adults regulate their affective responses.

Enhancements in self-referential processing

Although a lot of research has focused on emotion regulation as the set of controlled processes that underlie older adults' positivity effect, other types of controlled processes may also contribute to the effect. As discussed earlier (in "Negativity Biases Arise When Mnemonic Demands Are High and Detailed Recollection Is Required"), older adults' engagement of self-referential elaboration may contribute to these effects. Young adults tend to focus on how negative information relates to them (see Baumeister, Bratslavsky, Finkenauer, & Vohs, 2001), whereas older adults may be more likely to think about how positive information links to their self-concept (discussed by Kensinger & Leclerc, 2009).

Initial evidence suggestive of this pattern was revealed in a study in which young and older adults were asked to decide whether positive or negative adjectives described them (Gutchess, Kensinger, & Schacter, 2007). Young adults showed more activity in the ventromedial prefrontal cortex, a region associated with self-referential processing, during the viewing of negative adjectives as compared to positive ones. Older adults showed the opposite pattern of recruitment. As noted earlier (in "Positivity Effects Arise When Mnemonic Demands Are Low and Memory for 'Gist' Is Sufficient"), age-related valence reversals have been noted in a few other paradigms examining older adults' processing of photo objects (Leclerc & Kensinger, 2008a, 2008b, 2010) and words (Leclerc & Kensinger, 2008a, 2010).

The hypothesis that there is a connection between older adults' self-referential processing and their positivity effect needs to be tested more rigorously than it has been. But the extant data (e.g., see Tomaszczyk et al., 2008, for evidence that personal relevance modulates the positivity effect) suggest that it may be important to think about the positivity effect as arising not only from changes in emotion regulation but also from differences in other types of controlled processes such as self-referential processing.

CONCLUSIONS

This chapter has highlighted two ways in which emotion–memory interactions are affected by advancing age: Older adults remember the way that past experiences made them feel better than they remember nonaffective details of those events, and they remember proportionally more positive experiences than young adults. These changes may be caused by motivational changes in the way that older adults process affective information: Older adults may devote more attention to it and prioritize it for processing because it has additional self-relevance or is tied to their emotion regulation goals.

The changes may also reflect differences in mnemonic processing with aging, so older adults may focus on affective details or on positive information because this information relies on processes—such as self-referential encoding or gist-based retrieval—that are relatively well preserved in aging. As research continues to combine behavioral testing with the investigation of neural processes, the contributions of each of these dimensions will likely be elucidated, leading to a clearer answer for why emotion influences memory differently in older adults than in young adults.

ACKNOWLEDGMENTS

Preparation of this manuscript was supported by grants from the Dana Foundation and the Searle Scholars Program. I thank Donna Addis, Eric Allard, Ranga Atapattu, Lisa Feldman Barrett, Hiram Brownell, Angela Gutchess, Alisha Holland, Anne Krendl, Christina Leclerc, Brendan Murray, Jessica Payne, Katherine Schmidt, Scott Slotnick, Katherine Mickley Steinmetz, Robert Waldinger, and Jill Waring for thoughtful discussion related to the issues presented in this review.

REFERENCES

Adams, C., Labouvie-Vief. G., Hobart, C. J., & Dorosz, M. (1990). Adult age group differences in story recall style. *Journal of Gerontology, 45,* 17–27.

Addis, D. R., Leclerc, C. M., Muscatell, K., & Kensinger, E. A. (2010). There are age-related changes in neural connectivity during the successful encoding of positive, but not negative, information. *Cortex, 46,* 425–433.

Alea, N., Bluck, S., & Semegon, A. B. (2004). Young and older adults' expression of emotional experience: Do autobiographical narratives tell a different story? *Journal of Adult Development, 11,* 235–250.

Allard, E. S., & Isaacowitz, D. M. (2008). Are preferences in emotional processing affected by distraction? Examining the age-related positivity effect in visual fixation within a dual-task paradigm. *Aging, Neuropsychology, and Cognition, 15,* 725–743.

Anderson, A. K., Christoff, K., Panitz, D. A., & De Rosa, E., & Gabrieli, J. D. E. (2003). Neural correlates of the automatic processing of threat facial signals. *Journal of Neuroscience, 2,* 5627–5633.

Anderson, A. K., & Phelps, E. A. (2001). Lesions of the human amygdala impair enhanced perception of emotionally salient events. *Nature, 411,* 305–309.

Baumeister, R. F., Bratslavsky, E., Finkenauer, C., & Vohs, K. D. (2001). Bad is stronger than good. *Review of General Psychology, 5,* 323–370.

Baumeister, R. F., Vohs, K. D., & Tice, D. M. (2007). The strength model of self-control. *Current Directions in Psychological Science, 16,* 396–403.

Bernstein, L. J., Beig, S., Siegenthaler, A. L., & Grady, C. L. (2002). The effect of encoding strategy on the neural correlates of memory for faces. *Neuropsychologia, 40,* 86–98.

Blanchard-Fields, F. (2009). Flexible and adaptive socioemotional problem solving in adult development and aging. *Restorative Neurology and Neuroscience, 27,* 539–550.

Bless, H., Clore, G. L., Schwarz, N., Golisano, V., Rabe, C., & Wolk, M. (1996). Mood and the use of scripts: Does a happy mood really lead to mindlessness? *Journal of Personality and Social Psychology, 71,* 665–679.

Bohn, A., & Berntsen, D. (2007). Pleasantness bias in flashbulb memories: Positive and negative flashbulb memories of the fall of the Berlin Wall among East and West Germans. *Memory & Cognition, 35,* 565–577.

Braver, T. S., & Barch, D. M. (2002). A theory of cognitive control, aging cognition, and neuromodulation. *Neuroscience & Biobehavioral Reviews, 26,* 809–817.

Braver, T. S., & West, R. (2007). Working memory, executive control and aging. In F. I. M. Craik & T. A. Salthouse (Eds.), *The handbook of aging and cognition* (3rd ed.). New York, NY: Psychology Press.

Brown, S. B., & Ridderinkhof, K. R. (2009). Aging and the neuroeconomics of decision making: A review. *Cognitive, Affective, and Behavioral Neuroscience, 9,* 365–379.

Buchanan, T. W. (2007). Retrieval of emotional memories. *Psychonomic Bulletin, 133,* 761–779.

Buchanan, T. W., Etzel, J. A., Adolphs, R., & Tranel, D. (2006). The influence of autonomic arousal and semantic relatedness on memory for emotional words. *International Journal of Psychophysiology, 61,* 26–33.

Burke, D., & Light, L. (1981). Memory and aging: The role of retrieval processes. *Psychological Bulletin, 90,* 513–554

Bush, S. I., & Geer, J. H. (2001). Implicit and explicit memory of neutral, negative emotional, and sexual information. *Archives of Sexual Behavior, 30,* 615–631.

Cabeza, R. (2002). Hemispheric asymmetry reduction in older adults: The HAROLD model. *Psychology and Aging, 17,* 85–100.

Carstensen, L. L. (1993). Motivation for social contact across the life span: A theory of socioemotional selectivity. In J. E. Jacobs (Ed.), *Nebraska symposium on motivation: 1992, Developmental perspectives on motivation* (Vol. 40, pp. 209–254). Lincoln, NE: University of Nebraska Press.

Carstensen, L. L., Fung, H., & Charles, S. (2003). Socioemotional selectivity theory and the regulation of emotion in the second half of life. *Motivation and Emotion, 27,* 103–123.

Carstensen, L. L., Isaacowitz, D. M., & Charles, S. T. (1999). Taking time seriously: A theory of socioemotional selectivity. *American Psychologist, 54,* 165–181.

Carstensen, L. L., & Mikels, J. A. (2005). At the intersection of emotion and cognition: Aging and the positivity effect. *Current Directions in Psychological Science, 14*(3), 117–121.

Carstensen, L. L., Mikels, J. A. & Mather, M. (2006). Aging and the intersection of cognition, motivation and emotion. In J. Birren & K. W. Schaie (Eds.), *Handbook of the psychology of aging* (6th ed.). San Diego, CA: Academic Press.

Carstensen, L. L., & Turk-Charles, S. (1994). The salience of emotion across the adult life course. *Psychology and Aging, 9,* 259–264.

Castel, A. D., & Craik, F. I. (2003). The effects of aging and divided attention on memory for item and associative information. *Psychology and Aging, 18,* 873–885.

Comblain, C., D'Argembeau, A., & Van der Linden, M. (2005). Phenomenal characteristics of autobiographical memories for emotional and neutral events in older and younger adults. *Experimental Aging Research, 31,* 173–189.

Comblain, C., D'Argembeau, A., Van der Linden, M., & Aldenhoff, L. (2004). The effect of ageing on the recollection of emotional and neutral pictures. *Memory, 12,* 673–684.

Courtney, S. M., Petit, L., Haxby, J. V., & Ungerleider, L. G. (1998). The role of prefrontal cortex in working memory: Examining the contents of consciousness. *Philosophical Transactions of the Royal Society London, B, 353,* 1819–1828.

Craik, F. I. M., & Lockhart, R. S. (1972). Levels of processing: A framework for memory research. *Journal of Verbal Learning and Verbal Behavior, 11,* 671–684.

Davis, S. W., Dennis, N. A., Daselaar, S. M., Fleck, M. S., & Cabeza, R. (2008). Que PASA? The posterior–anterior shift in aging. *Cerebral Cortex, 18,* 1201–1209.

Dolan, R. J., & Vuilleumier, P. (2003). Amygdala automaticity in emotional processing. *Annals of the New York Academy of Sciences, 985,* 348–355.

Fleischman, D. A., Wilson, R. S., Gabrieli, J. D., Bienias, J. L, & Bennett, D. A. (2004). A longitudinal study of implicit and explicit memory in old persons. *Psychology and Aging, 19,* 617–625.

Fredrickson, B. L., & Branigan, C. (2005). Positive emotions broaden the scope of attention and thought–action repertoires. *Cognition & Emotion, 19,* 313–332.

Fung, H. H., & Carstensen, L. L. (2003). Sending memorable messages to the old: Age differences in preferences and memory for advertisements. *Journal of Personality & Social Psychology, 85,* 163–178.

Garoff, R. J., Slotnick, S. D., & Schacter, D. L. (2005). The neural origins of specific and general memory: The role of the fusiform cortex. *Neuropsychologia, 43,* 847–859.

Gasper, K., & Clore, G. L. (2002). Attending to the big picture: Mood and global versus local processing of visual information. *Psychological Science, 13,* 34–40.

Gross, J. J., Carstensen, L. L., Pasupathi, M., Tsai, J., Skorpen, C. G., & Hsu, A. Y. C. (1997). Emotion and aging: Experience, expression, and control. *Psychology and Aging, 12,* 590–599.

Gruhn, D., Scheibe, S., & Baltes, P. B. (2007). Reduced negativity effect in older adults' memory for emotional pictures: The heterogeneity–homogeneity list paradigm. *Psychology and Aging, 22,* 644–649.

Gunning-Dixon, F. M., Gur, R. C., Perkins, A. C., Schroder, L., Turner, T., Turetsky, B. I.,... Gur, R. E. (2003). Age-related differences in brain activation during emotional face processing. *Neurobiology of Aging, 24,* 285–295.

Gutchess, A. H., Kensinger, E. A., & Schacter, D. L. (2007). Aging, self-referencing, and medial prefrontal cortex. *Social Neuroscience, 2,* 117–133.

Gutchess, A. H., Kensinger, E. A., Yoon, C., & Schacter, D. L. (2007). Aging and the self-reference effect in memory. *Memory, 15,* 822–837.

Hahn, S., Carlson, C., Singer, S., & Gronlund, S. D. (2006). Aging and visual search: Automatic and controlled attentional bias to threat faces. *Acta Psychologica, 123,* 312–336.

Hamann, S. (2001). Cognitive and neural mechanisms of emotional memory. *Trends in Cognitive Sciences, 5,* 394–400.

Hashtroudi, S., Johnson, M. K., & Chrosniak, L. D. (1990). Aging and qualitative characteristics of memories for perceived and imagined complex events. *Psychology and Aging, 5,* 119–126.

Hashtroudi, S., Johnson, M. K., Vnek, N., & Ferguson, S. A. (1994). Aging and the effects of affective and factual focus on source monitoring and recall. *Psychology and Aging, 9,* 160–170.

Holland, A. C., & Kensinger, E. A. (in preparation). Younger and older adults' memories for the 2008 US presidential election.

Isaacowitz, D. M., Allard, E. S., Murphy, N. A., & Schlangel, M. (2009). The time course of age-related preferences toward positive and negative stimuli. *Journal of Gerontology: Psychological Sciences, 64,* 188–192.

Isaacowitz, D. M., Toner, K., Goren, D., & Wilson, H. R. (2008). Looking while unhappy: Mood-congruent gaze in young adults, positive gaze in older adults. *Psychological Science, 19,* 848–853.

Isaacowitz, D. M., Wadlinger, H. A., Goren, D., & Wilson, H. R. (2006). Selective preference in visual fixation away from negative images in old age? An eye-tracking study. *Psychology of Aging, 21,* 40–48.

Jacoby, L. L. (1991). A process dissociation framework: Separating automatic from intentional uses of memory. *Journal of Memory and Language, 30,* 513–541.

Jennings, J. M., & Jacoby, L. L. (1993). Automatic versus intentional uses of memory: Aging, attention, and control. *Psychology & Aging, 8,* 283–293.

Kahn, I., Davachi, L., & Wagner, A. D. (2004). Functional-neuroanatomic correlates of recollection: Implications for models of recognition memory. *Journal of Neuroscience, 24,* 4172–4180.

Kausler, D. H. (1994). *Learning and memory in normal aging.* San Diego, CA: Academic Press.

Kennedy, Q., Mather, M., & Carstensen, L. L. (2004). The role of motivation in the age-related positive bias in autobiographical memory. *Psychological Science, 15,* 208–214.

Kensinger, E. A. (2008a). How emotion affects older adults' memories for event details. *Memory, 17,* 1–12.

Kensinger, E. A. (2008b). Age differences in memory for arousing and nonarousing emotional words. *Journal of Gerontology: Psychological Sciences, 63,* P13–18.

Kensinger, E. A., & Corkin, S. (2003). Memory enhancement for emotional words: Are emotional words more vividly remembered than neutral words? *Memory and Cognition, 31,* 1169–1180.

Kensinger, E. A., & Corkin, S. (2004). Two routes to emotional memory: Distinct processes for valence and arousal. *Proceedings of the National Academy of Sciences, USA, 101,* 3310–3315.

Kensinger, E. A., & Leclerc, C. M. (2009). Age-related changes in the neural mechanisms supporting emotion processing and emotional memory. *European Journal of Cognitive Psychology, 21,* 192–215.

Kensinger, E. A., & Schacter, D. L. (2006). Amygdala activity is associated with the successful encoding of item, but not source, information for positive and negative stimuli. *Journal of Neuroscience, 26,* 2564–2570.

Kensinger, E. A., & Schacter, D. L. (2008). Neural processes supporting young and older adults' emotional memories. *Journal of Cognitive Neuroscience, 7,* 1–13.

Kensinger, E. A., Garoff-Eaton, R. J., & Schacter, D. L. (2006). Memory for specific visual details can be enhanced by negative arousing content. *Journal of Memory and Language, 54,* 99–112.

Kensinger, E. A., Garoff-Eaton, R. J., & Schacter, D. L. (2007). Effects of emotion on memory specificity in young and older Adults. *Journal of Gerontology, 62,* 208–215.

Kensinger, E. A., O'Brien, J., Swanberg, K., Garoff-Eaton, R. J., & Schacter, D. L. (2007). The effects of emotional content on reality-monitoring performance in young and older adults. *Psychology and Aging, 22,* 752–764.

Kensinger, E. A., Piguet, O., Krendl, A. C., & Corkin, S. (2005). Memory for contextual details: Effects of emotion and aging. *Psychology and Aging, 20,* 241–250.

Kern, R. P., Libkuman, T. M., Otani, H., & Holmes, K. (2005). Emotional stimuli, divided attention, and memory. *Emotion, 5,* 408–417.

Kirchhoff, B. A., Wagner, A. D., Maril, A., & Stern, C. E. (2000). Prefrontal-temporal circuitry for episodic encoding and subsequent memory. *Journal of Neuroscience, 20,* 6173–6180.

Koutstaal, W. (2006). Flexible remembering. *Psychonomic Bulletin & Review, 13,* 84–91.

Krendl, A. C., Heatherton, T. F., & Kensinger, E. A. (2009). Aging minds and twisting attitudes: An fMRI investigation of age differences in inhibiting prejudice. *Psychology and Aging, 24,* 530–541.

Kuskowski, M., & Pardo, J. V. (1999). The role of the fusiform gyrus in successful encoding of face stimuli. *Neuroimage, 9,* 599–610.

Labouvie-Vief, G., & Medler, M. (2002). Affect optimization and affect complexity: Modes and styles of regulation in adulthood. *Psychology and Aging, 17,* 571–588.

Larcom, M. J., & Isaacowitz, D. M. (2009). Rapid emotion regulation after mood induction: Age and individual differences. *Journal of Gerontology: Psychological Sciences, 64B*(6), 733–741,

Lawton, M. P., Kelban, M. H., Rajagopal, D., & Dean, J. (1992). Dimensions of affective experience in three age groups. *Psychology and Aging, 7,* 171–184.

Leclerc, C. M., Carpenter, S., & Kensinger, E. A. (submitted). Age-related differences in the cognitive up- and down-regulation of emotional images.

Leclerc, C. M., & Kensinger E. A. (2008a). Age-related differences in medial prefrontal activation in response to emotional images. *Cognitive, Affective, and Behavioral Neuroscience, 8,* 153–164.

Leclerc, C. M., & Kensinger E. A. (2008b). Effects of age on detection of emotional information. *Psychology and Aging, 23,* 209–215.

Leclerc, C. M., & Kensinger, E. A. (2010). Age-related valence-based reversal in recruitment of medial prefrontal cortex on a visual search task. *Social Neuroscience, 5,* 560–576.

Leclerc, C. M., & Kensinger, E. A. (2011). Neural processing of emotional pictures and words: A comparison of young and older adults. *Developmental Neuropsychology, 36,* 519–538.

Li, S.-C., Lindenberger, U., & Sikstrom, S. (2001). Aging cognition: From neuromodulation to representation. *Trends in Cognitive Science, 5,* 479–86.

Light, L. L. (1991). Memory and aging: Four hypotheses in search of data. *Annual Review of Psychology, 42,* 333–376.

Mandler, G. (1980). Recognizing: The judgment of previous occurrence. *Psychological Review, 87,* 252–271.

Markowitsch, H. J., Vandekerckhove, M. M., Laufermann, H., & Russ, M. O. (2003). Engagement of lateral and medial prefrontal areas in the ecphory of sad and happy autobiographical memories. *Cortex, 39,* 643–665.

Mather, M. (2006). Why memories may become more positive with age. In B. Uttl, N. Ohta, & A. L. Siegenthaler (Eds.), *Memory and emotion: Interdisciplinary perspectives* (pp. 135–159). Oxford, UK: Blackwell Publishing.

Mather, M., Canli, T., English, T., Whitfield, S., Wais, P., Ochsner, K., ... Carstensen, L. L. (2004). Amygdala responses to emotionally valenced stimuli in older and younger adults. *Psychological Science, 15,* 259–263.

Mather, M., & Carstensen, L. L. (2003). Aging and attentional biases for emotional faces. *Psychological Science, 14,* 409–415.

Mather, M., & Carstensen, L. L. (2005). Aging and motivated cognition: The positivity effect in attention and memory. *Trends in Cognitive Sciences, 9,* 496–502.

Mather, M., & Johnson, M. K. (2000). Choice-supportive source monitoring: Do our decisions seem better to us as we age? *Psychology and Aging, 15,* 596–606.

Mather, M., & Knight, M. (2005). Goal-directed memory: The role of cognitive control in older adults' emotional memory. *Psychology and Aging, 20,* 554–570.

Mather, M., & Knight, M. R. (2006). Angry faces get noticed quickly: Threat detection is not impaired among older adults. *Journals of Gerontology Series B: Psychological Sciences and Social Sciences, 61,* P54–P57.

May, C. P., Rahhal, T., Berry, E. M., & Leighton, E. A. (2005). Aging, source memory, and emotion. *Psychology of Aging, 20,* 571–578.

McDowd, J., & Botwinick, J. (1984). Rote and gist memory in relation to type of information, sensory mode, and age. *Journal of Genetic Psychology, 145,* 167–178.

Mickley, K. R., & Kensinger, E. A. (2008). Emotional valence influences the neural correlates associated with remembering and knowing. *Cognitive, Affective, and Behavioral Neuroscience, 8,* 143–152.

Mickley, K. R., & Kensinger, E. A. (2009). Phenomenological characteristics of emotional memories in younger and older adults. *Memory, 17,* 528–543.

Mickley Steinmetz, K. R., & Kensinger, E. A. (2009). The effects of valence and arousal on the neural activity leading to subsequent memory. *Psychophysiology, 46,* 1190–1199.

Mueller, J. H., Wonderlich, S., & Dugan, K. (1986). Self-referent processing of age-specific material. *Psychology and Aging, 1,* 293–299.

Murphy, N. A., & Isaacowitz, D. M. (2008). Preferences for emotional information in older and younger adults: A meta-analysis of memory and attention tasks. *Psychology and Aging, 23,* 263–286.

Naveh-Benjamin, M. (2000). Adult age differences in memory performance: Tests of an associative deficit hypothesis. *Journal of Experimental Psychology: Learning, Memory, and Cognition, 26,* 1170–1187.

Nielsen, L., & Phillips, J. W. (2008). Health economic choices in old age: Interdisciplinary perspectives on economic decisions and the aging mind. *Advances in Health Economics and Health Services Research, 20,* 227–270.

Northoff, G., & Bermpohl, F. (2004). Cortical midline structures and the self. *Trends in Cognitive Science, 8,* 102–107.

Nyberg, L., Habib, R., McIntosh, A. R., & Tulving, E. (2000). Reactivation of encoding-related brain activity during memory retrieval. *Proceedings of the National Academy of Sciences, USA, 97,* 11120–11124.

Ochsner, K. N. (2000). Are affective events richly "remembered" or simply familiar? The experience and process of recognizing feelings past. *Journal of Experimental Psychology: General, 129,* 242–261.

Ochsner, K. N., Bunge, S. A., Gross, J. J., & Gabrieli, J. D. (2002). Rethinking feelings: An FMRI study of the cognitive regulation of emotion. *Journal of Cognitive Neuroscience, 14,* 1215–1229.

Ochsner, K. N., Ray, R. D., Cooper, J. C., Robertson, E. R., Chopra, S., Gabrieli, J. D., & Gross, J. J. (2004). For better or for worse: Neural systems supporting the cognitive down- and up-regulation of negative emotion. *Neuroimage, 23,* 483–499.

Ohman, A., & Mineka, S. (2001). Fears, phobias, and preparedness: Toward an evolved module of fear and fear learning. *Psychological Review, 108,* 483–522.

Paller, K. A., & Wagner, A. D. (2002). Observing the transformation of experience into memory. *Trends in Cognitive Sciences, 6,* 93–102.

Park, D. C., & Payer, D. (2006). Working memory across the adult lifespan. In E. Bialystock & F. Craik (Eds.), *Lifespan cognition: Mechanisms of change.* New York, NY: Oxford University Press.

Park, D. C., & Schwarz, N. (Eds.). (2000). *Cognitive aging: A primer.* Philadelphia, PA: Psychology Press.

Pessoa, L. (2005). To what extent are emotional visual stimuli processed without attention and awareness? *Current Opinion in Neurobiology, 15,* 188–196.

Piefke, M., Weiss, P. H., Zilles, K., Markowitsch, H. J., & Fink, G. R. (2003). Differential remoteness and emotional tone modulate the neural correlates of autobiographical memory. *Brain, 126,* 650–668.

Rahhal, T., May, C. P., & Hasher, L. (2002). Truth and character: Sources that older adults can remember. *Psychological Science, 13,* 101–105.

Rajah, M. N., & D'Esposito, M. (2005). Region-specific changes in prefrontal function with age: A review of PET and fMRI studies on working and episodic memory. *Brain, 128,* 1964–1983.

Ranganath, C., & Knight, R. T., (2003). Prefrontal cortex and episodic memory: Integrating findings from neuropsychology and event-related functional neuroimaging. In A. Parker, E. Wilding, & T. Bussey (Eds.), *The Cognitive Neuroscience of Memory Encoding and Retrieval* (pp. 83–99). Philadelphia: Psychology Press.

Raz, N., Gunning-Dixon, F., Head, D., Rodrigue, K. M., Williamson, A., & Acker, J. D. (2004). Aging, sexual dimorphism, and hemispheric asymmetry of the cerebral cortex: Replicability of regional differences in volume. *Neurobiology of Aging, 25,* 377–396.

Richards, J. M., & Gross, J. J. (2000). Emotion regulation and memory: The cognitive costs of keeping one's cool. *Journal of Personality and Social Psychology, 79,* 410–424.

Rogers, T. B., Kuiper, N. A., & Kirker, W. S. (1977). Self-reference and the encoding of personal information. *Journal of Personality and Social Psychology, 35,* 677–688.

Rowe, G., Hirsh, J. B., & Anderson, A. K. (2007). Positive affect increases the breadth of attentional selection. *Proceedings of the National Academy of Sciences, USA, 104,* 383–388.

Salat, D. H., Buckner, R. L., Snyder, A. Z., Greve, D. N., Desikan, R. S. R., Busa, E.,... Fischl, B. (2004). Thinning of the cerebral cortex in aging. *Cerebral Cortex, 14,* 721–730.

Salat, D. H., Kaye, J. A., & Janowsky, J. S. (2001). Selective preservation and degeneration within the prefrontal cortex in aging and Alzheimer's disease. *Archives of Neurology, 58,* 1403–1408.

Schaefer, A., & Philippot, P. (2005). Selective effects of emotion on the phenomenal characteristics of autobiographical memories. *Memory, 13,* 148–160.

Scheibe, S., & Blanchard-Fields, F. (2009). Effects of regulating emotions on cognitive performance: What is costly for young adults is not so costly for older adults. *Psychology and Aging, 24,* 217–223.

Smith, A. P., Stephan, K. E., Rugg, M. D., & Dolan, R. J. (2006). Task and content modulate amygdala–hippocampal connectivity in emotional retrieval. *Neuron, 49,* 631–638.

Somerville, L. H., Wig, G. S., Whalen, P. J., & Kelley, W. M. (2006). Dissociable medial temporal lobe contributions to social memory. *Journal of Cognitive Neuroscience, 18,* 1253–1265.

Spencer, W. D., & Raz, N. (1995). Differential effects of aging on memory for content and context: A meta-analysis. *Psychology and Aging, 10,* 527–539.

St. Jacques, P. L., Bessette-Symons, B., & Cabeza, R. (2009). Functional neuroimaging studies of aging and emotion: Fronto-amygdalar differences during emotional perception and episodic memory. *Journal of the International Neuropsychological Society, 15,* 819–825.

St. Jacques, P. L., Dolcos, F., & Cabeza, R. (2009). Effects of aging on functional connectivity of the amygdala for subsequent memory of negative pictures: A network analysis of fMRI data. *Psychological Science, 20,* 74–84.

Symons, C. S., & Johnson, B. T. (1997). The self-reference effect in memory: A meta-analysis. *Psychological Bulletin, 121,* 371–394.

Talmi, D., Luk, T. C. B., McGarry, L., & Moscovitch, M. (2007). Are emotional pictures remembered better just because they are semantically related and relatively distinct? *Journal of Memory and Language, 56,* 555–574.

Tessitore, A., Hariri, A. R., Fera, F., Smith, W. G., Das, S., Weinberger, D. R., & Mattay, V. S. (2005). Functional changes in the activity of brain regions underlying emotion processing in the elderly. *Psychiatry Research, 139,* 9–18.

Tomaszczyk, J. C., Fernandes, M. A., & MacLeod, C. M. (2008). Personal relevance modulates the positivity bias in recall of emotional pictures in older adults. *Psychonomic Bulletin & Review, 15,* 191–196.

Tulving, E. (1972). Episodic and semantic memory. In E. Tulving, & W. Donaldson (Eds.), *Organization of Memory* (pp. 381–403). New York: Academic Press.

Urry, H. L., van Reekum, C. M., Johnstone, T., Kalin, N. H., Thurow, M. E., Schaefer, H. S.,... Davidson, R. J. (2006). Amygdala and ventromedial prefrontal cortex are inversely coupled during regulation of negative affect and predict the diurnal pattern of cortisol secretion among older adults. *Journal of Neuroscience, 26,* 4415–4425.

Vaidya, C. J., Zhao, M., Desmond, J. E., & Gabrieli, J. D. E. (2002). Evidence for cortical encoding specificity in episodic memory: Memory-induced re-activation of picture processing areas. *Neuropsychologia, 40,* 2136–2143.

Verhaeghen, P., Marcoen, A., & Goossens, L. (1993). Facts and fiction about memory aging: A quantitative integration of research findings. *Journals of Gerontology: Psychological Sciences, 48,* P157–P171.

Waring, J. D., & Kensinger E. A. (2009). Effects of emotional valence and arousal upon memory trade-offs with aging. *Psychology and Aging, 24,* 412–422.

Wheeler, M. E., Petersen, S. E., & Buckner, R. L., 2000. Memory's echo: Vivid remembering reactivates sensory-specific cortex. *Proceedings of the National Academy of Sciences, USA, 97,* 11125–11129.

Williams, L. M., Brown, K. J., Palmer, D., Liddell, B. J., Kemp, A. H., Olivieri, G.,... Gordon, E. (2006). The mellow years? Neural basis of improving emotional stability over age. *Journal of Neuroscience, 26,* 6422–6430.

Wright, C. I., Dickerson, B. C., Feczko, E., Negeira, A., & Williams, D. (2007). A functional magnetic resonance imaging study of amygdala responses to human faces in aging and mild Alzheimer's disease. *Biological Psychiatry, 62,* 1388–1395.

Xing, C., & Isaacowitz, D. M. (2006). Aiming at happiness: How motivation affects attention to and memory for emotional images. *Motivation and Emotion, 30,* 249–256.

Yoder, C. Y., & Elias, J. W. (1987). Age, affect, and memory for pictorial story sequences. *British Journal of Psychology, 78,* 545–549.

Yonelinas, A. P. (2002). The nature of recollection and familiarity: A review of 30 years of research. *Journal of Memory and Language, 46,* 441–517.

Zajonc, R. B. (1980). Feeling and thinking. Preferences need no inferences. *American Psychologist, 35,* 151–175.

10 Metamemory and memory efficiency in older adults

Learning about the benefits of priority processing and value-directed remembering

Alan D. Castel, Shannon McGillivray, and Michael C. Friedman

> Selection is the very keel on which our mental ship is built. And in the case of memory its utility is obvious. If we remembered everything, we should on most occasions be as ill off as if we remembered nothing.
>
> William James (1890, p. 680)

> [I]t is a triumph of life that old people lose their memories of inessential things, though memory does not often fail with regards to things that are of real interest to us. Cicero illustrated this with the stroke of a pen: No old man forgets where he has hidden his treasure.
>
> Gabriel Garcia Márquez (2005, p. 10)

INTRODUCTION/OVERVIEW

People need to remember important information in order to function efficiently. This includes remembering to buy necessary and important items at a grocery store, to pack essential items for a trip, to report important symptoms to a physician, or the main points from this chapter. Thus, the ability to select and remember important information is critical at any age. The ability to allocate attention and monitor memory capacity strategically can allow us to remember important or "high-value" information; we refer to this as value-directed remembering. In order to attend successfully to important information, which often occurs at the expense of other lower value but competing information, one has to be aware of how memory works and, more specifically, how memory can often fail. The ability to accomplish this requires metacognitive processes—more specifically, metamemory.

Metamemory is the knowledge and awareness about one's own memory and how memory works more generally. Thus, metamemory plays a key role when one is learning how to focus strategically on important information. The present chapter reviews age-related changes in metamemory, examines how goals and biases influence what is encoded by older adults, discusses when and how older adults can (and often need to) focus strategically on important information, and presents current research on this topic. A conceptual and computational framework is presented that demonstrates how metacognition and priority processing influence what information is later remembered. We conclude by discussing future directions and implications regarding age-related changes in memory, metamemory, and the value-directed remembering approach.

METAMEMORY IN OLDER ADULTS

During a recent conversation, an older adult revealed some interesting observations about his memory. He said his memory was declining, and as a result he realized he had to pay extra attention when something was important to remember (e.g., ask the person to say it again, write it down). While he claimed to remember important things often, when he did forget something important, he was again reminded about how his memory was declining. He noted that this cycle of events, while at times very frustrating, reminded him of how his memory works, and when it fails. This anecdote illustrates that age-related changes in memory are often accompanied by self-reported observations of this phenomenon, especially when individuals notice that they are forgetting something important or are forgetting more frequently. The present chapter reviews how memory, metacognition, and the value of what one remembers interact during advancing age, and it outlines current research that addresses this issue.

Older adults are aware of age-related changes in memory performance (Hertzog & Hultsch, 2000) and often feel they have less control over their memory abilities (Lachman, 2006). Older adults are also highly susceptible to stereotype threat, so even subtle "reminders" about aging lead to poorer memory performance (Hess, 2005; Levy, 1996; Stein, Blanchard-Fields, & Hertzog, 2002). In addition, older adults frequently report anxiety when faced with memory-demanding situations and challenges (Chasteen, Bhattacharyya, Horhota, Tam, & Hasher, 2005), which can then lead to poorer memory performance.

As mentioned earlier, metamemory is the knowledge and awareness about one's own memory and how memory works more generally. The anecdote at the beginning of the section is an example of metamemory (i.e., someone's observations about his or her own memory), and while personal observations such as these are often informative, experimental research on the topic has uncovered interesting and potentially useful findings. The literature regarding the impact of aging on metamemory abilities is mixed (see Hertzog & Hultsch, 2000). In some situations, older adults have exhibited either over- or underconfidence regarding how well they think they can remember information; in other instances, older adults display relatively accurate metacognitive judgments regarding both remembering and forgetting (e.g., Halamish, McGillivray, & Castel, in press; Hertzog, Kidder, Powell-Moman, & Dunlosky, 2002), possibly due to the lifelong experiences they have with memory use and the frequency in which they experience memory failures.

Interestingly, while older adults often express negative beliefs about their memories' capabilities, in some cases they may initially overestimate their ability to recall information (e.g., Bruce, Coyne, & Botwinick, 1982; Connor, Dunlosky, & Hertzog, 1997; Lachman & Jelalian, 1984; Murphy, Sanders, Gabriesheski, & Schmitt, 1981; Rast & Zimprich, 2009), whereas in other situations they may underestimate it (e.g., Coyne, 1985). An inability to monitor, predict, and assess one's own memory has obvious negative consequences. It can result in disappointment or embarrassment in situations where an individual is not able to remember what they think they will be able to remember. It can also lead to instances of forgetting, potentially resulting from the failure to allocate necessary time or effort needed to encode useful or important information. However, if one is aware of things that one might forget, one can learn to spend more time rehearsing that information, leading to better memory.

Optimal metamemory functioning involves accurately assessing one's own memory abilities and using memory principles to enhance memory performance. Experimental studies of metamemory tasks often involve asking participants to make judgments of learning (or JOLs) about what or how much they will later remember (a form of metacognitive *monitoring*) or asking participants what information they feel they need to restudy or study for shorter or longer periods of time (a form of metacognitve *control*). Bruce and colleagues (1982) found that although JOLs were similar for younger and older adults when learning a list of words, older adults recalled significantly fewer words (see also Connor et al., 1997), supporting the notion that older adults may suffer from metamemory monitoring as well as memory impairments (Pansky, Goldsmith, Koriat, & Pearlman-Avnion, 2009; but see Lovelace & Marsh, 1985; Rabinowitz, Craik, & Ackerman, 1982).

In regard to metacognitive control, Dunlosky and Connor (1997) observed that when older and younger adults were allowed to restudy words at their own pace, all participants spent more time studying items that they had assigned lower JOLs (i.e., words they judged as more difficult to recall) compared to those word that had been given higher JOLs (judged as more likely to remember). However, younger adults exhibited this effect to a much greater extent, indicating that age-related differences were present in the degree to which monitoring was used to allocate study time effectively. Dunlsoky and Connor suggest that this difference in study-time allocation may even contribute to the lower overall memory performance in older adults. However, Dunlosky and Hertzog (1997) found that younger and older adults used a "functionally identical algorithm" in their selection of items for restudy, with both groups selecting to restudy the items to which they had assigned lower JOLs. Thus, it appears that both younger and older adults learn to restudy information that they feel is more difficult to remember, suggesting that aging may not necessarily compromise monitoring and control skills.

This is a short and selective review of the metamemory and aging literature, but what we hoped to highlight is that while in some cases older adults do not display accurate metacognition, in many instances older adults' metamemory is as accurate as that of younger adults, if not even more insightful. For a more comprehensive discussion of metamemory and aging, including other types of metamemory assessments such as "feeling of knowing" (FOK) judgments, the "tip of the tongue" (TOT) phenomenon, and strategy use, see Hertzog and Hultsch (2000) or Dunlosky and Metcalfe (2009).

We will now review the factors that influence how older adults allocate attention and memory resources in a strategic fashion and how task goals and metacognitive monitoring can play a central role in later memory performance. Specifically, we will show that metacognitive processes can modify the scope of attention and the contents of memory; we will refer to this as the "metacognition modifying attention" (or MMA) hypothesis. The MMA hypothesis states that the need to encode high-value information and the awareness of a fixed or limited memory capacity can lead to the efficient allocation of attention toward important information at the expense of other, competing information. MMA involves the interaction between goals and evaluative processing (deciding what is important to remember), attentional control (being able to direct attention successfully to this information), and adjustment of metacognitive monitoring (learning about memory capacity) with appropriate feedback and task experience—factors that will be discussed in the following sections.

MEMORY EFFICIENCY AND THE STRATEGIC USE OF MEMORY CAPACITY

Most studies of episodic or working memory involve measures of memory capacity, accuracy, or quality, and older adults typically display deficits in these domains (but see Zacks & Hasher, 2006). However, very little research has examined measures of "memory efficiency," which involves evaluating how one focuses on important information, given memory capacity constraints. Older adults need to use memory efficiently, given memory impairments, and this involves prioritizing what is important to remember while being aware that not all information can be retained; we refer to this as value-directed remembering. Assigning value or utility to characteristics or options in the context of decision making has been a central component to theories regarding choice behavior (Tversky, 1969, 1972); however, in the context of memory research, very little emphasis has been placed on the value of to-be-remembered information and how older adults might use value to guide encoding and retrieval operations.

To determine if something is important to remember, people use "evaluative processing," which leads to the assignment of some sort of value to the information, and this process can be influenced by a variety of factors (see Castel, 2008). Most typically, value is based on how important the information is for the current goals of the individual, whether this information is consistent or inconsistent with prior knowledge, and motivation and anticipated future use of this information (e.g., Hess, Rosenberg, & Waters, 2001).

In the present chapter and viewpoint, the term *selectivity* refers to focusing on certain items or events that are perceived to be of high value, possibly at the expense of lower value information. As suggested by Riediger and Freund (2006), a more general form of "motivational" selectivity may involve two forms: (1) *focusing* on high value/important information, while also (2) *limiting* or *restricting* the access of lower value or more peripheral information. In the context of metacognition and goals influencing this process, one can consider the following example. When packing for a trip, one needs first to pack important and necessary items (e.g., clothes, money, etc.) and then include other, more peripheral items (e.g., books, camera, etc.), if space permits. In addition, it may be strategic first to pack the most important items, to ensure that these are not forgotten.

The conceptual framework of selection, optimization, and compensation (SOC; Baltes & Baltes, 1990; see also Riediger, Li, & Lindenberger, 2006, for the adaptive nature of SOC) posits that successful aging is related to a focused and goal-directed investment of limited resources into areas that yield optimal returns. Thus, older adults can selectively choose certain options in order to maximize performance based on goals, compensating for impairments by optimizing performance in specific, goal-related domains. This type of selectivity can be focused on achieving certain goals and can also be "loss based" (Freund & Baltes, 2002) as older adults adjust their goals in response to feedback or losses in order to attain desired and realistic outcomes eventually. In a similar vein, Heckhausen (1999; Heckhausen & Schulz, 1995) suggests that individuals have to take on the regulation of aging-related resource losses in order to function efficiently; this can lead to an improvement in efficient cognitive function. More recently, Hess (2005) has highlighted the "adaptive nature of cognition" and suggested that numerous factors (such as goals, social contexts, and characteristics of the individual) can influence selectivity and moderate age-related memory impairments.

Relating life span development theory to experimental studies of memory, a useful approach (although not typically incorporated in cognitive aging research) was outlined in Jenkins's (1979) tetrahedral model of memory experiments. Similarly to the SOC model, this model also emphasizes the sensitivity of memory to context, such that memory performance in a given situation is determined by interactions between four categories of variables: participant characteristics and goals, the cognitive strategy necessary for good performance, the nature of the to-be-remembered materials, and the manner in which one assesses performance. Extending Jenkins's ideas to cognitive aging, Hess (2005) has highlighted the need for a more multi-dimensional approach within the study of memory and aging in order to understand and explore the constellation of factors that influence and possibly mitigate the memory impairments so often observed in older adults.

THE EFFECTS OF GOALS AND RELEVANCE ON MEMORY IN OLDER ADULTS

People are often presented with more information than they can later remember, such as when listening to an hour-long lecture or, more practically for some older adults, when presented with a lengthy list of side effects of a given medication. Thus, it is critical to decide what information is important to remember, attend to this information, and encode it as valuable so that it can later be retrieved. This is especially true for older adults, who have widely documented impairments in attentional control and memory (Balota & Faust, 2001; McCabe, Roediger, McDaniel, Balota, & Hambrick, 2010) such that it is imperative to learn how to select what information should be remembered. Thus, the rememberer's goals play a key role in determining what information is attended to and how that information is deemed important to remember.

Typically, the goal in most experimental studies of episodic memory is to remember as much information as possible. Older adults usually show pronounced deficits in memory capacity (they remember less information), as well as deficits in memory quality and accuracy, compared to younger adults (see Koriat & Goldsmith, 1996). However, when more specific goals are set, the role of motivation to achieve these goals can lead to important insights regarding age-related differences in memory performance.

Several studies have examined how motivated cognition and goal-directed memory influence memory performance in old age. Much of this work has examined how emotional information is processed by younger and older adults and the strategic and adaptive use of goals in memory and decision making. It has been suggested that emotional regulation and emotional well-being are an important goal for older adults (e.g., Carstensen

1992, 1995). Investigations into the influence of emotional goals on memory have often found a "positivity bias" in older adults' memories.

Specifically, relative to younger adults, older adults are more likely to remember positive emotional information relative to negative emotional information (Mather & Carstensen, 2005, Tomaszczyk, Fernandes, & MacLeod, 2008). However, under divided attention, older adults do not show this positivity effect, suggesting that it may result from the strategic allocation of attention (Mather & Knight, 2005). Additionally, Fung and Carstensen (2003) found that older adults tend to favor and remember advertisements that are consistent with emotional goals, suggesting that emotional regulation can influence and motivate what older adults remember.

Older adults may perform well on more naturalistic memory and decision-making tasks because they involve more everyday forms of memory and reasoning (e.g., Castel, 2005; Rahhal, May, & Hasher, 2002; Rendell & Craik, 2002; Tentori, Osherson, Hasher, & May, 2001). Thus, it may be possible to reduce memory impairments by using materials that lend themselves well to typical memory and decision-making challenges faced by younger and older adults outside the laboratory. What remains unclear is how these groups weight various components of a task, and the MMA approach seeks to emphasize the role of evaluative processing by older adults, leading to adaptive and efficient performance (cf. Schacter, 1999).

The manner in which value is subjectively and internally assigned to information, such as choice features, positive and negative emotional valence, or components of a decision-making process, is critical. Older adults may be more aware of the need to use value to guide encoding and retrieval, relative to younger adults, and it is this observation that might reinforce the need to prioritize how information is processed (e.g., evaluating the relevance or priority of information) in order to lead to efficient memory performance.

Hess and colleagues (Germain & Hess, 2007; Hess et al., 2001; see also Hess & Emery, Chapter 8, this volume) have investigated the role of personal relevance and its impact on memory performance in older (and younger) adults. For example, Hess et al. (2001) found that older adults were more accurate in their recollection of information related to a narrative describing an older target person (increased relevance), compared to one describing a younger target person, and this accuracy increased under situations in which they were held accountable for their responses (increased motivation). Furthermore, older adults benefited to a greater extent from increasing motivation and relevance than did younger adults.

Extending these findings, Germain and Hess (2007) demonstrated that increased relevance was strongly associated not only with memory performance, but also with more efficient processing, and these effects were stronger within the older adult sample. Additionally, personally relevant material was shown to down-regulate the impact of the distracting information, suggesting that relevance can act to moderate the effects of interference from competing information. These findings suggest that older adults are able to allocate cognitive resources selectively when appropriate motivational influences are present (Hess et al., 2001; see also Tomaszczyk et al., 2008).

Older adults clearly have different goals relative to college students in terms of memory performance in the context of life span development and possibly also on laboratory-based memory tests (see also Carstensen, 1995), so it seems sometimes problematic to compare older adults to younger adults in these types of situations (see Castel, 2008). For example, Labouvie-Vief (1990) suggests that knowledge *acquisition* is more associated with young adulthood, whereas knowledge *utilization* may be more relevant in middle and later adulthood (see also Ardelt, 1997, 2000).

In a typical memory experiment setting, older adults may not be accustomed to memorizing large amounts of information or using esoteric methods to commit arbitrary information to memory, and often do not encounter the constant tests and exams that are common practice for college students. Younger adults who are college students could in fact be classified as "expert memorizers," in a much different sense than older adults, given the emphasis that is often placed on memorizing information and terminology when studying for exams, perhaps at the cost of being selective. Older adults may use evaluative processing to remember selectively only certain types of information, often at the cost of being able to remember large amounts of information or specific arbitrary details. Similarly, experts of various ages learn to attend to key features, such as when viewing a chess game or distinguishing between birds or different artistic styles, depending on the domain of expertise (Ericsson, Charness, Feltovich, & Hoffman, 2006). Beilock and Carr (2001) found that expert golfers focus on important features during domain-specific tasks (e.g., putting), but then later report lengthy but more generic or gist-base memory for the prior episode, relative to novices who report more specific episodic details (see also Castel, 2008).

Older adults may learn to become experts in terms of how to evaluate what information is important to remember, at the expense of details that are often not well remembered (Koutstaal, 2006). Adams (1991) and Adams, Smith, Nyquist, and Perlmutter (1997) have shown that older adults recall the gist of stories, as well as more interpretative information, whereas younger adults are better at recalling specific details of a story. This suggests that older adults use memory in different ways, especially in terms of the abstraction and retrieval of gist, and perhaps think that the retention and communication of the gist or main points are more important than recollection of specific details. Determining what information is important to remember and effectively retaining and communicating this information is a critical function and involves the strategic control of encoding and retrieval operations.

THE VALUE-DIRECTED REMEMBERING
APPROACH AND FINDINGS

Value-directed remembering requires the ability to allocate attention and monitor memory capacity in order to remember important or "high-value" information (see Castel, 2008). Thus, the value-directed remembering approach is concerned with how people can selectively remember important information at the expense of less important information. One method to examine the impact of value or importance on memory performance in an experimental setting is to have to-be-remembered items in a list assigned a range of different values. This differs from typical memory experiments in which each item, picture, or word pair is of equal importance to remember. By assigning different values to to-be-remembered items, one can determine how participants use value to guide encoding and retrieval processes and how they adaptively focus on high-value information.

In the "selectivity" paradigm (Castel, Balota, & McCabe, 2009; Castel, Benjamin, Craik, & Watkins, 2002; Castel, Farb, & Craik, 2007; Castel, Lee, Humphreys, & Moore, 2011; Hanten et al., 2007; Watkins & Bloom, 1999), participants are presented with a list of 12 words, and each word is paired with a different numeric value ranging from 1 to 12 (e.g., table 5, uncle 9, apple 2, pilot 6, etc.; see left panel in Figure 10.1). In some variants of this procedure, the value is presented immediately after the word to ensure that participants do not simply ignore low-value words. Participants are told that they should try to remember as many words as they can for a later recall test so that they maximize their score. The score is the sum of the associated values of the recalled words, and the experimenter informs participants of their scores once they have recalled the words. Following this feedback, participants are then tested with additional lists and encouraged to remember the high-value words in order to maximize their performance, although recalling any word will lead to a higher score.

The results from a selectivity experiment are displayed in the right panel of Figure 10.1, where the probability of recall is plotted as a function of point value. Younger adults perform quite well and on average recall more words than older adults, but in some instances do not appear as selective, recalling both high- and low-value words (Castel et al., 2002). Importantly, after some experience with the task (participants are given numerous unique lists, one after another), participants become aware that they cannot remember all of the words (because the words are presented fairly rapidly at encoding). Thus, participants begin to focus on or select the highest value words to remember in order to boost their score. Older adults are quite efficient at selectively remembering high-value words (i.e., the 12-, 11-, and 10-point value words) in light of knowing that they will likely only be able to remember three or four words. Thus, as can be seen in Figure 10.1, age-related differences in memory essentially disappear for high-value words and are greatest for the lower value words.

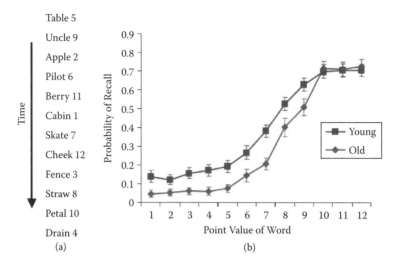

FIGURE 10.1 The selectivity procedure (panel A) and results (panel B) from the selectivity paradigm. Panel A: the participants are presented with a list of 12 words (one at a time), with each word having a unique value ranging from 1 to 12, and the values randomized across the serial positions. Participants recall the words with the goal to maximize their score, are given feedback about their score, and then engage in successive new lists and feedback about their score. Panel B: the results in terms of the probability of recall for younger and older adults as a function of point value. (Adapted from Castel, A. D. et al., 2002, *Memory & Cognition, 30,* 1078–1085; Castel, A. D. et al., 2007, *Memory & Cognition, 35,* 689–700.) There are no age differences for high-value items (12-, 11-, and 10-point words), whereas age differences exist in memory performance for other, lower values.

It is important to note that participants were told their score after the recall of each list and were then given another new list (in some cases doing this up to 48 times), so after the first few lists participants learned to become more selective in order to maximize their score (see Figure 10.2). An efficiency measure known as the "selectivity index" can also be calculated; this compares the participant's score relative to an ideal score based on the number of words recalled. For example, if an individual recalled three words, an ideal score would be 10 + 11 + 12 = 33 (i.e., recalling the top three words); however, if an individual's actual score was 8 + 10 + 12 = 30, then the selectivity index would be the actual score divided by the ideal score, actual/ideal = 30/33 = .91 (see Castel et al., 2002, for more details about the selectivity index).

In fact, under certain conditions (such as immediate free recall), older adults have displayed a higher selectivity than younger adults because they consistently recalled only the highest value words, whereas younger adults recalled high- and some additional low-value words (Castel et al., 2002).

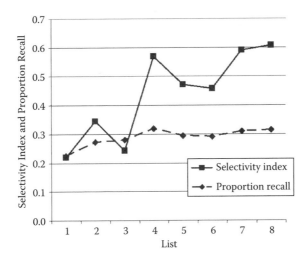

FIGURE 10.2 The selectivity index (derived from participants' overall point value score relative to an ideal score) and proportion of words recalled as a function of task experience (list number) for older adults. (Adapted from data in Castel, A. D. et al., 2002, *Memory & Cognition, 30,* 1078–1085; Castel, A. D. et al., 2007, *Memory & Cognition, 35,* 689–700.) While recall remained relatively stable across lists, the selectivity index increased with task experience.

Because younger adults' overall recall is typically higher than older adults' performance, the index may indeed be somewhat biased. However, it has provided a useful index of performance for several populations (see Castel et al., in press, for a recent study using a lifespan example). For example, children with attention-deficit/hyperactivity disorder (ADHD) and older adults with very mild Alzheimer's disease have shown specific impairments in selectivity (Castel et al., 2011; Castel, Balota, & McCabe, 2009), suggesting that selectivity is related to attentional control, as suggested by the MMA hypothesis. Thus, as it posits, a central component to the strategic use of memory is the ability to direct necessary attention to important information.

To illustrate how older adults learn to become more efficient in the selectivity task, Figure 10.2 shows performance (in terms of the selectivity index and proportion of words recalled) as a function of list. Recall performance improved slightly after the first few lists and then remained stable. Although older adults did not display high selectivity for the first few lists, after several lists, older adults became more selective by focusing on encoding higher value items, leading to higher efficiency scores (as reflected by the selectivity index). Although not shown in the figure, younger adults showed a similar trend, but with higher overall recall across all lists. Thus, it may be necessary to learn about how to be efficient, and this requires some experience with the task (and may be related to other changes in strategy and control by older adults; see Spieler, Mayr, & La Grone, 2006; Touron, 2006). It may be that older adults engage in an efficient form of event-based prospective memory with practice (e.g., McDaniel, Einstein, Stout, & Morgan, 2003) in terms of remembering to remember higher value information because this is reinforced with many trials and feedback about score in the selectivity paradigm.

Recent ongoing work from our laboratory has examined how younger and older adults learn about memory capacity in a "gambling" experiment (McGillivray & Castel, 2011). In this study, we used a modified version of the selectivity task. As each word-point value pair was presented, participants had to decide if they wanted to "bet" on whether or not they would be able to recall the word: If they recalled the word, they received the points associated with it, but if they failed to recall the word, they were penalized by that same point value. If participants did not bet on the pair, whether the word was remembered or not did not affect their score. How do older adults place their bets in such a task and how does this change with task experience? The results are displayed in Figure 10.3.

For the first list, younger adults received a low yet positive score, whereas older adults bet on more words than they actually later remembered, resulting in a negative score which suggests a metacognitive failure. However, with list experience, both groups increased their score as older adults

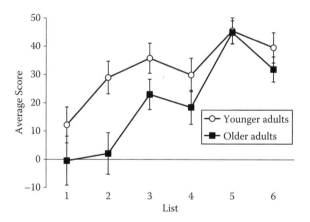

FIGURE 10.3 The average score on each list for both younger and older adults in the point-value "gambling" experiment. (Adapted from McGillivray, S., and Castel, A. D., 2011, *Psychology and Aging, 26*, 137–142.) Scores were calculated by adding the points associated with words that participants "bet" on and successfully recalled and then subtracting the points associated with the words they bet on and failed to recall. Both groups initially bet on more words than later remember (overconfidence). However, with task experience, both groups show improvement and learn to calibrate their bets to their actual memory capabilities, resulting in an increase in score.

learned to bet exclusively on and successfully recall the high-value items. In fact, by lists 5 and 6, older and younger adults obtained comparable scores, despite the fact that younger adults were able to recall significantly more words. This initial metacognitive failure for older adults on the first few lists then led to a recovery due to awareness about how focusing on less, but more important, information can improve performance on later lists. Thus, it may be necessary for both younger and older adults to learn about memory capacity and this requires some experience with the experimental task as well as feedback about score. These findings are consistent with research on the importance of task experience in updating and possibly improving metacognitive judgments and strategies (Dunlosky & Hertzog, 2000; Matvey, Dunlosky, Shaw, Parks, & Hertzog, 2002).

In a similar manner, Castel et al. (2007) employed a selectivity procedure in which words were paired with either negative or positive point values. Thus, participants had to focus on high-value items, but avoid encoding and later recall of the negative-value items. The incentive to focus on positive value in this case was reinforced because participants were instructed that recalling negative-value information would reduce their score. Both younger and older adults successfully recalled the positive, high-value information. Interestingly, much like younger adults, older adults did not recall any of the negative-value information. However, on a later surprise recognition test for all items, older adults were in fact more likely to recognize the negative-value words, relative to younger adults. This finding suggests that older adults did, in fact, process these words perhaps due to poorer inhibitory control (Hasher & Zacks, 1988) and perhaps took longer to code them as negative-value information, due to general cognitive slowing (Salthouse, 1996).

The observation that older adults do in fact initially encode negative, low-value, or irrelevant information is consistent with impairments in inhibitory control found in the directed forgetting paradigm (Bjork, Bjork, & Anderson, 1998). When given cues to remember or to forget certain items, older adults recall more of the "forget" items under certain conditions, suggesting that they have difficulty inhibiting the encoding and later recall of these items (e.g., Zacks, Radvansky, & Hasher, 1996). More recently, Sahakyan, Delaney, and Goodmon (2008) found that both younger and older adults could selectively forget the no longer relevant "forget" information. However, the directed forgetting paradigm does not allow for the examination of how value can influence control over encoding or how task experience can reduced age-related differences; these are critical issues in the present context, given that older adults can learn to rely on value to guide encoding operations. Thus, the idea that older adults can prioritize what information to commit to memory may have important implications for training efficient use of memory (e.g., Benjamin, 2008; Dunlosky & Hertzog, 1998).

We have recently examined how value influences binding in the context of associative memory and faces. A vast amount of research has shown that older adults display an associative deficit (for a review, see Old & Naveh-Benjamin, 2008), and this deficit is present for binding other information to faces, such as names, ages, and other faces (e.g., James, 2006; McGillivray & Castel, 2010; Naveh-Benjamin, Guez, Kilb, & Reedy, 2004; Rendell, Castel, & Craik, 2005; Rhodes, Castel, & Jacoby, 2008). However, the importance of selectively remembering certain "high-value" faces may have a strong effect on how well associative information is encoded by older adults.

To examine this issue, Friedman, Castel, McGillivray, and Flores (2010) had participants study faces, and each face was paired with a dollar amount ranging from $0 to $1,000. Participants were told that the dollar amount reflected how much money they had lent this person and that, if they later correctly recalled exactly how much the person owed them when cued with the face, they would "collect" the money. In general, both younger and older adults recalled a higher value for the faces that owed them more money (see Figure 10.4). Specifically, older adults were very accurate for the high-value faces, but less so for the lower value faces, relative to younger adults.

In a follow-up experiment, participants viewed faces that were paired with either a negative or positive amount of money (ranging from $1 to $100), with negative values indicating that the participant "owed" this person the stated value and positive values indicating that that person owed the participant the stated value. Interestingly, younger adults showed similar

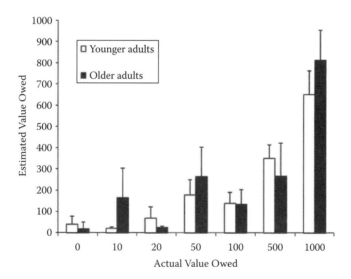

FIGURE 10.4 The average response for the amount of money that each face "owed" the participant. Participants were encouraged to guess if they could not remember the precise amount, and the average response is displayed as a function of the actual amount associated with each face. In general, both younger and older adults provided a greater estimate for the faces that owed more money, providing some evidence for remembering "gist-based" values associated with the faces.

performance for the negative and positive values, with better memory for the extreme values. However, older adults displayed better performance for the positive extreme values, but were significantly impaired for all of the negative extreme values, relative to younger adults. Thus, older adults may be more sensitive to value if it is framed in terms of gains, rather than losses, and this is consistent with their later associative memory performance observed in the present task (see also Denburg, Tranel, & Bechara, 2005; Kovalchik, Camerer, Grether, Plott, & Allman, 2005; Peters, Hess, Vastfjall, & Auman, 2007). This may also be consistent with the positivity bias literature (e.g., Mather & Carstensen, 2005), in that associative information that is presented as more positive relative to the individual is better remembered. In general, this finding indicates that older adults can bind certain valuable information with faces (see also Freund, Kourilova, & Kuhl, 2011; McGillivray, 2010) and may use strategies that bias how well they remember faces as well as the associated value information.

A PRIORITY-RECALL MODEL: THE PRODUCT OF PRIORITY PROCESSING

It is clear that older adults are capable of remembering information that is presented as being either more valuable or more in line with emotional and social goals. While these findings in and of themselves are quite revealing, it is necessary to try to understand how and why important information is better encoded and remembered, as well as factors that moderate the effect. The benefits of priority processing can be illustrated in a more computational manner by considering the interaction between the importance of information and when it actually needs to be recalled.

Anderson and Schooler (1991, 2000) note that the probability that a memory will be needed shows reliable relationships with frequency, recency, and patterns of prior exposures of that memory. They also introduce the "need" probability, which is the future probability that the rememberer will need a particular memory trace—a variable akin to value or priority of the information. To capture how memory is influenced by the perceived importance of the material, as well as the time interval that occurs between initial study and later retrieval, a simple two-parameter model can be derived that illustrates how memory is a product of several key variables that contribute to value-directed remembering.

The current conceptual and computation framework is based on the value-directed remembering approach, with value or priority dictating whether information will be needed and later remembered. The basic necessary computations and variables are such that the rememberer computes an assignment of priority value (PV)—how important the information is— and also time of recall value (TRV)—when this information needs to be recalled to satisfy the goals associated with the information. The product of these two variables would give an estimate regarding the probability of later recall, as shown in the following equation:

Probability of Recall = Product of the Priority Value (PV) × Time of Recall Value (TRV)

or, more simply, using the stated abbreviations:

p(later recall) = PV × TRV

where PV and TRV can be expressed as values between 0 and 1. Larger values of the priority variable (PV) indicate greater priority. Larger values of the time variable (TRV) reflect greater immediacy, whereas smaller values reflect more distance in time (i.e., a longer retention interval).

This equation and relationship between PV and TRV can be illustrated in the following examples. Imagine that while reading this chapter, you notice a reference to a paper you want to include in a book you are currently writing. You thus (either implicitly or explicitly) assign a priority value for the item (because it is important for the book that you are trying to finish, let us assign it .95), and also a time period to remember it later (later today, when you are writing your book, so it is assigned .90). The ensuing computation regarding the probability that you later recall this information would then be .95 × .90 = .86—a fairly high probability, which is a desirable result.

Alternatively, while reading this chapter, perhaps you are reminded about older adults and memory, which makes you think of your great aunt, which then reminds you that her birthday is coming up next month. You want to remember to buy a birthday card for her sometime soon and then put it in the mail. In this case, let us say the priority value is medium to high (e.g., .80), but the time period to remember this is in a week or two (e.g., .20). Thus, the probability that you later remember to do this is .80 × .20 = .16 (which might explain why the card arrives late or does not arrive at all!). It may be the case that older adults have a higher minimum threshold in terms of the probability of successfully remembering something (e.g., the probability must be .40 or greater to remember exact information fully), whereas a younger adult's threshold may be lower, leading to a greater chance of recall and perhaps greater precision of recall.

While the model is an overly simplistic approach, it does illustrate how value or priority (as well as when the information needs to be recalled) can greatly contribute to memory performance. There are many other variables that could be included—notably, age of the individual, the conditions of encoding and retrieval, and cues and prior knowledge that might aid encoding and later retrieval, such as level of expertise if the material is in a specific domain (see also Castel, 2008). The retention of emotional information could also be highlighted in the model because positive emotional information leads to an assignment of high value for older adults, reflecting a form of priority binding (e.g., MacKay & Ahmetzanov, 2005) for this type of salient information (see also Kensinger, 2009). Thus, the PV can be top-down, assigned consciously, and be based on the goals or agendas of the individual (Ariel, Dunlosky, & Bailey, 2009) or could be more data driven and based on certain characteristics of the information (e.g., McDaniel et al., 2003).

The TRV is typically goal driven, but is often dictated by external schedules because one would need to recall the information at a certain time (e.g., for a student, during an exam), as opposed to at any later time (e.g., once the exam is over, the retrieval of the needed answer is not as helpful). Variability in the TRV can result in recalling needed information well after the desired retrieval time, such as remembering a colleague's name 10 minutes after you failed to introduce him to a group of friends. Thus, another variable that could be added is the level of specificity in which you need to remember the information, and the specificity of the retrieval time period—something that is often modified with age (Craik, 2002). For example, remembering more generally to mail your great aunt's birthday card "sometime next week" versus remembering to send the card on Wednesday, before noon, could be introduced into this type of model. Lastly, this model requires empirical testing, and informative data can be generated only when to-be-remembered information differs in value.

It should also be noted that these examples involve retrospective memory for the material in question and how important it is to remember, as well as prospective memory to carry out the tasks (e.g., Kliegel, Martin, McDaniel, & Einstein, 2001, 2004). The research on value and memory discussed so far focused on retrospective memory for the most part and kept the retention interval constant, as dictated by the experimenter. Thus, in order to explore the parameters introduced in this priority processing model fully, one would need to incorporate items/tasks that differ in importance, as well as when the information needs to be later retrieved, and this would be a useful avenue for future research.

FUTURE DIRECTIONS

Much of this chapter has focused on psychological, lab-based assessments of metacognition and memory and how the processing of important information can be "improved" through specific manipulations of goals, motivation, value, and task experience. However, this concept of improving or aiding memory has been garnering increased attention within other disciplines as well. Currently, information technology can seemingly enhance and complicate how we remember important information (see Azevedo, 2007) and thus this area is one that is well suited to utilize and incorporate the lessons we have learned in lab.

As older adults may become less reluctant to use information technology to assist memory function (Charness & Boot, 2010), the judicious use of memory and the interplay between metacognition and the use of information technology in old age is an emerging field. For example, in order to assist with the recording of life events in "memory," Microsoft has developed a wearable digital camera (the SenseCam) that is designed to passively take timed photographs of the environment and personal encounters. In addition, other companies are developing ways to "lifelog" and record almost every minute of one's sensory life experience so that this information can later be accessed if necessary (see Benjamin, 2008; Finley, Tullis, & Benjamin, 2010).

The problematic part of this (excessively) constant recording process is determining what information will, in fact, be needed at a later time. The selection process, as Williams James stated in 1890, is the key to filtering what information is important to remember because being able to remember everything is just as bad as remembering nothing. Marking certain information as important might assist this process so that a memory-assisting device can allow for later and rapid access of this "marked" high-value information, as opposed to having to sift through volumes of irrelevant information. Thus, given the ease of being able to record and store vast amounts of information on a computer chip, the human is left with the critical task of determining what is important—something that perhaps the human memory system is already accomplishing while you read this sentence.

Given the fact that we are constantly bombarded with both useful and irrelevant information and need to be selective about what to attend to, developing a sense of what is important seems critical to leading an efficient and enjoyable life. The ability to focus on, or learn to focus on, important information is a central theme of the value-directed remembering approach. Within the lab, the development and acquisition of this "priority learning" process can occur over the course of a brief training session with a specific memory task (see Figures 10.2 and 10.3).

In a broader context, this ability develops over the course of a college education, in that one (hopefully) learns how to focus on and extract important information in classes and from textbooks. For older adults, this likely occurs over the course of a lifetime in terms of being discerning about what information is important to remember for one's work and daily life. This ability to prioritize and strategically allocate resources toward encoding important information becomes particularly valuable as one ages, given challenges in overall memory function. This ability may be preserved or enhanced despite decline in executive control (MacPherson, Phillips, & Della Sala, 2002) and may be related to older adults' ability to effectively regulate other domains, such as emotion, when attempting to solve problems (Blanchard-Fields, 2007).

In the real world, people obviously vary in terms of what information they find important or interesting and what they wish to remember, and tasks in which the value of the information is predetermined (such as in the selectivity task) do not capture how subjective assessments of importance influence memory. Thus, future research should assess memory under conditions in which the assignment of value is under the subjective control of the individual. For example, when most people pack for an upcoming trip, there are several essential items that they pack (e.g., toothbrush, clothes); the ability to choose which items are more important and how this varies depending on where you are going could offer insight into how individuals prioritize and later remember important information.

When clear and salient cues are used to communicate importance (e.g., point value or a loud voice communicating a message) or when importance within a domain with which one is familiar and has experience (such as packing for a trip) is being determined, older adults may be efficient in terms of later remembering important information. However, if one must first determine importance and then allocate resources to what one believes is important when faced with an unfamiliar situation or set of materials, this could prove to be overly taxing, and memory may suffer. That is, if resources are spent simply trying to figure out how important something is, this could prevent those resources from being allocated to remembering the information or engaging in memory-enhancing strategies. Therefore, future research is needed in order to determine more precisely the conditions under which encouraging and implementing selectivity and priority processing will be beneficial or possibly detrimental to memory performance.

Finally, additional research is also needed to investigate further how metacognition can modify what we attend to and what we then later remember. At present, numerous studies indicate that metacognitive monitoring and control remain fairly intact throughout the life span. Even studies that have found sizable metacognitive deficits in older adults (e.g., Bunnell, Baken, & Richards-Ward, 1999) have also usually found that these deficits are less so than those associated with actual memory ability. That is, metamemory abilities are likely better preserved in older adults than explicit memory abilities. This is encouraging in and of itself such that older adults may be able to use metacognitive strategies and awareness to help overcome or compensate for age-related declines in memory performance, consistent with the "metacognition modifying attention" hypothesis. The dynamic ability that individuals have to learn about their own memory capacity and how this knowledge can lead to the efficient allocation of attention toward important information is an area of research that is rife with possibilities.

CONCLUDING COMMENTS

The present chapter outlines how, despite a variety of memory impairments, older adults can efficiently use memory by focusing on important information. Metacognition and goals can modify attention, allowing older adults to be selective about what and how much information they encode by placing priority on high-value information. How older adults learn to identify and remember important information remains an open question, and what is in fact important may be directly related to life experience, culture, and wisdom (see Grossmann et al., 2010; Na et al., 2010). Given that memory declines in old age, but metamemory is often spared or even enhanced, it is both realistic and optimistic to consider how metacognition allows older adults to remember important information effectively.

ACKNOWLEDGMENTS

We would like to thank David McCabe, Matthew Rhodes, Aaron Benjamin, and Tom Hess, who provided useful feedback and discussion regarding topics presented in this chapter.

REFERENCES

Adams, C. (1991). Qualitative age difference in memory for text: A lifespan developmental perspective. *Psychology and Aging, 6,* 323–336.

Adams, C., Smith, M. C., Nyquist, L., & Perlmutter, M. (1997). Adult age-group differences in recall for the literal and interpretive meanings of narrative test. *Journal of Gerontology: Psychological Science, 57B,* P28–P40.

Anderson, J. R., & Schooler, L. J. (1991). Reflections of the environment in memory. *Psychological Science, 2,* 396–408.

Anderson, J. R., & Schooler, L. J. (2000). The adaptive nature of memory. In E. Tulving & F. I. M. Craik (Eds.), *The Oxford handbook of memory* (pp. 557–570). Oxford, England: Oxford University Press.

Ardelt, M. (1997). Wisdom and life satisfaction in old age. *Journal of Gerontology: Psychological Sciences, 52B,* P15–P27.

Ardelt, M. (2000). Intellectual versus wisdom-related knowledge: The case for a difference type of learning in the later year of life. *Educational Gerontology, 26,* 771–789.

Ariel, R., Dunlosky, J., & Bailey, H. (2009). Agenda-based regulation of study-time allocation: When agendas override item-based monitoring. *Journal of Experimental Psychology: General, 138,* 432–447.

Azevedo, R. (2007). Understanding the complex nature of self-regulatory processes in learning with computer-based learning environments: An introduction. *Metacognition and Learning, 2,* 57–65.

Balota, D. A., & Faust, M. E. (2001). Attention in dementia of the Alzheimer's type. In F. Bolla & S. Cappa (Eds.), *Handbook of neuropsychology: Vol. 6. Aging and dementia* (2nd ed., pp. 51–80). New York, NY: Elsevier Science.

Baltes, P. B., & Baltes, M. M. (1990). Psychological perspectives on successful aging: The model of selective optimization with compensation. In P. B. Baltes & M. M. Baltes (Eds.), *Successful aging: Perspectives from the behavioral sciences* (pp. 1–34). New York, NY: Cambridge University Press.

Beilock, S. L., & Carr, T. H. (2001). On the fragility of skilled performance: What governs choking under pressure? *Journal of Experimental Psychology: General, 130,* 701–725.

Benjamin, A. S. (2008). Memory is more than just remembering: Strategic control of encoding, accessing memory, and making decisions. In A. S. Benjamin & B. H. Ross (Eds.), *The psychology of learning and motivation* (Vol. 48, pp. 225–270). London, England: Academic Press.

Bjork, E. L., Bjork, R. A., & Anderson, M. C. (1998). Varieties of goal-directed forgetting. In J. M. Golding & C. MacLeod (Eds.), *Intentional forgetting: Interdisciplinary approaches* (pp. 103–137). Hillsdale, NJ: Lawrence Erlbaum Associates.

Blanchard-Fields, F. (2007). Everyday problem solving and emotion: An adult developmental perspective. *Current Directions in Psychological Science, 16,* 26–31.

Bruce, P. R., Coyne, A. C., & Botwinick, J. (1982). Adult age differences in metamemory. *Journal of Gerontology, 37,* 354–357.

Bunnell, J. K., Baken, D. M., & Richards-Ward, L. A. (1999). The effect of age on metamemory for working memory. *New Zealand Journal of Psychology, 28,* 23–29.

Carstensen, L. L. (1992). Social and emotional patterns in adulthood: Support for socioemotional selectivity theory. *Psychology and Aging, 7,* 331–338.

Carstensen, L. L. (1995). Evidence for a life-span theory of socioemotional selectivity. *Current Directions in Psychological Science, 4,* 151–156.

Castel, A. D. (2005). Memory for grocery prices in younger and older adults: The role of schematic support. *Psychology and Aging, 20,* 718–721.

Castel, A. D. (2008). The adaptive and strategic use of memory by older adults: Evaluative processing and value-directed remembering. In A. S. Benjamin & B. H. Ross (Eds.), *The psychology of learning and motivation* (Vol. 48, pp. 225–270). London, England: Academic Press.

Castel, A. D., Balota, D. A., & McCabe, D. P. (2009). Memory efficiency and the strategic control of attention at encoding: Impairments of value-directed remembering in Alzheimer's disease. *Neuropsychology, 23,* 297–306.

Castel, A. D., Benjamin, A. S., Craik, F. I. M., & Watkins, M. J. (2002). The effects of aging on selectivity and control in short-term recall. *Memory & Cognition, 30,* 1078–1085.

Castel, A. D., Farb, N., & Craik, F. I. M. (2007). Memory for general and specific value information in younger and older adults: Measuring the limits of strategic control. *Memory & Cognition, 35,* 689–700.

Castel, A. D., Lee, S. S., Humphreys, K. L., & Moore, A. N. (2011). Memory capacity, selective control, and value-directed remembering in children with and without attention-deficit/hyperactivity disorder (ADHD). *Neuropsychology, 25,* 15–24.

Castel, A. D., Humphreys, K. L., Lee, S. S., Galván, A., Balota, D. A., & McCabe, D. P. (in press). The development of memory efficiency and value-directed remembering across the lifespan: A cross-sectional study of memory and selectivity. *Developmental Psychology.*

Charness, N., & Boot, W. R. (2010). Aging and information technology use: Potential and barriers. *Current Directions in Psychological Science, 18,* 253–258.

Chasteen, A. L., Bhattacharyya, S., Horhota, M., Tam, R., & Hasher, L. (2005). How feelings of stereotype threat influence older adults' memory performance. *Experimental Aging Research, 31,* 235–260.

Connor, L. T., Dunlosky, J., & Hertzog, C. (1997). Age-related differences in absolute but not relative metamemory accuracy. *Psychology and Aging, 12,* 50–71.

Coyne, A. C. (1985). Adult age, presentation time, and memory performance. *Experimental Aging Research, 11,* 147–149.

Craik, F. I. M. (2002). Human memory and aging. In L. Bäckman & C. von Hofsten (Eds.), *Psychology at the turn of the millennium* (pp. 261–280). Hove, UK: Psychology Press.

Denburg, N. L., Tranel, D., & Bechara, A. (2005). The ability to decide advantageously declines prematurely in some normal older persons. *Neuropsychologia, 43,* 1099–1106.

Dunlosky, J., & Connor, L. T. (1997). Age differences in the allocation of study time account for age differences in memory performance. *Memory & Cognition, 25,* 691–700.

Dunlosky, J., & Hertzog, C. (1997). Older and younger adults use a functionally identical algorithm to select items for restudy during multitrial learning. *Journal of Gerontology: Psychological Sciences, 52,* P178–186.

Dunlosky, J., & Hertzog, C. (1998). Training program to improve learning in later adulthood: Helping older adults educate themselves. In D. J. Hacker, J. Dunlosky, & A. C. Graesser (Eds.), *Metacognition in educational theory and practice* (pp. 249–275). Mahwah, NJ: Lawrence Erlbaum Associates.

Dunlosky, J., & Hertzog, C. (2000). Updating knowledge about encoding strategies: A componential analysis of learning about strategy effectiveness from task experience. *Psychology and Aging, 15,* 462–474.

Dunlosky, J., & Metcalfe, J. (2009). *Metacognition.* Thousand Oaks, CA: Sage Publications, Inc.

Ericsson, K. A., Charness, N., Feltovich, P. J., & Hoffman, R. R. (2006). *The Cambridge handbook of expertise and expert performance.* New York, NY: Cambridge University Press

Finley, J. R., Tullis, J. G., & Benjamin, A. S. (2010). Metacognitive control of learning and remembering. In M. S. Khine & I. Saleh (Eds.), *New science of learning: Cognition, computers and collaboration in education.* New York, NY: Springer.

Freund, A. F., Kourilova, S., & Kuhl, P. (2011). Stronger evidence for own-age effects in memory for older as compared to younger adults. *Memory, 19,* 429–448.

Freund, A. M., & Baltes, P. B. (2002). Life-management strategies of selection, optimization, and compensation: Measurement by self-report and construct validity. *Journal of Personality and Social Psychology, 82,* 642–662.

Friedman, M. C., Castel, A. D., McGillivray, S., & Flores, C. C. (2010, April). *Associative memory for money and faces in young and old adults.* Poster presented at the 13th Biennial Cognitive Aging Conference, Atlanta, GA.

Fung, H., & Carstensen, L. L. (2003). Sending memorable messages to the old: Age differences in preferences and memory for advertisements. *Journal of Personality and Social Psychology, 85,* 163–178.

Garcia Márquez, G. J. (2005). *Memories of my melancholy whores* (p. 10). New York, NY: Alfred A. Knopf.

Germain, C. M., & Hess, T. M. (2007). Motivational influences on controlled processing: Moderating distractibility in older adults. *Aging Neuropsychology and Cognition, 14,* 462–486.

Grossmann, I., Na, J., Varnum, M. E. W., Park, D. C., Kitayama, S., & Nisbett, R. E. (2010). Reasoning about social conflicts improves into old age. *Proceedings of the National Academy of Sciences USA, 107,* 7246–7250.

Halamish, V., McGillivray, S., & Castel, A. D. (in press). Monitoring one's own forgetting in younger and older adults. *Psychology and Aging.*

Hanten, G., Li, X., Chapman, S. B., Swank, P., Gamino, J. F., Roberson, G., & Levin, H. S. (2007). Development of verbal selective learning. *Developmental Neuropsychology, 32,* 585–596.

Hasher, L., & Zacks, R. T. (1988). Working memory, comprehension, and aging: A review and a new view. In G. H. Bower (Ed.), *The psychology of learning and motivation* (Vol. 22, pp. 193–225). New York, NY: Academic Press.

Heckhausen, J. (1999). Developmental regulation in adulthood: Age normative and sociostructural constraints as adaptive challenges. New York, NY: Cambridge University Press.

Heckhausen, J., & Schulz, R. (1995). A life span theory of control. *Psychological Review, 102,* 284–304.

Hertzog, C., & Hultsch, D. F. (2000). Metacognition in adulthood and old age. In F. I. M. Craik & T. A. Salthouse (Eds.), *The handbook of aging and cognition* (2nd ed., pp. 417–466). Mahwah, NJ: Lawrence Erlbaum Associates.

Hertzog, C., Kidder, D. P., Powell-Moman, A., & Dunlosky, J. (2002). Aging and monitoring associative learning: Is monitoring accuracy spared or impaired? *Psychology and Aging, 17,* 209–225.

Hess, T. M. (2005). Memory and aging in context. *Psychological Bulletin, 131,* 383–406.

Hess, T. M., Rosenberg, D. C., & Waters, S. J. (2001). Motivation and representational processes in adulthood: The effects of social accountability and information relevance. *Psychology and Aging, 16,* 629–642.

James, L. (2006). Specific effects of aging on proper name retrieval: Now you see them, now you don't. *Journal of Gerontology, Psychological Science, 61,* P180–P183.

James, W. (1950). *The principles of psychology* (Vol. 1). New York, NY: Dover. (Original work published 1890.)

Jenkins, J. J. (1979). Four points to remember: A tetrahedral model of memory experiments. In L. S. Cermak & F. I. M. Craik (Eds.), *Levels of processing in human memory* (pp. 429–446). Hillsdale, NJ: Lawrence Erlbaum Associates.

Kensinger, E. A. (2009). How emotion affects older adults' memories for event details. *Memory, 17,* 208–219.

Kliegel, M., Martin, M., McDaniel, M. A., & Einstein, G. O. (2001). Varying the importance of a prospective memory task: Differential effects across time- and event-based prospective memory. *Memory, 9,* 1–11.

Kliegel, M., Martin, M., McDaniel, M. A., & Einstein, G. O. (2004). Importance effects in event-based prospective memory tasks. *Memory, 12,* 553–561.

Koriat, A., & Goldsmith, M. (1996). Monitoring and control processes in the strategic regulation of memory accuracy. *Psychological Review, 103,* 490–517.

Koutstaal, W. (2006). Flexible remembering. *Psychonomic Bulletin and Review,* 13(1), 84–91.

Kovalchik, S., Camerer, C. F., Grether, D. M., Plott, C. R., & Allman, J. M. (2005). Aging and decision making: A comparison between neurologically healthy elderly and young individuals. *Journal of Economic Behavior & Organization, 58,* 79–94.

Labouvie-Vief, G. (1990). Wisdom as integrated thought: Historical and developmental perspectives. In R. J. Sternberg (Ed.), *Wisdom: Its nature, origin, and development* (pp. 52–86). New York, NY: Cambridge University Press.

Lachman, M. E. (2006). Perceived control over aging-related declines: Adaptive beliefs and behaviors. *Current Directions in Psychological Science, 15,* 282–286.

Lachman, M. E., & Jelalian, E. (1984). Self-efficacy and attributions for intellectual performance in young and elderly adults. *Journal of Gerontology, 39,* 577–582.

Levy, B. (1996). Improving memory in old age through implicit self-stereotyping. *Journal of Personality and Social Psychology, 71,* 1092–1107.

Lovelace, E. A., & Marsh, G. R. (1985). Prediction and evaluation of memory performance by young and old adults. *Journal of Gerontology, 40,* 192–197.

MacKay, D. G., & Ahmetzanov, M. V. (2005). Emotion, memory, and attention in the taboo Stroop paradigm: An experimental analog of flashbulb memories. *Psychological Science, 16,* 25–32.

MacPherson, S. E., Phillips, L. H., & Della Sala, S. (2002). Age, executive function, and social decision making: A dorsolateral prefrontal theory of cognitive aging. *Psychology and Aging, 17,* 598–609.

Mather, M., & Carstensen, L. L. (2005). Aging and motivated cognition: The positivity effect in attention and memory. *Trends in Cognitive Sciences, 9*(10), 496–502.

Mather, M., & Knight, M. (2005). Goal-directed memory: The role of cognitive control in older adults' emotional memory. *Psychology and Aging, 20,* 554–570.

Matvey, G., Dunlosky, J., Shaw, R. J., Parks, C., & Hertzog, C. (2002). Age-related equivalence and deficit in knowledge updating of cue effectiveness. *Psychology and Aging, 17,* 589–597.

McCabe, D. P., Roediger, H. L., McDaniel, M. A., Balota, D. A., & Hambrick, D. Z. (2010). The relationship between working memory capacity and executive functioning: Evidence for an executive attention construct. *Neuropsychology, 24,* 222–243.

McDaniel, M. A., Einstein, G. O., Stout, A. C., & Morgan, Z. (2003). Aging and maintaining intentions over delays: Do it or lose it. *Psychology and Aging, 8,* 823–835.

McGillivray, S., & Castel, A. D. (2010). Memory for age–face associations: The role of generation and schematic support. *Psychology and Aging, 25,* 822–832.

McGillivray, S., & Castel, A. D. (2011). Betting on memory leads to metacognitive improvement by younger and older adults. *Psychology and Aging, 26,* 137–142.

Murphy, M. D., Sanders, R. E., Gabriesheski, A. S., & Schmitt, F. A. (1981). Metamemory in the aged. *Journal of Gerontology, 36,* 185–193.

Na, J., Grossmann, I., Varnum, M. E. W., Kitayama, S., Gonzalez, R., & Nisbett, R. E. (2010). Cultural differences are not always reducible to individual differences. *Proceedings of the National Academy of Sciences USA, 107,* 6192–6197.

Naveh-Benjamin, M., Guez, J., Kilb, A., & Reedy, S. (2004). The associative deficit of older adults: Further support using face-name associations. *Psychology and Aging, 19,* 541–546.

Old, S., & Naveh-Benjamin, M. (2008). Differential effects of age on item and associative measures of memory: A meta-analysis. *Psychology and Aging, 23,* 104–118.

Pansky, A., Goldsmith, M., Koriat, A., & Pearlman-Avnion, S. (2009). Memory accuracy in old age: Cognitive, metacognitive, and neurocognitive determinants. *European Journal of Cognitive Psychology, 21,* 303–329.

Peters, E., Hess, T. M., Vastfjall, D., & Auman, C. (2007). Adult age differences in dual information processes: Implications for the role of affective and deliberative processes in older adults' decision making. *Perspectives on Psychological Science, 21*, 1–23.

Rabinowitz, J. C., Craik, F. I. M., & Ackerman, B. P. (1982). A processing resource account of age differences in recall. *Canadian Journal of Psychology, 36*, 325–344.

Rahhal, T. A., May, C. P., & Hasher, L. (2002). Truth and character: Sources that older adults can remember. *Psychological Science, 13*, 101–105.

Rast, P., & Zimprich, D. (2009). Age differences in the underconfidence-with-practice effect. *Experimental Aging Research, 35*, 400–431.

Rendell, P. G., Castel, A. D., & Craik, F. I. M. (2005). Memory for proper names in old age: A disproportionate impairment? *Quarterly Journal of Experimental Psychology, 58A*, 54–71.

Rendell, P. G., & Craik, F. I. M. (2002). Virtual week and actual week: Age-related differences in prospective memory. *Applied Cognitive Psychology, 14*, 43–62.

Rhodes, M. G., Castel, A. D., & Jacoby, L. L. (2008). Associative recognition of face pairs by younger and older adults: The role of familiarity-based processing. *Psychology and Aging, 23*, 239–249.

Riediger, M., & Freund, A. M. (2006). Focusing and restricting: Two aspects of motivational selectivity in adulthood. *Psychology and Aging, 21*, 173–185.

Riediger, M., Li, S.-C., & Lindenberger, U. (2006). Selection, optimization, and compensation as developmental mechanisms of adaptive resource allocation: Review and preview. In J. E. Birren & K. W. Schaie (Eds.), *Handbook of the psychology of aging* (6th ed., pp. 289–313). Amsterdam, the Netherlands: Elsevier.

Sahakyan, L., Delaney, P., & Goodmon, L. (2008). Oh, honey, I already forgot that: Strategic control of directed forgetting in older and younger adults. *Psychology and Aging, 23*, 621–633.

Salthouse, T. A. (1996). The processing-speed theory of adult age differences in cognition. *Psychological Review, 103*, 403–428.

Schacter, D. L. (1999). The seven sins of memory: Insights from psychology and cognitive neuroscience. *American Psychologist, 54*, 182–203.

Spieler, D. H., Mayr, U., & LaGrone, S. (2006). Outsourcing cognitive control to the environment: Adult age differences in the use of task cues. *Psychonomic Bulletin & Review, 13*, 787–793.

Stein, R., Blanchard-Fields, F., & Hertzog, C. (2002). The effects of age stereotype priming on the memory performance of older adults. *Experimental Aging Research, 28*, 169–181.

Tentori, K., Osherson, D., Hasher, L., & May, C. (2001). Wisdom and aging: Irrational preferences in college students but not older adults. *Cognition, 81*, B87–B96.

Tomaszczyk, J. C., Fernandes, M. A., & MacLeod, C. M. (2008). Personal relevance modulates the positivity bias in recall of emotional pictures in older adults. *Psychonomic Bulletin & Review, 15*, 191–196.

Touron, D. R. (2006). Are item-level strategy shifts abrupt and collective? Age differences in cognitive skill acquisition. *Psychonomic Bulletin & Review, 13*, 781–786.

Tversky, A. (1969). Intransitivity of preferences. *Psychological Review, 76*, 31–48.

Tversky, A. (1972). Elimination by aspects. A theory of choice. *Psychological Review,* *79*, 281–299.

Watkins, M. J., & Bloom, L. C. (1999). *Selectivity in memory: An exploration of* *willful control over the remembering process.* Unpublished manuscript.

Zacks, R. T., & Hasher, L. (2006). Aging and long-term memory: Deficits are not inevitable. In E. Bialystok & F. I. M. Craik (Eds.), *Lifespan cognition: Mechanisms* *of change* (pp. 162–177). New York, NY: Oxford University Press.

Zacks, R. T., Radvansky, G., & Hasher, L. (1996). Studies of directed forgetting in older adults. *Journal of Experimental Psychology: Learning, Memory, and* *Cognition, 22,* 143–156.

Part 4

Neuroscientific, biological, epidemiological, and health perspectives

11 Multimodal neuroimaging in normal aging

Structure–function interactions

Grégoria Kalpouzos and Lars Nyberg

INTRODUCTION

Both biological and environmental factors influence brain structure and function throughout the life span. This is particularly obvious in development, when the brain undergoes maturational processes such as myelination and cortical architecture construction. These processes lead to specialization of networks accompanied by increasing cognitive performance (Casey, Tottenham, Liston, & Durston, 2005). In late adulthood, biological and environmental factors seem to impact the structure and function of the brain, such that the reverse pattern is observed: degeneration of myelin sheaths (Peters, 2002) and neuronal death, more diffuse and less specific neural networks engaged during cognitive tasks, and decreasing cognitive performance. So far, many studies have established links between cognition and brain structure as well as brain processes.

However, direct relationships between structural and functional cerebral changes have been little investigated and several key questions remain, including: To which extent do structural modifications related to the normal biological mechanisms that occur in normal aging influence brain function? To which extent do experience-driven functional changes (after training on a particular skill, for example) influence the architecture of the brain? In this chapter we begin to address these questions (see Figure 11.1). First, we report findings from the literature regarding structure–behavior and function–behavior relationships in aging. Second, results of studies in which structure–function links have been investigated are reported. Following this section about structural impact on function in aging, we discuss the impact of genetic and environmental factors on brain structure and function.

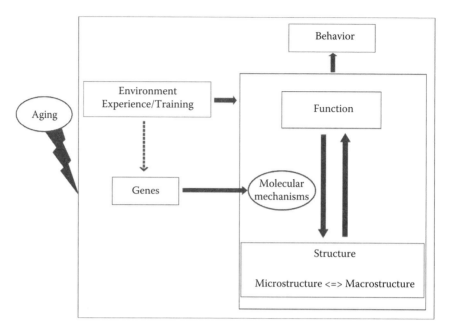

FIGURE 11.1 Schema illustrating the effects of genetic and environmental factors on the brain.

BRAIN STRUCTURE

Structural brain changes with advancing age

Macro- and microstructure of the aging brain has been extensively studied in vivo using magnetic resonance imaging (MRI). Specific MRI sequences have made possible the examination of the macrostructure of the brain. The T1-weighted sequence is most commonly used to measure gray matter (GM) and white matter (WM) volume or density with a resolution of 1 mm³. Microstructure of the brain, and especially of the WM, has mostly been examined using diffusion tensor imaging (DTI), where indices (fractional anisotropy, FA, and mean diffusivity, MD) extracted from water motion analysis provide information about the integrity of WM fibers (myelin, orientation, and regularity of WM fibers). Both cross-sectional and longitudinal studies converge toward frontal lobe shrinkage, with GM volume reduction and WM deterioration (Raz et al., 2005; Sowell et al., 2003).

More specifically within the prefrontal cortex (PFC), it is difficult to determine which of the subareas are more vulnerable with advancing age because of the different methods used as well as the different partitions adopted by various authors. It seems, however, that ventral areas of the PFC would be particularly vulnerable to aging effects, as well as lateral regions, but a large-scale meta-analysis is required for confirmation. Concerning WM, the corpus callosum, which connects the two hemispheres of the brain, seems to be mostly deteriorated in its anterior part (the genu), as well as frontal white matter.

Aging effects in other parts of the brain are less consistent across studies, due to several factors such as (1) the use of different methods of statistical analysis (region of interest [ROI]) versus whole-brain voxel-based methods (like voxel-based morphometry [VBM]); (2) the unwanted inclusion of subjects at preclinical stages of dementia, not detected at the time of scanning; and (3) design (cross-sectional studies where groups of different ages are compared versus longitudinal studies where the same individuals are scanned at different time points).

The hippocampus, a structure in the medial temporal lobes, provides a good example of the first two factors. Studies that have used the ROI approach reported hippocampal atrophy in normal aging (Raz et al., 2005). However, when using a whole-brain approach, it appears that relative to global GM loss, the hippocampus is one of the structures that undergoes moderate or no atrophy in comparison to other regions (Good et al., 2001; Grieve, Clarck, Williams, Peduto, & Gordon, 2005; Sullivan, Marsh, & Pfefferbaum, 2005). In addition, VBM studies showed that different subfields or parts of the hippocampus do not show similar GM changes. The head of the structure seems to be preserved while the posterior part (body and tail) may undergo GM volume loss (Kalpouzos, Chételat, Baron, et al., 2009; Kalpouzos, Persson, & Nyberg, 2011).

Chételat et al. (2008) demonstrated that the subiculum may be more sensitive to GM density loss while the CA1 and other subfields would be preserved. These results highlight an important difference between normal aging and Alzheimer's disease (AD) in which the hippocampus is the most structurally deteriorated region of the brain. Moreover, in AD, the anterior part of the hippocampus and the CA1 subfield show the greatest deterioration. Some authors have proposed the "last in, first out" or "developmental" hypothesis in normal aging, where the most ancient structures (both phylogenetically and ontogenetically) are more resistant to biological aging processes, and the most recent ones to develop (neocortical areas, especially the prefrontal lobe) are the first to deteriorate (Fjell et al., 2009; Grieve et al., 2005; Kalpouzos, Chételat, Baron, et al., 2009). MRI analyses on fetal brains showed early maturation of the hippocampal region—especially of its anterior part, which contains the most archaic substructures—and late maturation of the neocortical structures, more particularly of the prefrontal lobe (Prayer et al., 2006; Radoš, Judaš, & Kostović, 2006; Toga, Thompson, & Sowell, 2006).

Other descriptive models have emerged concerning WM maturation and age-related deterioration (relying in great part on myelination). In normal aging, several studies provided strong evidence for an anterior–posterior gradient of WM shrinkage. Indeed, the most systematically deteriorated WM was found in the frontal lobes and the anterior corpus callosum, with decreased anisotropy and increased diffusivity (for review, see Sullivan &

Pfefferbaum, 2006). A reverse description has been provided regarding development, where myelination proceeds from posterior to anterior—fitting well with the developmental theory of aging, but also from inferior to superior.

Another description has been provided in relation to the fibers' length and function: Proximal pathways would be myelinated before distal pathways, sensory before motor, and projection tracts before association tracts (for review, see Lenroot & Giedd, 2007). A DTI study on aging examined the three main fiber structures: callosal tracts connecting contralateral regions of the two hemispheres, association tracts connecting intrahemispheric cortical regions, and projection tracts connecting the cortex to the thalamus, brainstem, and spinal cord (Stadlbauer, Salomonowitz, Strunk, Hammen, & Ganslandt, 2008). The strongest age effect on anisotropy was found in associative fibers; a moderate effect was found on callosal fibers, and nonsignificant effects on projection fibers. A significant difference of correlations between associative and projection fibers was found, in line with the developmental hypothesis. The latter has been supported by Davis et al. (2009), who used a state-of-the-art method to analyze white matter tracts—tractography—that allows investigation of gradual effects on long white matter tracts. The authors specifically investigated tracts that connect the frontal lobe to other more posterior areas (uncinate fasciculus and cingulate bundle) and evidenced that age effects increase along these tracts linearly from posterior to anterior regions.

Overall, the previously mentioned findings converge toward the developmental hypothesis of aging, which is seductive and appears logical. A description of evolution and aging processes in more brain areas and a discussion can be found in Raz (2000) and is illustrated in Figure 11.2. To our knowledge, a systematic study of this kind of evolutionary model has not yet been done. Moreover, the effects of genetic/biological and environmental factors may increase the complexity, and this model may require adjustments.

Two recent studies do not support this model. Westlye and colleagues analyzed T1-weighted signal intensity and thickness (Westlye et al., 2010a) and DTI measures (Westlye et al., 2010b) in subjects aged 8–85 years old. Signal intensity likely indicates intracortical axonal myelination and synaptic density, while DTI provides indices regarding WM properties. The former was accurate in dissociating maturational processes and aging-related mechanisms. The authors found a peak of maturation at 8 years old for the occipital cortex, and about 30 years old for the frontal cortex. A plateau was observed at middle age, and after the age of 60 deterioration was first seen in posterior parietal and occipital regions, and later in the frontal lobe. DTI analyses did not support the developmental hypothesis either, but it must be noted that the authors extracted diffusivity indices from the center of the pathways, whereas more distal fibers connecting the neocortex, which are finer, may be more vulnerable to aging effects, in line with the proximal-distal gradient.

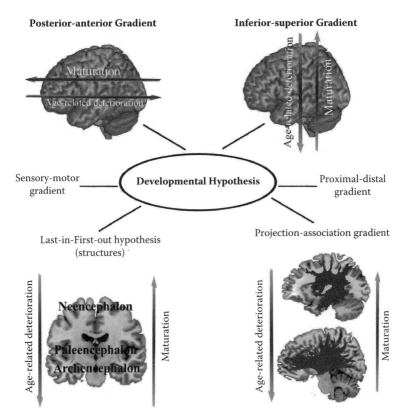

Posterior-anterior Gradient

Inferior-superior Gradient

Sensory-motor gradient

Developmental Hypothesis

Proximal-distal gradient

Last-in-First-out hypothesis (structures)

Projection-association gradient

FIGURE 11.2 Illustration of the different aspects of the developmental hypothesis. Several descriptive gradients have been suggested regarding development and age-related deterioration of gray matter and white matter tracts. The hypothesis is that the last regions and tracts to mature during development are those that deteriorate first in aging. This hypothesis has been notably suggested for brain structures ("last-in-first-out" hypothesis; Raz, 2000). The human brain is composed of three hierarchical systems, which successively appeared throughout evolution (phylogenesis). These systems are the archencephalon (the oldest one), the paleencephalon, and the neencephalon. The archencephalon is composed (in humans) of sensory-integrative cortical structures (archeo-cortex) such as the hippocampus and the reticulate matter. The paleencephalon has a paleo-cortex composed of the cingulate gyrus, the entorhinal circumvolution, and the olfactory system. Its sensory system is the thalamus, and its motor system is composed of the pallidum and motor nuclei of the thalamus (paleo-striatum). The neencephalon is composed of the cerebral cortex (or neocortex), primary areas, and nuclei of the basal ganglia (caudate nucleus, and putamen, or neostriatum). On the ontogenetic axis, the order of appearance and development of the structures seems to roughly follow the phylogenetic axis (Radoš et al., 2006). As shown in the figure, several gradients related to development and aging have been described, especially regarding structure. When it comes to function, some support for the developmental hypothesis can be found in some specific networks (e.g., the late matured and early deteriorated fronto-parietal network), but no further attempt has been made so far to test this model at the functional level.

Structure–behavior relationships

Assessing correlations between structural cerebral data and performance obtained at different cognitive tasks is useful in revealing a relationship between GM volume, WM integrity, and cognition. Most of the published studies failed to reveal relationships between GM loss in certain regions of the brain and memory in normal aging. Van Petten's meta-analysis (2004) across 33 studies and 107 memory tasks did not support the "bigger is better" hypothesis, postulating that more cortex would contribute to better performance. Correlations between hippocampal volume and memory performance in childhood and young adulthood were negative, reflecting the pruning process during development where GM reduction and WM increase are part of maturational processes. Strong variability was found in older subjects, resulting in no consistent association between hippocampal volume and memory. While the authors provided methodological reasons to explain this surprising result, we can evoke again the issue regarding the subfields of this structure, as well as the hypothesis that, in normal aging, structural hippocampal changes may not primarily support memory impairment, in contrast to preclinical Alzheimer's disease (Chételat et al., 2003).

Because most of the studies on age-related structural changes showed frontal deterioration rather than hippocampal deterioration, it is reasonable to assume that a significant link should exist between frontal structural deterioration and memory impairment. However, findings remain inconclusive (Van Petten et al., 2004), especially when using wide regions of interest. A few studies where voxel-based correlations between brain volume and performance were assessed did reveal a significant relationship between the volume of specific areas of the PFC and memory impairment (Kalpouzos, Chételat, Landeau, et al., 2009).

Another factor may explain the inconsistency of results: Simple brain-performance correlations may not be optimal in revealing direct relationships. The PFC is primarily involved in executive functioning, and it is possible that episodic memory impairment in healthy older adults is mediated by the alteration of other cognitive functions. Thus, the use of appropriate statistics such as mediation analyses, hierarchical regressions, and commonality analyses could be a solution in relating age-related PFC volume decrease and memory impairment. Head, Rodrigue, Kennedy, and Raz (2008) hypothesized that age may directly influence regional brain volume, which in turn may impact basic cognitive functions such as processing speed and executive functions, which may be responsible for a high-order cognitive function such as episodic memory. The authors measured the volume of several brain areas, and PFC volume did not exert a direct effect on memory (but the hippocampus did). However, a path analysis revealed that age had a direct effect on PFC volume and that the effect of PFC volume on memory was mediated by working memory and inhibition (which were impaired with advancing age).

Finally, we can invoke a third factor of sensitivity in highlighting structure–behavior links: longitudinal measurement instead of cross-sectional measurement of age-related changes. Kramer et al. (2007) investigated structure–behavior relationships on a longitudinal axis in 50 healthy older subjects (mean age at baseline ~ 74 years old; mean follow-up ~ 45 months, range 13–82 months). Using a hierarchical multiple regression analysis, the authors showed a significant impact of longitudinal hippocampal GM loss on memory impairment. This study demonstrated that longitudinal assessment may increase the sensitivity of the detection of structure–behavior links. However, age of the subjects included in this study may also explain the significant result. Indeed, it has been suggested that age-related GM loss of the hippocampus is not linear and would show a significant acceleration in older age after 65 years old (Allen, Bruss, Brown, & Damasio, 2005).

Structure–behavior correlations have also been shown between white matter integrity as measured with DTI and cognition in relation to age— although inconsistently, as for GM–behavior relationships. Correlations between indices of WM integrity and declining cognitive performance have been found in several domains—mainly, executive functioning, processing speed, visual search, and memory. Some authors have suggested the existence of a disconnection syndrome (O'Sullivan et al., 2001). This disconnection syndrome may be partly responsible for cognitive impairment in relation to aging (for review, see Gunning-Dixon, Brickman, Cheng, & Alexopoulos, 2009) and is supported by both ROI (Kennedy & Raz, 2009) and voxel-based (Sasson, Doniger, Pasternak, & Assaf, 2010) analyses. These studies showed that the age-related disruption of a distributed set of regions and extended fiber tracts (fronto-temporal, fronto-occipital, fronto-parietal) correlated with episodic and working memory, executive functions, and processing speed (see also Davis et al., 2009). The limited available data, especially concerning memory, do not allow strong conclusions regarding relationships between WM integrity and cognition in aging.

FUNCTIONAL BRAIN CHANGES WITH ADVANCING AGE

Functional MRI (and also positron emission tomography—PET), based on blood oxygenation level-dependent (BOLD) signal, allows the visualization of local brain activity during a given cognitive task. Models and theories have emerged to describe age-related modifications of the brain areas engaged while performing episodic memory tasks. As described later, a strong focus has been on the frontal lobe because the bulk of findings concerned age-related differences in this wide brain area.

In a seminal study, Grady et al. (1994) demonstrated for the first time reduced occipital activity and increased prefrontal activity in older adults during the perception of faces and locations. A hypothesis was put forward that older individuals compensated for sensory processing decline (in

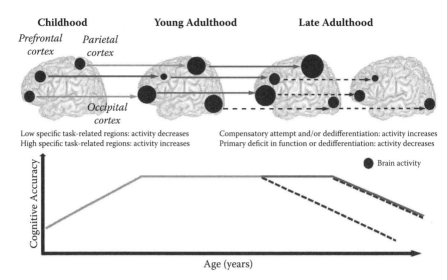

FIGURE 11.3   Schematic representation of brain activity changes from childhood to late adulthood in the prefrontal, parietal, and occipital cortices. In childhood, low performance in comparison to young adults is mainly related to the immaturity of the fronto-parietal system involved in high-order cognitive functions. From childhood to young adulthood, activity of prefrontal regions that are not task specific tends to attenuate, while that of prefrontal and parietal regions that are task specific increases. From young to late adulthood, two patterns can be seen: (1) increased prefrontal and parietal activity related to failed or successful compensation, and (2) decreased prefrontal activity related to decreased performance (primary deficit in function). Dedifferentiation can go along with compensation or primary deficit in function. Occipital activity decreases with increasing age and may reflect primary deficit in function.

this study, visual processing related to occipital cortex) by over-recruiting prefrontal areas (Figure 11.3). This pattern of results has been replicated several times and has been named PASA, for "posterior–anterior shift in aging" (Davis, Dennis, Daselaar, Fleck, & Cabeza, 2008).

This idea of functional compensation by over-recruitment of prefrontal areas has been investigated by Cabeza, Anderson, Locantore, and McIntosh (2002). In that study, 16 young and 16 older subjects were enrolled and asked to retrieve information from episodic memory. Afterward, high- and low-performing older adults were separated. The neuroimaging analyses showed that the high performers (who performed at the same level as the young subjects) overactivated the prefrontal cortex, while the low performers displayed similar activity to that of the younger group. Thus, overactivation seemed beneficial and may reflect functional reorganization of the prefrontal cortex in order to cope with cognitive demands. The authors noticed that while young adults' prefrontal activity was right lateralized, that of the high-performing older subjects was bilateral. More precisely, the contralateral prefrontal region was additionally engaged in this group of older subjects.

Functional prefrontal hemispheric specialization had been previously described in episodic memory in young adults, such that the left PFC is more engaged than the right PFC in encoding, and the right PFC is more engaged than the left one in retrieval (the hemispheric encoding/retrieval asymmetry [HERA] model; Habib, Nyberg, & Tulving, 2003; Nyberg, Cabeza, & Tulving, 1996; Tulving, Kapur, Craik, Moscovitch, & Houle, 1994). Thus, it seems that in aging, this asymmetry is lost, but bilateralization could be beneficial in improving performance. This observation gave rise to the *h*emispheric *a*symmetry *r*eduction in *old*er adults (HAROLD) model (Cabeza et al., 2002).

This phenomenon of bilateralization has not always been replicated. First, prefrontal overactivation related to aging is not systematic. On the contrary, many studies showed underactivation in older subjects (for review, see Persson & Nyberg, 2006). Second, in the case of bilateral recruitment, the exact prefrontal sites remained unspecific, whereas PFC structure varies from one region to the other and these subdivisions do subserve different functions. In an attempt to specify which age-related, overactivated prefrontal regions were related to compensation, dedifferentiation, and deficit in function, Rajah and D'Esposito (2005) conducted a qualitative meta-analysis on working and episodic memory findings. Globally, they found that left dorsal and anterior prefrontal cortex activity may reflect effective functional compensation in older subjects, whereas right dorsal and anterior frontal cortex disruption contributes to age-related memory impairment. Finally, ventral prefrontal under- or overactivation would be related to dedifferentiation in older people.

More recently, Park and Reuter-Lorenz (2009) integrated this notion of compensation by the PFC by elaborating the "scaffolding theory" of the aging brain (or STAC, standing for scaffolding theory of aging and cognition). This theory provides a dynamic and optimistic view of the aging brain. It relies on the observation that despite cognitive decline and GM and WM structural deterioration, increased prefrontal activity is often seen in older adults. This theory stipulates that increased prefrontal activity is a marker of compensatory mechanisms, adaptively elaborated in response to decline in order to optimize performance. STAC also stipulates that these compensatory processes can be further developed and maintained through cognitive engagement.

At least two issues must be raised regarding these models and theories. The first point is that they focus on the PFC, neglecting the other regions of the brain. A reason may be that the strongest age-related differences do occur in the PFC (see the meta-analysis performed by Spreng, Wojtowicz, & Grady, 2010). Another reason may be the variability of findings in other regions of the brain. An example is the regions of the medial temporal lobe.

As for structural neuroimaging results, very divergent findings and there-fore interpretations have been provided. It seems that a majority of studies did not find differences in hippocampal activity between younger and older subjects (see Persson, Kalpouzos, Nilsson, Ryberg, & Nyberg, 2011, for review). However, Hedden and Gabrieli (2004) reported studies where an age-related decline in hippocampal activity was found. Also, other authors showed that alteration with age was seen in the parahippocampal cortex rather than the hippocampus; this underactivity was accompanied by mem-ory impairment (Daselaar, Veltman, Rombouts, Raaijmakers, & Jonker, 2003; Gutchess et al., 2005).

In our laboratory, we conducted a study that aimed at testing whether hippocampal activity was affected in normal aging (Persson et al., 2011). We used the face–name paired-associates task, which consists of encod-ing pairs of faces associated with names and retrieving the corresponding names to the presented faces. This task elicited robust hippocampal activity in the young subjects, and we found no difference in hippocampal activity between younger and older subjects, who performed the task equally well. However, we did find moderate underactivation of the entorhinal cortex in the older group at encoding. Daselaar, Fleck, Dobbins, Madden, and Cabeza (2006) showed decreased activity of the hippocampus in a group of older subjects during episodic retrieval, but increased parahippocam-pal activity. The authors hypothesized that the overactivation seen in the parahippocampal cortex was compensatory. The older subjects had deficits in recollection processes at retrieval (supported by the hippocampus) and the authors hypothesized that compensation occurred by using familiarity-based mechanisms, which are preferentially underpinned by parahippo-campal areas.

The discrepancy between Persson and colleagues' (2011) and Daselaar and colleagues' (2006) studies may be due to differences in how the pro-tocols were designed and how the statistical analyses were conducted. In Persson et al., brain activity was measured by blocks of items without differentiating hits and misses and without considering the processes on which retrieval was based (recollection or familiarity); in Daselaar et al., brain activity was modeled for each item in a parametric fashion, accord-ing to the nature of the recognition (based more on recollection or more on familiarity).

In a longitudinal PET study, Beason-Held, Kraut, and Resnick (2008a, 2008b) showed increased activity of the hippocampus over a period of 9 years in resting state and episodic memory. Performance remained stable over this period. Also, the authors found that the regions that exhibited the strongest changes (both decreases and increases) were the PFC and the temporal cortex, suggesting ongoing functional reorganization over time in these regions. Occipital decreases and increases were also noticed. Finally, quite late during the follow-up (in years 7 and 9), inferior parietal activity decrease was observed. Interhemispheric compensation was suggested over time, reminiscent of the HAROLD model: While left entorhinal activity decreased in year 3, increased right hippocampal activity was observed in year 5 and left-sided increase in year 7.

Interestingly, a strong global contralateral compensation seemed to occur in the specific figural recognition task, where a right-sided decrease was accompanied with a left-sided increase in activity (this mostly concerned the lateral temporal cortex). This right-sided decrease in activity fits well with an older model of aging that we have not discussed yet: the right hemi-aging model.

The right hemi-aging model is the earliest model where integration of brain modifications and cognitive decline has been attempted (for review, see Dolcos, Rice, & Cabeza, 2002). It was initially based on the observation that older individuals showed more impairment on spatial tasks (which preferentially depend upon the right hemisphere) than on verbal tasks (which preferentially depend upon the left hemisphere). This model has been reevaluated together with the HAROLD model in a review by Dolcos and colleagues (2002), in favor of HAROLD. The authors also provided an overview of the weak validity of the right hemi-aging model.

The greatest impairment previously found in nonverbal tasks in older individuals may be due to task complexity, where verbal material already has a representation in mind, while spatial material is, most of the time, abstract. Other domains have been explored in relation to the right hemi-aging hypothesis, but have remained inconclusive. In general, structural neuroimaging studies did not support the hypothesis that the right hemisphere is more vulnerable than the left one; atrophy seems to be symmetric. Although this model is not considered anymore in the framework of aging, Rajah and D'Esposito (2005) highlighted in their meta-analysis some results compatible with the hypothetical fragility of the right hemisphere, notably based on the dopaminergic system.

Similarities and differences between structure–behavior and function–behavior findings

Structure–behavior relationships in aging showed most significant results in the PFC, and volume reduction would be related to cognitive impairment. Functional studies showed two opposite patterns in the PFC: under- and overactivation. While underactivation was related to low performance, overactivation would reflect cognitive compensation and thus higher performance. Underactivation can be easily linked to volume loss. However hypothetical structure–function relationship in the case of over-recruitment of the PFC is more difficult to interpret, especially in regard to the compensation theories described earlier. One issue to consider would be nonuniformity of atrophy within the frontal lobe. Indeed, an idea would be that under-recruitment may be seen in strongly atrophied prefrontal subareas, while over-recruitment may occur in prefrontal subareas that undergo moderate or no atrophy. The same logic can be applied to other brain areas as a general structure–function association.

Completely different patterns emerged when looking at the occipital cortex. Studies did not report any relationship between performance and structural integrity in aging. Functional studies quite systematically reported underactivation of occipital areas in older individuals. How to relate these opposite patterns is problematic. Here, too, it is possible that some specific regions of the occipital cortex undergo atrophy, as shown by some voxel-based studies (Abe et al., 2008; Kalpouzos, Chételat, Baron, et al., 2009; Salat et al., 2004).

While no consensus has yet been reached concerning structure–behavior relationship in regions of the medial temporal lobe, we can cautiously acknowledge a relative structural and functional preservation of the hippocampus in normal aging, at least up to a certain age, where the decline is more pronounced (estimated to be between 60 and 70 years old). Even though gray matter loss and hypofunction have been shown in this structure, normal aging effects are stronger in other areas of the brain—mainly, the neocortex. A significant structural and/or functional deterioration of the hippocampus may be linked to genuine memory impairment and perhaps constitute an early sign of AD.

Other regions of the brain have been less considered in aging, and it seems difficult to draw any conclusion regarding the parietal and temporal cortices, as well as the thalamus and cerebellum. Regarding the basal ganglia, while structural findings have not reached a consensus, we can, however, enlighten the fact that multimodal neuroimaging studies combining molecular (PET) and functional (MRI) data evidenced age-related disorders of the fronto-striatal dopaminergic system as subserving cognitive impairment (Nyberg & Bäckman, 2010).

STRUCTURE–FUNCTION RELATIONSHIPS: MULTIMODAL IMAGING

Until recently, multimodal neuroimaging in general and on aging in particular has rarely been considered. As one can deduce from the first two sections, studies on structure and studies on function are typically dissociated, although structural studies sometimes refer to functional findings and vice versa. While we attempted in the previous sections to establish links between structural and functional findings, it should be noted that one major difficulty in integrating information from several neuroimaging modalities lies in the methods available for subsequent analyses. Indeed, a limited number of specific tools is available, often resulting in suboptimal analyses.

Overall, three kinds of structure–function relationships have been investigated. The first one relies on the hypothesis that global reduction of the size of the brain may impact local function. Because these relationships lack specificity, we did not report these findings and refer the reader to Brodtmann, Puce, Darby, and Donnan (2009). In a second set of studies, the aim was to identify distal structure–function relationships such that structural deterioration of structure A would modify activity in structure B. In a third set of studies, regional and local structure–function relationships have been examined such that structural deterioration of structure A may be responsible for modified activity in structure A. We differentiate (1) "regional" and (2) "local" interactions by referring to (1) a predefined structure or part of the structure (e.g., the whole hippocampus or the head of the hippocampus) and (2) the voxel (volumetric pixel) level where structure–function interactions were assessed for each voxel of the brain.

Most of the studies concern distal structure–function relationships. Indeed, to the best of our knowledge in the field of normal aging, we are aware of only four studies (in addition to ours) in which regional/local structure–function relationships have been investigated. As noted before, the difficulty in performing voxel-by-voxel analyses is due to the lack of specific tools. Many factors must be controlled in direct multimodal analyses: Due to the nature of the acquisitions, within-subject brains may be different in their shape, intermodality variance is obviously different because the nature of the collected data is different (signal intensity related to GM volume, signal intensity related to BOLD), intermodality realignment must approach perfection, voxel size must be identical, and so on. As developed in the previous sections, subdivisions of a lobe (e.g., the PFC) may undergo different structural and functional changes in aging. Thus, in addition to distal structure–function links, it seemed of primary importance to examine whether age-related under- and over-recruitment could primarily be explained by local GM changes.

Distal structure–function interactions

Brassen and colleagues (2009) examined young and elderly women's brain structure and activation during an episodic retrieval memory task in which the older group globally performed worse than the younger one. The authors focused on the PFC and the temporal lobe. They used the ROI approach, so the GM density of the PFC was calculated as a mean of the dorsolateral and orbital prefrontal cortices. Individual GM density means were also extracted from the medial temporal lobe (hippocampus and parahippocampal cortex). For correctly retrieved items, the older subjects showed underactivation of the right dorsolateral PFC and over-recruitment of middle lateral temporal cortex bilaterally.

Across all subjects, GM density of each of the preselected ROIs negatively correlated with left lateral temporal activity, but positively with right PFC activity. When considering the older subjects separately, only positive correlations were found, and they were significant for the left temporal cortex but not for the right PFC. Finally, across all subjects, a positive correlation was found between PFC activity and the average of PFC and medial temporal lobe GM density. Thus, decreased PFC and increased lateral temporal activity in aging were associated with GM loss in the PFC and the medial temporal lobe. These findings showed how structural deterioration of a region may be related to functional compensation in another region and that this compensation may be possible under the condition of limited structural damage.

In a trimodal neuroimaging study including DTI, T1-weighted, and fMRI acquisitions, Persson, Nyberg, et al. (2006) investigated the structural and functional neural substrates of cognitive decline in normal aging and structure–function interactions. The authors separated older subjects on the basis of their episodic memory decline over 10 years. The individuals were scanned during incidental encoding. In comparison to the subjects who remained stable over time, the ones who later declined showed smaller hippocampi, over-recruitment of the right ventral PFC, and shrinkage of the anterior corpus callosum (the genu). Hippocampal volume did not significantly correlate with right ventral PFC activity, but a negative correlation was found between FA of the genu of the corpus callosum and activity of the right ventral PFC, such that the deterioration of anterior WM microstructure would be associated with additional recruitment of PFC and both were associated with cognitive decline.

Madden et al. (2007) examined visual attention in aging. They collected DTI and fMRI data in addition to behavioral data and performed bimodal imaging analyses. The authors focused on the fronto-parietal network, which is involved in top-down attention, when attention is directed toward the periphery in search for specific items (goal directed). Based on the disconnection hypothesis, the authors expected that age-related WM disruption would mediate differences in activation. Top-down attention was found to be preserved in the older subjects. The fronto-parietal network was over-recruited in the older subjects, and activity in the frontal eye field and the superior parietal lobule was positively correlated to performance.

According to the authors, this overactivation reflected compensation for declining bottom-up attention processes subtended by the visual areas (which, however, were not under-recruited in the older adults). DTI analyses showed more pronounced white matter deterioration in anterior regions (mainly superior and pericallosal frontal white matter), and FA of the pericallosal frontal WM was significantly correlated to parietal activity, such that lower frontal WM integrity was associated with increased parietal activity in the older group. A regression analysis did not confirm the result of the correlation and finally did not fully support the disconnection hypothesis; however, methodological issues (such as suboptimal DTI parameters) may have weakened statistical power.

These studies showed distal structure–function relationships with substantial discrepancies, notably regarding the hypothetical role of the structural deterioration of medial temporal lobe structures on prefrontal recruitment (Brassen et al., 2009; Persson, Nyberg, et al., 2006). However, they highlighted interesting results such that the deterioration of anterior WM fibers may induce prefrontal and parietal over-recruitment (Madden et al., 2007; Persson, Nyberg, et al., 2006). Also, Brassen et al. (2009) highlighted the overactivation of lateral temporal cortex in response to MTL and PFC damage, and this region has rarely been considered as a potential site for functional compensation in aging, as for parietal overactivity (Madden et al., 2007).

Regional and local structure–function interactions

In the perspective of evaluating top-down attention in aging, Thomsen et al. (2004) used the dichotic listening paradigm and fMRI. Cortical volumetry was also assessed. The authors found that for the condition where top-down attention was required, the older participants performed less well (in contradiction with the aforementioned study where top-down mechanisms were preserved; Madden et al., 2007). In this older group, the left middle frontal cortex (BA 8/9) was less activated, and a separate VBM analysis showed that this region was the only one to show significant GM density reduction. The authors hypothesized that this local structural shrinkage may have induced less activity in left prefrontal cortex and therefore impairment of top-down control. The authors did not report any statistical relationship between local frontal GM loss and reduced activity; however, the overlap between the underactivated region and the voxel-based results of the VBM analysis is indicative of a structure–function relationship.

Johnson et al. (2000) assessed a semantic categorization task using fMRI (and structural MRI) in normal aging and Alzheimer's disease. The authors limited the multimodal analyses to two activated clusters located in the left superior temporal gyrus and left inferior frontal gyrus. They further extracted an approximate volume of these regions and calculated an index of atrophy. No significant correlation between activity of the two regions and global or regional atrophy was found in the healthy group. A significant correlation was found in the Alzheimer's group, where more atrophy of the left inferior frontal gyrus was associated to more activity of this region. The authors concluded that this may be a compensatory neural or vascular response to neuronal loss in AD. Perhaps the suboptimal method used to extract volumes precluded their finding significant results in the healthy older adults.

A recent study addressed structure–function relationships in normal aging, examining word-finding failures that typically occur in the elderly, the tip-of-the-tongue states (Shafto, Stamatakis, Tam, & Tyler, 2010). The authors used both fMRI and VBM. They found a structure–function relationship in the older individuals in the left anterior insula, such that the elderly showed less insular activity during tip-of-the-tongue states than younger subjects, and this decrease in activity was related to reduced regional GM density.

To our knowledge, only one study used a voxel-based approach to investigate local structure–function relationships in aging (Bartrés-Faz et al., 2009). We have reported the results of this study in the following section, in relation to cognitive reserve.

In our laboratory, we overcame the limitations of regional measurements by conducting a voxel-based fMRI-GM study in aging (Kalpouzos et al., under review). This was done in order to disentangle whether the most common differences seen in age-related changes in activity were due to local GM loss. This study consisted of encoding and retrieval of face–name pairs by a group of young subjects and a group of older individuals. Both groups performed well, with no significant difference in performance. The functional results showed no significant difference of activity in the hippocampus between groups (Persson et al., 2011). Additional analysis of GM volume (using VBM) showed no age-related GM loss in the hippocampus except in the tail, supporting the idea that this structure is not of the most deteriorated, both structurally and functionally, with advancing age—at least in high-performing older adults.

As expected, we found functional differences in most age-sensitive regions such as the PFC, but also in the parietal and occipital cortices. The occipital cortex was less activated in the old group, especially during encoding, while the PFC and parietal cortex were more activated during retrieval. In order to consider GM volume at the voxel level, we used BPM (biological parametric mapping; Casanova et al., 2007). This toolbox allowed us to perform analyses of covariance, contrasting functional activation between the two groups while controlling for GM volume, voxel by voxel, providing a more subtle whole-brain structure–function analysis than using the ROI approach and calculation of mean values.

We found that occipital under-recruitment was due to a substantial GM volume loss occurring in this part of the brain—most strongly in the lingual gyrus. Increased prefrontal and parietal activity was partly explained by a decrease in GM volume. However, atrophy in these specific overactivated regions of the PFC (dorsomedial and dorsolateral PFC) and lateral parietal cortex was relatively minor in comparison to other PFC regions located more ventrally in our group of subjects and to more anterior parietal regions. Moreover, these overactivated regions were correlated to performance in the older group, providing evidence for compensatory mechanisms such that the aging brain would recruit regions that are moderately deteriorated in order to compensate for structural deterioration that occurs in other parts of the brain. However, performance was differentially correlated to frontal and parietal regions: We found negative function–behavior correlations in the PFC, but positive correlations in the parietal cortex, suggesting a lack of specificity in the selected over-recruited regions.

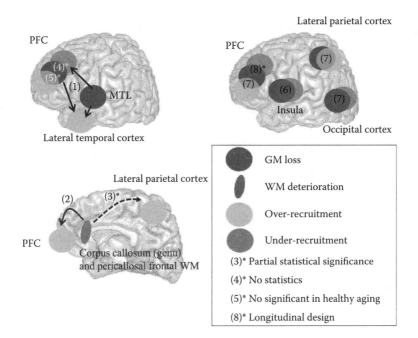

FIGURE 11.4 Schematic illustration of distal and regional/local structure–function interactions in aging, according to the findings of the following studies: (1) Brassen et al. (2009), (2) Persson et al. (2006), (3) Madden et al. (2007), (4) Thomsen et al. (2004), (5) Johnson et al. (2000), (6) Shafto et al. (2010), (7) Kalpouzos et al. (2011), and (8) Nyberg et al. (2010). Arrows represent distal structure–function interactions, while overlaid circles represent regions/local structure–function interactions. PFC: prefrontal cortex; MTL: medial temporal lobe; WM: white matter.

To sum up, the inspection of Figure 11.4, which reports the structure–function interactions described previously, tends to conclude that both age-related distal and local structural deterioration induces either over-recruitment or underactivation of the PFC. Although the few number of studies precludes any firm conclusion, it seems, however, that structural deterioration would preferentially induce prefrontal overactivation—as for the parietal cortex. All the studies that have demonstrated over-recruitment of the PFC and the parietal and temporal cortex also showed compensation or preservation of cognitive accuracy. (Even Persson, Nyberg, et al., 2006, who showed prefrontal over-recruitment in the declining group, also found a trend toward a positive function–behavior correlation within this group.) Our study and Brassen and colleagues' study showed that compensatory over-recruitment is possible when structural shrinkage is mild or moderate.

Because a few multimodal imaging studies have been performed in children, it would be interesting to draw a parallel between structure–function interactions in childhood and late adulthood in the framework of the developmental theory. As stipulated in the previous sections, the frontal lobe is the last structure to undergo maturation, expressed by decrease in synapses resulting in specialized neural networks (Thompson & Nelson, 2001). In activation studies, maturation is expressed as reduced and more efficient regional engagement (also termed differentiation). In other words, before the PFC has reached maturation, more regions are activated, with low specificity (no significant correlation with performance) and suboptimal performance (for a longitudinal fMRI study of PFC maturation, see Durston et al., 2006).

This pattern characterizing the nonmatured brain may mirror that of older brains, where over-recruitment could reflect dedifferentiation instead of—or together with—compensation (see Figure 11.3). A multimodal neuroimaging study showed interactions between microstructural integrity measured with DTI and activation as measured with fMRI: Olesen, Nagy, Westerberg, and Klingberg (2003) scanned 23 children aged 8–18 years during a working memory task. A correlation analysis showed significant relationships between FA values of WM located at the junction of the frontal and parietal lobes and BOLD signal of the superior frontal and inferior parietal cortices. Significant correlations were also found between FA of the anterior corpus callosum and fronto-parietal activity and caudate activity, FA of temporo-occipital WM and parietal activity, and caudate activity. Moreover, correlations between performance and activity in the superior frontal cortex, the inferior parietal cortex, and the caudate nucleus were significant. Finally, correlations between performance and FA in the anterior corpus callosum, temporo-occipital WM, anterior frontal WM, and fronto-parietal WM were also significant. Importantly, these correlations were related to individual age. Thus, this study demonstrated that age-related increase in WM organization contributes to increased task-related brain activity.

The few structure–function findings available in aging research are promising and this topic should be further explored in the future. The study of distal and local structure–function interactions provides important information to the understanding of age-related cognitive decline or preservation or compensation. Notably, the parallel we drew between maturational processes and mechanisms that occur in late adulthood is intriguing and seems to support the developmental hypothesis in aging. At least, the few findings we reported here support this view regarding the fronto-parietal network involved in high-order cognitive processes. Structural and functional late maturation of this network seems to determine optimal accuracy in high-order cognitive functions, while structural integrity of these regions in late adulthood may be a prerequisite for efficient functional compensation.

GENETIC AND ENVIRONMENTAL EFFECTS
ON STRUCTURE AND FUNCTION IN AGING

Brain structure, function, and related behavior (e.g., memory performance) are under the influence of both genetic and environmental factors. It has been hypothesized that different brain areas would be differentially influenced by these two factors (Thompson et al., 2001). A way to test this hypothesis is to use the twin design. The study of monozygote and dizygote twins allows estimation of the heritability of specific brain areas; monozygote twins are genetically identical and dizygote twins share approximately half similar genetic material.

Thompson and colleagues (2001) used a twin design and measured cortical thickness. They found that the frontal cortex and cortical areas involved in language (Broca's and Wernicke's areas) are under strong genetic control, and sensory-motor regions and parieto-occipital cortices undergo more genetic control in dizygote twins than unrelated persons. These results suggest a genetic continuum where frontal, language-related, and parieto-occipital association cortices would be highly dependent on genetics (the authors found a 95%–100% correlation between monozygote twins in these areas). This percentage remained significant between dizygote twins in Wernicke's area and the parieto-occipital cortex (60%–70%). It is noteworthy to report that left Broca's and Wernicke's areas were under genetic control while contralateral regions were not, providing perhaps a left-lateralized genetic advantage.

The authors also reported significant correlations between frontal structure and differences in general intelligence as measured by Spearman's *g* factor. This suggests that structure–behavior relationships are under genetic control in some brain areas. However, the study was conducted in a limited sample of individuals (10 pairs of dizygote twins and 10 pairs of monozygote twins) of an average age ~ 48 years old, precluding a definite conclusion.

A more recent study included 404 paired twins and evaluated the degree of genetic/shared (common) and environmental-/individual-specific (unique) influence in 96 regions of interest, including cortical areas with subdivisions (e.g., of the prefrontal cortex), subcortical areas, and the ventricles (Kremen et al., 2009). The age range of the subjects (all males) was limited to 51–59 years. This study, which provided a review of previous findings, is not in agreement with several assumptions or previous results. Even though the authors reported no significant differences, in most of the ROIs left gray and white matter showed more heritability than in the right hemisphere. In complement to Thompson et al. (2001), some frontal regions showed high heritability (left superior frontal gyrus, 75%), but others moderate to low (right frontal pole, 14%). Finally, the hippocampus, basal ganglia, thalamus, amygdala, and nucleus accumbens showed higher genetic influence than neocortical regions. The authors rejected the developmental hypothesis, arguing that "one might expect that genetic variance (and, thus, heritability) would be low for older structures because natural selection processes might be nearer to 'completion' for those structures" (p. 221).

The genetics-to-environment ratio on brain structure likely changes with age. To our knowledge, there is no large-scale twin study including age as a factor. However, we report two studies of interest in which the hippocampus and the corpus callosum were specifically considered in older subjects. Regarding the hippocampus, Sullivan, Pfefferbaum, Swan, and Carmelli (2001) showed that its volume was more influenced by the environment than genes in older male twins aged 68–78 years (there was no decline of the hippocampal volume with age). Even though the well-known neurogenesis that occurs in the hippocampus cannot account for volume maintenance over age, its existence constitutes strong proof for the possibility of malleability by environmental inputs. Moreover, as discussed previously, the hippocampus is an important structure for encoding, consolidating, and retrieving information in memory; in other words, it contributes to learning, and this characteristic is conditioned by its plasticity.

Pfefferbaum, Sullivan, and Carmelli (2001) studied the heritability of the corpus callosum. They found different effects according to the section of the structure: The proportion of genetic to environmental contributions to anisotropy was 1:1 for the anterior corpus callosum and 3:1 for its posterior part. These findings suggest that anterior regions (the two frontal hemispheres are mainly connected by the genu of the corpus callosum) are more dependent on environmental factors, while posterior regions are strongly influenced by genetic factors. The finding that the structure of the anterior corpus callosum is influenced by the environment supports the hypothesis that it is receptive to external changes. Because it mainly connects prefrontal areas of the two hemispheres, one could expect close pattern of genetic-to-environmental ratio for the PFC. This finding contradicts that of Thompson et al. (2001). One possibility that could explain such discrepancy may be, as mentioned before, differential age effects on genetic versus environmental influence on brain structure.

The study of genetic and environmental effects on brain structure provided some clues regarding global patterns. However, this framework will only be complete when different genetic polymorphisms are considered and when how the environment impacts genes' effects on brain and cognition is studied. Imaging genetics is a new research area. Among the thousands of genes, the most studied genes' polymorphisms in relation to aging are the *APOE* (apolipoprotein E), *COMT* (catechol-O-methyl-transferase) and *BDNF* (brain-derived neurotrophic factor), which showed significant effects on cognition (Raz, Rodrigue, Kennedy, & Land, 2009), brain structure, and function (for a detailed review on this topic, see Mattay, Goldberg, Sambataro, & Weinberger, 2008).

Concerning the *APOE*, carriers of the ε4 allele have poorer memory performance, smaller hippocampi (Lind, Larsson, et al., 2006), and are more at risk to develop Alzheimer's disease than noncarriers of this allele.

Persson, Lind, and colleagues (2006) investigated differences in white matter integrity using DTI in nondemented older individuals according to their *APOE* genotype. Carriers of the ε4 allele showed diminished FA in the middle and posterior part of the corpus callosum, the fronto-occipital fasciculus/anterior cingulum, and in the hippocampus. Thus, the *APOE* genotype modulates the anisotropic properties of the brain, and notably, the ε4 allele exerts an effect on posterior regions and the medial temporal lobe that are primarily affected in AD.

Honea, Vidoni, Harsha, and Burns (2009) investigated cognition, GM volume loss (using VBM), and white matter integrity (using DTI) in healthy older individuals. In ε4-carriers, they found reduced memory performance, reduced GM volume in several regions of the medial temporal lobe and also in fronto-parietal areas, and diminished white matter integrity in the parahippocampal region. Brain activity is also reduced in several regions in healthy older ε4-carriers, as shown by Lind, Persson, and colleagues (2006) during a semantic categorization task. Carriers of ε4 showed less activity than non-ε4-carriers in the anterior cingulate gyrus and left inferior lateral parietal cortex. The latter also showed a dose effect, such that homozygous ε4-carriers displayed even less activity than heterozygous ε3/ε4 carriers, who in turn displayed less activity than non-ε4-carriers. Moreover, a dysfunction of the hippocampus has been revealed in ε4-carriers, where a reverse pattern was found: While non-ε4-carriers activated the hippocampus more to novel in comparison to familiar items (the novelty effect), ε4-carriers displayed more hippocampal activity to familiar than novel items.

We must, however, report that several studies found overactivation in subjects at risk for Alzheimer's disease carrying the ε4 allele—notably in the PFC, but also the parietal and temporal cortices and regions of the medial temporal lobe, reflecting a compensatory response to early pathological deterioration. This overactivity seems to occur in this population when the task is particularly effortful (e.g., Bookheimer et al., 2000, where episodic encoding and retrieval were assessed).

BDNF val66met polymorphism affects episodic memory, brain activity, and the volume of the hippocampus (but other regions as well; see Nemoto et al., 2006) in aging. Sambataro et al. (2010) conducted an fMRI study of episodic encoding and retrieval in 125 individuals aged 19–85 years old. Val/val and met-carriers showed similar performance on the retrieval task. However, the met-carriers showed a steeper slope in age-related reduction in hippocampal activity at both encoding and retrieval, even when hippocampal volume was statistically controlled, suggesting an accelerated decline of hippocampal functioning in met-carriers with advancing age. *COMT* (mainly expressed in the PFC) is particularly interesting to study in aging because it regulates dopaminergic synaptic transmission, which undergoes deterioration with advancing age. Briefly, the valine-to-methionine substitution (Val158Met polymorphism) leads to increased dopamine availability and cognitive performance. Age magnifies the effects of val/met polymorphism, such that older met-carriers generally perform better than val-carriers (for review, see Lindenberger et al., 2008).

Also, synergetic effects of genes occur. Even though single genes' effects on cognition and brain structure and function have been detected, they are relatively low (see, for example, Small, Rosnick, Fratiglioni, and Bäckman, 2004, for a meta-analysis on *APOE* polymorphism effect on cognition in healthy older individuals). *BDNF-COMT* synergetic effects have been shown at the cognitive level in older individuals (for review, see Lindenberger et al., 2008). Hashimoto et al. (2009) recently carried out a 3-year longitudinal study and showed, in preclinical Alzheimer's disease patients, that in addition to a more rapid atrophy of the medial temporal lobe in the *APOE* ε4-carriers over the first year of follow-up (in comparison to non-ε4-carriers), *BDNF* polymorphism was also associated with disease progression; met-carriers showed more atrophy in limbic and paralimbic regions than the val-carriers. However, due to a low number of subjects, interaction between the two genes could not be assessed. Overall, available data are rare and therefore genetic effects on the aging brain need to be further explored, together with multimodal neuroimaging, which is missing in genetics-neuroimaging research.

Although we emphasized genetic effects on the aging brain, environmental effects may also exert a strong influence, sometimes stronger than genetic effects. Environmental factors usually include education (formal and informal), cognitive engagement, social interactions, leisure activities, and physical fitness, as well as expertise in different skills and training. These factors have been related to cognitive and brain reserve, such that high education, rich social interactions, and cognitive and physical training may delay dementia and contribute to successful aging by recruiting alternative networks in order to respond efficiently to task demands. Differences in cognitive reserve influence cognition, brain structure, and function (for review, see Stern, 2009).

Solé-Padullés et al. (2009) examined structure–function links in healthy older subjects, subjects with mild cognitive impairment, and patients with AD in relation to cognitive reserve. Cognitive reserve was evaluated with intellectual quotient, education–occupation, and intellectual and social activities. The authors estimated whole-brain volume derived from structural MRI (sum of both GM and WM volumes) and local brain activity during a visual encoding memory task (functional MRI). In normal older subjects, higher cognitive reserve was associated with higher brain volume and lower functional activity. In MCI subjects and AD patients, the inverse pattern was found: higher cognitive reserve was linked to smaller brain volume and more activity. However, the authors revealed that cognitive reserve status was better explained by brain activity than brain volume.

As demonstrated in the structure-function study we recently conducted in our laboratory and described in the previous section (Kalpouzos et al.,

2011), local structural deterioration associated with aging may determine which alternative networks can be used. Thus, using a measure of global brain volume probably disadvantaged the strength of its role on cognitive reserve in Solé-Palludés and colleagues' study and lacked specificity. Bartrés-Faz et al. (2009) overcame this limitation by introducing in their study local GM volume, and they used the BPM toolbox to assess voxel-by-voxel structure–function relationships in relation to aging and cognitive reserve. First, the authors found positive correlations between GM volume and cognitive reserve estimates in the right superior, left medial frontal cortex, and left inferior parietal cortex. Negative correlations between cognitive reserve estimates and brain activity during a working memory task were found in the right inferior frontal cortex, suggesting that older individuals with higher cognitive reserve activated this region less than those who had lower cognitive reserve. However, this relationship disappeared when controlling for local GM, suggesting that this correlation was primarily driven by local GM differences.

This study refined the findings of the previous one by showing that, in the elderly, environmental factors may influence brain volume locally in fronto-parietal areas. This result contrasts with Thompson and colleagues' findings (2001), where the frontal lobe seemed to be under strong control by genetic rather than environmental factors. In the previous sections, we have shown the importance of the fronto-parietal network maturation and integrity in high-level cognitive functions. More particularly, we demonstrated the existence of structure–function relationships in aging in these brain areas, such that a moderate reduction of local GM volume may induce increased compensatory activity in these same areas. Thus, a structural preservation of these areas in aging via a high cognitive reserve would guarantee optimal functioning of high-level cognitive operations. The reduction of activity in the right inferior PFC in older persons with high cognitive reserve underlies the hypothesis that less activity is related to the use of more efficient networks (see the section about reduction in activity during maturation). In line with our multimodal study in aging, Bartrés-Faz et al. (2009) found a link between frontal activity and GM, testifying that GM integrity has an impact on function.

So far, we have examined structure–behavior, function–behavior, and the impact of structure on function. We have also illustrated the influence of genetic and environmental factors on cognition, brain structure, and function. Among the environmental factors, we mentioned training on a particular skill or cognitive ability. Training can induce changes in cognitive performance associated with the involvement of a particular network. A phenomenon that is usually neglected is the impact of training on structure (structural plasticity). As shown on Figure 11.1, structure may influence function, but function associated to behavior can also modify brain structure, probably via molecular mechanisms. We here provide an example of short-term structural modifications by training on a particular skill (and aging effects), as well as an example of long-term structural modifications by expertise in a specific domain.

Functional plasticity of the brain has been shown by using training on specific cognitive abilities. Recently, in our laboratory, we showed which specific areas of the brain were functionally associated with training on updating and the aging effects on such plasticity (Dahlin, Stigsdotter Neely, Larsson, Bäckman, & Nyberg, 2008). Updating is an important executive function called upon in everyday life and consists of deleting nonrelevant information in memory and adding new, incoming relevant information. Younger and older subjects were trained for 5 weeks on tasks requiring updating. They were scanned twice, before and after the training period on three tasks, two updating tasks, and one inhibition task. Both younger and older groups showed increase in performance in the main updating task after training; however, the improvement was less strong in the older group. Younger subjects, but not older subjects, also showed a specific transfer effect on the other updating task (increased performance).

Before training, a fronto-parietal network was activated in both groups during updating, and the striatum was additionally activated in the young group only. In both groups, the striatum was the only region to show a training-related increase in activity, suggesting that this region may exhibit functional plasticity in aging related to increased performance after training, but this plasticity is weaker than in younger individuals because training effect was reduced and transfer effect nonexistent. Hypothetical training-related structural plasticity has not been investigated in this study in conjunction with functional plasticity. By contrast, in other studies, structural plasticity after training has been demonstrated, although functional plasticity has not.

Boyke, Driemeyer, Gaser, Büchel, and May (2008) examined short-term structural plasticity in younger and older subjects over 6 months on a particular skill: juggling. After 3 months' practice, increased GM in visual areas, left hippocampus, and bilateral nucleus accumbens was observed in all subjects. Then, after 3 months of no practice, GM of these specific areas decreased. Thus, in normal aging, short-term structural remodeling of the brain is relatively preserved, although less strong than in younger subjects, probably reflecting the fact that the older ones did not achieve the same level of performance.

Long-term structural plasticity has been demonstrated quite often in diverse populations of experts, such as taxi drivers and professional musicians. Here, structural plasticity is related to long-term practice, or expertise. Aging effects have not been specifically evaluated. However populations enrolled in these studies contain middle-aged and older subjects because expertise is obviously associated with years of practice. Many functional studies have shown the crucial involvement of the hippocampus in spatial memory (for review, see Burgess, Maguire, & O'Keefe, 2002).

Maguire et al. (2000) examined the size of this structure in licensed taxi drivers who undoubtedly had navigation skills. The authors found increased posterior but reduced anterior hippocampal size in the taxi drivers; these results were further confirmed by an analysis showing these size differences in link with the time the taxi drivers had been in practice. Thus, long-term practice of navigation contributes to the remodeling of the hippocampus, which supports spatial memory. This is also true for other structures of the brain and other skills. Professional musicians, for example, have increased GM of motor, auditory, and visuospatial brain areas in comparison to amateur musicians and nonmusicians (e.g., Gaser & Schlaug, 2003).

CONCLUSION AND FUTURE DIRECTIONS

The aim of this chapter was to link brain structural and functional modifications that occur in normal aging with cognitive performance. The driving assumption was that structure undoubtedly exerts an effect on function and vice versa. A first observation that can be made is the lack of available data on direct structure–function assessment. Despite this, we highlighted some similarities between structure–behavior and function–behavior that may constitute a basis for future investigations. In order to enlarge our understanding of structure–function interactions, we also considered brain maturation that occurs during development and cognitive improvement. A first general feature that appeared is the reverse structural and functional patterns that take place during development and aging. Known as the "developmental theory" or "last-in-first-out" hypothesis, it seems globally true that the first structures to mature show relative structural and functional stability with increasing age. The most striking example was provided by the hippocampus. Its structural and functional deterioration may be related to signs of pathological processes.

The last structures to mature also seem to be the most vulnerable with increasing age, as is the case of the prefrontal lobe. During development, structural organization of the prefrontal lobe subtends its functional specialization (*differentiation*). This phenomenon is functionally expressed by more focal activity in the frontal lobe (or in other words, specialized subregions of the PFC and also the parietal cortex are more activated during a specific task, while the engagement of nonrelevant subareas decreases). These maturational changes underlie cognitive improvement.

While the opposite phenomenon has been described in normal aging (*dedifferentiation*), another event, termed functional compensation, has been described. Compensation is characterized by increased activity, mainly in the prefrontal cortex, but also, as shown in a recent study that we conducted in our laboratory, the parietal cortex. The few structure–function studies tend to conclude that functional compensation is possible under the condition of mild to moderate structural shrinkage. Moreover, as a preliminary assumption, it is likely that the aging brain reacts to structural deterioration of some regions by over-recruiting other brain areas that are not or are minimally structurally deteriorated and can cope with cognitive demands. Structure and function are under the influence of both genetic and environmental factors, which may differentially modulate structure–function–behavior interactions on the individual level. We notably reported the different impact of genetic polymorphisms, as well as the impact of environmental factors, on structural and functional brain plasticity.

Finally, a factor that should be taken into account in future investigations is the design of the studies. We mainly reported the findings of cross-sectional studies because longitudinal studies are rare. Many factors may confound the results when using a cross-sectional design, such as a bias in population selection (high-performing older adults). In our laboratory, we conducted a structural–functional longitudinal experiment in which 37 middle-aged and older individuals were followed and scanned twice over the course of 6 years (Nyberg et al., 2010). The functional task was a categorization task that served as an incidental encoding for future recall.

Over the 6 years, a cognitive decline was observed. Longitudinal structural analyses showed that the most structurally deteriorated regions were the thalamus, postcentral areas, left inferior parietal cortex, the cerebellum, the left caudate nucleus, and left lateral temporal and right ventral prefrontal cortices. Functional MRI analyses demonstrated a reduction in right prefrontal and occipital activity and an increase in the left parahippocampal gyrus. Importantly, joint cross-sectional analyses within the same sample of subjects at the two time points demonstrated the higher sensitivity of longitudinal assessment over cross-sectional assessment; in contradiction with the longitudinal results, a trend toward an overactivation of the PFC was observed.

Further longitudinal structure–function analyses showed a positive correlation between prefrontal GM decrease and prefrontal under-recruitment over time (increased GM loss was associated with decreased activity), also in contradiction with our cross-sectional results. Although these results are unique and need to be replicated, they challenge current views and theories regarding brain structure and function with associated age-related cognitive decline, and they constitute a basis for future investigations. In other words, theories based on cross-sectional studies may be limited to successful aging due to the biased selection of high-performing subjects and may not portray the structure–function profile of the general aging population with decline in episodic memory and other cognitive functions.

REFERENCES

Abe, O., Yamasue, H., Aoki, S., Suga, M., Yamada, H., Kasai, K.,... Ohtomo, K. (2008). Aging in the CNS: Comparison of gray/white matter volume and diffusion tensor data. *Neurobiology of Aging, 29,* 102–116.

Allen, J. S., Bruss, J., Brown, C. K., & Damasio, H. (2005). Normal neuroanatomical variation due to age: The major lobes and a parcellation of the temporal region. *Neurobiology of Aging, 26,* 1245–1260.

Bartrés-Faz, D., Solé-Padullés, C., Junqué, C., Rami, L., Bosch, B., Bargalló, N.,... Molinuevo, J. L. (2009). Interactions of cognitive reserve with regional brain anatomy and brain function during a working memory task in healthy elders. *Biological Psychiatry, 80,* 256–259.

Beason-Held, L. L., Kraut, M. A., & Resnick, S. M. (2008a). I. Longitudinal changes in aging brain function. *Neurobiology of Aging, 29,* 483–496.

Beason-Held, L. L., Kraut, M. A., & Resnick, S. M. (2008b). II. Temporal patterns of longitudinal change in aging brain function. *Neurobiology of Aging, 29,* 497–513.

Bookheimer, S. Y., Strojwas, M. H., Cohen, M. S., Saunders, A. M., Pericak-Vance, M. A., Mazziotta, J. C., & Small, G. W. (2000). Patterns of brain activation in people at risk for Alzheimer's disease. *New England Journal of Medicine, 343,* 450–456.

Boyke, J., Driemeyer, J., Gaser, C., Büchel, C., & May, A. (2008). Training-induced brain structure changes in the elderly. *Journal of Neuroscience, 28,* 7031–7035.

Brassen, S., Büchel, C., Weber-Fahr, W., Lehmbeck, J. T., Sommer, T., & Braus, D. F. (2009). Structure–function interactions of correct retrieval in healthy elderly women. *Neurobiology of Aging, 30,* 1147–1156.

Brodtmann, A., Puce, A., Darby, D., & Donnan, G. (2009). Regional fMRI brain activation does correlate with global brain volume. *Brain Research, 1259,* 17–25.

Burgess, N., Maguire, E. A., & O'Keefe, J. (2002). The human hippocampus and spatial and episodic memory. *Neuron, 35,* 625–641.

Cabeza, R., Anderson, N. D., Locantore, J. K., & McIntosh, A. R. (2002). Aging gracefully: Compensatory brain activity in high-performing older adults. *NeuroImage, 17,* 1394–1402.

Casanova, R., Srikanth, R., Baer, A., Laurienti, P. J., Burdette, J. H., Hayasaka, S.,... Maldjian, J. A. (2007). Biological parametric mapping: A statistical toolbox for multimodality brain image analysis. *NeuroImage, 34,* 137–143.

Casey, B. J., Tottenham, N., Liston, C., & Durston, S. (2005). Imaging the developing brain: What have we learned about cognitive development? *Trends in Cognitive Sciences, 9,* 104–110.

Chételat, G., Desgranges, B., de la Sayette, V., Viader, F., Berkouk, K., Landeau B.,... Eustache, F. (2003). Dissociating atrophy and hypometabolism impact on episodic memory in mild cognitive impairment. *Brain, 126,* 1955–1967.

Chételat, G., Fouquet, M., Kalpouzos, G., Denghien, I., de la Sayette, V., Viader, F.,... Desgranges, B. (2008). Three-dimensional surface mapping of hippocampal atrophy progression from MCI to AD and over normal aging as assessed using voxel-based morphometry. *Neuropsychologia, 46,* 1721–1731.

Dahlin, E., Stigsdotter Neely, A., Larsson, A., Bäckman, L., & Nyberg, L. (2008). Transfer of learning after updating training mediated by the striatum. *Science, 320,* 1510–1512.

Daselaar, S. M., Fleck, M. S., Dobbins, I. G., Madden, D. J., & Cabeza, R. (2006). Effects of healthy aging on hippocampal and rhinal memory functions: An event-related fMRI study. *Cerebral Cortex, 16,* 1771–1782.

Daselaar, S. M., Veltman, D. J., Rombouts, S. A., Raaijmakers, J. G., & Jonker, C. (2003). Neuroanatomical correlates of episodic encoding and retrieval in young and elderly subjects. *Brain, 126,* 43–56.

Davis, S. W., Dennis, N. A., Buchler, N. G., White, L. E., Madden, D. J., & Cabeza, R. (2009). Assessing the effects of age on long white matter tracts using diffusion tensor tractography. *NeuroImage, 46,* 530–541.

Davis, S. W., Dennis, N. A., Daselaar, S. M., Fleck, M. S., & Cabeza, R. (2008). Qué PASA? The posterior–anterior shift in aging. *Cerebral Cortex, 18,* 1201–1209.

Dolcos, F., Rice, H. J., & Cabeza, R. (2002). Hemispheric asymmetry and aging: Right hemispheric decline or asymmetry reduction? *Neuroscience and Biobehavioral Reviews, 26,* 819–825.

Durston, S., Davidson, M. C., Tottenham, N., Galvan, A., Spicer, J., Fossella, J. A., & Casey, B. J. (2006). A shift from diffuse to focal cortical activity with development. *Developmental Science, 9,* 1–20.

Fjell, A. M., Westlye, L. T., Amlien, I., Espeseth, T., Reinvang, I., Raz, N.,... Walhovd, K. B. (2009). High consistency of regional cortical thinning in aging across multiple samples. *Cerebral Cortex, 19,* 2001–2012.

Gaser, C., & Schlaug, G. (2003). Brain structures differ between musicians and non-musicians. *Journal of Neuroscience, 23,* 9240–9245.

Good, C. D., Johnsrude, I. S., Ashburner, J., Henson, R. N. A., Friston, K. J., & Frackowiak, R. S. J. (2001). A voxel-based morphometric study of ageing in 465 normal adult human brains. *NeuroImage, 14,* 21–36.

Grady, C. L., Maisog, J. M., Horwitz, B., Ungerleider, L. G., Mentis, M. J., Salerno, J. A.,... Haxby, J. V. (1994). Age-related changes in cortical blood flow activation during visual processing of faces and locations. *Journal of Neuroscience, 14,* 1450–1462.

Grieve, S. M., Clarck, C. R., Williams, L. M., Peduto, A. J., & Gordon, E. (2005). Preservation of limbic and paralimbic structures in aging. *Human Brain Mapping, 25,* 391–401.

Gunning-Dixon, F. M., Brickman, A. M., Cheng, J. C., & Alexopoulos, G. S. (2009). Aging of cerebral white matter: A review of MRI findings. *International Journal of Geriatric Psychiatry, 24,* 109–117.

Gutchess, A. H., Welsh, R. C., Hedden, T., Bangert, A., Minear, M., Liu, L. L., & Park, D. C. (2005). Aging and the neural correlates of successful picture encoding: Frontal activations compensate for decreased medial-temporal activity. *Journal of Cognitive Neuroscience, 17,* 84–96.

Habib, R., Nyberg, L., & Tulving, E. (2003). Hemispheric asymmetries of memory: The HERA model revisited. *Trends in Cognitive Sciences, 7,* 241–245.

Hashimoto, R., Hirata, Y., Asada, T., Yamashita, F., Nemoto, K., Mori, T.,... Ohnishi, T. (2009). Effect of the brain-derived neurotrophic factor and the apolipoprotein E polymorphisms on disease progression in preclinical Alzheimer's disease. *Genes, Brain and Behavior, 8,* 43–52.

Head, D., Rodrigue, K. M., Kennedy, K. M., & Raz, N. (2008). Neuroanatomical and cognitive mediators of age-related differences in episodic memory. *Neuropsychology, 22,* 491–507.

Hedden, T., & Gabrieli, J. D. (2004). Insights into the ageing mind: A view from cognitive neuroscience. *Nature Reviews Neuroscience, 5,* 87–96.

Honea, R. A., Vidoni, E., Harsha, A., & Burns, J. M. (2009). Impact of *APOE* on the healthy aging brain: A voxel-based MRI and DTI study. *Journal of Alzheimer's Disease, 18,* 553–564.

Johnson, S. C., Saykin, A. J., Baxter, L. C., Flashman, L. A., Santulli, R. B., McAllister, T. W., & Mamourian, A. C. (2000). The relationship between fMRI activation and cerebral atrophy: Comparison of normal aging and Alzheimer's disease. *NeuroImage, 11,* 179–187.

Kalpouzos, G., Chételat, G., Baron, J. C., Landeau, B., Mevel, K., Godeau, C.,... Desgranges, B. (2009). Voxel-based mapping of brain gray matter volume and glucose metabolism profiles in normal aging. *Neurobiology of Aging, 30,* 112–124.

Kalpouzos, G., Chételat, G., Landeau, B., Clochon, P., Viader, F., Eustache, F., & Desgranges, B. (2009). Structural and metabolic correlates of episodic memory in relation to the depth of encoding in normal aging. *Journal of Cognitive Neuroscience, 21,* 372–389.

Kalpouzos, G., Persson, J., & Nyberg, L. (2011). Local brain atrophy accounts for functional activity differences in normal aging. *Neurobiology of Aging,* in press. doi:10.1016/jneurobiolaging.2011.02.021

Kennedy, K. M., & Raz, N. (2009). Aging white matter and cognition: Differential effects of regional variations in diffusion properties on memory, executive functions, and speed. *Neuropsychologia, 47,* 916–927.

Kramer, J. H., Mungas, D., Reed, B. R., Wetzel, M. E., Burnett, M. M., Miller, B. L.,... Chui, H. C. (2007). Longitudinal MRI and cognitive change in healthy elderly. *Neuropsychology, 21,* 412–418.

Kremen, W. S., Prom-Wormley, E., Panizzon, M. S., Eyler, L. T., Fischl, B., Neale, M. C.,... Fennema-Notestine, C. (2009). Genetic and environmental influences on the size of specific brain regions in midlife: The VETSA MRI study. *NeuroImage, 49,* 1213–1223.

Lenroot, R. K., & Giedd, J. N. (2007). The structural development of the human brain as measured longitudinally with magnetic resonance imaging. In D. Coch, K. W. Fischer, & G. Dawson (Eds.), *Human behavior, learning, and the developing brain: Typical development* (pp. 50–73). New York, NY: Guilford Press.

Lind, J., Larsson, A., Persson, J., Ingvar, M., Nilsson, L. G., Bäckman, L.,... Nyberg, L. (2006). Reduced hippocampal volume in nondemented carriers of the apolipoprotein E ε4: Relation to chronological age and recognition memory. *Neuroscience Letters, 396,* 23–27.

Lind, J., Persson, J., Ingvar, M., Larsson, A., Cruts, M., Van Broeckhoven, C.,... Nyberg, L. (2006). Reduced functional brain activity response in cognitively intact apolipoprotein E ε4 carriers. *Brain, 129,* 1240–1248.

Lindenberger, U., Nagel, I. E., Chicherio, C., Li, S. C., Heekeren, H. R., & Bäckman, L. (2008). Age-related decline in brain resources modulates genetic effects on cognitive functioning. *Frontiers in Neuroscience, 2,* 234–244.

Madden, D. J., Spaniol, J., Whiting, W. L., Bucur, B., Provenzale, J. M., Cabeza, R.,... Huettel, S. A. (2007). Adult age differences in the functional neuroanatomy of visual attention: A combined fMRI and DTI study. *Neurobiology of Aging, 28,* 459–476.

Maguire, E. A., Gadian, D. G., Johnsrude, I. S., Good, C. D., Ashburner, J., Frackowiak, R. S. J., & Frith, C. D. (2000). Navigation-related structural change in the hippocampi of taxi drivers. *Proceedings of the National Academy of Sciences USA, 97,* 4398–4403.

Mattay, V. S., Goldberg, T. E., Sambataro, F., & Weinberger, D. R. (2008). Neurobiology of cognitive aging: Insights from imaging genetics. *Biological Psychiatry, 79,* 9–22.

Nemoto, K., Ohnishi, T., Mori, T., Moriguchi, Y., Hashimoto, R., Asada, T., & Kunugi, H. (2006). The Val66Met polymorphism of the brain-derived neurotrophic factor gene affects age-related brain morphology. *Neuroscience Letters, 397*, 25–29.

Nyberg, L., & Bäckman, L. (2010). Memory changes and the aging brain: A multimodal imaging approach. In K. W. Schaie & S. L. Willis (Eds.), *Handbook of the psychology of aging* (7th ed., pp. 121–133). New York, NY: Elsevier.

Nyberg, L., Cabeza, R., & Tulving, E. (1996). PET studies of encoding and retrieval: The HERA model. *Psychonomic Bulletin & Review, 3*, 135–148.

Nyberg, L., Salami, A., Andersson, M., Eriksson, J., Kalpouzos, G., Kauppi, K.,... Nilsson, L. G. (2010). Longitudinal evidence for frontal cortex under-recruitment in aging. *Proceedings of the National Academy of Sciences USA, 107*, 22682–22686.

Olesen, P. J., Nagy, Z., Westerberg, H., & Klingberg, T. (2003). Combined analysis of DTI and fMRI data reveals a joint maturation of white and gray matter in a fronto-parietal network. *Cognitive Brain Research, 18*, 48–57.

O'Sullivan, M., Jones, D. K., Summers, P. E., Morris, R. G., Williams, S. C., & Markus, H. S. (2001). Evidence for cortical "disconnection" as a mechanism of age-related cognitive decline. *Neurology, 57*, 632–638.

Park, D. C., & Reuter-Lorenz, P. (2009). The adaptive brain: Aging and neurocognitive scaffolding. *Annual Review of Psychology, 60*, 173–196.

Persson, J., Kalpouzos, G., Nilsson, L. G., Ryberg, M., & Nyberg, L. (2011). Preserved hippocampus activation in normal aging as revealed by fMRI. *Hippocampus, 21*, 753–766.

Persson, J., Lind, J., Larsson, A., Ingvar, M., Cruts, M., Van Broeckhoven, C.,... Nyberg, L. (2006). Altered brain white matter integrity in healthy carriers of the *APOE* ε4 allele. A risk for AD? *Neurology, 66*, 1029–1033.

Persson, J., & Nyberg, L. (2006). Altered brain activity in healthy seniors: What does it mean? *Progress in Brain Research, 157*, 45–56.

Persson, J., Nyberg, L., Lind, J., Larsson, A., Nilsson, L. G., Ingvar, M., & Buckner, R. L. (2006). Structure–function correlates of cognitive decline in aging. *Cerebral Cortex, 16*, 907–915.

Peters, A. (2002). The effects of normal aging on myelin and nerve fibers: A review. *Journal of Neurocytology, 31*, 581–593.

Pfefferbaum, A., Sullivan, E. V., & Carmelli, D. (2001). Genetic regulation of regional microstructure of the corpus callosum in late life. *Neuroreport, 12*, 1677–1681.

Prayer, D., Kasprian, G., Krampl, E., Ulm, B., Witzani, L., Prayer, L., & Brugger, P. C. (2006). MRI of normal fetal brain development. *European Journal of Radiology, 57*, 199–216.

Radoš, M., Judaš, M., & Kostović, I. (2006). In vitro MRI of brain development. *European Journal of Radiology, 57*, 187–198.

Rajah, M. N., & D'Esposito, M. (2005). Region-specific changes in prefrontal function with age: A review of PET and fMRI studies on working and episodic memory. *Brain, 128*, 1964–1983.

Raz, N. (2000). Aging of the brain and its impact on cognitive performance: Integration of structural and functional findings. In F. I. M. Craik & T. A. Salthouse (Eds.), *The handbook of aging and cognition* (pp. 1–90). Mahwah, NJ: Lawrence Erlbaum Associates.

Raz, N., Lindenberger, U., Rodrigue, K. M., Kennedy, K. M., Head, D., Williamson, A.,... Acker, J. D. (2005). Regional brain changes in aging healthy adults: General trends, individual differences and modifiers. *Cerebral Cortex, 15,* 1676–1689.

Raz, N., Rodrigue, K. M., Kennedy, K. M., & Land, S. (2009). Genetic and vascular modifiers of age-sensitive cognitive skills: Effects of *COMT, BDNF, ApoE,* and hypertension. *Neuropsychology, 23,* 105–16.

Salat, D. H., Buckner, R. L., Snyder, A. Z., Greve, D. N., Desikan, R. S. R., Busa, E.,... Fischl, B. (2004). Thinning of the cerebral cortex in aging. *Cerebral Cortex, 14,* 721–730.

Sambataro, F., Murty, V. P., Lemaître, H. S., Reed, J. D., Das, S., Goldberg, T. E.,... Mattay, V. S. (2010). BDNF modulates normal human hippocampal ageing. *Molecular Psychiatry, 15,* 116–118.

Sasson, E., Doniger, G. M., Pasternak, O., & Assaf, Y. (2010). Structural correlates of memory performance with diffusion tensor imaging. *NeuroImage, 50,* 1231–1242.

Shafto, M. A., Stamatakis, E. A., Tam, P. P., & Tyler, L. K. (2010). Word retrieval failures in old age: the relationship between structure and function. *Journal of Cognitive Neuroscience, 22,* 1530–1540.

Small, B. J., Rosnick, C. B., Fratiglioni, L., & Bäckman, L. (2004). Apolipoprotein E and cognitive performance: A meta-analysis. *Psychology and Aging, 19,* 592–600.

Solé-Padullés, C., Bartrés-Faz, D., Junqué, C., Vendrell, P., Rami, L., Clemente, I. C.,... Molinuevo, J. L. (2009). Brain structure and function related to cognitive reserve variables in normal aging, mild cognitive impairment and Alzheimer's disease. *Neurobiology of Aging, 30,* 1114–1124.

Sowell, E. R., Peterson, B. S., Thompson, P. M., Welcome, S. E., Henkenius, A. L., & Toga, A. W. (2003). Mapping cortical change across the human life span. *Nature Neuroscience, 6,* 309–315.

Spreng, R. N., Wojtowicz, M., & Grady, C. L. (2010). Reliable differences in brain activity between young and old adults: A quantitative meta-analysis across multiple cognitive domains. *Neuroscience and Biobehavioral Reviews, 34,* 1178–1194.

Stadlbauer, A., Salomonowitz, E., Strunk, G., Hammen, T., & Ganslandt, O. (2008). Age-related degradation in the central nervous system: Assessment with diffusion-tensor imaging and quantitative fiber tracking. *Radiology, 247,* 179–188.

Stern, Y. (2009). Cognitive reserve. *Neuropsychologia, 47,* 2015–2028.

Sullivan, E. V., Marsh, L., & Pfefferbaum, A. (2005). Preservation of hippocampal volume throughout adulthood in healthy men and women. *Neurobiology of Aging, 26,* 1093–1098.

Sullivan, E. V., & Pfefferbaum, A. (2006). Diffusion tensor imaging and aging. *Neuroscience and Biobehavioral Reviews, 30,* 749–761.

Sullivan, E. V., Pfefferbaum, A., Swan, G. E., & Carmelli, D. (2001). Heritability of hippocampal size in elderly twin men: Equivalent influence from genes and environment. *Hippocampus, 11,* 754–762.

Thompson, P., Cannon, T. D., Narr, K. L., van Erp, T., Poutanen, V. P., Huttunen, M.,... Toga, A. W. (2001). Genetic influences on brain structure. *Nature Neuroscience, 4,* 1253–1258.

Thompson, R. A., & Nelson, C. A. (2001). Developmental science and the media. Early brain development. *American Psychologist, 56,* 5–15.

Thomsen, T., Specht, K., Hammar, Å., Nyttingnes, J., Ersland, L., & Hugdahl, K. (2004). Brain localization of attentional control in different age groups by combining functional and structural MRI. *NeuroImage, 22,* 912–919.

Toga, A. W., Thompson, P. M., & Sowell, E. R. (2006). Mapping brain maturation. *Trends in Neurosciences, 29,* 148–159.

Tulving, E., Kapur, S., Craik, F. I. M., Moscovitch, M., & Houle, S. (1994). Hemispheric encoding retrieval asymmetry in episodic memory: Positron emission tomography findings. *Proceedings of the National Academy of Sciences USA, 91,* 2016–2020.

Van Petten, C. (2004). Relationship between hippocampal volume and memory ability in healthy individuals across the lifespan: Review and meta-analysis. *Neuropsychologia, 42,* 1394–1413.

Van Petten, C., Plante, E., Davidson, P. S. R., Kuo, T. Y., Bajuscak, L., & Glisky, E. L. (2004). Memory and executive function in older adults: Relationships with temporal and prefrontal gray matter volumes and white matter hyperintensities. *Neuropsychologia, 42,* 1313–1335.

Westlye, L. T., Walhovd, K. B., Dale, A. M., Bjørnerud, A., Due-Tønnessen, P., Engvig, A.,... Fjell, A. M. (2010a). Differentiating maturational and aging-related changes of the cerebral cortex by use of thickness and signal intensity. *NeuroImage, 52,* 172–185.

Westlye, L. T., Walhovd, K. B., Dale, A. M., Bjørnerud, A., Due-Tønnessen, P., Engvig, A.,... Fjell, A. M. (2010b). Life-span changes of the human brain white matter: Diffusion tensor imaging (DTI) and volumetry. *Cerebral Cortex, 20,* 2055–2068.

12 Dopaminergic modulation of memory aging

Neurocomputational, neurocognitive, and genetic evidence

Shu-Chen Li

When I was younger, I could remember anything, whether it had happened or not; but I am getting old, and soon I shall remember only the latter.

Mark Twain

INTRODUCTION

This chapter is about the potential neurochemical and genetic underpinnings that contribute to Mark Twain's complaint about his memory as an old man. As is often the case with widely celebrated writers, in this quote from his autobiography, Twain spoke of a core issue in human conditions that most people experience when they become older: the problem of less reliable memory.

Aging affects three main aspects of memory functions: working memory, episodic memory, and source memory. Concerning working memory—the ability to keep certain information in mind for a short period while doing other mental operations—ample studies have shown reduced verbal and spatial memory span, memory updating capacity, and plasticity in older adults in comparison to younger adults (e.g., Gazzaley et al. 2005; Li et al., 2008; Nagel et al. 2009; Schneider-Graces et al., 2010; for reviews, see Bopp & Verhaeghen, 2005; Salthouse, 1994). Similarly, converging evidence points to age-related decline in episodic memory—the ability to remember details and associations of experienced episodes (e.g., Kalpouzos et al., 2009; Kliegl & Lindenberger, 1993; Leshikar, Gutchess, Hebrank, Sutton, & Park, 2010; Mitchell, Johnson, Raye, & D'Esposito, 2000; Naveh-Benjamin, 2000; Plancher, Gyselinck, Nicolas, & Piolino, 2010; Verhaeghen & Marcoen, 1993).

Episodic memory plasticity is also evidently more limited in old age (Baltes & Kliegl, 1992; Brehmer, Li, Müller, von Oertzen, & Lindenberger, 2007; Shing, Werkle-Bergner, Li, & Lindenberger, 2008; Singer, Lindenberger, & Baltes, 2003). As for the ability to verify the veridicality of recollected events (e.g., the correct source or context of the experienced episodes), older adults are more prone to false memory (misrecollections) than younger adults (Dennis, Kim, & Cabeza, 2007; Dodson, Bawa, & Krueger, 2007; McCabe, Roediger, McDaniel, & Balota, 2009; Rajah, Languay, & Valiquette, 2010; Shing, Werkle-Bergner, Li, & Lindenberger, 2009).

Age-related declines in the frontal-hippocampal memory circuitry at the neuroanatomical (e.g., Charlton, Barrick, Lawes, Markus, & Morris, 2010; Head, Rodrigue, Kennedy, & Raz, 2008; Raz et al., 2005; Yassa, Matfield, Stark, & Stark, 2011), neurofunctional (e.g., Daselaar, Fleck, Dobbins, Madden, & Cabeza, 2006; Dennis et al., 2008; Gutchess et al., 2005; Mitchell et al., 2000), and neurochemical (e.g., Bäckman et al., 2000; Mozley, Gur, Mozley, & Gur, 2001; see also Bäckman, Lindenberger, Li, & Nyberg, 2010; Li, Lindenberger, & Bäckman, 2010, for reviews) levels contribute to older adults' memory problems.

Guided by neurocomputational theories relating dopaminergic modulation to neuronal noise and distinctiveness of memory representations (Li, Lindenberger, & Sikström, 2001; Servan-Schreiber, Printz, & Cohen, 1990), the focus of this chapter is on age-related decline in dopaminergic modulation and its contributions to the common memory problems that older adults experience. In the first part of the chapter, the effects of deficient dopaminergic modulation on older adults' working memory and episodic memory deficits will be illustrated in results from two sets of computational simulations. Evidence from recent functional and receptor imaging as well as behavioral genetic studies supporting these theoretical links will then be reviewed in the remaining sections.

NEUROMODULATION AND NOISE IN NEURAL INFORMATION PROCESSING

The central nervous system is a communication system with an enormous complexity: The brain is estimated to have about 100 billion nerve cells, and on average each of these nerve cells communicates with 1,000 other neurons. Whether these intercellular communications across the synapses of neurons were electrical or chemical in nature underwent a long period of debate from the 1930s to the 1960s; current consensus is that over 99% of the synapses in the brain use chemical transmissions involving neurotransmitters (Greengard, 2000). A prominent source of intrinsic variability of neural information processing is synaptic noise that arises, in part, from fluctuations of postsynaptic activations reflecting probabilistic neurotransmitter releases (e.g., Hessler, Shirke, & Malinow, 1993).

Various transmitter systems are important for signal transmissions in the brain, with clear implications on cognition and behavior (see Harris-Warrick & Marder, 1991; Marder & Thirumalai, 2002, for reviews). The specificities of the different transmitter systems (e.g., acetylcholine, noradrenaline, serotonin, dopamine, and glutamate) and their influences on cortical processes and cognitive functions differ as well. However, at an abstract level, many of their computational effects can be captured as dynamic regulatory mechanisms of adaptive systems, including regulating the signal-to-noise ratio of neural information processing (see Doya, Dayan, & Hasselmo, 2002, for reviews of computational works on this topic in an edited special issue).

In the early 1990s, dopamine's role in regulating the signal-to-noise ratio of neural information processing was first highlighted in a theory of cognitive deficits in schizophrenics. In this context, dopamine's noise regulation effect was modeled by the gain parameter of the sigmoidal activation function of neural networks (Cohen & Servan-Schreiber, 1992; Servan-Schreiber et al., 1990). Based on cross-sectional data, a range of studies provided converging evidence for steady declines in the dopaminergic systems during the course of usual aging, be it the binding efficacy of the presynaptic (e.g., dopamine transporter; Erixon-Lindroth et al., 2005) or postsynaptic (e.g., dopamine receptors; Kassinen & Rinne, 2002) components in various striatal and extrastriatal regions (e.g., Suhara et al., 1991; Kassinen & Rinne, 2002; Wong et al., 1984; see also Bäckman et al., 2010; Li, Lindenberger, Nyberg, Heekeren, & Backman, 2009, for recent reviews).

It should be noted, however, cross-sectional estimates of negative age gradients may be steeper than actual longitudinal declines of the dopamine systems. Moreover, recent research on the etiopathogenesis of Parkinson's disease (e.g., Le, Chen, & Jankovic, 2009) suggested that the negative effects of age-related attenuation of dopamine functions on cognition may be nonlinear, showing consequences only when dopamine efficacy falls below a critical threshold.

In light of steady age-related declines, the earlier theory of dopamine regulation of neuronal signal-to-noise ratio (Servan-Schreiber et al., 1990) was augmented with a stochastic gain, as opposed to the original static gain, regulation (Li & Lindenberger, 1999; Li et al., 2001; Li, Lindenberger & Frensch, 2000) to model age-related deficits in dopamine modulation. The extended model accounted for a wide range of commonly observed cognitive aging deficits, including impairments in working memory (Li & Sikström, 2002) and episodic associative memory (Li, Naveh-Benjamin, & Lindenberger, 2005). Specifically, the neuromodulation of the cognitive aging model captures age-related decline in dopaminergic neuromodulation by stochastically attenuating the gain control (G) of the sigmoidal activation function that captures the presynaptic to postsynaptic input-response transfer (Figure 12.1a).

With large inputs, a direct consequence of reducing the G (and hence the slope) of the activation function is increased within-network random activation variability (Figure 12.1b). This, in turn, leads to increased performance variability in simulated aging networks (Figure 12.1c). In contrast, if G is increased to excessive values, the activation function becomes a step function and activation variability depends critically on the amplitudes of inputs. Activation variability is markedly reduced with large positive or negative inputs and increased with intermediate inputs. Processing units

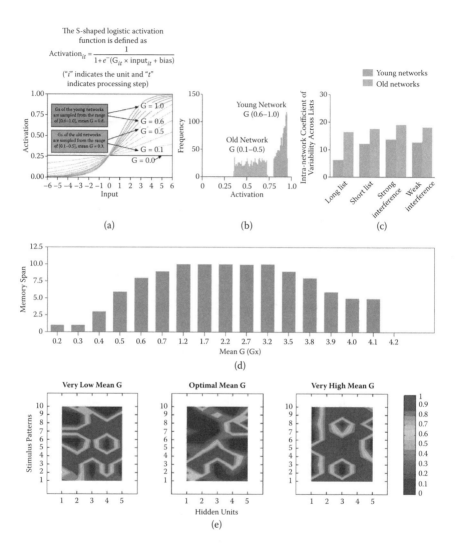

FIGURE 12.1 Modeling deficient neuromodulation in aging. (a) Simulating aging-related DA modulation by reducing stochastic gain tuning. Reduced gain tuning increases (b) random activation variability and (c) performance variability in simulated old networks. (Adapted with permission from Li, S.-C. et al., 2001, *Trends in Cognitive Sciences, 5,* 479–486. Copyright Elsevier 2001.) Stochastic gain tuning captures the inverted-U function relating DA modulation and functional outcomes of (d) working memory performance and (e) distinctiveness of activation patterns. (Adapted with permission from Li, S.-C., & Sikström, S., 2002, *Neuroscience and Biobehavioral Reviews, 26,* 795–808. Copyright Elsevier, 2002.)

with excessive gain modulation thus act as high-pass filters, detecting only strong inputs while losing amplitude discriminability past a given threshold (Wolfart et al., 2005).

These properties of stochastic G tuning predict an inverted-U function (Figure 12.1d, 12.1e) between the levels of dopaminergic modulation, neuronal representation distinctiveness, and cognitive outcomes such as working-memory capacity that has been confirmed empirically (Arnsten, 1998; Goldman-Rakic, Muly, & Williams, 2000; Mattay et al., 2003; Vijayraghavan, Wang, Birnbaum, Williams, & Arnsten, 2007). In summary, both deficient and excessive neuromodulation hamper neural information processing and result in less distinctive neuronal representations, which then compromise cognition. This model had also been applied more specifically to account for age-related differences in working memory and episodic associative memory, which are reviewed in the following two sections.

WORKING MEMORY DEFICIT AND DEFICIENT DOPAMINERGIC MODULATION: COMPUTATIONAL ACCOUNT

Since Baddeley and Hitch coined the term in 1974, the components of "working memory" (i.e., the two-modality-dependent, short-term storages of information and the central executive system) have been investigated extensively (see Baddeley, 2007, for recent views). Most current views consider working memory as a set of related cognitive control functions that involve the maintenance, goal-directed monitoring and manipulation, and flexible updating of information that are subserved by the prefrontal-parietal network. Various computational approaches have been proposed to model working memory and cognitive control (see O'Reilly, Herd, & Pauli, 2010, for review). Of particular interest here are models that capture dopamine's regulation of the stability of working memory representations (Durstewitz, Seamans, & Sejnowski, 2000), its role in affecting the dynamic connectivity between prefrontal cortex and the basal ganglia (O'Reilly & Frank, 2006), and its effect on the signal-to-noise ratio of neuronal signal transduction in general (Cohen & Servan-Schreiber, 1992).

Age-related decline in the different aspects of working memory is a well-established phenomenon (for reviews, see Bopp & Verhaeghen, 2005; Salthouse, 1994). One paradigm often used for accessing working memory function is the so-called n-back task, which involves showing a series of to-be-remembered stimuli. The memory load in this task is manipulated by varying the trial lag as to which stimuli need to be held in mind (e.g., one, two, or three trials ago). This task can be simulated with neural networks that also incorporate recurrent connections from the output layer to a working memory context module at the intermediate layer (see Figure 12.2a for a schematic diagram for one such network). These recurrent connections

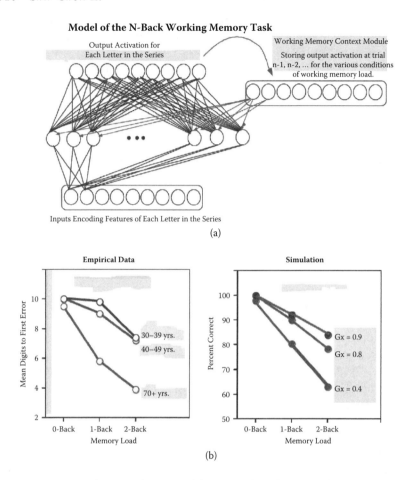

FIGURE 12.2 (a) Schematic diagram of the network architecture for simulating the *n*-back task. (b) Empirical data (Dobbs & Rule, 1989) comparing *n*-back performance in individuals at different ages (left panel) and simulation results showing *n*-back performance with different mean G (right panel), simulating aging-related differences in dopaminergic modulation. (Adapted with permission from Li, S.-C., & Sikström, S., 2002, *Neuroscience and Biobehavioral Reviews, 26,* 795–808. Copyright Elsevier, 2002.)

can temporarily store output patterns from current trial (*n*), trial (*n*-1), trial (*n*-2), and trial (*n*-3).

One computational model specifically accounted for the relation between deficient dopamine modulation and working memory deficit in old age. Focusing on dopamine's role in signal tuning, Li and Sikström (2002) combined the recurrent network architecture with the stochastic gain manipulation to explore the effects of deficient dopaminergic modulation and working memory deficits in older adults by lowering the G parameter of the activation function. In line with empirical findings showing that older adults in their 70s performed significantly worse in an *n*-back task compared to younger adults in their 30s and 40s (see Figure 12.2b; Dobbs & Rule, 1989), networks with a lower mean G, simulating deficient dopamine modulation, performed worse in the *n*-back task and were more affected by increasing memory load (see Figure 12.2c).

EPISODIC ASSOCIATIVE MEMORY DEFICIT AND DEFICIENT DOPAMINERGIC MODULATION: COMPUTATIONAL ACCOUNT

Memory of daily events often involves various components, such as the content of a conversation, the persons involved, and the time and place at which the conversation took place. Relative to younger adults, older adults are particularly impaired in episodic memory tasks requiring associative binding of separate components into compound episodes, such as tasks requiring item–context and item–item binding (e.g., Chalfonte & Johnson, 1996; Kliegl & Lindenberger, 1993; Light, 1991). Furthermore, older adults show deficits in remembering contextual details, such as whether an event was seen or heard and whether it happened at one or another possible location (e.g., Kliegl & Lindenberger, 1993; Spencer & Raz, 1995). Together, these various forms of memory declines have been taken to indicate that older adults have a deficit in associative binding (Naveh-Benjamin, 2000), whether it involves associating content and context, concatenating features into a compound memory item, or generating relations between different items.

Older adults' associative-binding deficit has been systematically investigated using the associative recognition task (e.g., Naveh-Benjamin, 2000; Naveh-Benjamin, Hussain, Guez, & Bar-On, 2003). One study specifically demonstrated that aging affects associative more than item memory (Naveh-Benjamin, 2000, Experiment 2). The participants were presented with pairs of unrelated words (e.g., piano–stove) during study and were instructed to study each pair either as two single words (the "words" instruction) or as a pair (the "pairs" instruction). Later, recognition tests were given to assess both associative and item memory. The associative test required the participants to distinguish studied (target) pairs from new pairs (lures) formed by recombining words in studied pairs; the item test entailed distinguishing between studied (target) and nonstudied (lure) words.

Older adults performed worse than younger adults on the item and the associative tests. Specifically, older adults showed a greater memory deficit for the associative test than for the item test. Moreover, when the associations between word pairs were memorized intentionally (i.e., under the pair instruction), older adults' deficit relative to younger adults was particularly large. Unlike the younger adults, older adults could not benefit from the study instruction of explicitly encoding the associations.

Theories of associative networks suggest that efficient conjunctive coding requires a neural network's processing units to be selectively sensitive to subsets of features, rather than to all features (e.g., Graham & Willshaw, 1995). As reviewed previously, simulating age-related decline in neuromodulation by stochastically reducing the gain parameter (G) of the activation function at each processing step led to less distinctive internal stimulus representations (Li et al., 2001). Less distinctive representation is the flip side of efficient conjunctive coding because more processing units are required to code feature combinations of different stimuli. Less distinctive representation can lead to erroneous conjunctions, which are deleterious in distributed and context-dependent coding, undermining memory binding and spreading memory errors (e.g., Roediger & McDermott, 2000).

Combining a dual-path feature-association conjunctive binding model with the stochastic gain manipulation, the link between age-related decline in dopaminergic modulation and older adults' deficit in associative binding was explored (Li et al., 2005). The model (see Figure 12.3a) has parallel processing paths for intraitem feature binding and interitem associative binding. Features of each item in a given pair were distributedly processed (i.e., all features contributed jointly to the internal feature representations in the intermediate layer) within the corresponding feature-binding path, whereas the associative-binding path processed interitem associations.

The simulation accounted for differential effects of aging on item and associative memory, particularly for age-related deficit in associative binding. Old networks' performance was relatively spared in the item test and more impaired in the associative test. In particular, the simulation results (see Figure 12.3c) capture the empirical three-way interaction between age, instruction, and test type (see Figure 12.3b; Naveh-Benjamin, 2000). This indicated that deficient dopamine modulation may be a source for why older adults could not benefit from explicit encoding instruction to focus on the associations during encoding.

Furthermore, results from analyzing the networks' internal activation patterns also revealed that the old network's disproportionately poor associative binding was due to the less efficient conjunctive coding of associative information. The distributed conjunctive coding of associations between different pairs of items was less distinctive in the old than in the young network. Specifically, although the old network's processing units at the internal representation layer were more highly activated, they responded in a rather nondifferentiated manner to different stimulus pairs (Li et al., 2005).

The less distinctive representation of associations between memory items or between items and encoding context can lead to illusory conjunctions and spread memory errors (Roediger & McDermott, 2000). Indeed, older adults are more susceptible to false memory, as illustrated in Mark Twain's own description about his memory in old age as well as in a range of empirical results (Dennis et al., 2007; Gallo, Foster, & Johnson, 2009; Gallo & Roediger, 2003; Skinner & Fernandes, 2009; Thapar & Westerman, 2009).

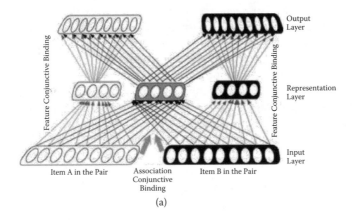

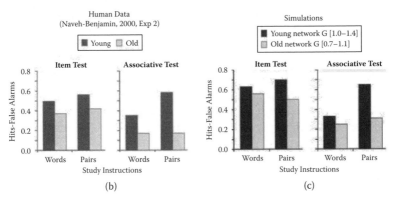

FIGURE 12.3 (a) Schematic diagram of the network architecture for simulating the associative recognition task. (b) Empirical data (Naveh-Benjamin, 2000) and (c) stimulation results (Li, et al., 2005) of age-related associative binding deficit. (Adapted with permission from Li, S.-C. et al., 2005, *Psychological Science, 16,* 445–450. Copyright APS.)

Moreover, the more highly activated but less distinctive representations of associative binding as observed in the old network may contribute to older adults' tendency to be highly confident about a certain remembrance, although the memory is actually false (e.g., Dodson et al., 2007; Shing et al., 2009).

EMPIRICAL FINDINGS SUPPORTING THEORETICAL ACCOUNTS OF DOPAMINERGIC MODULATION OF AGING OF WORKING MEMORY

Recent advancements in molecular imaging (see Cumming, 2009, for review) and genomic (Green, Munafo, & DeYoung, 2008, for review) approaches opened up new avenues for empirical evaluations of the aforementioned theoretical links between age-related declines in dopaminergic modulation and memory deficits. The focus here will be recent behavioral genetic, receptor imaging, and genomic imaging studies on dopaminergic modulation of working memory and episodic memory.

Dopamine's involvement in working memory has been well documented in animal research for more than two decades (e.g., Castner & Goldman-Rakic, 2004; Sawaguchi & Goldman-Rakic, 1991; Vijayraghavan et al., 2007; Williams & Goldman-Rakic, 1995). In vivo observations of dopamine's effect in humans have not been possible until lately. In a recent PET study that investigated the effect of aging on dopamine transporter (DAT) binding in the caudate and putamen, clear age-related loss of striatal DAT binding from early to late adulthood was observed. Furthermore, individual differences in DAT binding accounted for age-related impairment in visual working memory (Erixon-Lindroth et al., 2005).

This influence of the striatal dopamine transporter on working memory may be mediated through the frontal-striatal dopaminergic pathway. In terms of age-related deficit in dopamine receptor and its impact on working memory, one recent pharmaco-imaging study (Fischer et al., 2010) and one multimodal imaging study (Bäckman et al., 2011) nicely demonstrated that age-related differences in load-dependent functional brain activity in the working memory circuitry (e.g., left and right prefrontal cortex as well as the left parietal cortex) is very much mediated by age-related differences in D1 receptor mechanisms.

Other evidence supporting dopamine's contribution to age-related working memory deficits comes from behavior genetic research. For instance, the catechol-O-methyltransferase (COMT) enzyme degrades dopamine in the frontal cortex and subsequently affects the endogenous level of dopamine in the prefrontal cortex. The enzymatic activity of the val carrier of the COMT gene in degrading dopamine is about three to four times higher than that of the met carrier (Lotta et al., 1995), thus resulting in a lower dopamine level in val homozygotes than in met carriers. Recently, Nagel et al. (2008) found that COMT genotype affected the reaction times in a spatial working memory task, particularly in older adults. Older COMT val homozygotes were slower than met carriers in deciding whether a spatial location had been seen or had not been seen before (see Figure 12.4, right panel); no genotype effect was found in younger adults (Figure 12.4, left panel).

In addition to the overall level of working memory performance per se, other studies suggest that dopamine modulation is also important for working memory plasticity. A recent PET receptor imaging study showed that, in younger adults, intensive working memory training is associated with changes in the density of cortical dopamine receptors. Individuals whose working memory improved more as a function of training also showed a greater training-induced change in D1 receptor binding potential, suggesting a training-related enhancement in the release of endogenous dopamine (McNab et al., 2009). Another related finding comes from a behavioral

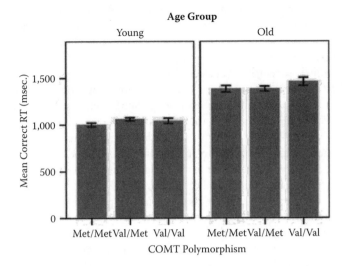

FIGURE 12.4 Effects of COMT genotype on reaction times of a spatial working-memory task in younger and older adults. (Adapted with permission from Nagel, I. E. et al., 2008, *Frontiers in Human Neuroscience, 2*, Article No. 1. Copyright Frontiers in Human Neuroscience.)

genetic study, which showed that individuals who carried the dopamine transporter genotype (i.e., DAT 9-repeat carriers) associated with a higher level of striatal dopamine benefited more from working memory training (Brehmer et al., 2009).

Of specific interest to memory aging, age-related differences in working memory plasticity (Li et al., 2008) and transfer effects of memory training (Dahlin, Neely, Larsson, Bäckman, & Nyberg, 2008) may also be related to older adults' deficient dopamine function. Specifically, functional brain activity in the dopamine innervated striatal region was found to be critical for the transfer of training effect to a 3-back verbal working memory task in younger adults. Older adults did not show significant striatal activation before training, which may underlie the lack of transfer effect in this age group (Dahlin et al., 2008).

EMPIRICAL FINDINGS SUPPORTING THEORETICAL ACCOUNTS OF DOPAMINERGIC MODULATION OF EPISODIC MEMORY AGING

A wide range of evidence from pharmacological and brain imaging studies in animals and humans supports dopamine's role in modulating working memory, although there are also some inconsistencies in the observed effects due to study differences in task demands and the type and dose of drugs administered. Futhermore, individual differences in dopamine geno-types (see Bäckman, Nyberg, Lindenberger, Li, & Farde, 2006; Bäckman et al., 2010, for reviews) add to the complexity in the findings.

In comparison to evidence for dopamine modulation of working mem-ory, the empirical relation between dopamine and episodic memory is less established. A few recent functional brain imaging studies showed that dopamine affects episodic encoding (e.g., Schott et al., 2006; Wittmann et al., 2005). Specifically, carriers of the dopamine transporter gene that is associated with a higher level of extracellar dopamine (i.e., DAT 9-repeat carriers) showed higher midbrain activation during encoding than 10-repeat carriers. Relatedly, a recent pharmacological study with younger adults showed that applying apomorphine at low doses to stimulate presynaptic receptors and thereby decrease extracelluar dopamine impaired episodic memory (Montoya et al., 2006).

As for episodic memory deficit in old age, one recent pharmacological imaging study showed that older adults' episodic memories was more sensi-tive to drug intervention of the dopamine systems than those of younger adults (Morcom et al., 2010). Age differences in drug effects on functional brain activations associated with episodic memory, however, were harder to pin down, given age differences in performance and drug reactivity and the potential interactions between age and genetic differences (Li, Chicherio et al., 2010; Lindenberger et al., 2008; Nagel et al., 2008).

Taking a multimodal imaging approach, Nyberg et al. (2009) recently showed in a sample of middle-aged and older adults (ages 52–67) that stria-tal D2 binding activity is positively correlated with the magnitude of pre-frontal brain activation during a long-term memory updating task. This finding indicates that, through the frontal-striatal pathway, age-related decline in the striatal dopamine system may affect prefrontal activation when long-term memories are updated. It also highlights the close interac-tions between the working memory and episodic memory systems. Other than its contribution to age-related impairment in the level of episodic memory performance per se, early results from computational studies (Li et al., 2001) suggested that the substantial age-related reduction in episodic memory plasticity, as shown by the testing-the-limit paradigm (Baltes & Kliegl, 1992), may also be attributable to deficient dopamine modulation in old age (see Figure 12.5). This prediction, however, still needs to be veri-fied empirically.

OUTLOOK

This chapter very selectively focused on dopaminergic modulation of working memory and episodic memory in human aging. Future studies, however, should also consider other transmitter systems and genotypes.

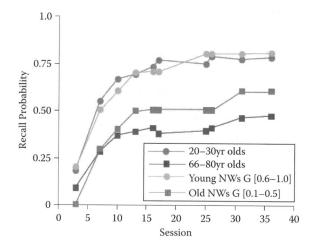

FIGURE 12.5 Simulating deficient dopamine modulation in older adults with reduced G in neural networks accounts for age-related deficit in episodic memory plasticity. (Data from Baltes, P. B., & Kliegl, R., 1992, *Developmental Psychology, 28,* 121–125; Li, S.-C. et al., 2001, *Trends in Cognitive Sciences, 5,* 479–486; adapted with permission. Copyright Elsevier.)

On the one hand, computational theories of dopaminergic modulation suggest that DA receptor stimulation could lead to long-lasting NMDA current and increased inhibition to sharpen working-memory representations (Durstewitz et al., 2000). On the other hand, some empirical evidence shows that dopamine-relevant genes interact with genes relevant for glutamate (GRM3) or brain-derived neurotrophic factor (BDNF) in affecting working memory (Nagel et al., 2008; Tan et al., 2007). Dopamine may also interact with other genes that have been shown to affect episodic memory and aging, such as the KIBRA gene (e.g., Preuschhof et al., 2010) and the BDNF gene (e.g., Li, Chicherio, et al., 2010). The fact that dopamine is involved in both the aging of working and episodic memory also leaves open the question as to whether the functions of different memory systems dedifferentiate or, in other words, become less independent in old age.

A century after Mark Twain's death, indisputable cures for his complaint about his unreliable memory as an old man are still not available. However, findings from modern research of memory aging have paved ways to uncover some of the neurochemical and genetic sources for the problem. En route to understanding the neurobiological and genetic processes of memory aging, a further challenge would be to unravel how these processes may interact with environmental and contextual supports in order to arrive at optimal interventions to lessen the inconvenient human condition of memory aging.

ACKNOWLEDGMENTS

I would like to give special thanks to members of the "DA-Study," which is a part of the Neuromodulation of Lifespan Cognition Project at the Center for Lifespan Psychology, Max Planck Institute for Human Development (See Project Website:http://www.mpibberlin.mpg.de/en/research/lifespan-psychology/projects/neuromodulation-of-lifespan-cognition). Some of the published studies reviewed in this chapter are the products of intensive collaborations with current and past members of the DA-Study—in particular, Lars Bäckman, Aga Burzynska, Christian Chicherio, Hauke Heekeren, Ulman Lindenberger, Irene Nagel, Lars Nyberg, Goran Papenberg, Claudia Preuschhof, and Thomas Sanders.

REFERENCES

Arnsten, A. F. T. (1998). Catecholamine modulation of prefrontal cortical cognitive function. *Trends in Cognitive Sciences, 2,* 436–447.

Bäckman, L., Ginovart, N., Dixon, R. A., Wahlin, T. B., Wahlin, A., Halldin, C., & Farde, L. (2000). Age-related cognitive deficits mediated by changes in the striatal dopamine system. *American Journal of Psychiatry, 157,* 635–637.

Bäckman, L., Karlsson, S., Fischer, H., Karlsson, P., Brehmer, Y., Rieckman, A., MacDonald, S. W. S., Farde, L., & Nyberg, L. (2011). Dopamine D1 receptors and age differences in brain activation during working memory. *Neurobiology of Aging, 32,* 1849–1856.

Bäckman, L., Lindenberger, U., Li, S.-C., & Nyberg, L. (2010). Linking cognitive aging to alterations in dopamine neurotransmitter functioning: Recent data and future avenues. *Neuroscience and Biobehavioral Reviews, 34,* 670–677.

Bäckman, L., Nyberg, L., Lindenberger, U., Li, S.-C., & Farde, L. (2006). The correlative triad among aging, dopamine, and cognition: Current status and future prospects. *Neuroscience and Biobehavioral Reviews, 30,* 791–807.

Baddeley, A. D. (2007). *Working memory, thought, and action.* New York, NY: Oxford University Press.

Baddeley, A. D., & Hitch, G. (1974). Working memory. In G. H. Bower (Ed.), *The psychology of learning and motivation: Advances in research and theory* (Vol. 8, pp. 47–89). New York, NY: Academic Press.

Baltes, P. B., & Kliegl, R. (1992). Further testing of limits of cognitive plasticity: Negative age differences in a mnemonic skill are robust. *Developmental Psychology, 28,* 121–125.

Bopp, K. L., & Verhaeghen, P. (2005). Aging and verbal memory span: A meta-analysis. *Journals of Gerontology: Series B. Psychological Sciences and Social Sciences, 60,* P223–P233.

Brehmer, Y., Li, S.-C., Müller, V., von Oertzen, T., & Lindenberger, U. (2007). Memory plasticity across the life span: Uncovering children's latent potential. *Developmental Psychology, 43,* 465–478.

Brehmer, Y., Westerberg, H., Bellander, M., Fürth, D., Karlsson, S., & Bäckman, L. (2009). Working memory plasticity modulated by dopamine transporter genotype. *Neuroscience Letters, 467,* 117–120.

Castner, S. A., & Goldman-Rakic, P. S. (2004). Enhancement of working memory in aged monkeys by a sensitizing regimen of dopamine D1 receptor stimulation. *Journal of Neuroscience, 24,* 1446–1450.

Chalfonte, B. L., & Johnson, M. K. (1996). Feature memory and binding in young and older adults. *Memory & Cognition, 24,* 403–416.

Charlton, R. A., Barrick, T. R., Lawes, I. N. C., Markus, H. S., & Morris, R. G. (2010). White matter pathways associated with working memory in normal aging. *Cortex, 46,* 474–489.

Cohen, J. D., & Servan-Schreiber, D. (1992). Context, cortex, and dopamine: A connectionist approach to behavior and biology in schizophrenia. *Psychological Review, 99,* 45–77.

Cumming, P. (2009). *Imaging dopamine.* Cambridge, UK: Cambridge University Press.

Dahlin, E., Stigsdotter-Neely, A., Larsson, A., Bäckman, L., & Nybergm L. (2008). Transfer of learning after updating training mediated by the striatum. *Science, 320,* 1510–1512.

Daselaar, S. M., Fleck, M. S., Dobbins, I. G., Madden, D. J., & Cabeza, R. (2006). Effects of healthy aging on hippocampal and rhinal memory functions: An event-related fMRI study. *Cerebral Cortex, 16,* 1771–1782.

Dennis, N. A., Hayes, S. M., Prince, S. E., Madden, D. J., Huettel, S. A., & Cabeza, R. (2008). Effects of aging on the neural correlates of successful item and source memory encoding. *Journal of Experimental Psychology: Learning, Memory, and Cognition, 34,* 791–808.

Dennis, N. A., Kim, H., & Cabeza, R. (2008). Effects of aging on true and false memory formation: An fMRI study. *Neuropsychologia, 45,* 3157–3166.

Dobbs, A. R., & Rule, B. G. (1989). Adult age differences in working memory. *Psychology and Aging, 4,* 500–503.

Dodson, C. S., Bawa, S., & Krueger, L. E. (2007). Aging, metamemory, and high-confidence errors: A misrecollection account. *Psychology and Aging, 22,* 122–133.

Doya, K., Dayan, P., & Hasselmo, M. E. (Eds.). (2002). Computational models of neuromodulation. *Neural Networks* (special issue), *4*(6).

Durstewitz, D., Seamans, J. K., & Sejnowski, T. J. (2000). Dopamine-mediated stabilization of delay-period activity in a network model of prefrontal cortex. *Journal of Neurophysiology, 83,* 1733–1750.

Erixon-Lindroth, N., Farde, L., Robbins-Wahlin, T.-B., Sovago, J., Halldin, C., & Bäckman, L. (2005). The role of the striatal dopamine transporter in cognitive aging. *Psychiatry Research Neuroimaging, 138,* 1–12.

Fischer, H. et al. (2010). Simulating neurocognitive aging: Effects of a dopaminergic antagonist on brain activity during working memory. *Biological Psychiatry, 67,* 575–580.

Gallo, D. A., Forster, K. T., & Johnson, E. L. (2009). Elevated false recollection of emotional pictures in young and older adults. *Psychology and Aging, 24,* 981–988.

Gallo, D. A., & Roediger, H. L. (2003). The effects of associations and aging on illusory recognition. *Memory and Cognition, 31,* 1036–1044.

Gazzaley, A. et al. (2005). Top-down suppression deficit underlies working memory impairment in normal aging. *Nature Neuroscience, 8,* 1298–1300.

Goldman-Rakic, P. S., Muly, E. C., & Williams, G. V. (2000). D1 receptors in prefrontal cells and circuits. *Brain Research Review, 31,* 295–301.

Graham, B., & Willshaw, D. (1995). Improving recall from an associative memory. *Biological Cybernetics, 72,* 337–346.

Green, A. E., Munafo, M. R., & DeYoung, C. G. (2008). Using genetic data in cognitive neuroscience: from growing pains to genuine insights. *Nature Reviews Neuroscience, 9,* 710–720.

Greengard, P. (2000). The neurobiology of dopamine signaling. Nobel Lecture (Stockholm, Sweden, Dec. 8, 2000).

Gutchess, A. H., Welsh, R. C., Hedden, T., Bangert, A., Minear, M., Liu, L. L., & Park, D. C. (2005). Aging and the neural correlates of successful picture encoding: Frontal activations compensate for decreased medial-temporal activity. *Journal of Cognitive Neuroscience, 17,* 84–96.

Harris-Warrick, R. M., & Marder, E. (1991). Modulation of neural networks for behavioral. *Annual Review of Neuroscience, 14,* 39–57.

Head, D., Rodrigue, K. M., Kennedy, K. M., & Raz, N. (2008). Neuroanatomical and cognitive mediators of age-related differences in episodic memory. *Neuropsychology, 22,* 491–507.

Hessler, N. A., Shirke, A. M., & Malinow, R. (1993). The probability of transmitter release at a mammalian central synapse. *Nature 366,* 569–572.

Kalpouzos, G. et al. (2009). Structural and metabolic correlates of episodic memory in relation to the depth of encoding in normal aging. *Journal of Cognitive Neuroscience, 21,* 372–389.

Kassinen, V., & Rinne, J. O. (2002). Functional imaging studies of dopamine system and cognition in normal aging and Parkinson's disease. *Neuroscience and Biobehavioral Reviews, 26,* 785–793.

Kliegl, R., & Lindenberger, U. (1993). Modeling intrusions and correct recall in episodic memory: Adult age-differences in encoding of list context. *Journal of Experimental Psychology: Learning, Memory, and Cognition, 19,* 617–637.

Le, W., Chen, S., & Jankovic, J. (2009). Etiopathogenesis of Parkinson disease: A new beginning? *Neuroscientist, 15,* 28–35.

Leshikar, E. D., Gutchess, A. H., Hebrank, A. C., Sutton, B. P., & Park, D. C. (2010). The impact of increased relational encoding demands on frontal and hippocampal function in older adults. *Cortex, 46,* 507–521.

Li, S.-C., Chicherio, C., Nyberg, L., von Oertzen, T., Nagel, I. E., Sander, T., Heekeren, H. R.,... Bäckman, L. (2010). Ebbinghaus revisited: Influences of the BDNF Val66Met polymorphism on backward serial recall are modulated by human aging. *Journal of Cognitive Neuroscience, 22,* 2164–2173.

Li, S.-C., & Lindenberger, U. (1999). Cross-level unification: A computational exploration of the link between deterioration of neurotransmitter systems and dedifferentiation of cognitive abilities in old age. In L.-G. Nilsson & H. J. Markowitsch (Eds.), *Cognitive neuroscience of memory* (pp. 103–146). Göttingen, Germany: Hogrefe & Huber.

Li, S.-C., Lindenberger, U., & Bäckman, L. (2010). Dopaminergic modulation of cognition across the life span. *Neuroscience and Biobehavioral Reviews, 34,* 625–630.

Li, S.-C., Lindenberger, U., & Frensch, P. A. (2000). Unifying cognitive aging: From neuromodulation to representation to cognition. *Neurocomputing, 32–33,* 879–890.

Li, S.-C., Lindenberger, U., Nyberg, L., Heekeren, H. R., & Bäckman, L. (2009). Dopaminergic modulation of cognition in human aging. In W. Jagust & M. D'Esposito (Eds.), *Imaging the aging brain* (pp. 71–91). New York, NY: Oxford University Press.

Li, S.-C., Lindenberger, U., & Sikström, S. (2001). Aging cognition: From neuro-modulation to representation to cognition. *Trends in Cognitive Sciences, 5*, 479–486.

Li, S.-C., Naveh-Benjamin, M., & Lindenberger, U. (2005). Aging neuromodulation impairs associative binding: a neurocomputational account. *Psychological Science, 16*, 445–450.

Li, S.-C., Schmiedek, F., Huxhold, O., Röcke, C., Smith, J., & Lindenberger, U. (2008). Working memory plasticity in old age: Practice gain, transfer, and maintenance. *Psychology and Aging, 23*, 731–742.

Li, S.-C., & Sikström, S. (2002). Integrative neurocomputational perspectives on cognitive aging, neuromodulation, and representation. *Neuroscience and Biobehavioral Reviews, 26*, 795–808.

Light, L. L. (1991). Memory and aging: Four hypotheses in search of data. *Annual Review of Psychology, 42*, 333–376.

Lindenberger, U., Nagel, I. E., Chicherio, C., Li, S.-C., Heekeren, H. R., & Bäckman, L. (2008). Age-related decline in brain resources modulates genetic effects on cognitive functioning. *Frontiers in Neuroscience, 2*, 234–244.

Lotta, T., Vidgren, J., Tilgmann, C., Ulmanen, I. Melen, K., Julkunen, I. & Taskinen, J. (1995). Kinetics of human soluble and membrane-bound catechol-O-meth-yltransferase: A revised mechanism and description of the termolabile variant of the enzyme. *Biochemistry, 34*, 4202–4210.

Marder, E., & Thiirumalai, V. (2002). Celluar, synaptic and network effects of neu-romodulation. *Neural Networks, 15*, 479–493.

Mattay, V. S. et al. (2003). Catechol-O-methyltransferase val(258)-met genotype and individual variation in the brain responses to amphetamine. *Proceedings of the National Academy of Sciences USA, 100*, 6186–6191.

McCabe, D. P., Roediger, H. L., McDaniel, M. A., & Balota, D. A. (2009). Aging reduces veridical remembering but increases false memory: Neuropsychological test correlates of remember–know judgments. *Neuropsychologia, 47*, 2164–2173.

McNab, F., Varrone, A., Farde, L., Jucaite, A., Bystritsky, P., Forssberg, H., & Klingberg, T. (2009). Changes in cortical dopamine D1 receptor binding asso-ciated with cognitive training. *Science, 323*, 800–802.

Mitchell, K. J., Johnson, M. K., Raye, C. L., & D'Esposito, M. (2000). FMRI evi-dence of age-related hippocampal dysfunction in feature binding in working memory. *Cognitive Brain Research, 10*, 197–206.

Montoya, A., Lai, S., Menear, M., Duplessis, E., Thavundayil, J., Schmitz, N., & Lepage, M. (2006). Apomorphine effects on episodic memory in young healthy volunteers. *Neuropsychologia, 46*, 292–300.

Morcom, A. M. et al. (2010). Memory encoding and dopamine in the aging brain: A psychopharmacological neuroimaging study. *Cerebral Cortex, 20*, 743–757.

Mozley, L. H., Gur, R. C., Mozley, P. D., & Gur, R. E. (2001). Striatal dopamine transporters and cognitive functioning in healthy men and women. *American Journal of Psychiatry, 158*, 1492–1499.

Nagel, I. E., Chicherio, C., Li, S.-C., von Oertzen, T., Sander, T., Villringer, A.,... Lindenberger, U. (2008). Human aging magnifies genetic effects on executive functioning and working memory. *Frontiers in Human Neuroscience, 2*, article number 1.

Nagel, I. E., Preuschhof, C., Li, S.-C., Nyberg, L., Bäckman, L. Lindenberger, U., & Heekeren, H. R. (2009). Performance level modulates adult age differences in brain activation during spatial working memory. *Proceedings of National Academy of Sciences, 106,* 22552–22557.

Naveh-Benjamin, M. (2000). Adult age differences in memory performance: Tests of an associative deficit hypothesis. *Journal of Experimental Psychology: Learning, Memory, and Cognition, 26,* 1170–1187.

Naveh-Benjamin, M., Hussain, Z., Guez, J., & Bar-On, M. (2003). Adult age differences in episodic memory: Further support for an associative-deficit hypothesis. *Journal of Experimental Psychology: Learning, Memory, and Cognition, 29,* 826–837.

Nyberg, L., Andresson, M., Jakobsson-Mo, S., Larsson, A., Marklund, P., Riklund, K., & Bäckman, L. (2009). Striatal dopamine D2 binding is related to frontal bold response during updating of long-term memory representations. *NeuroImage, 46,* 1194–1199.

O'Reilly, R. C., & Frank, M. J. (2006). Making working memory work: A computational model of learning in the frontal cortex and basal ganglia. *Neural Computation, 18,* 283–328.

O'Reilly, R. C., Herd, S. A., & Pauli, W. M. (2010). Computational models of cognitive control. *Current Opinion in Neurobiology, 20,* 257–261.

Plancher, G., Gyselinck, V., Nicolas, S., & Piolino, P. (2010). Age effect on components of episodic memory and feature binding: A virtual reality study. *Neuropsychology, 24,* 379–390.

Preuschhof, C., Heekeren, H. R., Li, S.-C., Sander, T., Lindenberger, U., & Bäckman, L. (2010). KIBRA and CLSTN2 polymorphisms exert interactive effects on human episodic memory. *Neuropsychologia, 48,* 402–408.

Rajah, M. N., Languay, R., & Valiquette, L. (2010). Age-related changes in prefrontal cortex activity are associated wit behavioral deficits in both temporal and spatial context memory retrieval in older adults. *Cortex, 46,* 535–549.

Raz, N., Lindenberger, U., Rodrigue, K. M., Kennedy, K. M., Head, D., Williamson, A.,... Acker, J. D. (2005). Regional brain changes in aging healthy adults: General trends, individual differences and modifiers. *Cerebral Cortex, 15,* 1676–1689.

Roediger, H. L., III., & McDermott, K. B. (2000). Tricks of memory. *Current Directions in Psychological Science, 9,* 123–127.

Salthouse, T. A. (1994). The aging of working memory. *Neuropsychology, 8,* 535–543.

Sawaguchi, T., & Goldman-Rakic, P. S. (1991). D1 dopamine receptors in prefrontal cortex: involvement in working memory. *Science, 251,* 947–950.

Schneider-Graces, N. J., Gordon, B. A., Brumback-Peltz, C. R., Shin, E., Lee Y., Sutton, B. P.,... Fabiani, M. (2010). Span, crunch, and beyond: Working memory capacity and the aging brain. *Journal of Cognitive Neuroscience, 22,* 655–669.

Schott, B. H., Seidenbecher, C. I., Fenker, D. B., Lauer, C. J., Bunzeck, N., Bernstein, H.-G.,... Düzel, E. (2006). The dopaminergic midbrain participates in human episodic memory formation: Evidence from genetic imaging. *Journal of Neuroscience, 26,* 1407–1417.

Servan-Schreiber, D., Printz, H. W., & Cohen, J. D. (1990). A network model of catecholamine effects: Gains, signal-to-noise ratio and behavior. *Science, 249,* 892–895.

Shing, Y. L., Werkle-Bergner, M., Li, S.-C., & Lindenberger, U. (2008). Associative and strategic components of episodic memory: A life span dissociation. *Journal of Experimental Psychology: General, 137,* 495–513.

Shing, Y. L., Werkle-Bergner, M., Li, S.-C., & Lindenberger, U. (2009). Committing memory errors with high confidence: older adults do but children don't. *Memory, 17,* 169–179.

Singer, T., Lindenberger, U., & Baltes, P. B. (2003). Plasticity of memory for new learning in very old age: A story of major loss? *Psychology and Aging, 18,* 306–317.

Skinner, E. I., & Fernades, M. A. (2009). Illusory recollection in older adults and younger adults under divided attention. *Psychology and Aging, 24,* 211–216.

Smith, H. E. (Ed.) (2010). *Autobiography of Mark Twain.* Berkeley, CA: University of California Press.

Spencer, W. D., & Raz, N. (1995). Differential effects of aging on memory for content and context: A meta-analysis. *Psychology and Aging, 10,* 527–539.

Suhara, T., Fukuda, H., Inoue, O., Itoh, T., Suzuki, K., Yamasaki, T., & Tateno, Y. (1999). Age-related changes in human D1 dopamine receptors measured by positron emission tomography. *Psychopharmacology, 103,* 41–45.

Tan, H. Y., Chen, Q., Sust, S., Buckholtz, J. W., Meyers, J. D., Egan, M.F. et al. (2007). Epistasis between catechol-O-methyltransferase and type II metabotrophic glutamate receptor 3 genes on working memory brain fuction. *Proceedings of National Academy of Sciences USA, 104,* 12536–12541.

Thapar, A., & Westerman, D. L. (2009). Aging and fluency-based illusions in recognition memory. *Psychology and Aging, 24,* 595–603.

Verhaeghen, P., & Marcoen, A. (1993). Memory aging as a general phenomenon: Episodic recall of older adults is a function of episodic recall of young adults. *Psychology and Aging, 8*(3), 380–388.

Vijayraghavan, S., Wang, M., Birnbaum, S. G., Williams, G. V., & Arnsten, A. F. T. (2007). Inverted-U dopamine D1 receptor actions on prefrontal neurons engaged in working memory. *Nature Neuroscience, 10,* 376–384.

Williams, G. V., & Goldman-Rakic, P. S. (1995). Modulation of memory field by dopamine D1 receptors in prefrontal cortex. *Nature, 376,* 572–575.

Wittmann, B. C., Schott, B. H., Guderian, S., Frey, J. U., Heinze, H. J., & Düzel, E. (2005). Reward-related fMRI activation of dopaminergic midbrain is associated with enhanced hippocampus-dependent long-term memory formation. *Neuron, 45,* 459–467.

Wolfart, J. Debay, D., Le Masson, G., Destexhe, A., & Ball, T. (2005). Synaptic background activity controls spike transfer from thalamus to cortex. *Nature Neuroscience, 8,* 1760–1767.

Wong, D. F., Wagner, H. N., Jr., Dannals, R. F., Links, J. M., Frost, J. J., Ravert, H. T., et al. (1984). Effects of age on dopamine and serotonin receptors measured by positron tomography in the living human brain. *Science, 226,* 1393–1396.

Yassa, M. A., Mattfeld, A. T., Stark, S. M., & Stark, C. E. L. (2011). Age-related memory deficits linked to circuit-specific disruptions in the hippocampus. *Proceedings of the National Academy of Sciences USA, 108,* 8873–8878.

13 Yes, memory declines with aging—but when, how, and why?

*Roger A. Dixon, Brent J. Small,
Stuart W. S. MacDonald,
and John J. McArdle*

INTRODUCTION

Research on memory and aging focuses on (a) processes through (and levels at) which individuals recall previously experienced events and information, (b) the timing, extent, and variability with which these processes and associated performances differ and change with aging, and (c) the conditions and factors that control, predict, or modulate these differences and changes dynamically and interactively throughout adulthood. Decades of research have produced numerous provocative and robust findings, but also an ever widening purview and increasingly integrative perspective on the phenomena of memory changes with aging (see Cabeza, Nyberg, & Park, 2004; Craik & Salthouse, 2008; Dixon, Bäckman, & Nilsson, 2004; Zacks, Hasher, & Li, 2006).

Today, research on memory and aging recurrently addresses specific aspects of underlying mechanisms of memory per se. In addition, the field of memory and aging has come to involve progressively complex questions regarding conditions, modulators, factors, and correlates from neurological, genetic, lifestyle, biological, health, affective, social, and cultural domains. Moreover, contemporary memory and aging research includes methods and designs reflecting the very best in experimental procedures, as well as techniques and approaches derived from longitudinal, quantitative, computational, neuroimaging, neurogenetics, epidemiological, microbiological, biomedical, and sociocultural perspectives. Such adventures in integrative or cross-disciplinary research in memory are not unique; in the field of aging, they apply with growing theoretical significance and clinical implications to other aspects of cognition and psychosocial functioning (Dixon, 2011).

The narrative of this chapter is designed to chart a path that reflects, if not integrates, novel developments in both of these two clusters: (a) new domains and sources of influence and (b) new methods and approaches to research. We sketch an approach to understanding normal aging-related changes in performance on a traditional form of memory. Specifically, declarative memory includes both episodic and semantic memory systems (Nyberg et al., 2003; Tulving, 1995). As indicated in the chapter title, we concede at the outset the fact that declarative memory performance *generally* declines with advancing age, but we focus theoretical attention on three guiding (and qualifying) questions: *When*, *how*, and *why* does memory change with aging?

Accordingly, the chapter addresses four main topics regarding the aging of declarative memory. First, we describe longitudinal and epidemiological approaches to memory and aging, noting that their combination provides the possibility to address when, how, and why memory declines with aging. Second, we describe our own ongoing large-scale project that yields (longitudinally) both within- and between-person information on memory aging and (epidemiologically) a platform for examining a broad range of modulators (such as risk and protective factors) of both typical and neuropathological memory change. Third, we summarize some recent research results flowing from the convergence of this approach with our project. Fourth, we conclude with new data pertaining to the opportunities and challenges inherent in applying these approaches for directly representing normative memory change functions in ways that reflect the fact that they are differential, variable, and complex and include both growth and decline functions (within and across persons).

MERGING LONGITUDINAL AND EPIDEMIOLOGICAL APPROACHES TO MEMORY AGING

Several years ago, three collaborators representing three larger-scale longitudinal and epidemiological studies of aging convened a conference and edited a subsequent volume in which the goal was to explore the emerging theoretical, methodological, and substantive frontiers of "pluralistic and epidemiological" approaches to cognitive aging (Dixon, Backman, & Nilsson 2004). The three longitudinal and epidemiological aging projects were known as the Betula Project (Sweden), Kungsholmen Project (Sweden), and the Victoria Longitudinal Study (Canada). Other corresponding projects represented among the contributors were the Berlin Aging Study, Canberra Longitudinal Study, and the Swedish Adoption/Twin Study on Aging.

We noted that the evolving discipline of cognitive aging, dazzling in its growth in the previous decade, was becoming more of an "interdiscipline." By this term we observed that the field was not so much impeded by multiple approaches and theories, but rather enhanced by the energy and opportunities they embodied. A similar explicitly interdisciplinary perspective informed a more recent conference-to-book enterprise (Hofer & Alwin, 2008). In both cases, contributors not only addressed fine-grained and theoretically trenchant research on mechanisms of cognitive performance in older adults, but also forecast new developments and directions for understanding influences on cognitive changes occurring across aging, with the influences ranging through a variety of dynamic and interactive contexts. Accordingly, chapters from these books covered crucial theoretical movements (Park & Minear, 2004), methodological issues (Hertzog, 2004), neurological changes (Raz, 2004; Wilson, 2008), biological markers (Anstey, 2008; Herlitz & Yonker, 2004), health influences (Spiro & Brady, 2008; Wahlin, 2004), genetic aspects (Pedersen, 2004; Reynolds, 2008), and many others.

The key notion was not that every study of cognitive or memory aging would be required to measure and evaluate influences from such widely ranging (and changing) sources, but rather that, overall, as a field addressing a set of complex and changing phenomena, some benefit would accrue to promoting more such research (Dixon, 2011). In this chapter, we consider this provisional lesson as applying to all processes within cognitive aging, including the current topic—the prominent and well-researched area of declarative memory.

Briefly, longitudinal and epidemiological approaches are applied in a coordinated fashion to understand the development, distribution, and future projections of health and illness phenomena. They produce implications for theoretical (e.g., identifying causes, conditions, and sequelae of diseases), clinical (e.g., identifying possibilities for intervention, protection, and prevention), and public health (e.g., marshalling large-scale recovery or contingency policies, promotion of healthy outcomes) initiatives. An immediate goal is to identify the causes, distributions, risk factors, and protective factors associated with a given outcome.

Memory-related outcomes may be involved in the same manner for (a) neurocognitive diseases (e.g., sporadic Alzheimer's disease), (b) classifications of at-risk memory-related conditions (e.g., mild cognitive impairment), (c) variability in memory decline within normal or typical ranges, or even (d) the potential for sustained high levels of memory performance into unexpectedly late periods of adulthood (Dixon, 2010). Whereas risk factors to memory aging are thought to accelerate decline or hinder maintenance, protective factors may promote maintenance or buffer decline. With aging, the increasing hazards are conferred by accumulating risk factors, comorbidities, biomedical health, neurobiological integrity, and consequent neurocognitive dysfunction (e.g., Anstey, 2008; Park & Reuter-Lorenz, 2009; Raz, 2004).

Among the corresponding resources and protective factors operating to support some aspects of declarative memory are lifestyle engagement (cognitive, social, physical activities), adaptive processes (compensation, optimization, selection, management), and various forms of plasticity and resilience (e.g., Ball et al., 2002; Baltes, Lindenberger, & Staudinger, 2006; Dixon, 2010; Ghisletta, Bickel, & Lövdén, 2006; Hertzog, Kramer, Wilson, & Lindenberger, 2008; Stern, 2007). Although they may operate to interrupt the downward press from the expanding and deepening pool of hazards of aging, these protective resources are typically diminishing in number and efficacy with aging. Thus, with aging, we may expect that the probability of maintaining all domains or subtypes of memory functioning is dynamically reduced by the number of, severity of, and interactions among risk and protection factors.

Where does this leave us theoretically? In a recent review, it was disclosed that theories of psychological aging, as represented in the perennial "theories" chapters in a major handbook series dating back to 1977, were not typically cast as the search for (a) global reach or purview, (b) immutable or universal principles, or (c) broadly generalizable logical or formal structures (e.g., Baltes & Willis, 1977; Birren, 1999; Dixon, 2011). Moreover, this pattern seemed to fit other sciences dealing with complex, evolving, adapting, dynamic, and interactive systems. Instead, many theories of psychological aging focused on accounting for relatively local phenomena with specific and adapted constructs and mechanisms. Where does this leave us methodologically?

This leads us to the importance of including a variety of procedures and designs in the overall field of memory aging. Some of these will be in the scientifically productive category of experimental, quasi-experimental, univariate, and cross-sectional designs. These include the possibilities of examining (a) more direct causality, partly through the control of alternative explanations, and (b) potentially new covariates and modulators of aging-memory relationships. Some of these will be in the general areas of longitudinal epidemiological research, and there are very good reasons for these to be pursued. Among these is the fact that many such studies have in their protocols and batteries (a) multiple measures of risk and protective factors relevant to specific memory phenomena, (b) multiple indicators from the main epidemiological clusters relevant to memory (including biological vitality, neurobiological integrity, neurocognitive resources, cognitive status, lifestyle and environment, social–cultural factors), and (c) multiple measures of all major systems and subtypes of memory

In addition, these studies feature multiple assessments over time, such that the dynamic operation of epidemiological factors operating through the prism of epidemiological functions can be associated with changes and differences in memory performance (e.g., Dixon, 2010; McArdle, 2009). In the next section, we turn to a discussion of one example research project that serves as the platform for the present work on memory and aging.

THE VLS: A PLATFORM FOR STUDIES OF MEMORY AGING

The Victoria Longitudinal Study (VLS) operates in two western provinces of Canada. It was begun in the late 1980s and has continued since that time. The original rationale was to recruit successive cohorts of healthy adults (initially aged 55–85 years) and follow them longitudinally as they developed various aging-related conditions, including memory decline, memory impairment, and neurodegenerative diseases. Accordingly, research on memory aging in the VLS has attended to such issues as actual group-level average change over time (Dixon, Wahlin, et al., 2004), structural models of cognitive resource influences on memory change (Hertzog, Dixon, Hultsch, & MacDonald, 2003), biological vitality (BioAge) effects on memory change (MacDonald, Dixon, Cohen, & Hazlitt, 2004), general health influences on memory aging (Small, Dixon, & McArdle, 2011; Wahlin, MacDonald, de Frias, Nilsson, & Dixon, 2006), emergent health conditions such as type 2 diabetes (Yeung, Fischer, & Dixon, 2009), role of neurocognitive inconsistency (Dixon et al., 2007; MacDonald, Hultsch, & Dixon, 2003), and acute health conditions such as stroke (Mansueti, de Frias, Bub, & Dixon, 2008), as well as dynamics of memory and memory compensation (Dixon & de Frias, 2007).

The design of the VLS is longitudinal sequential, with three main cohorts (or samples) followed at 3- to 4-year intervals (see Dixon & de Frias, 2004, for additional information). The three cohorts were initiated in the 1980s, 1990s, and 2000s, and each included roughly 500–600 participants, plus multiple control groups. At each wave about 12–14 hours of testing for each individual occurs. Overall, about 2,000 participants have run the VLS gauntlet at least once and many of them multiple times. As can be seen in Figure 13.1, at present we have collected longitudinal data from all available members of each sample as follows: VLS Sample 1 has seven waves (18 years) of data, VLS Sample 2 has five waves (12 years of data), and VLS Sample 3 has three waves (6 years) of data. Multiple indicators from several clusters highlight the VLS battery. The clusters include:

- Wide-ranging cognitive and neurocognitive performance and status
- Health conditions, health beliefs, and all medications
- Biomarkers and "BioAge," sensory functioning, fitness, DNA–genetics
- Memory compensation and metacognitive knowledge and beliefs
- Life and family history, concurrent lifestyle and activities
- Psychosocial affect and depression

In the next section, we turn to a brief review of some research results following the longitudinal epidemiological approach.

VLS AND MEMORY AGING: SEEKING PROVISIONAL ANSWERS TO THE *WHEN, HOW,* AND *WHY* QUESTIONS

To some extent, the VLS began as a project emphasizing individual differences in memory changes, with all major systems of memory represented

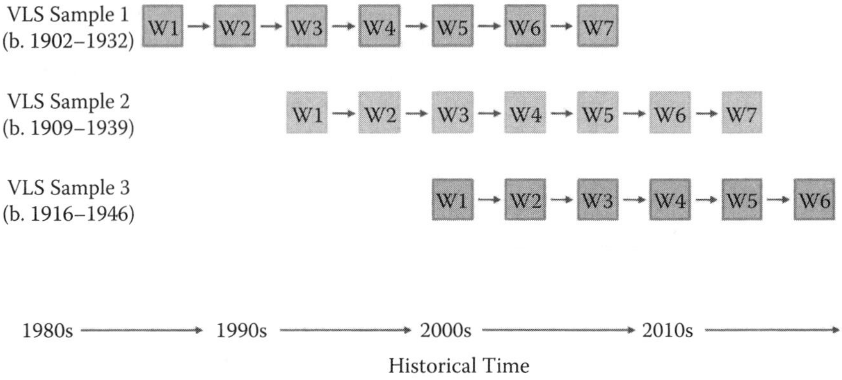

VLS Sample 1
(b. 1902–1932)   W1 → W2 → W3 → W4 → W5 → W6 → W7

VLS Sample 2
(b. 1909–1939)   W1 → W2 → W3 → W4 → W5 → W6 → W7

VLS Sample 3
(b. 1916–1946)   W1 → W2 → W3 → W4 → W5 → W6

1980s ──────→ 1990s ──────→ 2000s ──────→ 2010s ──────→
Historical Time

FIGURE 13.1 The VLS sequential longitudinal design.

and investigated. Memory was viewed as a focus for both theoretical and applied reasons, but the early dual emphasis was on charting declarative memory changes both independently and as a function of cognitive primitives (e.g., Dixon, Backman, & Nilsson, 2004; Hertzog et al., 2003; Hultsch, Hertzog, Dixon, & Small, 1998; Small, Dixon, Hultsch, & Hertzog, 1999). Research was carried out at both the manifest and latent variable levels depending on the research question. At that time, very few longitudinal data were available with which to explore the prevailing question of how memory performance might actually change with aging, so virtually anything was interesting, if not novel. In addition, however, we attended to the subquestions of whether:

- Memory changed uniformly (or differentially) across systems or forms
- Memory changed uniformly (or differentially) across aging individuals
- Actual memory change patterns were consonant with the commanding patterns of group differences observed with cross-sectional data
- Select cognitive resources (e.g., speed), other memory phenomena (e.g., working), or demographic factors (e.g., age, gender) affected observed patterns of declarative memory aging

For the VLS, the epidemiological aspect was at first grafted onto the growing longitudinal part. The two initiatives began to appear together when we examined selected individual difference characteristics such as:

- The moderating role of lifestyle activities on memory change (only cognitively engaging lifestyle activities; Hultsch, Hertzog, Small, & Dixon, 1999)
- Spin-Off studies showing the benefits of recruitment and collaboration in memory performance (e.g., Dixon, 1999)

- The role that everyday memory compensation might play in overall memory competence in normal (Dixon & Backman, 1995; Dixon, de Frias, & Bäckman, 2001) and clinical (Dixon, Hopp, Cohen, de Frias, & Bäckman, 2003) populations
- Cross-national comparisons of episodic memory performance (Dixon, Wahlin, et al., 2004)

In this section, we briefly review more recent work combining longitudinal and epidemiological agendas.

Declarative memory: Intraindividual change and variability

As noted earlier, declarative memory includes both episodic and semantic memory (Nyberg et al., 2003; Tulving, 1995). Regarding aging, a received view, based on much excellent cross-sectional research, is that episodic memory displays regular, step-like (perhaps decade-related) decrements in group mean performance across successively older ages. In contrast, the decrement function for semantic memory performance was acknowledged as not so steep, with even a hint of stability in mean-level age-related performance (Nyberg et al., 2003; Park & Minear, 2004). The emergence of longitudinal data, however, presented the field with a dilemma of both theoretical and methodological proportions (e.g., Hertzog, 2004; McArdle, 2009; McArdle, Fisher, & Kadlec, 2007; Schaie, 2011; Zelinski & Kennison, 2007): Given similar measures, do patterns and interpretations differ according to research design? If the template pattern is represented by the cross-sectionally derived step-like decrements across decades from young adulthood through late life, then an affirmative answer would be appropriate.

Several international longitudinal studies were producing multiwave data that, even when adjusted for qualifying factors, presented differential, if not modest, decline. To test whether this might apply across manifest indicators of episodic memory and across two countries (Canada, Sweden), the VLS partnered with the Kungsholmen Project. We assembled a data set that featured 15 different measures of episodic memory in a 40-year span of 54- to 94-year-olds ($n = 568$), who were tested twice at about a 3-year interval. The main result was 3-year patterns (of group mean-level change) that reflected notably modest or gradual decrements (Dixon, Wahlin, et al., 2004).

Subsequently, we examined longer periods (e.g., 12 years) as qualified by initial age group (comparing young-old, mid-old, and old-old adults) and as contrasted with the patterns of intraindividual variability lurking behind the means. For word recall, Figure 13.2 displays, on the one hand, the raw startling contrast behind 12-year gradual mean-level change (with minor age differences) and, on the other hand, individual trajectories that have produced the means (Dixon, 2007). The figures show the means and intraindividual patterns for a subset of the sample, as well as for the full sample (including dropouts for all reasons).

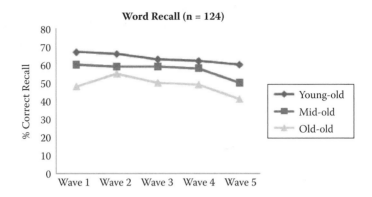

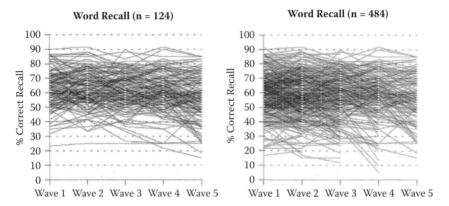

FIGURE 13.2 VLS 12-year mean-level intraindividual change and variability patterns by age (young-old, mid-old, old-old) for episodic memory (word recall).

More recently, we explored 18-year mean-level, wave-by-wave data, with the patterns displayed in Figure 13.3. These informal analyses imply the possibility that the aging of declarative memory—even episodic memory— could be characterized as much more gradual (at least in the 55+ age range) than would have been expected by cross-sectional data. We recently tested this idea more formally (Small et al., 2011) by fitting piecewise (spline) random-effects models to long-term age-based change profiles of a VLS sample (n = 952; age = 55–95 years). We specifically tested whether there were differences in trajectory in the 55–75 age range versus the 75–95 age range. The results showed that, across six cognitive measures (two episodic, two semantic, two speed), there was relatively little significant decline in the young-old phase, although uniformly significant decline occurred in the old-old phase. Word recall and fact recall seemed to be the most sensitive to earlier decline. As presented later in this chapter, we have conducted a new set of analyses on these data to investigate a related issue. For now, the conclusion of this line of inquiry is threefold (Dixon, 2011; Hertzog, 2004):

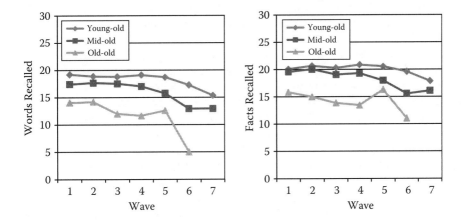

FIGURE 13.3 VLS 18-year mean-level change results (by wave) for episodic memory (left) and semantic memory (right).

- There are wide individual differences in change trajectories in late life, but overall mean-level patterns would not always support the notion of dramatic decrements in memory aging.
- At the very least, these qualifications would not have been known with cross-sectional data.
- The emerging long-term longitudinal results require careful integration into theories of memory and aging.

Biological and health factors in memory aging

Since the earliest theorizing in human aging, the underlying role of biological (and, by extension, health) factors in shaping or interacting with cognitive changes has been acknowledged (e.g., Baltes & Willis, 1977; Birren, 1999; Birren & Cunningham, 1985; see review by Dixon, 2011). As an alternative way of measuring developmental time, the concept of "biological age" as a supplement (if not replacement) to chronological age has been available (at least conceptually) for half a century. The BioAge concept is based on the long-held premise that chronological age is merely an index of developmental time. A corollary is that, although increasing chronological age is clearly associated with increasing morbidity, age itself does not cause disease or death (Peto & Doll, 1997).

Regarding cognition, age (years since birth) conveys no causal implications (i.e., aging per se is not a cause of memory decline) or explanatory weight (i.e., aging per se is not an explanation of memory decline). Instead, chronological age is a proxy for the true mechanistic factors that lead to changes and variability in cognition and memory over time. Not to despair, however: from another perspective, it is also a potentially valuable marker of biological age (Dixon, 2011). Nevertheless, both descriptive and explanatory agendas in memory aging could be enhanced by the availability of mechanism-related functional markers of aging.

Although BioAge is clearly more complicated to estimate than chronological age, candidate markers have been tested and even assembled in provisional multivariate representations (e.g., Anstey, Dear, Christensen, & Jorm, 2005; Klemera & Doubal, 2006; Lindenberger & Ghisletta, 2009; MacDonald et al., 2004; Nakamura & Miyao, 2007). Nevertheless, no specific or widely adopted procedures are yet available, but the long advanced notion of evaluating the biological and health context of cognitive aging is alive and well (e.g., Anstey, 2008; Dixon, 2011; Spiro & Brady, 2008).

In addition, one active notion is that (direct) neurobiological, (indirect) biological, and a variety of health factors may contribute to aging-related changes and variability in cognition in a multicausal, interactive, dynamic manner. Worth emphasizing is that even indirect biological-health markers may be related to specific memory decline or impairment. For example, research has shown that aging-related memory effects are related to indirect physiological indicators (such as grip strength and gait–balance; Atti et al., 2008), vascular indicators (such as diastolic and systolic blood pressure; Qiu, Winblad, & Fratiglioni, 2005), and genetic or epigenetic indicators (e.g., National Institute on Aging, 2008).

In the VLS, we have approached this issue at an empirical level in several promising ways. First, we have addressed BioAge specifically. Based on a principal components analysis of a set of VLS biological markers (e.g., blood pressure, grip strength, vision, audition, peak expiratory flow, body mass index), we developed a composite measure of BioAge, assigning a value to each participant in a five-wave (12-year) postdiction study (MacDonald et al., 2004). Notably, BioAge was correlated moderately with chronological age (r = .48), leaving room to investigate two main research questions. Whereas the first research question addressed the simple issue of whether BioAge was even related to concurrent cognitive performance or 12-year change in performance, the second addressed the more fundamental issue of whether BioAge accounts for substantial variance (more than, or independent from, chronological age) in individual differences in 12-year change.

For the two episodic memory tasks (word and story recall), BioAge (unlike chronological age) accounted for substantial independent variance and shared substantial variance with chronological age. In a later cross-sectional study (n = 386; ages = 61–95), we found that BioAge mediated the effect of chronological age on episodic memory (Wahlin et al., 2006). More recently, the possibility that neurocognitive speed tasks may reflect some of the construct domain of biological markers—and be productive contributors to cognitive aging research—has been promoted (Deary, Johnson, & Starr, 2010).

Accordingly, our own research program on neurocognitive speed and inconsistency has incidentally provided some support for this notion, showing some relationship to 6-year memory change (MacDonald et al., 2003) and concurrent cognitive and memory status, including mild cognitive impairment (Dixon et al., 2007). Although this is promising, some challenges remain for continuing research on biological markers and cognitive aging (Anstey, 2008; Dixon, 2011). These include developing a common framework, battery, and metric for estimating BioAge, as well as demonstrating that it indeed contributes substantially and differentially—as compared to chronological age—to understanding cognitive and memory change with aging.

A second direction of memory change research in this general category reflects the health side of this epidemiological continuum. Like BioAge, where a variety of biological or functional markers have been tested with some commonality and some success (Anstey, 2008), health can be (and has been) operationalized in multiple potentially (but not always) overlapping and functional ways (Spiro & Brady, 2008). These include global health estimates (e.g., reflecting health chronicity or burden), subjective or instrumental health (e.g., health beliefs or functional health), and the role of actual aging-related health conditions in affecting memory change (e.g., cardio/cerebrovascular health, type 2 diabetes). VLS research on memory change has benefited from the availability and empirical vitality of markers from each of these domains (e.g., Small et al., 2011; Wahlin et al., 2006).

For present purposes, we will briefly summarize a recent initiative exploring the extent to which type 2 diabetes (T2D), a disease increasing in prevalence in North America, may be related to exacerbated cognitive and memory decline, as well as dementia. Although not principally a neurological disease, T2D is linked through indirect biological factors to possible peripheral and central neuropathic changes and may, in fact, be associated with atrophy in cortical and hippocampal structures. Reviewers have noted that accumulating studies revealed inconsistent patterns of cognitive and neurocognitive T2D-related deficits (Nilsson, 2006). For example, episodic memory effects were inconsistently indicated in the neuropsychological literature, but a close examination of the research revealed vast differences in the techniques with which memory was assessed (as well as many other methodological challenges).

By tapping (a) the broad VLS battery as a resource, (b) the large data archives as a base pool for well-diagnosed T2D patients and well-characterized control participants, and (c) both cross-sectional and longitudinal designs, the VLS has entered this new literature (e.g., Fischer, de Frias, Yeung, & Dixon, 2009; Yeung et al., 2009). The recent result most relevant to the present chapter is that T2D has a direct effect on episodic memory performance (but not semantic memory performance). However, this effect was mediated by two biological markers (systolic blood pressure and gait–balance) and a subjective-functional health composite (McFall, Geall, Dolcos, Fischer, & Dixon, 2010).

That proximal neurological health conditions (e.g., neurodegenerative diseases or mild stroke) affect memory and cognition in predictable ways is not surprising. However, that a distal health condition (with indirect projections into neural functioning) may have profound effects on memory performance and change with aging is encouraging to health-cognition hypotheses (Small et al., 2011; Spiro & Brady, 2008). At present, three varieties of biological health were involved: specific health condition, specific biological markers, and a composite subjective–instrumental health indicator. In the next section, we shift from brief reviews of VLS longitudinal epidemiological research to an overview of new data reflecting this perspective.

LONG-TERM MEMORY CHANGE IN MULTIWAVE LONGITUDINAL RESEARCH: DESIGNS AND BATTERIES FOR ATTRITION AND RETEST ADJUSTMENTS

Differentiating change and "no change" through designs and analyses

The theoretical and methodological opportunities that accrue from examining actual memory change trajectories over multiple waves and ages are substantial (McArdle, 2009; Schaie & Hofer, 2001). Because of understandable exigencies in managing and funding longitudinal studies, available long-term data may vary in regularity and frequency of waves, span of age actually covered, and data quality (e.g., missing data, theoretically relevant measures). The VLS contributes to this climate in that it has multiple occasions, a broad-age initial age band (55–85 years) that could widen with the merging of samples, and a large theoretically selected cognitive battery repeated at each wave.

However, in addition to the advantages of intraindividual designs for studying intraindividual change, there are some methodological challenges and theoretical opportunities, including checking on attrition effects or retest/practice effects (see Figure 13.4). Notably, some longitudinal studies have detected selective attrition (e.g., lower performers dropping out of the study) and retest effects (later assessments being affected by earlier test performance). Naturally, such an effect, if systematic and of significant degree, can lead to underestimations of the magnitude and function of longitudinally observed changes (see Ferrer, Salthouse, Stewart, & Schwartz, 2004; McArdle et al., 2007; Rabbitt, Lunn, & Wong, 2008; Salthouse, 2009; Schaie, 2009; Thorvaldsson, Hofer, Berg, & Johansson, 2006).

Moreover, studies vary in the design features that might protect or promote such contaminating effects; these include longitudinal interval (shorter more problematic for retest effects, but better for minimizing attrition), characteristics of measures (simpler, memorable tasks may be more prone to retest effects), characteristics of batteries (single forms of measures versus multiple forms), initial characteristics of participants (demographics,

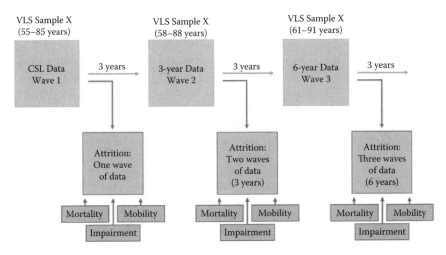

FIGURE 13.4 Longitudinal vignette: a detailed view of the mechanics of wave-to-wave assessment. The figure presents the hypothetical VLS "Sample X" followed over 6 years, with illustrations of research complications and opportunities related to cross-sectional comparisons (CSL), longitudinal follow-ups, and three prominent attrition analyses.

homogeneity–heterogeneity on pertinent characteristics), exclusionary criteria (e.g., Alzheimer's disease or psychiatric condition), and others. The VLS, for example, selected an intermediate 3- to 4-year interval design, used tasks that are comprehensive and not easily repeatable, and developed multiple forms of key constructs (Dixon & de Frias, 2004). Regarding the latter, two common measures of episodic memory (word and story) are implemented in the VLS with the assistance of a set of six equivalent forms, rotated by pairs through the longitudinal design. This means that for such a task, commonly thought to be vulnerable to practice effects, participants will not see the same form for at least 9 years (three successive waves).

Methodological notes for new data

We assembled a 12-year (up to five-wave) data set to examine age-based (as distinct from the more traditional wave-based) longitudinal changes in episodic and semantic memory. An additional goal was to control the influence of traditional covariates (gender, education) in the context of important moderators (practice, attrition) (Ferrer et al., 2004; McArdle et al., 2007). The initial sample included n = 952 adults (M age = 68.6 years; 63% female; M education = 14.2 years), some of whom contributed 12-year (five-wave) data, with demographic and background characteristics consonant with all previous VLS studies (Dixon & de Frias, 2004). Whereas episodic memory was measured with the VLS word recall task (six equivalent lists) and VLS story recall task (six equivalent narratives), semantic memory was measured with the VLS standard fact recall (also counterbalanced).

After converting all test scores to T-scores (based on the mean and SD at wave 1), we applied random effects models (SAS Proc Mixed; Littell, Milliken, Stroup, Wolfinger, & Schabenberger, 2006) to analyze age-based (centered at age 75) changes in memory performance. The advantage of using age rather than wave as the basis measure is that it permits the estimation of an accelerated longitudinal design. This produces longitudinal gradients of changes between the youngest age at the start of the study and the oldest age at the end of the study (Duncan, Duncan, & Hops, 1996). As a result, although we have a maximum of 12 years of longitudinal data available for any individual in this particular sample, we derive longitudinal change gradients that span about 40 years of adulthood (55–95 years of age). Finally, in addition to gender and education, we examined the influence of attrition and practice on individual differences (a) at the intercept (age 75) and (b) in the slope (changes over time). Specifically, we created group-specific variables for practice and attrition following published procedures that could be enacted given the VLS sequential design (McArdle & Bell, 2000).

First results: Intraindividual changes in memory performance

The results of our analyses are shown in Figure 13.5. To illustrate the raw data that contribute to the results that are observed, we present a spaghetti plot whereby the actual changes (across age, on the X axis) for all individuals participating in this study are shown. The change patterns are remarkably diverse and variable (across individuals). From these data the answer to the question of *when* memory aging begins to decline would appear to be "it depends":

- On the individual, in that some appear to be performing equivalently over relatively long periods at both higher and moderate levels
- On the task, in that word recall appears to be a more sensitive indicator of aging change than story recall
- On the procedure for determining the advent or inflection point of decline

Second results: Growth curves with and without adjustments

In addition to the raw data that are presented in Figure 13.5, we have prepared a set of derived figures from a random sample of 200 individuals (see Figure 13.6). Superimposed on these intraindividual plots are the results of

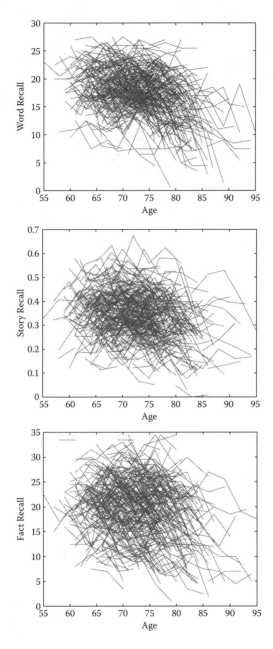

FIGURE 13.5 Intraindividual changes (*n* = 952) in declarative memory performance, including word (score), story (proportion), and fact (score) recall.

the random effects models that describe change in each of three declarative memory measures. The solid line represents aging changes that are independent of age at baseline, gender, and years of education. The dotted line represents changes that are independent of each of those covariates, as well as independent of the effects of attrition and practice. The growth curves superimposed over the intraindividual patterns indicate that overall decline does not appear to begin in general until the 70s. A key issue is whether the adjustments for attrition and practice affect the patterns of observed aging-related changes.

As would be expected, given the intraindividual results in Figures 13.5 and 13.6, word recall patterns show the earliest (early 70s) and steepest (almost 2 SD) decline across age. However, controlling for attrition and practice did not substantially alter the nature of age-related declines that were observed, as can be seen by the overlapping gradients in Figure 13.6. Recall that word memory performance is measured with a set of six equivalent and extensive tests rotated such that no test is seen twice by any participant until 9 years have elapsed. Notably, an inspection of the parameter estimates from the random effects models revealed that the linear and quadratic age terms were statistically significant in both the unadjusted and adjusted models.

Although also an indicator of episodic memory, the decline observed for story recall generally began later (roughly mid-70s) and was relatively more shallow (less than 1 SD) than for word recall. The models that did or did not adjust for the effects of practice and attrition exhibited slightly less overlap among the adjustment-related functions; this suggests the possibility that the fully adjusted model resulted in participants beginning with better performance than did the unadjusted model—an order less evident in the 70s but reappearing in the 90s. This was also evidenced in the parameter estimates, in that the linear and quadratic age terms were both statistically significant in the model that did not adjust for attrition and practice, but only the linear age term was statistically significant in the model that adjusted for both factors.

Next, accumulated over the 40-year span, the overall observed decline for fact recall was about 1.5 SD units, with an apparent inflection point at about 70 years of age. The adjustment-related functions were generally overlapping. The change estimates exhibited substantial overlap between the models, and the linear and quadratic age effects were statistically significant in both cases. In sum, the magnitude of aging-related change in declarative memory functions varies widely across individuals and tasks. Taken as a computed latent growth curve, it can be seen to suggest a baseline pattern that is gradual among relatively healthy adults aging from their 50s to their 90s. Finally, although not shown or analyzed in these new VLS data, the sources of these individual differences in intraindividual changes in declarative memory with aging—as well as the overall curve representing change and variability of memory aging—are to be found (in part) in the aforementioned epidemiological risk and protective factors.

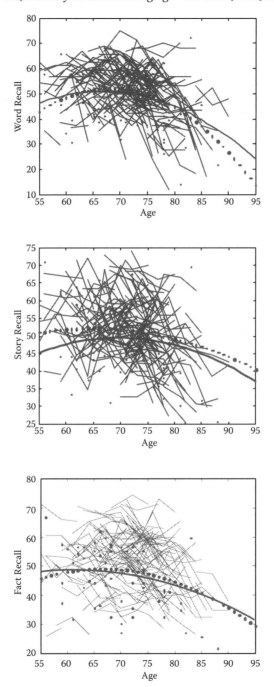

FIGURE 13.6 Latent growth curves for VLS declarative memory performance, both unadjusted (bold) and adjusted (dotted) for attrition effects. Performance is represented in T-score units.

CONCLUSION

Longitudinal and epidemiological studies provide unique opportunities to examine patterns, profiles, and predictors of memory aging. In this chapter we portrayed several characteristics of such studies that can contribute to enhancing our knowledge about the aging of declarative memory. The Canadian Victoria Longitudinal Study was taken as an example, and a set of recent studies that embody the principles of change, variability, and interdisciplinarity were described. We concluded with new data pertaining to an interesting aspect of longitudinal studies of aging.

As longitudinal studies "age," they accumulate substantial theoretical potential and methodological advantages, and yet they also encounter notable challenges. Not only do older adults drop out of studies, but they also do not always do so randomly. Moreover, being involved in an intraindividual study may provide incidental opportunities to experience the materials or procedures in a way that could implicitly enhance participants' performances. For these reasons, it is imperative that longitudinal studies be designed to promote long-term participation and to protect against potential retest or practice effects. Under all circumstances, it is crucial for such studies to collect information about dropouts or decedents and to conduct the occasional check on retest effects. At its inception, the VLS benefited from lessons learned by earlier longitudinal studies and incorporated an interest in these two sets of phenomena into the research design and research plan.

In the present chapter we have taken as our premise that declarative memory performance declines with normal aging. Our three guiding conceptual questions of memory aging were axiomatic. The question of *when* refers to the point in aging at which declarative memory processes begin to decline at detectable or clinically significant levels. The question of *how* refers to the common patterns and degrees of variability, across subsets of individuals and tasks, through which changes are manifested. The question of *why* refers to the controls, causes, precursors, and modulators of these changes.

The new VLS results presented in this chapter paint a notable picture of memory aging. Yes, there is decline with aging, but (a) *when* it happens is not as early or as universal as some cross-sectional studies may indicate, (b) *how* it happens depends on dynamic and interactive aspects of the changing biological and environmental contexts of aging, and (c) *why* it happens can be addressed at each "local" level by new theoretical efforts as integrated with new methodological advances. As noted by Birren and Schroots (2001), ambitious answers to primordial questions of human aging have stumped scholars for centuries. Final resolutions to even our local *when–how–why* questions of memory aging await future researchers and projects of formidable scope and clarity.

ACKNOWLEDGMENT

The VLS is supported by a grant from the National Institutes of Health (National Institute on Aging; R37 AG008235) to Roger Dixon, who also acknowledges support from the Canada Research Chairs program. We thank Jill Friesen and Bonnie Whitehead for technical assistance in the preparation of this chapter, and an anonymous reviewer for helpful suggestions on an earlier version of the manuscript.

REFERENCES

Anstey, K. (2008). Cognitive aging and functional biomarkers: What do we know, and where to from here? In S. M. Hofer & D. F. Alwin (Eds.), *The handbook of cognitive aging: Interdisciplinary perspectives* (pp. 327–339). Thousand Oaks, CA: Sage.

Anstey, K., Dear, K., Christensen, H., & Jorm, A. F. (2005). Biomarkers, health, lifestyle and demographic variables as correlates of reaction time performance in early, middle and late adulthood. *Quarterly Journal of Experimental Psychology, 58A,* 5–21.

Atti, A. R., Palmer, K., Volpato, S., Winblad, B., De Ronchi, D., & Fratiglioni, L. (2008). Late-life body mass index and dementia incidence: Nine-year follow-up data from the Kungsholmen Project. *Journal of the American Geriatric Society, 56,* 111–116.

Ball, K., Berch, D. B., Helmers, K. F., Jobe, J. B., Leveck, M. D., Marsiske, M.,... Willis, S. L. (2002). Effects of cognitive training interventions with older adults: A randomized control trial. *Journal of the American Medical Association, 288,* 2271–2281.

Baltes, P. B., Lindenberger, U., & Staudinger, U. M. (2006). Lifespan theory in developmental psychology. In W. Damon & R. M. Lerner (Eds.), *Handbook of child psychology: Vol. 1. Theoretical models of human development* (6th ed., pp. 569–664). New York, NY: Wiley.

Baltes, P. B., & Willis, S. L. (1977). Toward psychological theories of aging and development. In J. E. Birren & K. W. Schaie (Eds.), *Handbook of the psychology of aging* (pp. 128–154). New York, NY: Van Nostrand Reinhold.

Birren, J. E. (1999). Theories of aging: A personal perspective. In V. L. Bengtson & K. W. Schaie (Eds.), *Handbook of theories of aging.* New York, NY: Springer.

Birren, J. E., & Cunningham, W. R. (1985). Research on the psychology of aging: Principles, concepts, and theory. In J. E. Birren & K. W. Schaie (Eds.), *Handbook of the psychology of aging* (2nd ed., pp. 3–34). New York, NY: Van Nostrand Reinhold.

Birren, J.E., & Schroots, J.J.F. (2001). The history of geropsychology. In J.E. Birren & K.W. Schaie (Eds.), *Handbook of the psychology of aging* (5th ed.; pp. 3–28). San Diego: Academic Press.

Cabeza, R., Nyberg, L., & Park, D. C. (Eds.). (2004). *Cognitive neuroscience of aging: Linking cognitive and cerebral aging.* New York, NY: Oxford University Press.

Craik, F. I. M., & Salthouse, T. A. (Eds.). (2008). *Handbook of aging and cognition* (3rd ed.). New York, NY: Psychology Press.

Deary, I. J., Johnson, W., & Starr, J. M. (2010). Are processing speed tasks biomarkers of cognitive ageing? *Psychology and Aging, 25,* 219–228.

Dixon, R. A. (1999). Exploring cognition in interactive situations: The aging of N+1 minds. In T. M. Hess & F. Blanchard-Fields (Eds.), *Social cognition and aging* (pp. 267–290). San Diego, CA: Academic Press.

Dixon, R. A. (2007, August). *Memory health and aging: Exploring epidemiological perspectives.* Invited address at the International Cognitive Aging Conference, Adelaide, Australia.

Dixon, R. A. (2010). An epidemiological approach to cognitive health in aging. In L. Bäckman & L. Nyberg (Eds.), *Memory, aging, and the brain* (pp. 144–166). London, England: Psychology Press.

Dixon, R. A. (2011). Enduring theoretical themes in psychological aging: Derivation, functions, perspectives, and opportunities. In K. W. Schaie & S. L. Willis (Eds.), *Handbook of the psychology of aging* (7th ed., pp. 3–23). San Diego, CA: Academic Press.

Dixon, R. A., & Bäckman, L. (Eds.). (1995). *Compensating for psychological deficits and declines: Managing losses and promoting gains.* Hillsdale, NJ: Lawrence Erlbaum Associates.

Dixon, R. A., Bäckman, L., & Nilsson, L.-G. (Eds.). (2004). *New frontiers in cognitive aging.* Oxford, England: Oxford University Press.

Dixon, R. A., & de Frias, C. M. (2004). The Victoria Longitudinal Study: From characterizing cognitive aging to illustrating changes in memory compensation. *Aging, Neuropsychology, and Cognition, 11,* 346–376.

Dixon, R. A., & de Frias, C. M. (2007). Mild memory deficits differentially affect six-year changes in compensatory strategy use. *Psychology and Aging, 22,* 632–638.

Dixon, R. A., de Frias, C. M., & Bäckman, L. (2001). Characteristics of self-reported memory compensation in late life. *Journal of Clinical and Experimental Neuropsychology, 23,* 650–661.

Dixon, R. A., Garrett, D. D., Lentz, T. L., MacDonald, S. W. S., Strauss, E., & Hultsch, D. F. (2007). Neurocognitive markers of cognitive impairment: Exploring the roles of speed and inconsistency. *Neuropsychology, 21,* 381–399.

Dixon, R. A., Hopp, G. A., Cohen, A.-L., de Frias, C. M., & Bäckman, L. (2003). Self-reported memory compensation: Similar patterns in Alzheimer's disease and very old adult samples. *Journal of Clinical and Experimental Neuropsychology, 25,* 382–390.

Dixon, R. A., Wahlin, Å., Maitland, S. B., Hultsch, D. F., Hertzog, C., & Bäckman, L. (2004). Episodic memory change in late adulthood: Generalizability across samples and performance indices. *Memory & Cognition, 32,* 768–778.

Duncan, S. E., Duncan, T. E., & Hops, H. (1996). Analysis of longitudinal data within accelerated longitudinal designs. *Psychological Methods, 1,* 236–248.

Ferrer, E., Salthouse, T. A., Stewart, W. F., & Schwartz, B. S. (2004). Modeling age and retest processes in longitudinal studies of cognitive abilities. *Psychology and Aging, 19,* 243–259.

Fischer, A. L., de Frias, C. M., Yeung, S. E., & Dixon, R. A. (2009). Short-term longitudinal trends in cognitive performance in older adults with type 2 diabetes. *Journal of Clinical and Experimental Neuropsychology, 31,* 809–822.

Ghisletta, P., Bickel, J.-F., & Lövdén, M. (2006). Does activity engagement protect against cognitive decline in old age? *Journal of Gerontology: Psychological Sciences, 61B,* P253–261.

Herlitz, A., & Yonker, J. E. (2004). Hormonal effects on cognition in adults. In R. A. Dixon, L. Bäckman, & L.-G. Nilsson (Eds.), *New frontiers in cognitive aging* (pp. 253–277). Oxford, England: Oxford University Press.

Hertzog, C. (2004). Does longitudinal evidence confirm theories of cognitive aging derived from cross-sectional data? In R. A. Dixon, L. Bäckman, & L.-G. Nilsson (Eds.), *New frontiers in cognitive aging* (pp. 41–64). Oxford, England: Oxford University Press.

Hertzog, C., Dixon, R. A., Hultsch, D. F., & MacDonald, S. W. S. (2003). Latent change models of adult cognition: Are changes in processing speed and working memory associated with changes in episodic memory? *Psychology and Aging, 18,* 755–770.

Hertzog, C., Kramer, A. F., Wilson, R. S., & Lindenberger, U. (2008). Enrichment effects on adult cognitive development: Can the functional capacity of older adults be preserved and enhanced? *Psychological Science in the Public Interest, 9*(1), 1–65.

Hofer, S. M., & Alwin, D. F. (Eds.). (2008). *The handbook of cognitive aging: Interdisciplinary perspectives.* Thousand Oaks, CA: Sage.

Hultsch, D. F., Hertzog, C., Dixon, R. A., & Small, B. J. (1998). *Memory change in the aged.* New York, NY: Cambridge University Press.

Hultsch, D. F., Hertzog, C., Small, B. J., & Dixon, R. A. (1999). Use it or lose it: Engaged lifestyle as a buffer of cognitive decline in aging? *Psychology and Aging, 14,* 245–263.

Klemera, P., & Doubal, S. (2006). A new approach to the concept and computation of biological age. *Mechanisms of Ageing and Development, 127,* 240–248.

Lindenberger, U., & Ghisletta, P. (2009). Cognitive and sensory declines in old age: Gauging the evidence for a common cause. *Psychology and Aging, 24,* 1–16.

Littell, R. C., Milliken, G. A., Stroup, W. W., Wolfinger, R. D., & Schabenberger, O. (2006). *SAS for mixed models* (2nd ed.). Cary, NC: SAS Press.

MacDonald, S. W. S., Dixon, R. A., Cohen, A.-L., & Hazlitt, J. E. (2004). Biological age and 12-year cognitive change in older adults: Findings from the Victoria Longitudinal Study. *Gerontology, 50,* 64–81.

MacDonald, S. W. S., Hultsch, D. F., & Dixon, R. A. (2003). Performance variability is related to change in cognition: Evidence from the Victoria Longitudinal Study. *Psychology and Aging, 18,* 510–523.

Mansueti, L., de Frias, C. M., Bub, D., & Dixon, R. A. (2008). Exploring cognitive effects of self-reported mild stroke in older adults: Selective but robust effects on story memory. *Aging, Neuropsychology, and Cognition, 15,* 545–573.

McArdle, J. J. (2009). Latent variable modeling of differences and changes with longitudinal data. *Annual Review of Psychology, 60,* 577–605.

McArdle, J. J., & Bell, R. Q. (2000). Recent trends in modeling longitudinal data by latent growth curve methods. In T. D. Little, K. U. Schnabel, & J. Baumert (Eds.), *Modeling longitudinal and multi-group data: Practical issues, applied approaches, and scientific examples* (pp. 69–108). Mahwah, NJ: Lawrence Erlbaum Associates.

McArdle, J. J., Fisher, G. G., & Kadlec, K. M. (2007). Latent variable analyses of age trends of cognition in the health and retirement study, 1992–2004. *Psychology and Aging, 22,* 525–545.

McFall, G. P., Geall, B. P., Fischer, A. L., Dolcos, S., & Dixon, R. A. (2010). Testing covariates of type 2 diabetes-cognition associations in older adults: Moderating or mediating effects? *Neuropsychology, 24,* 547–562.

Nakamura, E., & Miyao, K. (2007). A method for identifying biomarkers of aging and constructing an index of biological age in humans. *Journal of Gerontology: Biological Sciences, 62A,* 1096–1105.

National Institute on Aging. (2008). *Workshop summary: Genetic methods and life course development.* Washington, DC: National Institutes of Health.

Nilsson, E. (2006). *Diabetes and cognitive functioning: The role of age and comorbidity.* Unpublished doctoral dissertation, Karolinska Institutet, Stockholm.

Nyberg, L., Maitland, S. B., Rönnlund, M., Bäckman, L., Dixon, R. A., Wahlin, Å., & Nilsson, L.-G. (2003). Selective adult age differences in an age-invariant multifactor model of declarative memory. *Psychology and Aging, 18,* 149–160.

Park, D., & Minear, M. (2004). Cognitive aging: New directions for old theories. In R. A. Dixon, L. Bäckman, & L.-G. Nilsson (Eds.), *New frontiers in cognitive aging* (pp. 19–40). Oxford, England: Oxford University Press.

Park, D. C., & Reuter-Lorenz, P. (2009). The adaptive brain: Aging and neurocognitive scaffolding. *Annual Review of Psychology, 60,* 173–196.

Pedersen, N. L. (2004). New frontiers in genetic influences on cognitive aging. In R. A. Dixon, L. Bäckman, & L.-G. Nilsson (Eds.), *New frontiers in cognitive aging* (pp. 235–252). Oxford, England: Oxford University Press.

Peto, R., & Doll, R. (1997). Old age is associated with disease but does not cause it. *British Medical Journal, 315,* 1030–1032.

Qiu, C., Winblad, B., & Fratiglioni, L. (2005). The age-dependent relation of blood pressure to cognitive functions and dementia. *Lancet Neurology, 4,* 487–499.

Rabbitt, P., Lunn, M., & Wong, D. (2008). Death, dropout, and longitudinal measurements of cognitive change in old age. *Journal of Gerontology: Psychological Sciences, 63,* 271–278.

Raz, N. (2004). The aging brain: Structural changes and their implications for cognitive aging. In R. A. Dixon, L. Bäckman, & L.-G. Nilsson (Eds.), *New frontiers in cognitive aging* (pp. 115–133). Oxford, England: Oxford University Press.

Reynolds, C. A. (2008). Genetic and environmental influences on cognitive change. In S. M. Hofer & D. F. Alwin (Eds.), *The handbook of cognitive aging: Interdisciplinary perspectives* (pp. 557–574). Thousand Oaks, CA: Sage.

Salthouse, T. A. (2009). When does age-related cognitive decline begin? *Neurobiology of Aging, 30,* 507–514.

Schaie, K. W. (2009). When does age-related cognitive decline begin? Salthouse again reifies the "cross-sectional fallacy." *Neurobiology of Aging, 30,* 528–529.

Schaie, K. W. (2011). Historical influences on aging and behavior. In K. W. Schaie & S. L. Willis (Eds.), *Handbook of the psychology of aging* (7th ed.). San Diego, CA: Elsevier.

Schaie, K. W., & Hofer, S. M. (2001). Longitudinal studies in aging research. In J. E. Birren & K. W. Schaie (Eds.), *Handbook of the psychology of aging* (5th ed., pp. 53–77). San Diego, CA: Academic Press.

Small, B. J., Dixon, R. A., Hultsch, D. F., & Hertzog, C. (1999). Longitudinal changes in quantitative and qualitative indicators of word and story recall in young-old and old-old adults. *Journal of Gerontology: Psychological Sciences, 54B,* P107–115.

Small, B. J., Dixon, R. A., & McArdle, J. J. (2011). Tracking cognition–health changes from 55 to 95 years of age. *Journal of Gerontology: Psychological Sciences, 66B,* i153–i161.

Spiro, A., III, & Brady, C. .B. (2008). Integrating health into cognitive aging research and theory: Quo vadis? In S. M. Hofer & D. F. Alwin (Eds.), *The handbook of cognitive aging: Interdisciplinary perspectives* (pp. 260–282). Thousand Oaks, CA: Sage.

Stern, Y. (Ed.). (2007). *Cognitive reserve*. New York, NY: Taylor & Francis.

Thorvaldsson, V., Hofer, S. M., Berg, S., & Johansson, B. (2006). Aging and late-life terminal decline in perceptual speed: A comparison of alternative modeling approaches. *European Psychologist, 11,* 196–203.

Tulving, E. (1995). Organization of memory: Quo vadis? In M. S. Gazzaniga (Ed.), *The cognitive neurosciences* (pp. 839–847). Cambridge, MA: MIT Press.

Wahlin, Å. (2004). Health, disease, and cognitive aging. In R. A. Dixon, L. Bäckman, & L.-G. Nilsson (Eds.), *New frontiers in cognitive aging* (pp. 279–302). Oxford, England: Oxford University Press.

Wahlin, Å., MacDonald, S. W. S., de Frias, C. M., Nilsson, L.-G., & Dixon, R. A. (2006). How do health and biological age influence chronological age and sex differences in cognitive aging: Moderating or mediating or both? *Psychology and Aging, 21,* 318–332.

Wilson, R. S. (2008). Neurological factors in cognitive aging. In S. M. Hofer & D. F. Alwin (Eds.), *The handbook of cognitive aging: Interdisciplinary perspectives* (pp. 298–307). Thousand Oaks, CA: Sage.

Yeung, S. E., Fischer, A. L., & Dixon, R. A. (2009). Exploring effects of type 2 diabetes on cognitive functioning in older adults. *Neuropsychology, 23,* 1–9.

Zacks, R. T., Hasher, L., & Li, K. Z. H. (2006). Human memory. In F. I. M. Craik & T. A. Salthouse (Eds.), *The handbook of aging and cognition* (2nd ed., pp. 293–358). Mahwah, NJ: Lawrence Erlbaum Associates.

Zelinski, E. M., & Burnight, K. P. (1997). Sixteen-year longitudinal and time-lag changes in memory and cognition in older adults. *Psychology and Aging, 12,* 503–523.

Zelinski, E. M., & Kennison, R. F. (2007). Not your father's test scores: Cohort reduces psychometric aging effects. *Psychology and Aging, 22,* 546–557.

14 Biomarkers and memory aging

A life-course perspective

Kaarin J. Anstey

BIOMARKER RESEARCH: DEFINITIONS, HISTORY, AND RELEVANCE TO COGNITIVE AGING

Functional biomarkers are measures that index functional capacity and also decline with age (Butler et al., 2004). They typically include measures of visual function (acuity, accommodation, contrast sensitivity), auditory acuity, lung function, muscle strength (grip, quadriceps, or ankle dorsiflexion), blood pressure, and reaction time or processing speed (Anstey, Lord, & Smith, 1996). Vibration sense, touch sensitivity, and reach are also used (Anstey et al., 1996). These biomarkers generally have high test–retest reliability (Anstey, Smith, & Lord, 1997). Selected batteries of functional biomarkers strongly predict functional outcomes such as falls (Lord, Ward, Williams, & Anstey, 1994; Stalenhoef, Diederiks, Knottnerus, Kester, & Crebolder, 2002; van Schoor, Smit, Pluijm, Jonker, & Lips, 2002), mortality (Anstey, Luszcz, Giles, & Andrews, 2001), general mobility, and driving (Wood, Anstey, Kerr, Lacherez, & Lord, 2008).

Biomarker research was popular in the 1960s and 1970s as early gerontologists attempted to identify alternative means of measuring biological or functional aging. It has long been recognized that chronological age is simply an index of time since birth and that there are very large individual differences in functional capacity among groups of individuals at any given age.

The concept of a functional assessment as opposed to chronological age has also been used as an approach to combat perceived ageism associated with "age cutoffs" for employment or specific tasks such as flying aircraft. It also appeals to the intuitive and anecdotal observation that people age at different rates and human performance is highly variable in later life. Another important characteristic of functional biomarkers is that they operationalize the effects of disease. In this sense, they avoid the need to measure disease itself as they index the impact of disease on function. For example, diabetes may affect peripheral sensation and visual acuity as well as reaction time. However, the impact of diabetes differs between individuals. Hence, measuring the functional impact of disease via functional biomarkers will give a fairer and more accurate estimate of functional capacity than simply using disease status as an indicator. This enables objective evaluation of competency based on physical function rather than on age, disease, or health.

There have been hundreds of variables used as putative biomarkers in research. A review by Anstey et al. in 1996 surveyed the biomarker literature to identify the most commonly used biomarkers and calculate their consistency in relation to chronological age. This review found that visual acuity, visual accommodation, hearing, muscle strength, pulmonary function, simple reaction time, digit symbol, and systolic and diastolic blood pressure were identified as the most reliable biomarkers. Psychosocial variables had the weakest associations with age.

Functional biomarkers involve measuring perception and cognitive function and therefore overlap with core psychological abilities and outcomes. There is a strong overlap among the measures used in functional age research and individual differences studies in psychology (Dirken, 1972). Since its inception, functional age research has included cognitive measures as potential indices of function. In particular, measures of psychomotor speed have long been recognized as factors that show declines with decline in general functional capacity.

From a broader perspective, it is also clear that cognition is another functional biomarker. Fluid cognition including working memory has similar relationships with several major functional outcomes; it declines in normal aging and also predicts mortality (Anstey et al., 2001; Anstey, Mack, & von Sanden, 2006; Bosworth & Schaie, 1999; Geerlings et al., 1999). The longitudinal trajectories of decline in memory and decline in functional biomarkers are similar. Figure 14.1 shows spaghetti plots of memory aging and visual aging over 8 years in the Australian Longitudinal Study of Aging (ALSA).

Birren and Cunningham (1985) applied the theory of primary and secondary aging to cognitive decline, proposing the first model to link biomarkers and memory aging. Primary aging was traditionally thought to reflect innate maturational processes and is operationalized by functional age indices. Secondary aging was thought to reflect the impact of disease and environment on the organism. Figure 14.2 illustrates this proposal.

An important tenet of early biomarker research was that a single biological aging process can be indexed by multiple measures. Increasingly, however, it has been recognized that different body systems (and brain regions) age at different rates (Aihie Sayer, Osmond, Briggs, & Cooper, 1999; Raz et al., 2005). This initially called into question the utility of the concept of biomarkers. However, as their utility in predicting functional outcomes has been demonstrated and more flexible statistical and theoretical models of aging have been developed, concerns over this early simplistic view appear to have dissipated.

In the field of individual differences, sensorimotor abilities have long been viewed as part of the structure of human intelligence (Carroll, 1993). Specific theories of intelligence have included visual and auditory abilities

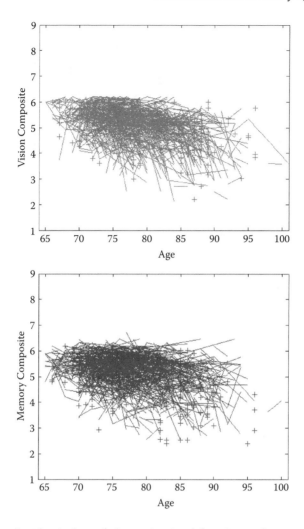

FIGURE 14.1 Spaghetti plots of change in visual function and memory function over 8 years in the Australian Longitudinal Study of Aging (Anstey, Hofer, & Luszcz, 2003. *Psychology and Aging, 18*(4), 714–726).

(Horn, 1982, 1985, 1987). These provide some context for understanding biomarkers in relation to memory. The observation of shared variance between sensory and cognitive function in the cognitive aging literature raised theoretical questions about shared versus unique causal factors underlying cognitive and sensory aging (Allen et al., 2001; Anstey, Hofer, & Luszcz, 2003b; Anstey, Luszcz, & Sanchez, 2001a; Christensen, Mackinnon, Korten, & Jorm, 2001; Hofer & Sliwinski, 2001; Lindenberger & Baltes, 1994; Mackinnon, Christensen, & Jorm, 2006; Salthouse, Hancock, Meinz, & Hambrick, 1996).

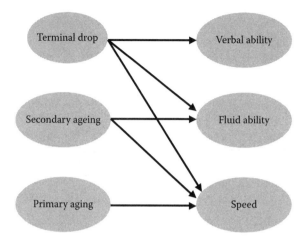

FIGURE 14.2 Birren and Cunningham's (1985) model relating biomarkers to cognitive decline. Biomarkers operationalized primary aging. This original model does not specify memory; however, working memory and episodic memory may be categorized as fluid abilities.

The examination of memory in relation to biomarkers involves taking a different perspective to that usually taken by cognitive psychologists. Drawing more on theories of gerontology and life-course development, memory and biomarkers can be understood in terms of interrelationships between different aspects of functional capacity over the life course, as influenced by biology, disease, culture, and experience.

MEMORY RESEARCH IN THE CONTEXT OF A LIFE-COURSE APPROACH TO COGNITIVE DEVELOPMENT AND DEMENTIA

A broad view of memory aging incorporates both normal and pathological changes in memory occurring in later life. Alzheimer's disease (AD) is the most common cause of dementia and has specific neuropathology including neurofibrillary tangles (NFTs) and amyloid plaques. Vascular disease is the second most prevalent cause of dementia, leading to vascular dementia. In addition to the memory loss that occurs with dementia, memory loss in late life occurs with mild cognitive impairment and other preclinical dementia syndromes that affect approximately 20% of nondemented adults over age 70 (Plassman et al., 2008). Normative memory loss also occurs in adults without impairment.

Taking a life-course perspective for both normal and pathological memory aging allows for consideration of the spectrum of biological, contextual, and social influences on memory development and risk of disease leading to pathological memory aging in later life (Anstey, 2008; Whalley, Dick, & McNeill, 2006). When measured at a specific time point in late life, memory function is evaluated at a moment in a life-course trajectory that has been determined by many interacting factors. It results from health, medical conditions, social environment, education and occupational experiences, and genetic influences. Likewise, functional capacity, as indexed by functional biomarkers, reflects the outcome of previous historical influences on the individual. Cognitive performance and functional capacity (in the physical sense, e.g., physical strength, sensory function, lung function) jointly determine the maximum level of function of an individual and the risk of injury and mobility. They are also strongly related to longevity—in terms of both time since birth and time till death.

It is argued here that a life-course approach to memory aging provides the context and framework in which to understand the development of human memory and pathological conditions such as dementia (Anstey, 2008; Whalley et al., 2006). It also provides a context in which human performance and memory can be interrelated. The life-course approach involves several key facets (Baltes, Staudinger, & Lindenberger, 1999; Ben-Shlomo & Kuh, 2002; Kuh & Ben-Shlomo, 2004). First is the acknowledgment of intergenerational influences. Social and biological contexts may be transferred from one generation to another and influence brain development and memory function. These influences are most apparent in instances of extreme deprivation or alcohol abuse during pregnancy leading to fetal alcohol syndrome and memory deficits in later life (Wacha & Obrzut, 2007).

However, positive biological environments and stimulating home and educational environments also influence brain development and may build cognitive and brain reserve (Whalley, Deary, Appleton, & Starr, 2004). The building of cognitive reserve in the first two decades of life may set the optimal level of memory function for an individual and hence influence the level at which normal memory aging begins. Cognitive and brain reserve also influence the risk of dementia and cognitive impairment in the context of injury, disease, and genetic factors, as well as the interactions among them (Whalley et al., 2006).

A life-course approach to memory aging also requires careful interpretation of research findings based on studies of aging using older cohorts. Such studies only represent one part of the overall trajectory of memory development; hence, evaluating how other factors, such as biomarkers, relate to memory may be biased when restricting observations to late life (Anstey, 2008).

Nonlinear relationships among variables in relation to cognitive function and age may also occur over the life course. Alcohol use has been shown to have a U-shaped association with memory function in young, middle, and older aged adults such that light to moderate drinkers show better performance than abstainers and heavy drinkers (Rodgers et al., 2005). This association has also been demonstrated in relation to alcohol consumption and risk of dementia (Anstey, Mack, & Cherbuin, 2009).

Taking a life-course approach to memory and cognitive aging highlights the difficulty in isolating whether associations among biomarkers such as sensory function and grip strength, and memory, are due to a common cause. A number of functional capacities show similar trajectories over the life course, reaching their peak in the 20s and then declining gradually until a more rapid decline takes place in the 70s. This pattern is seen for episodic memory, fluid intelligence, lung function, vision, hearing, and grip strength. This needs to be recognized before associations in cross-sectional studies are interpreted as indicating "causal" relationships among variables.

A life-course approach also recognizes that gene expression may occur at different points in the adult life course to influence memory decline and risk of memory impairment. This seems to be particularly true for the Apolipoprotein E (APOE) genotype. In early and middle adulthood, the E4 allele has not been associated with worse memory; there have even been reports of it being associated with better memory function (Han & Bondi, 2008). While a review concluded that the APOE E4 allele is not associated with cognitive decline in normal aging (Small et al., 2000), there is very strong evidence that it is the strongest genetic risk factor for memory impairment caused by Alzheimer's disease (Bertram & Tanzi, 2008).

Another conceptual distinction important for understanding how memory aging occurs in the context of biological aging is that between short-term fluctuations and long-term structural change (S. C. Li, Huxhold, & Schmiedek, 2004; K. Z. Li & Lindenberger, 2002). Factors that may influence memory in the laboratory, such as improvement seen after administration of nicotine (Elrod, Buccafusco, & Jackson, 1988), may not have similar effects over years or decades. There is now strong evidence that smoking is a risk factor for memory decline and dementia (Anstey, von Sanden, Salim, & O'Kearney, 2007).

WHY STUDY BIOMARKERS IN RELATION TO MEMORY AGING?

Viewing memory aging in the context of biomarkers allows gerontologists to incorporate an understanding memory function into the broader range of characteristics that enable successful performance of high-level instrumental activities of daily living. It is the combination of sensory and physical capacity as well as cognitive and memory capacity that enables performance in the workplace, managing finances, and managing vehicles and transport. Decline in one body system influences decline in another or may be due to a common pathology or process. For example, decline in visual acuity or visual contrast sensitivity may influence memory performance in everyday life. Rapid decline in some specific functional biomarkers in late life may be indicative of a pathological process that also underlies pathological memory aging (Anstey, Luszcz, & Sanchez, 2001b).

In the following sections the link between sensory biomarkers and memory aging is examined in more detail, first focusing specifically on sensory biomarkers, which have a special role in memory aging due to their direct relationship to encoding. The intriguing relationships between lung function and memory and muscle strength memory are then discussed prior to an overview of cross-sectional and longitudinal studies of biomarkers and experimental approaches.

SENSORY BIOMARKERS AND MEMORY AGING

Visual and auditory abilities have long been viewed as part of the structure of intelligence within hierarchical theories. These are well described by Carroll (1993). John Horn included both visual and auditory factors in the broader theory of fluid and crystallized intelligence (Horn, 1982, 1985, 1987), and very early psychologists included grip strength and sensory abilities in their test batteries. Hence, the recent renewed interest in the relationship between memory aging and sensory biomarkers (Anstey & Smith, 1999; Anstey, Stankov, & Lord, 1993; Anstey, Windsor, Jorm, Christensen, & Rodgers, 2004; Lindenberger & Baltes, 1994; Lindenberger, Scherer, & Baltes, 2001; Salthouse et al., 1996; Wahlin, MacDonald, deFrias, Nilsson, & Dixon, 2006) relates back to very early psychological research.

In aging, the impact of disease and injury at the level of the end organ places additional demands on visual and auditory perception, thus influencing memory performance in the laboratory in addition to intrinsic memory aging. A continuing challenge for research in this field is to identify whether sensory changes at the level of the end organ reflect only peripheral factors and hence "confound" the measurement of true cognitive ability.

Alternatively, they could also be indicators of biological aging and be indicative of faster neurological aging. There is some evidence for eye disease being associated with increased mortality (Cugati et al., 2007; Lee, Gomez-Marin, Lam, & Zheng, 2002; Murphy, Craik, Li, & Schneider, 2000), which supports the view that these peripheral changes still index some overall biological age. Hence, theoretically, it is extremely difficult to disentangle the shared and unique factors underlying sensory and cognitive function in late life (Anstey, 2002). This raises the question of how to evaluate whether impaired memory performance resulting from reduced encoding from poorer visual perception is "true" memory impairment.

APPROACHES TO EXPLAINING THE STRONG RELATIONSHIPS BETWEEN SENSORY BIOMARKERS AND MEMORY

Various approaches have been taken to explaining the observation of strong associations between sensory acuity and memory performance in older adults. The different approaches stem from different research methodologies—namely, experimental cognitive psychology, individual differences, and neuropsychology. These are not necessarily mutually exclusive. Perhaps the most clearly specified and hence best tested model of how sensory aging affects memory performance in late life is the cognitive resource model, or effortfulness hypothesis. This proposes that sensory deficits reduce the quality of mental representations of stimuli, thus increasing the resources required (or effort) to encode information. This leaves fewer resources for processing of information and increases errors in retrieval (Murphy et al., 2000; Rabbitt, 1990; Tun, McCoy, & Wingfield, 2009).

The sensory deprivation theory argues that the association between sensory function and memory performance in later life is caused by brain changes that result from lack of mental stimulation occurring when older adults develop sensory impairment through disease or normal aging (Schneider & Pichora-Fuller, 2000; Sekuler & Blake, 1987). This theory has rarely been investigated, largely due to the difficulty in conducting experimental research that imposes sensory deficits for any length of time. Researchers have attempted to evaluate whether removal of sensory deficit improved cognitive function by evaluating cognitive function before and after cataract surgery. A randomized controlled trial and a longitudinal study examined memory change after cataract removal and neither observed improvement (Anstey, Lord, et al., 2006; Valentijn et al., 2005).

Common factor models are derived from cross-sectional correlational research and propose that the association between sensory function and cognition is due to common neurological causes. These models are not amenable to experimental manipulation and can only be evaluated by examining shared variance in correlational studies. Figure 14.3 depicts the hypothetical relationships among a biomarker, memory, and age in a common factor model, a common plus specific factor model, and a model with no common factor underlying memory and the hypothetical biomarker. It has been argued that a major limitation for common factor models is that they cannot be falsified (Allen et al., 2001). Finding that variance is shared between two variables or factors suggests an association, but there is always the possibility that a third variable or variables explain the association. Hence, correlational approaches, even those involving longitudinal research, cannot establish absolute causation.

Finally, another less investigated but promising theory is that the *common neuropathological* changes underlying AD, the most common cause of dementia, may also cause declines in abilities measured by functional biomarkers, including sensory function. The neuropathological changes that lead to AD have been shown to commence as early as the fifth decade (Braak & Braak, 1991). Hence, it is possible that in individuals at risk of AD, decline in sensory and cognitive function occurs years prior to the disease. Such individuals would not be screened out of studies of "normal

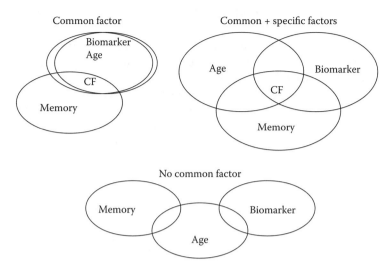

FIGURE 14.3 Depiction of the shared variance in the common factor model, common and specific factor models, and no common factor models.

aging" because their general cognitive function remains above a screening threshold for several years during the prodromal period.

The primary pathology of AD include NFTs and amyloid plaques. Although there is typically a low density of NFTs in the primary visual areas, the NFT distribution is related to the regional distribution of pyramidal neurons, which are the source of corticocortical projections (Cronin-Golomb, Corkin, & Growdon, 1995). Hence, the view of AD as a neural disconnection syndrome, whereby NFTs and amyloid plaques disrupt neuronal circuits or tracts connecting different brain regions (Zhang et al., 2009), may explain the association between visual and cognitive deficits in late life.

Evidence for this is seen in impairment of higher order visual functions in clinical studies comparing AD patients to controls (Cronin-Golomb et al., 1995) and in the disruption of resting state networks in functional magnetic resonance imaging (fMRI) studies (Zhang et al., 2009). Given the very long prodromal period for AD, it is possible that degradation of the cortical connectivity occurs slowly in adults who do not meet any diagnostic criteria and are hence included in cognitive aging studies. This cortical disconnection may also explain the association between cognitive function and other functional biomarkers such as motor control and muscle strength.

It is important to acknowledge that none of these theories is mutually exclusive and that the strong associations observed between biomarkers and memory aging are likely to result from a number of performance factors and neurological factors, which may be interrelated.

LUNG FUNCTION AND MEMORY AGING

Aging of the pulmonary system involves reduced work capacity of the skeletal muscles of the chest wall and the smooth muscles in the bronchi, chest wall, and diaphragm, while loss of bone mass from the rib thoracic cage affects pulmonary function through a reduction in chest capacity (Hagberg, Yerg, & Seals, 1988). Performance on a lung function test also requires a participant to follow instructions and blow air out as quickly as he or she can. Hence, the commonly used measure of forced expiratory volume in one second (FEV_1) involves a speeded response. The view of pulmonary function as a biomarker is not inconsistent with lifestyle and disease explanations because biomarkers are thought to operationalize physical function, which is the outcome of both innate maturational processes and disease and lifestyle factors. However, the assumption that FEV_1 becomes more strongly associated with memory specifically in old age remains to be tested adequately in longitudinal studies and cross-sectional studies that sample the entire adult age range.

A growing number of cross-sectional and longitudinal studies have now reported reliable associations between indices of lung function and cognitive (including memory) test performance. Several studies report results specifically for older age groups (Anstey, 1999; Cook et al., 1995; Whitfield et al., 1997), while one study has reported the effect in a sample of middle-aged adults (Cerhan et al., 1998) and others have also reported the association in cross-sectional studies of young adulthood to old age (Anstey et al., 2004; Emery, 1997; van Boxtel et al., 1997). Lung function has also been shown to predict cognitive decline in large longitudinal aging studies (Albert et al., 1995; Emery, Pedersen, Svartengren, & McClearn, 1998), and pulmonary function in midlife (average age 52 years) has been shown to predict cognitive function 26 years later in a large epidemiological study of men (Chyou et al., 1996).

Theories explaining the association between lung function and cognitive test performance generally invoke either lifestyle or disease factors as indirect causes of individual differences in pulmonary function that then influence cognitive test performance. Smoking and physical activity are two such lifestyle factors that have been hypothesized to influence cognitive function indirectly.

Smoking may affect lung capacity by placing individuals at risk for respiratory disease and by reducing cardiopulmonary fitness generally. Physical activity has been associated with increased pulmonary capacity and hence has been hypothesized to protect against cognitive impairment and decline. Mechanisms proposed for this effect include:

- Exercise-induced increases in cerebral blood flow
- Maintenance of the nigrostriatal dopamine system in aging leading to reduced motor aging seen in faster movement and reaction times (MacRae, Spirduso, Walters, Farrar, & Wilcox, 1987)

- Improved cardiovascular fitness (Spirduso, 1980)
- Improved health of the central nervous system (Dustman et al., 1984, 1990)

Support for the moderating effect of physical fitness on cognitive function, including memory, comes from cross-sectional studies. Exercise interventions have been shown to improve lung function (Steinhaus et al., 1990), although their benefit for cognition appears to be weak based on currently available randomized controlled trials (Williams, Plassman, Burke, Holsinger, & Benjamin, 2010). The disease factors thought to influence cognitive function via lung function include asthma, chronic obstructive airway disease (COPD), and sleep disorders. Further research is required to link lung function specifically to a wide range of memory measures to better describe the strength and nature of the relationship between this biomarker and memory aging. Functional MRI and structural brain imaging studies will be especially important for identifying neurological explanations for the observed associations.

MUSCLE STRENGTH, MOTOR FUNCTION, AND MEMORY AGING

Aging may be associated with loss of motor units affecting muscle strength; hence, over time, correlations may emerge between these functional biomarkers and memory. Grip strength has been shown to predict cognitive decline in the oldest old and mortality (Anstey et al., 2001; Ling et al., 2010). Conversely, poor cognitive function has been shown to predict decline in muscle strength in late life (Raji et al., 2005). Grip has been viewed as an indicator of vitality, and low grip is an indicator of frailty. However, longitudinal research evaluating shared variance in the aging of motor systems and memory is sparse.

Some studies have evaluated more general functional decline in relation to memory aging—where functional decline is measured by a test battery or a general latent variable is derived from a set of functional age measures. Using data from the Victoria Longitudinal Study (VLS), MacDonald, Dixon, Cohen, and Hazlitt (2004) showed that a composite of sensorimotor measures predicted memory decline over 12 years better than chronological age. In another 12-year follow-up of 750 older adults who were healthy at baseline, physical function measures (grip strength, timed walk, fatigue, and body composition) predicted conversion to mild cognitive impairment and faster rate of decline in episodic memory, semantic memory, and working memory (Boyle, Buchman, Wilson, Leurgans, & Bennett, 2010).

Other authors have evaluated whether loss of physical function precedes cognitive decline, cognitive decline precedes cognitive impairment, or both occur simultaneously. In one study, 1,793 healthy older women were followed for 8 years. At baseline, they were measured on gait speed, grip strength, and chair stands, as well as the 3MS, which is a global cognitive measure including measures of memory. These authors found that baseline global cognitive function and change in global cognitive function were associated with decline in physical performance, but baseline physical performance was not associated with cognitive decline, supporting the hypothesis that cognitive decline occurs simultaneously with declines in physical function, or precedes it (Atkinson et al., 2010).

It is possible that aging of the prefrontal cortex results in cognitive decline followed by greater difficulty with motor coordination and control (Anstey, Wood, Kerr, Caldwell, & Lord, 2009). Further research is required to link aspects of brain aging, such as cortical and subcortical atrophy, degradation of cortical connectivity, and white matter changes, to memory declines and physical function. Longitudinal neuroimaging studies may assist in delineating the interrelationships among these domains and the temporal ordering of loss of function in memory and functional capacities.

CROSS-SECTIONAL STUDIES ON BIOMARKERS AND MEMORY AGING

Several early studies of functional age published in the 1960s reported strong associations between functional biomarkers and memory. A study published in 1993 showed that a set of functional biomarkers used in predicting falls explained all the age-related variance in cognitive function (Anstey et al., 1993). This study concluded that "the decline in sensorimotor processing is an important indicator of cognitive functioning" (p. 569). Similarly, a report from the Berlin Aging Study (BASE) demonstrated a very strong association between sensory function (vision and hearing) and cognition (Lindenberger & Baltes, 1994). This was attributed to a common cause: the aging brain. This cross-sectional association among cognitive and sensorimotor variables was replicated in other population-based studies (Anstey et al., 2001a; Christensen et al., 2001), although not all authors interpreted the findings in terms of a common cause.

In a specific investigation of the association between visual function and memory aging, Drobny, Anstey, and Andrews (2005) correlated visual tests with measures of both visual and verbal memory. They found that visual function was associated with memory tested in both domains and concluded that the association between visual function and visual memory in late life was not due to peripheral visual changes. Similarly, in a previous study including measures of visual acuity and pure-tone thresholds and visually and aurally presented reaction time tests, cross-domain associations were observed for all reaction time measures, suggesting that sensory modality was not the key common factor explaining associations between sensory function and reaction time (Anstey, 1999).

Table 14.1 Correlations between biomarkers and memory in the PATH cohorts aged 20–24,[a] 40–44,[b] and 60–64[c]

		Male				Female			
		Vision	FEV	FVC	Grip	Vision	FEV	FVC	Grip
DSB	20–24	–.004	.089[e]	.102[e]	.038	.016	.097[d]	.095[e]	.074[e]
	40–44	.024[d]	.084[e]	.074[d]	.017	.079[e]	.119[e]	.095[e]	.094[e]
	60–64	.075[e]	.157[e]	.171[e]	.103[e]	.155[e]	.121[e]	.135[e]	.088[e]
Immed. recall	20–24	.024	.164[e]	.099[e]	.000	–.006	.082[e]	.057[d]	.055
	40–44	.057[e]	.164[e]	.157[e]	.080[e]	.077[e]	.137[d]	.127[e]	.133[e]
	60–64	.097[e]	.122[e]	.148[e]	.127[e]	.130[e]	.063[d]	.059[d]	.107[e]
Delayed recall	20–24	.029	.129[e]	.076[d]	–.012	–.036	.064[d]	.031	.030
	40–44	.082[e]	.149[d]	.129[e]	.099[d]	.065[d]	.143[e]	.124[e]	.113[e]
	60–64	.098[e]	.115[e]	.35[e]	.131[e]	.138[e]	.074[e]	.056	.112[e]

Notes: FEV = forced expiratory volume; FVC = forced vital capacity; Grip = grip strength in kilograms; vision = vision measured on a Snellen scale; DSB = digit span backward; Immed = immediate.

[a] *n* = 2353–2389.
[b] *n* = 2496–2528.
[c] *n* = 2496–2551.
[d] $p < .05$.
[e] $p < .01$.

A limitation of some studies demonstrating associations between memory and sensory function cross sectionally has been that they have used samples comprising only older adults. It is possible that sensory function explains individual differences in cognitive function across the life span. This possibility was explored in the PATH Through Life Study. Table 14.1 shows the raw correlations between functional biomarkers in three cohorts randomly selected from the electoral roll in Canberra, Australia (where voting is compulsory). Importantly, associations between functional biomarkers and memory are evident in young, middle-aged, and young-old adults. This demonstrates that the association between memory and these other abilities is present throughout adulthood.

LONGITUDINAL RESEARCH LINKING VISUAL AND AUDITORY ACUITY WITH MEMORY AGING

There are now a few reports from longitudinal studies examining how sensory and cognitive variables are interrelated over time. The first longitudinal analyses that estimated the strength of associations between rate of change in sensory function and memory aging were conducted in the ALSA. This unique study includes measures of visual acuity, auditory acuity, and episodic memory with measurements taken on three occasions over

8 years (Anstey et al., 2003b). Although trajectories of decline in vision, hearing, memory, and processing speed were similar, there was no shared variance between rates of decline in sensory measures and rate of decline in processing speed.

Hence, despite the strong associations among sensory measures and processing speed in cross-sectional analyses (Anstey et al., 2001a), it appears that decline in these factors occurs in parallel and does not involve a common factor. However, there was a moderate degree of shared variance between decline in visual acuity and decline in episodic memory, consistent with earlier analyses of two waves of data from this study (Anstey et al., 2001b). A similar analysis conducted in the BASE also found that although there was some shared variance among sensory and memory decline, there was also unique variance (Lindenberger & Ghisletta, 2009).

This longitudinal association between visual acuity and memory aging was also found in the Maastricht Longitudinal Aging Study (MAAS) (Valentijn et al., 2005). In this study, 418 adults aged 55 and older were followed for 6 years. Measures included visual acuity, pure tone thresholds, a visual verbal learning test (VVLT), and other cognitive measures. The authors found that change in visual acuity predicted change in the VVLT and other cognitive measures. Contrary to results from the ALSA and BASE, findings from the MAAS also indicated that change in auditory acuity predicted the total memory scores and change in memory, although this effect was weaker than that of vision. Compared with decline in visual acuity that occurs in normal aging, hearing loss is more likely to result from environmental factors, such as occupational exposures, and hence may be less likely to indicate general neurological aging. Analyses conducted on the MAAS did not evaluate whether rates of decline in visual aging and memory aging actually shared variance.

Another study of 1,668 adults aged 69 and older (the Study of Osteoporotic Fractures, SOF) (Lin et al., 2004) examined visual and hearing impairment as predictors of decline in performance on the mini-mental state examination (MMSE). Clinically defined impairment in vision but not hearing predicted decline on the MMSE, with the effect again stronger for visual impairment. In another longitudinal study using the MMSE as an outcome, researchers found that near-vision impairment (but not distance-vision or auditory impairment) was associated with decline in MMSE in Mexican Americans (n = 2,140 followed for 7 years) (Reyes-Ortiz et al., 2005). Hence, the findings from longitudinal studies are consistent in showing that visual decline or visual impairment is more strongly related with cognitive and memory decline than auditory acuity and hearing impairment.

Another hypothesis relevant to memory aging and functional biomarkers is the dedifferentiation hypothesis (Babcock, Laguna, & Roesch, 1997; Balinsky, 1941). According to this hypothesis, abilities become more strongly correlated in late life. If there are common causal factors

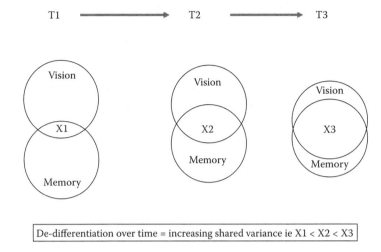

De-differentiation over time = increasing shared variance ie X1 < X2 < X3

FIGURE 14.4 Dedifferentiation between vision and memory would result in increasing shared variance at each measurement occasion.

underlying sensory and cognitive aging, the associations among sensory function and memory performance would be expected to strengthen in late life. Figure 14.4 depicts the associations between vision and memory according to the dedifferentiation hypothesis.

However, an investigation of dedifferentiation among memory and sensory factors over 8 years in ALSA did not find support for this (Anstey, Hofer, & Luszcz, 2003a). This study adjusted for gender, depression, physical health, self-rated health, and sample attrition; other authors investigating dedifferentiation have rarely adjusted for these contextual variables (Ghisletta & Lindenberger, 2004). It is possible, therefore, that disease accounts for some of the observed dedifferentiation or that dedifferentiation emerges over longer periods of time than that studied in ALSA.

However, other recent findings have not supported the dedifferentiation hypothesis, even within cognitive domains (Sims, Allaire, Gamaldo, Edwards, & Whitfield, 2009; Tucker-Drob, 2009; Tucker-Drob & Salthouse, 2008). Despite elegant work evaluating lead–lag relationships between processing speed, verbal knowledge, and visual acuity (Ghisletta & Lindenberger, 2005), no bivariate dual change score model (McArdle et al., 2004) that evaluates the lead–lag relationships between memory and sensory function has been published.

EXPERIMENTAL STUDIES

More detailed relationships between sensory aging and cognitive test performance have been studied in experimental settings. The general theme underlying this has been to determine how visual and auditory function affected by aging and disease is directly or indirectly related to cognitive processing and true cognitive ability. Researchers investigating the impact of age-related declines in vision on cognitive performance have reported results that are in general support of the cognitive resource theory, finding that memory performance is poorer for tasks using degraded visual stimuli. For example, Anstey, Butterworth, Borzycki, and Andrews (2006) found that older adults took longer to perform associative memory tasks when test stimuli were presented at low-contrast levels to simulate age-related visual declines. Another recent study of simulated cataract in 50 older drivers aged 66–87 found that accuracy and speed for cognitive tasks were significantly impaired when visual input was degraded (see Anstey, & Wood, 2011).

In contrast to earlier work on auditory stimuli manipulation and memory (Murphy et al., 2000), this study did not find that visual degradation of stimuli or simulated cataract differentially influenced primary versus secondary memory (See et al., 2010). This study concluded that age-related declines in visual function may reduce the accuracy and speed of cognitive performance; therefore, the cognitive abilities of older adults may be underestimated in neuropsychological testing. However, a caveat relating to research where visual stimuli are degraded is that it is not possible to make this equivalent to the impact of eye disease on visual function. The degradation of visual stimuli does not necessarily mimic the effects of eye disease that reduce contrast sensitivity and visual acuity because these may involve intraocular light scatter and glare sensitivity (Wood et al., 2009). It is likely that a similar caveat applies to methods used to mimic the effects of age-related hearing loss. In addition, eye disease may be an indicator of more rapid biological aging, so interpretations of how function, disease, and memory interrelate need to take place in the broader perspective of biological aging.

Using biomarkers jointly to measure "bioage"

The fact that several functional measures correlate with one another has enabled researchers to construct a composite Bioage factor or factors and use this higher order factor to explain various outcomes (e.g., Anstey & Smith, 1999; Wahlin et al., 2006). Anstey and Smith (1999) created a latent variable of Bioage that measured sensory and physical function (visual acuity, pure tone thresholds, FEV1, grip strength, vibration strength). In a cross-sectional study, this latent variable explained all the age-related variance in working memory in a sample of older women. The Bioage factor also explained the relationship between physical activity and cognition, and health and cognition. Hence, it proved to be a very efficient method of measuring functional health status in a meaningful way that operationalized the effects of disease and lifestyle as well as innate maturation.

In a similar study, Wahlin and colleagues (2006) created a sensory Bioage factor (visual acuity and pure tone thresholds) and a physical Bioage factor indicated by peak flow and grip strength. These authors also found that Bioage accounted for 54% of age-related variance in working memory and 45% of age-related variance in episodic memory in a sample of 386 males and females from the VLS. In a longitudinal study of the VLS where a single Bioage factor that included both sensory and physical measures was created, Bioage was found to predict cognitive decline (MacDonald et al., 2004).

The construct of Bioage has therefore been demonstrated to have broad utility in explaining how health and physiological aging relate to cognitive function and cognitive decline. It provides a means by which the impact of chronic disease on functional capacity can be operationalized in a manner that relates to cognitive function. For example, chronic pulmonary diseases result in less vital capacity and frailty, lack of physical exercise leads to reduced grip strength, and diabetes may reduce sensory function.

In large-scale multivariate studies of aging, the Bioage construct allows researchers to develop metamodels of the relationships among the many variables that influence memory in late life. It provides a better index for explaining individual differences in cognitive performance than chronological age does because chronological age is an index of time, whereas Bioage is an index of sensory and physical function. The Bioage construct also has potential as an outcome measure in intervention research that aims to improve memory aging by reducing the rate of biological aging through lifestyle changes. For example, an exercise intervention may improve lung function and grip strength, hence improving an individual's score on a measure of Bioage.

CONCLUSION

Memory in late life is measured by psychologists using laboratory tests that require sensory input. Visual and auditory changes occur in normal aging, and eye disease and hearing impairment are increasingly prevalent in later life (Schneider & Pichora-Fuller, 2000). Hence, memory aging and its assessment are inextricably linked with age-related changes in sensory function. More broadly, declines in physical capacity including muscle strength, lung function, and the integration of sensorimotor systems occur alongside declines in memory in late life. Although longitudinal studies are now providing the information to enable researchers to evaluate how the trajectories of decline in memory and biomarkers overlap in late life, much is still unknown about the temporal ordering of change and the causes of decline.

A life-course approach to understanding both memory development and functional aging and performance provides the breadth of perspective required to incorporate the many complex influences on memory development in late adulthood and the development of memory impairment. Three areas of research stand out as priorities in this field:

- We need further research linking longitudinal change in memory to functional biomarkers, specifically involving multiple measures of memory and multiple occasions of measurement.
- We need further experimental work investigating the effect of age-related changes in sensory function (due to both disease and normal aging) on cognitive processing.
- We need to increase our understanding of how NFTs and other AD pathology reduce cortical connectivity in ways that cause memory deficits and deficits in functional biomarkers.

ACKNOWLEDGMENT

Anstey is funded by NHMRC Fellowship no. 1002560.

REFERENCES

Aihie Sayer, A., Osmond, C., Briggs, R., & Cooper, C. (1999). Do all systems age together? *Gerontology, 45*(2), 83–86.

Albert, M. S., Jones, K., Savage, C. R., Berkman, L., Seeman, T., Blazer, D., & Rowe, J. W. (1995). Predictors of cognitive change in older persons: MacArthur studies of successful aging. *Psychology and Aging, 10*(4), 578–589.

Allen, P. A., Hall, R. J., Druley, J. A., Smith, A. F., Sanders, R. E., & Murphy, M. D. (2001). How shared are age-related influences on cognitive and noncognitive variables? *Psychology and Aging, 16*(3), 532–549.

Anstey, K. (2002). The interpretation of shared age-related variance among factors in cross-sectional cognitive aging studies. *Gerontology, 48*(1), 2–4; discussion, 22–29.

Anstey, K. J. (1999). Sensorimotor variables and forced expiratory volume as correlates of speed, accuracy, and variability in reaction time performance in late adulthood. *Aging Neuropsychology and Cognition, 6*, 84–95.

Anstey, K. J. (2008). Alcohol exposure and cognitive development: An example of why we need a contextualized, dynamic life course approach to cognitive aging—A mini-review. *Gerontology, 54*(5), 283–291.

Anstey, K. J., Butterworth, P., Borzycki, M., & Andrews, S. (2006). Between- and within-individual effects of visual contrast sensitivity on perceptual matching, processing speed, and associative memory in older adults. *Gerontology, 52*(2), 124–130.

Anstey, K. J., Hofer, S. M., & Luszcz, M. A. (2003a). Cross-sectional and longitudinal patterns of dedifferentiation in late-life cognitive and sensory function: The effects of age, ability, attrition, and occasion of measurement. *Journal of Experimental Psychology General, 132*(3), 470–487.

Anstey, K. J., Hofer, S. M., & Luszcz, M. A. (2003b). A latent growth curve analysis of late-life sensory and cognitive function over 8 years: Evidence for specific and common factors underlying change. *Psychology and Aging, 18*(4), 714–726.

Anstey, K. J., Lord, S. R., Hennessy, M., Mitchell, P., Mill, K., & von Sanden, C. (2006). The effect of cataract surgery on neuropsychological test performance: A randomized controlled trial. *Journal of International Neuropsychology Society, 12*(5), 632–639.

Anstey, K. J., Lord, S. R., & Smith, G. A. (1996). Measuring human functional age: A review of empirical findings. *Experiments in Aging Research, 22*(3), 245–266.

Anstey, K. J., Luszcz, M. A., Giles, L. C., & Andrews, G. R. (2001). Demographic, health, cognitive, and sensory variables as predictors of mortality in very old adults. *Psychology and Aging, 16*(1), 3–11.

Anstey, K. J., Luszcz, M. A., & Sanchez, L. (2001a). A reevaluation of the common factor theory of shared variance among age, sensory function, and cognitive function in older adults. *Journal of Gerontology B Psychological Sciences Social Sciences, 56*(1), P3–11.

Anstey, K. J., Luszcz, M. A., & Sanchez, L. (2001b). Two-year decline in vision but not hearing is associated with memory decline in very old adults in a population-based sample. *Gerontology, 47*(5), 289–293.

Anstey, K. J., Mack, H., & von Sanden, C. (2006). The relationship between cognition and mortality in patients with stroke, coronary heart disease or cancer. *European Psychologist, 11*, 182–195.

Anstey, K. J., Mack, H. A., & Cherbuin, N. (2009). Alcohol consumption as a risk factor for dementia and cognitive decline: meta-analysis of prospective studies. *American Journal of Geriatric Psychiatry, 17*(7), 542–555.

Anstey, K. J., & Smith, G. A. (1999). Interrelationships among biological markers of aging, health, activity, acculturation, and cognitive performance in late adulthood. *Psychology and Aging, 14*(4), 605–618.

Anstey, K. J., Smith, G. A., & Lord, S. (1997). Test–retest reliability of a battery of sensory motor and physiological measures of aging. *Perceptual and Motor Skills, 84*(3 Pt 1), 831–834.

Anstey, K. J., Stankov, L., & Lord, S. R. (1993). Primary aging, secondary aging, and intelligence. *Psychology and Aging, 8*(4), 562–570.

Anstey, K. J., von Sanden, C., Salim, A., & O'Kearney, R. (2007). Smoking as a risk factor for dementia and cognitive decline: A meta-analysis of prospective studies. *American Journal of Epidemiology, 166*, 367–378.

Anstey, K. J., Windsor, T. D., Jorm, A. F., Christensen, H., & Rodgers, B. (2004). Association of pulmonary function with cognitive performance in early, middle and late adulthood. *Gerontology, 50*(4), 230–234.

Anstey, K. J., & Wood, J. (2011). Chronological age and age-related cognitive deficits are associated with an increase in multiple types of driving errors in late life. *Neuropsychology, 25*(5), 613–621.

Anstey, K. J., Wood, J., Kerr, G., Caldwell, H., & Lord, S. R. (2009). Different cognitive profiles for single compared with recurrent fallers without dementia. *Neuropsychology, 23*(4), 500–508.

Atkinson, H. H., Rapp, S. R., Williamson, J. D., Lovato, J., Absher, J. R., Gass, M.,… Espeland, M. A. (2010). The relationship between cognitive function and physical performance in older women: Results from the women's health initiative memory study. *Journals of Gerontology Series A: Biological Sciences and Medical Sciences, 65*(3), 300–306.

Babcock, R. L., Laguna, K. D., & Roesch, S. C. (1997). A comparison of the factor structure of processing speed for younger and older adults: Testing the assumption of measurement equivalence across age groups. *Psychology and Aging, 12*(2), 268–276.

Balinsky, B. (1941). An analysis of the mental factors of various age groups from nine to sixty. *Genetic Psychology Monographs, 23,* 191–234.

Baltes, P. B., Staudinger, U. M., & Lindenberger, U. (1999). Lifespan psychology: Theory and application to intellectual functioning. *Annual Review of Psychology, 50,* 471–507.

Ben-Shlomo, Y., & Kuh, D. (2002). A life course approach to chronic disease epidemiology: Conceptual models, empirical challenges and interdisciplinary perspectives. *International Journal of Epidemiology, 31,* 285–293.

Bertram, L., & Tanzi, R. E. (2008). Thirty years of Alzheimer's disease genetics: The implications of systematic meta-analyses. *Nature Reviews Neuroscience, 9*(10), 768–778.

Birren, J. E., & Cunningham, W. (1985). Research on the psychology of aging: Principles, theory and concepts. In J. E. Birren & K. W. Schaie (Eds.), *Handbook of the psychology of aging* (pp. 3–34). New York, NY: Van Nostrand Reinhold.

Bosworth, H. B., & Schaie, K. W. (1999). Survival effects in cognitive function, cognitive style, and sociodemographic variables in the Seattle Longitudinal Study. *Experimental Aging Research, 25*(2), 121–139.

Boyle, P. A., Buchman, A. S., Wilson, R. S., Leurgans, S. E., & Bennett, D. A. (2010). Physical frailty is associated with incident mild cognitive impairment in community-based older persons. *Journal of the American Geriatrics Society, 58*(2), 248–255.

Braak, H., & Braak, E. (1991). Neuropathological staging of Alzheimer-related changes. *Acta Neuropathology (Berlin), 82*(4), 239–259.

Butler, R. N., Sprott, R., Warner, H., Bland, J., Feuers, R., Forster, M.,...Wolf, N. (2004). Biomarkers of aging: from primitive organisms to humans. *Journals of Gerontology Series A: Biological Science and Medical Science, 59*(6), B560–B567.

Carroll, J. B. (1993). *Human cognitive abilities: A survey of factor analytic studies.* Cambridge, England: Cambridge University Press.

Cerhan, J. R., Folsom, A. R., Mortimer, J. A., Shahar, E., Knopman, D. S., McGovern, P. G.,... Heiss, G. (1998). Correlates of cognitive function in middle-aged adults. *Gerontology, 44*(2), 95–105.

Christensen, H., Mackinnon, A. J., Korten, A., & Jorm, A. F. (2001). The "common cause hypothesis" of cognitive aging: Evidence for not only a common factor but also specific associations of age with vision and grip strength in a cross-sectional analysis. *Psychology and Aging, 16*(4), 588–599.

Chyou, P. H., White, L. R., Yano, K., Sharp, D. S., Burchfiel, C. M., Chen, R.,... Curb, J. D. (1996). Pulmonary function measures as predictors and correlates of cognitive functioning in later life. *American Journal of Epidemiology, 143*(8), 750–756.

Cook, N. R., Albert, M. S., Berkman, L. F., Blazer, D., Taylor, J. O., & Hennekens, C. H. (1995). Interrelationships of peak expiratory flow rate with physical and cognitive function in the elderly: MacArthur Foundation studies of aging. *Journals of Gerontology Series A: Biological Sciences and Medical Sciences, 50*(6), M317–323.

Cronin-Golomb, A., Corkin, S., & Growdon, J. H. (1995). Visual dysfunction predicts cognitive deficits in Alzheimer's disease. *Optometry and Vision Science,* 72(3), 168–176.

Cugati, S., Cumming, R. G., Smith, W., Burlutsky, G., Mitchell, P., & Wang, J. J. (2007). Visual impairment, age-related macular degeneration, cataract, and long-term mortality: The Blue Mountains Eye Study. *Archives of Ophthalmology, 125*(7), 917–924.

Dirken, J. M. (1972). *Functional age of industrial workers.* Groningen, the Netherlands: Wolters–Noordhof.

Drobny, J. V., Anstey, K. J., & Andrews, S. (2005). Visual memory testing in older adults with age-related visual decline: A measure of memory performance or visual functioning? *Journal of Clinical and Experimental Neuropsychology,* 27(4), 425–435.

Dustman, R. E., Emmerson, R. Y., Ruhling, R. O., Shearer, D. E., Steinhaus, L. A., Johnson, S. C., ... Shigeoka, J. W. (1990). Age and fitness effects on EEG, ERPs, visual sensitivity, and cognition. *Neurobiology of Aging, 11*(3), 193–200.

Dustman, R. E., Ruhling, R. O., Russell, E. M., Shearer, D. E., Bonekat, H. W., Shigeoka, J. W., ... Bradford, D. C. (1984). Aerobic exercise training and improved neuropsychological function of older individuals. *Neurobiology of Aging, 5*(1), 35–42.

Elrod, K., Buccafusco, J. J., & Jackson, W. J. (1988). Nicotine enhances delayed matching-to-sample performance by primates. *Life Science, 43*(3), 277–287.

Emery, C. F. (1997). Cognitive functioning among patients in cardiopulmonary rehabilitation. *Journal of Cardiopulmonary Rehabilitation, 17*(6), 407–410.

Emery, C. F., Pedersen, N. L., Svartengren, M., & McClearn, G. E. (1998). Longitudinal and genetic effects in the relationship between pulmonary function and cognitive performance. *Journal of Gerontology Series B: Psychological Science and Social Science, 53*(5), P311–317.

Geerlings, M. I., Deeg, D. J., Penninx, B. W., Schmand, B., Jonker, C., Bouter, L. M., & van Tilburg, W. (1999). Cognitive reserve and mortality in dementia: The role of cognition, functional ability and depression. *Psychological Medicine,* 29(5), 1219–1226.

Ghisletta, P., & Lindenberger, U. (2004). Static and dynamic longitudinal structural analyses of cognitive changes in old age. *Gerontology, 50*(1), 12–16.

Ghisletta, P., & Lindenberger, U. (2005). Exploring structural dynamics within and between sensory and intellectual functioning in old and very old age: Longitudinal evidence from the Berlin Aging Study. *Intelligence, 33,* 555–587.

Hagberg, J. M., Yerg, J. E., II, & Seals, D. R. (1988). Pulmonary function in young and older athletes and untrained men. *Journal of Applied Physiology, 65*(1), 101–105.

Han, S. D., & Bondi, M. W. (2008). Revision of the apolipoprotein E compensatory mechanism recruitment hypothesis. *Alzheimer's Dementia, 4*(4), 251–254.

Hofer, S. M., & Sliwinski, M. J. (2001). Understanding ageing. An evaluation of research designs for assessing the interdependence of ageing-related changes. *Gerontology, 47*(6), 341–352.

Horn, J. L. (1982). The aging of human abilities. In B. B. Wolman (Ed.), *Handbook of developmental psychology* (pp. 847–869). Englewood Cliffs, NJ: Prentice Hall.

Horn, J. L. (1985). Remodeling old models of intelligence. In B. Wolman (Ed.), *Handbook of intelligence: Theories, measurements and applications.* New York, NY: Wiley.

Horn, J. L. (1987). A context for understanding information processing studies of human abilities. In P. A. Vernon (Ed.), *Speed of information processing and intelligence* (pp. 201–238). Norwood, NJ: Ablex.

Kuh, D., & Ben-Shlomo, Y. (2004). *The lifecourse approach to chronic disease epidemiology* (2nd ed.). Oxford, England: Oxford University Press.

Lee, D. J., Gomez-Marin, O., Lam, B. L., & Zheng, D. D. (2002). Visual acuity impairment and mortality in US adults. *Archives of Ophthalmology, 120*(11), 1544–1550.

Li, K. Z., & Lindenberger, U. (2002). Relations between aging sensory/sensorimotor and cognitive functions. *Neuroscience and Biobehavioral Reviews, 26*(7), 777–783.

Li, S. C., Huxhold, O., & Schmiedek, F. (2004). Aging and attenuated processing robustness: Evidence from cognitive and sensorimotor functioning. *Gerontology, 50*(1), 28–34.

Lin, M. Y., Gutierrez, P. R., Stone, K. L., Yaffe, K., Ensrud, K. E., Fink, H. A.,... Mangione, C. M. (2004). Vision impairment and combined vision and hearing impairment predict cognitive and functional decline in older women. *Journal of the American Geriatrics Society, 52*(12), 1996–2002.

Lindenberger, U., & Baltes, P. B. (1994). Sensory functioning and intelligence in old age: A strong connection. *Psychology and Aging, 9*(3), 339–355.

Lindenberger, U., & Ghisletta, P. (2009). Cognitive and sensory declines in old age: Gauging the evidence for a common cause. *Psychology and Aging, 24*(1), 1–16.

Lindenberger, U., Scherer, H., & Baltes, P. B. (2001). The strong connection between sensory and cognitive performance in old age: Not due to sensory acuity reductions operating during cognitive assessment. *Psychology and Aging, 16*(2), 196–205.

Ling, C. H., Taekema, D., de Craen, A. J., Gussekloo, J., Westendorp, R. G., & Maier, A. B. (2010). Handgrip strength and mortality in the oldest old population: The Leiden 85-plus Study. *Canadian Medical Association Journal, 182*(5), 429–435.

Lord, S. R., Ward, J. A., Williams, P., & Anstey, K. J. (1994). Physiological factors associated with falls in older community-dwelling women. *Journal of the American Geriatrics Society, 42*(10), 1110–1117.

MacDonald, S. W., Dixon, R. A., Cohen, A. L., & Hazlitt, J. E. (2004). Biological age and 12-year cognitive change in older adults: Findings from the Victoria Longitudinal Study. *Gerontology, 50*(2), 64–81.

Mackinnon, A., Christensen, H., & Jorm, A. F. (2006). Search for a common cause factor amongst cognitive, speed and biological variables using narrow age cohorts. *Gerontology, 52*(4), 243–257.

MacRae, P. G., Spirduso, W. W., Walters, T. J., Farrar, R. P., & Wilcox, R. E. (1987). Endurance training effects on striatal D2 dopamine receptor binding and striatal dopamine metabolites in presenescent older rats. *Psychopharmacology (Berlin), 92*(2), 236–240.

McArdle, J. J., Hamgami, F., Jones, K., Jolesz, F., Kikinis, R., Spiro, A., III, & Albert, M. S. (2004). Structural modeling of dynamic changes in memory and brain structure using longitudinal data from the normative aging study. *Journal of Gerontology Series B: Psychological Science and Social Science, 59*(6), P294–P304.

Murphy, D. R., Craik, F. I., Li, K. Z., & Schneider, B. A. (2000). Comparing the effects of aging and background noise on short-term memory performance. *Psychology and Aging, 15*(2), 323–334.

Plassman, B. L., Langa, K. M., Fisher, G. G., Heeringa, S. G., Weir, D. R., Ofstedal, M. B., ... Wallace, R. B. (2008). Prevalence of cognitive impairment without dementia in the United States. *Annals of Internal Medicine, 148*(6), 427–434.

Rabbitt, P. (1990). Mild hearing loss can cause apparent memory failures which increase with age and reduce with IQ. *Acta Otolaryngoly Supplement, 476,* 167–175; discussion 176.

Raji, M. A., Kuo, Y. F., Snih, S. A., Markides, K. S., Peek, M. K., & Ottenbacher, K. J. (2005). Cognitive status, muscle strength, and subsequent disability in older Mexican Americans. *Journal of the American Geriatrics Society, 53*(9), 1462–1468.

Raz, N., Lindenberger, U., Rodrigue, K. M., Kennedy, K. M., Head, D., Williamson, A., ... Acker, J. D. (2005). Regional brain changes in aging healthy adults: General trends, individual differences and modifiers. *Cerebral Cortex, 15,* 1676–1689.

Reyes-Ortiz, C. A., Kuo, Y. F., DiNuzzo, A. R., Ray, L. A., Raji, M. A., & Markides, K. S. (2005). Near vision impairment predicts cognitive decline: Data from the Hispanic established populations for epidemiologic studies of the elderly. *Journal of the American Geriatrics Society, 53*(4), 681–686.

Rodgers, B., Windsor, T. D., Anstey, K. J., Dear, K. B., Jorm, F. J., & Christensen, H. (2005). Non-linear relationships between cognitive function and alcohol consumption in young, middle-aged and older adults: The PATH through life project. *Addiction, 100*(9), 1280–1290.

Salthouse, T. A., Hancock, H. E., Meinz, E. J., & Hambrick, D. Z. (1996). Interrelations of age, visual acuity, and cognitive functioning. *Journal of Gerontology Series B: Psychological Science and Social Science, 51*(6), P317–330.

Schneider, B. A., & Pichora-Fuller, M. K. (2000). Implications of perceptual deterioration for cognitive aging research. In F. I. M. Craik & T. A. Salthouse (Eds.), *Handbook of aging and cognition* (pp. 155–220). Mahwah, NJ: Lawrence Erlbaum Associates.

See, A., Anstey K. J., & Wood, J. (2010). Simulated cataract and low contrast stimuli impair cognitive performance in older adults: Implications for neuropsychological assessment and everyday function. *Aging, Neuropsychology, & Cognition, 18,* 1–21.

Sekuler, R., & Blake, R. (1987). Sensory underload. *Psychology Today, 21,* 48–51.

Sims, R. C., Allaire, J. C., Gamaldo, A. A., Edwards, C. L., & Whitfield, K. E. (2009). An examination of dedifferentiation in cognition among African-American older adults. *Journal of Cross Cultural Gerontology, 24*(2), 193–208.

Small, B. J., Graves, A. B., McEvoy, C. L., Crawford, F. C., Mullan, M., & Mortimer, J. A. (2000). Is APOE-ε-4 a risk factor for cognitive impairment in normal aging? *Neurology, 54*(11), 2082–2088.

Spirduso, W. W. (1980). Physical fitness, aging, and psychomotor speed: A review. *Journal of Gerontology, 35,* 850–865.

Stalenhoef, P. A., Diederiks, J. P., Knottnerus, J. A., Kester, A. D., & Crebolder, H. F. (2002). A risk model for the prediction of recurrent falls in community-dwelling elderly: A prospective cohort study. *Journal of Clinical Epidemiology, 55*(11), 1088–1094.

Steinhaus, L. A., Dustman, R. E., Ruhling, R. O., Emmerson, R. Y., Johnson, S. C., Shearer, D. E., … Bonekat, W. H. (1990). Aerobic capacity of older adults: A training study. *Journal of Sports Medicine and Physical Fitness, 30*(2), 163–172.

Tucker-Drob, E. M. (2009). Differentiation of cognitive abilities across the life span. *Developmental Psychology, 45*(4), 1097–1118.

Tucker-Drob, E. M., & Salthouse, T. A. (2008). Adult age trends in the relations among cognitive abilities. *Psychology and Aging, 23*(2), 453–460.

Tun, P. A., McCoy, S., & Wingfield, A. (2009). Aging, hearing acuity, and the attentional costs of effortful listening. *Psychology and Aging, 24*(3), 761–766.

Valentijn, S. A., van Boxtel, M. P., van Hooren, S. A., Bosma, H., Beckers, H. J., Ponds, R. W., … Jolles, J. (2005). Change in sensory functioning predicts change in cognitive functioning: Results from a 6-year follow-up in the Maastricht Aging Study. *Journal of the American Geriatrics Society, 53*(3), 374–380.

van Boxtel, M. P., Paas, F. G., Houx, P. J., Adam, J. J., Teeken, J. C., & Jolles, J. (1997). Aerobic capacity and cognitive performance in a cross-sectional aging study. *Medical Science and Sports Exercise, 29*(10), 1357–1365.

van Schoor, N. M., Smit, J. H., Pluijm, S. M., Jonker, C., & Lips, P. (2002). Different cognitive functions in relation to falls among older persons. Immediate memory as an independent risk factor for falls. *Journal of Clinical Epidemiology, 55*(9), 855–862.

Wacha, V. H., & Obrzut, J. E. (2007). Effects of fetal alcohol syndrome on neuropsychological function. *Journal of Developmental and Physical Disabilities, 19*(3), 217–226.

Wahlin, A., MacDonald, S. W., deFrias, C. M., Nilsson, L. G., & Dixon, R. A. (2006). How do health and biological age influence chronological age and sex differences in cognitive aging: Moderating, mediating, or both? *Psychology and Aging, 21*(2), 318–332.

Whalley, L. J., Deary, I. J., Appleton, C. L., & Starr, J. M. (2004). Cognitive reserve and the neurobiology of cognitive aging. *Aging Research Reviews, 3*(4), 369–382.

Whalley, L. J., Dick, F. D., & McNeill, G. (2006). A life-course approach to the aetiology of late-onset dementias. *Lancet Neurology, 5*(1), 87–96.

Whitfield, K. E., Seeman, T. E., Miles, T. P., Albert, M. S., Berkman, L. F., Blazer, D. G., & Rowe, J. W. (1997). Health indices as predictors of cognition among older African Americans: MacArthur Studies of Successful Aging. *Ethnicity and Disease, 7*(2), 127–136.

Williams, J. W., Plassman, B. L., Burke, J. R., Holsinger, T., & Benjamin, S. (2010). *Preventing Alzheimer's disease and cognitive decline. Evidence report/technical assessment No. 193.* Durham, NC: National Institutes of Health.

Wood, J. M., Anstey, K. J., Kerr, G. K., Lacherez, P. F., & Lord, S. (2008). A multidomain approach for predicting older driver safety under in-traffic road conditions. *Journal of the American Geriatrics Society, 56*(6), 986–993.

Wood, J. M., Chaparro, A., Anstey, K. J., Hsing, Y. E., Johnsson, A. K., Morse, A. L., & Wainwright, S. E. (2009). Impact of simulated visual impairment on the cognitive test performance of young adults. *British Journal of Psychology, 100*(Pt 3), 593–602.

Zhang, H. Y., Wang, S. J., Xing, J., Liu, B., Ma, Z. L., Yang, M., … Teng, G.J. (2009). Detection of PCC functional connectivity characteristics in resting-state fMRI in mild Alzheimer's disease. *Behavioral Brain Research, 197*(1), 103–108.

Author Index

A

Subject Index